MW00560798

BARRON'S

HOW TO PREPARE FOR THE

EMT-

PARAMEDIC EXAM

Mark L. Marchetta, B.S., R.N., NREMT-P
EMS Coordinator, Continuing Medical Education Program Director
  Summa Health System, Akron, Ohio
State of Ohio EMS Board Member
Chairman, State of Ohio Education Committee
Chairman, State of Ohio EMS Testing Committee
Member, *2001 International Who's Who of Public Service Historical Society*
Research Associate, UCLA Medical Center of Prehospital Care

BARRON'S

DEDICATION

To my wife Loretta, the biggest supporter of my work.
Thank you for your tolerance, understanding, and sense of humor.

To my children Mark Jr. and Austin. You are truly the light of my life.
Thanks for making every day so precious.

To my parents who have supported me through all my endeavors.

© Copyright 2003 by Barron's Educational Series, Inc.

All rights reserved. No part of this book may be reproduced in
any form, by photostat, microfilm, xerography, or any other
means, or incorporated into any information retrieval
system, electronic or mechanical, without the written
permission of the copyright owner.

All inquiries should be addressed to:

Barron's Educational Series, Inc.
250 Wireless Boulevard
Hauppauge, New York 11788
http://www.barronseduc.com

Library of Congress Catalog Card No. 2002034526

International Standard Book No. 0-7641-2229-0

Library of Congress Cataloging-in-Publication Data

Marchetta, Mark.
     How to prepare for the EMT—paramedic exam / Mark Marchetta.
       p. ; cm.
     ISBN 0-7641-2229-0
       1. Emergency medicine—Examinations, questions, etc. 2. Emergency medical
technicians—Licenses—United States—Study guides. I. Title
     [DNLM: 1. Emergencies—United States—Examination Questions. 2. Emergency
Medical Services—United States—Examination Questions. 3. Emergency Medical
Technicians—United States—Examination Questions. WB 18.2 M317h 2003]
     RC86.9 .M367 2003
     616.02'5'076—dc21   2002034526

PRINTED IN THE UNITED STATES OF AMERICA

9 8 7 6 5 4 3 2

Contents

Contributors

How To Prepare for the EMT—Paramedic Exam was written with the assistance of several educators who have demonstrated excellence in the clinical and classroom settings. The following individuals contributed to this book.

P. A. Ambrose, NREMT-P
EMS/Continuing Medical Education
   Coordinator
St. Vincent and Medical College of Ohio
Life Flight / Mobile Life
Critical Care Transport Network
Toledo, Ohio

K. A. Ballman, R.N., CEN, EMT-P
Director, Paramedic Training
Bethesda Hospital
Cincinnati, Ohio

William S. Krost, BSAS, NREMT-P
Administrative Director EMS and
   Trauma Services
St. Vincent Charity Hospital
Cleveland, Ohio

Alan F. Mistler, MEd, R.N., NREMT-P
Director, EMS Educational Programs
Field Service Professor
University of Cincinnati
Cincinnati, Ohio

Megan K. Shaw, MEd, B.S.N., R.N.
Staff Development Instructor
Summa Health System
Akron, Ohio

Brian Tritchler, B.S.N., R.N., CEN, EMT-P
Director, Paramedic Education
Summa Health System
Akron, Ohio

Medical Advisor and Contributing
   Author:
Mike Mackan, MD, FACEP
Director, EMS Activities
Summa Health System
Clinical Professor, Emergency Medicine
North East Ohio College of Medicine
Akron, Ohio

Manuscript Review:
Loretta L. Marchetta, R.N.
Quality Management Coordinator
Cardiovascular Services
Mercy Medical Center
Canton, Ohio

Preface

The purpose of this book is to help you prepare for examinations in your EMT-Paramedic education course and your state paramedic certification exam. If you are currently certified, this book will provide you with an effective review for a refresher or any recertification exam you may need to take.

How to Prepare for the EMT—Paramedic Exam consists of multiple-choice questions accompanied by answers with the rationale. The material is based on information in the 1998 United States Department of Transportation National Standard EMT-Paramedic Curriculum and the 2000 National Registry of Emergency Medical Technicians Practice Analysis.

This book consists of ten chapters. I strongly encourage you to start with Chapter One, "Tips for Preparing and Taking a Test." You can then move on to Chapters Two through Seven, which contain exam questions. When reviewing the questions, it is important to have confidence choosing the correct answer. Confidence comes through understanding the material. If you find yourself missing several questions on one topic (i.e., management of seizures) or even if you get a question correct with a "lucky guess," it is essential that you go back to the course material presented to you and make certain you *truly* understand the information. Memorizing the questions and answers to every question in this book will not ensure a passing grade on any examination. This book must be used as a tool to identify areas that require additional studying and understanding.

Once you review the questions and brush up on any material you may have found difficult, you can move on to Chapters Eight through Ten, which contain practice tests.

The practice tests will be a helpful assessment of how well you know the material. The practice tests are not divided into individual sections or chapters; the questions are in no particular order. You may answer two questions on cardiology, followed by three questions on pediatrics, followed by one question on trauma, etc.

This book will assist you in your studies and ultimately passing your examination. Just remember, you have the luxury of thinking about what you are going to choose for your answer on your exam. When it actually comes to providing patient care, you must be able to call upon your education to assist you in decision making. That is why it's important to understand your course material and *not* memorize it.

Good luck in your EMS career.
Mark Marchetta

CHAPTER 1

Tips for Preparing for and Taking the Test

This chapter contains essential information on test preparation including:

- Studying for the test
- Preparation the day before the test
- Test-taking techniques
- Advice for after the test

BRING ON THE TEST!

Ever wonder how some people can get all the answers right on a test without ever studying? Are you one of the those people or one of the others who get so anxious that in spite of memorizing the material you can't remember a thing?

Most adults get a bit stressed when they have an exam coming up. It often hits adults harder than younger people. Children and teenagers take tests routinely in school, so test taking is a familiar part of their lives. But if you've been out of school for a while, you're less accustomed to being judged in this manner. You may also have more pressure to succeed on a test if you are taking it to obtain or advance a career.

The secret of being a good test taker isn't only understanding the material. A big part of it has to do with attitude—how do you approach the test, with confidence or timidly like a scared rabbit? Another part has to do with the following tips for preparing for and taking a test.

STUDYING FOR THE TEST

First—When will the test be given? Once you have that information you can decide how much you are able to study and then fit studying into your already full schedule. Developing a plan to include study time in your day is very important. When taking an important test you want to allow as much time as possible. Starting early also allows you to spend a little time each day studying. More intense studying can be done for a few days before the exam.

Second—Find out what will be covered on the test, how many questions, and how long you have to take the exam. You're already off to a good start here; you've got a book that reviews the material that could be on the test. Talking with others who have taken the exam is another way to get an idea of what may be on the test. Just remember, questions vary from test to test and although the topics emphasized in this review manual may be similar, it will probably not be identical. Also, when talking with others keep in mind that you are getting their perception of the test, which may not always be accurate.

Third—Take the practice tests in this book. This will help you become familiar with the format and wording of the questions and also help identify areas of weakness. If you find yourself missing multiple questions on trauma and airway, you should plan on spending more study time on these areas. Taking the practice exams will also give you an idea of how long you can spend on a question and still have enough time to safely finish the exam on time.

Fourth—Elicit support from your family. Studying will probably affect your family, in some way. It may take time away from activities or you may need quiet time or a quiet place, all of which may be very difficult to find in a typical family. Your family needs to understand the importance of the test so they can understand the schedule and give the support and encouragement you need.

PREPARATION THE DAY BEFORE THE TEST

Conduct a final review. This is not the time to try and learn new material; this should truly be a review.

Get a good night's rest. It is important to be well rested before a big test. It is easier to think when you are rested. Studies show that we can function on very little sleep, but the activities are not performed at your highest level of mental functioning. It will be harder to pull the information from the crevices of your brain and you don't want that to happen during the test.

Make sure you know where to go to take the test. If the location is unfamiliar it is probably a good idea to take a "trial run" and find the testing site. Getting lost on your way to the test can be frustrating and will only add to your anxiety. This can be even more of a problem if you are prone to test anxiety.

Get all your materials and supplies ready. For some tests you need a special admission card. Do you need a #2 pencil? If so, make sure you have an adequate supply that are sharpened and have erasers. It may be helpful to have a watch; not all rooms have clocks. This allows you to budget the amount of time spent on each question. Some people like to take a supply of small hard candies to help them stay awake. If you are one of those people make sure that this is allowed.

Plan to arrive a few minutes early on the day of the test. In case there are problems on the way to the test site, such as a traffic jam or car trouble. It also gives you time to relax and select your seat. Do you want to be able to see a clock, look out a window, or avoid any distractions? If you are left-handed you may want a left-handed desk or use a second desk, but make sure this is acceptable. Talk with others but avoid discussions of what they studied or think will be on the test. That can lead to more intense test anxiety or it may make it harder to recall the material you do know.

TEST-TAKING TECHNIQUES

During the Test Itself—Tips for Answering Questions

Be confident! When you first look at the test, take a deep breath and approach it with a take-charge attitude. Who is the boss here? The test, which is flat and lifeless, or you, an adult ready to succeed?

When you first receive the test read or listen to *all* the directions. Are there specific requirements for completing the answer sheet? How should you change an answer? How long will you have to complete the test? Will there be any breaks? Can you write on the test? Are there penalties for incorrect answers? Be confident and approach the test with a positive attitude.

General Test-Taking Strategies

1. Read each question *and* all the options carefully. Look for words that may alter the meaning, i.e., always, never, usually, most, except, primary, most important, etc. Often they are highlighted in some way to make them more noticeable. However if they are not, and you are permitted to write on the test, mark them.

2. Answer the easy questions first. Do not spend a lot of time trying to answer a difficult question the first time through the test. If you skip a question make sure you mark it so you can come back to it if time permits. Sometimes a question further on will trigger your memory for the question you skipped. Also, as you are answering the remaining questions make sure you mark the answers in the correct location. It is a good idea to check about every 15 minutes to make sure the answers are in the correct places on the answer sheet.

3. When you have gone through the entire test once, go back and spend a little more time on the questions you skipped. If you know the answer now, great—mark it! If you are still unsure, guess only if you are not penalized for incorrect answers. Here are some tips for guessing that may help:

   a. Eliminate any of the options you are sure are incorrect. That way, if you still have to guess, you increase the odds for selecting the right answer.
   b. Read the question again all the way through. Is there one answer that fits grammatically? If so, it is more likely to be the correct answer.
   c. Go with the middle range if the answer is a number and you are not sure—that is usually the best guess.
   d. If "all of the above" is a choice then it is probably correct. However, you can check this by looking to see if at least two of the answer options are correct. Sometimes this may *not* help, especially if the question is asking for the most important, the next step, or the highest priority.
   e. If you are still stuck, reread the answer options. Are there a couple that are similar? If so, choose the one that is the most inclusive. Generally, the option that is very different is not the correct choice.
   f. Be careful not to read anything into the question; base your choice only on the information given. Think in terms of the usual not the unusual. Sometimes it is

helpful to ask yourself exactly what the question is asking by rephrasing it in your own words.

g. If there are unfamiliar terms in any of the answers try and decipher them. If the term is still unfamiliar it is probably an incorrect option.

h. It is not unusual in patient care scenarios to have questions that ask you to select several different options and group them in the correct order. Generally, if you need to guess on this type of a question start by eliminating incorrect information since it is usually easier to pick out.

Resist the urge to get up and leave the minute you finish the test; this is not a race to see who can finish first! Always take a few minutes when you have finished to review and make sure you have answered all of the questions and they are marked correctly.

Remember, your first choice is usually correct. Go with your gut instinct and don't change the answer unless you are *absolutely* certain the one you marked is not correct.

Check to make sure you have answered all the questions with only one answer. Count the total number of responses filled in; generally, it should be the same as the number of questions on the test. Don't go through and review too many times when you have finished as that will only increase your anxiety.

ADVICE FOR AFTER THE TEST

Once you have completed the test, turn it in and leave. It is not a good idea to talk about the test with the others. This tends to increase your anxiety, especially if you find they have answered differently. The test is finished and you cannot go back and change any of your answers. Besides, everyone's perception of the test—hard or easy—and what they remember will be different based on what they studied and what their own personal strengths and weaknesses are. You have made it this far; the worst is over and all you can do now is wait for the results! Reward yourself for making it through the test. You (and your family) deserve to spend some time on something fun for a change.

CHAPTER 2

Airway and Breathing

This chapter contains questions on airway and breathing assessment, proper interventions for patients with respiratory compromise, oxygen delivery systems, ventilatory support, and respiratory anatomy and physiology.

There are also questions on basic airway management and basic cardiopulmonary resuscitation. Give these questions due consideration because *it is a fact* that you must do *basic* interventions before you can perform *advanced* interventions.

It is common for paramedic students to answer basic airway and breathing questions incorrectly because they want to go directly to the advanced interventions. Don't fall into this trap!

1. Total lung capacity is:
   (A) the amount of gas moved in and out of the respiratory tract each minute.
   (B) the amount of gas contained in the lungs at the end of a maximal inspiration.
   (C) the amount of gas inhaled or exhaled during a normal breath.
   (D) the amount of gas that remains in the respiratory system after forced expiration.

2. Respiratory acidosis is caused by
   (A) an excess of bicarbonate.
   (B) excess carbon dioxide retention.
   (C) a loss of bicarbonate.
   (D) excess carbon dioxide excretion.

Questions 3 and 4 are based on the following scenario:

You are using an end-tidal carbon dioxide detector as a tool to assist for proper endotracheal intubation placement.

3. The absence of carbon dioxide in exhaled air indicates the endotracheal tube has been
   (A) placed in the right mainstem bronchus.
   (B) correctly placed in the trachea.
   (C) placed in the esophagus.
   (D) placed in the left mainstem bronchus.

4. Your next action is to
   (A) deflate the cuff, pull the endotracheal tube back 2 cm, and reassess placement.
   (B) secure the endotracheal tube and confirm correct placement by auscultation.
   (C) inflate the distal cuff with 7–10 cc of air and secure the endotracheal tube.
   (D) remove the endotracheal tube and provide several ventilations prior to attempting intubation again.

---

5. Anatomical dead space is
   (A) the volume of air in the trachea, bronchi, and air passages that does not reach the alveoli during respiration.
   (B) the volume of air in the trachea, bronchi, and air passages that is available for gas exchange during respiration.
   (C) the volume of air in the alveoli that does not contribute to oxygen-carbon dioxide exchange.
   (D) the volume of air in the alveoli that contributes to oxygen-carbon dioxide exchange during respiration.

6. You are called for a 54-year-old woman who is unconscious. Your assessment reveals the patient to be apneic and pulseless. Initial management of this patient's airway should include
   (A) assisted ventilation with a bag-valve device at 6–10 LPM.
   (B) assisted ventilation with a nonrebreather mask at 10–15 LPM.
   (C) immediate nasotracheal intubation and ventilation with a bag-valve device.
   (D) insertion of an oropharyngeal airway and ventilation with a bag-valve device.

7. Normal intrathoracic pressure
   (A) exceeds atmospheric pressure.
   (B) is equal to atmospheric pressure.
   (C) is less than atmospheric pressure.
   (D) None of the above.

8. Breath sounds such as crackles and rhonchi that are not normally heard are defined
   as _____ breath sounds.
   (A) bronchial
   (B) adventitious
   (C) vesicular
   (D) bronchovesicular

9. Which of the following correctly describes the flow of air from outside the body into
   the trachea?
   (A) Nose, nasopharynx, laryngopharynx, oropharynx, larynx, trachea
   (B) Nose, nasopharynx, larynx, laryngopharynx, oropharynx, trachea
   (C) Nose, nasal cavities, nasopharynx, oropharynx, laryngopharynx, larynx, trachea
   (D) Nose, nasal cavities, laryngopharynx, nasopharynx, oropharynx, larynx, trachea

10. You are called for an unresponsive 29-year-old man. Bystanders report he has been
    drinking heavily all day. Assessment reveals the patient to be responsive only to
    painful stimuli. His breathing is shallow at a rate of four to six times per minute.
    How would you manage this patient's airway?
    (A) Nasal cannula at 2–4 LPM
    (B) Simple face mask at 4–6 LPM
    (C) Nonrebreather mask at 10–15 LPM
    (D) Bag-valve device with a reservoir at 10–15 LPM

11. The normal arterial pH range in the human body is
    (A) 7.0–7.15
    (B) 7.15–7.35
    (C) 7.35–7.45
    (D) 7.45–7.80

12. You have orally intubated a patient. While your partner ventilates the patient with a
    bag-valve device, you assess for proper placement. Auscultation reveals sounds
    heard over the right chest and an absence of breath sounds over the left chest.
    Your best course of action would be to:
    (A) hyperventilate the patient and prepare the equipment necessary for a surgical
        cricothyrotomy.
    (B) deflate the endotracheal tube cuff, withdraw the tube 2 cm, reinflate the cuff,
        and reevaluate breath sounds.
    (C) deflate the endotracheal tube cuff, remove the endotracheal tube, and
        hyperventilate the patient with a bag-valve device.
    (D) insert a large diameter needle into the fourth or fifth intercostal space,
        midaxillary line.

13. The Sellick maneuver
    (A) is used to clear a foreign body airway obstruction in an infant or child.
    (B) is used to clear blood or mucus from an endotracheal tube or the nasopharynx.
    (C) may be used to minimize gastric distention and facilitate placement of an endotracheal tube into the glottic opening.
    (D) is the preferred method for opening the airway of an unconscious patient when cervical spine injury is suspected.

14. The area where the trachea divides into the right and left mainstem bronchi is known as the
    (A) pleura.
    (B) xiphoid process.
    (C) carina.
    (D) sternal angle.

15. The administration of which of the following may result in a decrease in the respiratory rate?
    (A) Nubain
    (B) Diltiazem
    (C) Cordarone
    (D) Morphine sulphate

16. The anatomical structure between the base of the tongue and the epiglottis into which the tip of the curved blade (Macintosh blade) is placed during orotracheal intubation is the
    (A) carina.
    (B) vallecula.
    (C) glottis.
    (D) esophagus.

17. The term used to describe normal breath sounds heard over most of the chest wall is
    (A) bronchial.
    (B) adventitious.
    (C) vesicular.
    (D) bronchovesicular.

18. When blood levels of carbon dioxide or hydrogen ions increase above normal, the respiratory center of the brain responds by
    (A) decreasing the rate and increasing the depth of respiration.
    (B) increasing the rate and depth of respiration.
    (C) increasing the rate and decreasing the depth of respiration.
    (D) decreasing the rate and decreasing the depth of respiration.

19. The blood component responsible for transporting oxygen from the lungs to the body tissues and transporting carbon dioxide from the body tissues to the lungs is the
    (A) plasma.
    (B) platelets.
    (C) leukocytes.
    (D) erythrocytes.

20. Residual volume is
    (A) the amount of gas moved in and out of the respiratory tract each minute.
    (B) the amount of gas contained in the lungs at the end of a maximal inspiration.
    (C) the amount of gas inhaled or exhaled during a normal breath.
    (D) the amount of gas that remains in the respiratory system after forced expiration.

21. You have a female patient with a long history of COPD who complains of worsening shortness of breath. She is on continuous 2 LPM of home oxygen. You are concerned that increasing the oxygen flow may eliminate the hypoxic drive to breathe because the hypoxic drive is regulated by
    (A) high PaO_2.
    (B) low PaO_2.
    (C) high oxygen saturation.
    (D) low oxygen saturation.

22. During inspiration the
    (A) diaphragm contracts and the intercostal muscles relax.
    (B) diaphragm relaxes and the intercostal muscles contract.
    (C) diaphragm relaxes and the intercostal muscles relax.
    (D) diaphragm contracts and the intercostal muscles relax.

23. The simplest airway management technique in a patient *without* suspected cervical spine injury is
    (A) head-tilt/chin-lift maneuver.
    (B) modified jaw-thrust maneuver.
    (C) endotracheal intubation.
    (D) nasotracheal intubation.

24. The proper size oropharyngeal airway is determined by measuring
    (A) from the tip of the nose to the center of the chin.
    (B) from the corner of the mouth to the tip of the chin.
    (C) from the corner of the mouth to the tip of the earlobe at the angle of the jaw.
    (D) from the center of the mouth to the tip of the earlobe at the angle of the jaw.

25. The normal value for PCO_2 is
    (A) 7.00 to 7.15.
    (B) 22 to 26 mEq/liter.
    (C) 35 to 45 mmHg.
    (D) 80 to 100 mmHg.

26. Respiration
    (A) is the exchange of gases between a living organism and its environment.
    (B) is the process that moves air into and out of the lungs.
    (C) is inadequate oxygenation at the cellular level.
    (D) is a respiratory rate greater than that metabolically necessary for gas exchange.

27. Manual maneuvers used to open a patient's airway
    (A) are contraindicated in most patients.
    (B) are difficult to perform.
    (C) include head tilt/chin lift and jaw thrust.
    (D) do not usually work without more extensive intervention.

28. Tidal volume is
    (A) the amount of gas moved in and out of the respiratory tract per minute.
    (B) the amount of gas contained in the lungs at the end of a maximal inspiration.
    (C) the amount of gas inhaled and exhaled during a normal breath.
    (D) the amount of gas that remains in the respiratory system after forced expiration.

29. The thoracic cavity is covered by a smooth, moist epithelial layer called the:
    (A) visceral pleura.
    (B) parietal pleura.
    (C) visceral peritoneum.
    (D) parietal peritoneum.

30. Advantages of the Esophageal Tracheal CombiTube include all of the following except
    (A) insertion is rapid and easy.
    (B) it can be used on trauma patients.
    (C) it can provide ventilation if placed in the esophagus.
    (D) it can be used with pediatric patients.

31. The lungs are covered by a smooth, moist epithelial layer called the
    (A) visceral pleura.
    (B) parietal pleura.
    (C) visceral peritoneum.
    (D) parietal peritoneum.

Questions 32 and 33 are based on the following scenario:

You are caring for a male patient in ventricular tachycardia. He is lethargic, diaphoretic, pale, and has vomited once. His vital signs are: BP 74/P, pulse 184, respirations 14. You are assigned to manage the airway.

32. Initial management should include:
    (A) high-flow oxygen by nonrebreather mask.
    (B) preparation for intubation.
    (C) bag-valve mask ventilations.
    (D) suctioning the airway for vomitus.

33. Your patient becomes unresponsive and apneic. Further airway management should include
    (A) providing ventilations through a nonrebreather mask.
    (B) bag-valve mask ventilation at 12 times per minute.
    (C) endotracheal intubation.
    (D) oral airway insertion and supplemental oxygen by nonrebreather mask.

---

34. Minute volume is

    (A) the amount of gas moved in and out of the respiratory tract per minute.
    (B) the amount of gas contained in the lungs at the end of a maximal inspiration.
    (C) the amount of gas inhaled or exhaled during a normal breath.
    (D) the amount of gas that remains in the respiratory system after forced expiration.

35. What effects does hyperventilation have on cerebral circulation and intracranial pressure?
    (A) More pronounced decrease in circulation than decrease in intracranial pressure
    (B) Vasoconstriction and increased intracranial pressure
    (C) Vasodilation and decreased intracranial pressure
    (D) Little or no effect on cerebral circulation or intracranial pressure

36. You arrive at the scene of an accident in which a car has struck a telephone pole. You find a 17-year-old female ejected from her vehicle, lying 25 feet from the point of impact. Which of the following is an acceptable method of opening her airway?
    (A) Modified jaw thrust
    (B) Neck extension
    (C) Neck flexion
    (D) Sellick's maneuver

37. Which of the following is not considered a sign or symptom indicating a tension pneumothorax?
    (A) Dyspnea
    (B) Hyperresonance to percussion
    (C) Distended jugular veins
    (D) Clear lung sounds

38. After decompressing the chest of the victim with a tension pneumothorax, you determine your intervention was successful by observing for
    (A) air rushing from the catheter.
    (B) a decrease in the patient's cyanosis.
    (C) an improvement in the patient's level of consciousness.
    (D) an improvement in the patient's ventilatory and circulatory status.

39. During needle decompression, the needle is inserted on the top of the rib for what purpose?
    (A) To ensure that the vein, artery, and nerve bundle under each rib are not damaged
    (B) To ensure proper placement
    (C) To ensure that the catheter enters the pleural space at the correct angle
    (D) To ensure that the site does not become a sucking chest wound

40. The phrenic nerve originates from which spinal nerves?
    (A) C1 – C2 – C3
    (B) C3 – C4 – C5
    (C) C5 – C6 – C7
    (D) C6 – C7 – T1

41. A drop in systolic blood pressure of 10 mmHg or more or the absence of a radial pulse during inspiration is known as
    (A) pericardial tamponade.
    (B) pulsus paradoxus.
    (C) orthostatic change.
    (D) pulse pressure change.

42. A nasal cannula will deliver ___ % of oxygen at a flow rate of 6 LPM in optimal conditions.
    (A) 30
    (B) 40
    (C) 50
    (D) 65

43. A nonrebreather mask can deliver an oxygen concentration of _____% at a flow rate of 15 LPM.
    (A) 40 to 60
    (B) 60 to 80
    (C) 80 to 95
    (D) 90 to 100

44. A bag-valve mask device with a reservoir and an adequate oxygen source (at least 15 LPM) will deliver an oxygen concentration of
    (A) 21%.
    (B) 40% to 60%.
    (C) 80%.
    (D) 100%.

45. The minimum size bag-valve mask device used for neonates, infants, and children should be
    (A) 250 ml.
    (B) 450 ml.
    (C) 750 ml.
    (D) 1000 ml.

46. You respond to a 72-year-old man with syncope. He is sitting in the kitchen when you arrive. He is alert and oriented to person, place, and time. He complains of dizziness. Current vitals are BP 108/60, pulse 96 slightly irregular, and respirations of 28. Pulse oximeter reading is 97%. ECG shows a sinus rhythm with occasional PVC's. This patient should receive oxygen
    (A) by nasal cannula at 3 LPM.
    (B) by nonrebreather mask.
    (C) oxygen application is not required.
    (D) by nasal cannula at 6 LPM.

47. Suctioning (application of negative pressure) should be activated
    (A) upon insertion of the suction catheter.
    (B) upon extraction of the suction catheter.
    (C) both upon insertion and extraction.
    (D) either upon insertion or extraction (it makes no difference).

48. The nasopharyngeal airway should be measured
    (A) from the corner of the mouth to the earlobe.
    (B) from the tip of the nose to the earlobe.
    (C) from the tip of the nose to the corner of the mouth.
    (D) from the tip of the nose to the chin.

49. When using a straight blade (Miller blade) to intubate an adult patient, the tip of the blade should be placed
    (A) directly on or under the epiglottis.
    (B) above the epiglottis.
    (C) in the vallecula.
    (D) past the epiglottis at the vocal cords.

50. When intubating an adult patient with a curved blade (Macintosh blade), the tip of the blade should be placed
    (A) under the epiglottis.
    (B) in the vallecula, at the base of the tongue.
    (C) in the vallecula, at the opening of the vocal cords.
    (D) to the right of the epiglottis.

51. When confirming endotracheal tube placement, it is imperative to auscultate
    (A) at the midaxillary line.
    (B) over the trachea.
    (C) over the epigastrium.
    (D) All of the above.

52. A respiratory pattern characterized by a gradually increasing rate and tidal volume followed by a gradual decrease with intermittent periods of apnea is
    (A) Cheyne-Stokes.
    (B) Biot's (ataxic).
    (C) central neurogenic hyperventilation.
    (D) agonal.

53. A respiratory pattern characterized by an irregular pattern, rate, and volume with intermittent periods of apnea is
    (A) Cheyne-Stokes.
    (B) Biot's (ataxic).
    (C) central neurogenic hyperventilation.
    (D) agonal.

54. A respiratory pattern characterized by deep, rapid respirations is
    (A) Cheyne-Stokes.
    (B) Biot's (ataxic).
    (C) central neurogenic hyperventilation.
    (D) agonal.

55. A respiratory pattern characterized by slow, shallow, irregular respirations is
    (A) Cheyne-Stokes.
    (B) Biot's (ataxic).
    (C) central neurogenic hyperventilation.
    (D) bradypnea.

56. All of the following can affect the accuracy reading of a pulse oximeter except
    (A) hypoperfusion.
    (B) anemia.
    (C) carbon monoxide poisoning.
    (D) hyperthermia.

57. Complications of endotracheal intubation include all of the following except
    (A) trauma to the teeth.
    (B) gastric distension.
    (C) esophageal intubation.
    (D) laryngospasm.

58. Confirmation of endotracheal tube placement should be evaluated
    (A) immediately after insertion.
    (B) each time the patient is moved.
    (C) by at least two methods.
    (D) All of the above.

59. A high-pitched noise associated with upper airway constriction is known as
    (A) wheezing.
    (B) rhonchi.
    (C) stridor.
    (D) rales.

60. Before providing rescue breathing to an unresponsive victim, you must check for breathing. You do this by
    (A) opening the airway.
    (B) shaking and shouting to stimulate the victim to breathe.
    (C) looking, listening, and feeling airflow through the victim's nose or mouth.
    (D) establishing unresponsiveness.

61. You are performing rescue breathing. When you initially open the airway, how many breaths do you give?
    (A) 1
    (B) 2
    (C) 3
    (D) 4

62. Where should you place your hands on the chest of an adult victim when you are performing chest compressions?
    (A) On the top of the sternum
    (B) On the lower one third of the sternum
    (C) On the lower half of the sternum, at the nipple line
    (D) Over the very bottom of the sternum

63. What is the ratio of compressions to ventilations when performing one-person CPR on an adult?
    (A) 5 compressions to 1 ventilation
    (B) 15 compressions to 1 ventilation
    (C) 15 compressions to 2 ventilations
    (D) 5 compressions to 2 ventilations

64. What is the correct speed you should use to perform chest compressions for an adult victim of cardiac arrest?
    (A) 100 times per minute
    (B) 60 times per minute
    (C) 120 times per minute
    (D) 80 times per minute

65. You are performing rescue breathing with a bag-mask device for an apneic child. How often should you provide rescue breaths?
    (A) Once every 3 seconds
    (B) Once every 4 seconds
    (C) Once every 5 seconds
    (D) Once every 6 seconds

Questions 66 to 68 are based on the following scenario:

You are caring for a 77-year-old male patient who is short of breath. He has a history of COPD and is on home oxygen at 3 LPM by nasal cannula. He is alert and oriented to person, place, and time but is able to speak in only two- to three-word sentences. BP is 148/92, pulse 124, respirations of 28.

66. What does the patient's ability to speak in two- to three-word sentences indicate?
    (A) Respiratory alkalosis is present.
    (B) There is inadequate tidal volume.
    (C) His condition is improving.
    (D) Respiratory acidosis is present.

67. You observe this patient utilizing pursed-lip breathing technique. Which statement is correct regarding pursed-lip breathing?
    (A) It is not usually used by COPD patients.
    (B) It may eliminate the hypoxic drive to breathe.
    (C) It helps improve tidal volume.
    (D) It helps maintain pressure within the airways.

68. The development of which sign/symptom in this patient would lead you to believe he is significantly decompensating?
    (A) Decreased level of consciousness
    (B) JVD
    (C) Cyanosis
    (D) Increase in blood pressure

---

69. You respond to a cafeteria for a 16-year-old patient who is choking. Your patient is conscious and coughing forcefully. She appears anxious and is difficult to communicate with due to the coughing but is able to follow commands. Assessment reveals a respiratory rate of 28, shallow, diminished breath sounds on the right side, and a SpO_2 reading of 96%. Based on the history and assessment findings, you suspect

    (A) aspiration of food into the right mainstem bronchus causing obstruction.
    (B) a spontaneous pneumothorax on the left side secondary to the forceful coughing.
    (C) that the choking episode has subsided and the patient is recovering.
    (D) a spontaneous pneumothorax on the right side secondary to the forceful coughing.

70. Nasotracheal intubation is contraindicated in a patient with
    (A) clenched teeth.
    (B) a history of recent sinus infections.
    (C) a suspected basilar skull fracture.
    (D) facial trauma.

71. Blind nasotracheal intubation
    (A) should be attempted only on an apneic patient.
    (B) is preferred over oral intubation.
    (C) should be attempted on a patient with spontaneous respirations.
    (D) is contraindicated when facial trauma is present.

72. An infant should not be suctioned for more than
    (A) 15 seconds.
    (B) 5 seconds.
    (C) 10 seconds.
    (D) 20 seconds.

73. One reason the respiratory system of a geriatric patient becomes less effective is that
    (A) the muscles of the diaphragm weaken.
    (B) tidal volume increases.
    (C) there is decreased chest wall compliance.
    (D) the lungs become more compliant.

74. You respond to the home of a 17-year-old male because his father was unable to wake him. The father states that his son was at a party last night and has a history of recreational drug use. He is unconscious and unresponsive. BP is not obtainable, pulse 42 and weak, and respirations of 4. You have orally intubated the patient. Auscultation of lung sounds post intubation reveal breath sounds heard over the right chest and an absence of breath sounds over the left chest. Your next action would be to
    (A) hyperventilate the patient and reassess lung sounds.
    (B) deflate the endotracheal tube cuff, withdraw the tube 2 cm, reinflate the cuff, and reevaluate breath sounds.
    (C) deflate the endotracheal tube cuff, remove the endotracheal tube, and hyperventilate the patient with a bag-valve device.
    (D) observe the patient and monitor his SpO_2 reading for several minutes.

75. All of the following are reasons for a pulse oximeter to read "Error" except
    (A) low capillary blood flow.
    (B) peripheral vasoconstriction.
    (C) extremity movement.
    (D) hyperthermia.

76. Field extubation is indicated if the patient
    (A) is awake and able to maintain his or her own airway.
    (B) is unconscious and continually bites the endotracheal tube.
    (C) is not suspected of alcohol intoxication.
    (D) becomes combative and starts to delay additional treatment.

77. You have successfully resuscitated a patient who suffered a cardiac arrest. You
    are enroute to the hospital when the patient wakes up and is not tolerating the
    endotracheal tube. The medical director at the receiving hospital has ordered you to
    extubate the patient. All of the following should be done except
    (A) removing the endotracheal tube on a cough or expiration.
    (B) deflating the endotracheal tube cuff completely.
    (C) removing the endotracheal tube slowly.
    (D) providing supplemental oxygen once the tube is removed.

78. You arrive on the scene of a 40-year-old male with a complaint of palpations and
    dizziness. Vitals are BP 102/78, pulse 128 slightly irregular, and respirations of 26.
    A pulse oximeter reading of 86% is obtained. He has no past medical problems.
    With this information, you suspect
    (A) hyperventilation syndrome.
    (B) hypoxemia.
    (C) congestive heart failure.
    (D) pending respiratory arrest.

79. The presence of rhonchi in a patient diagnosed with pneumonia indicates
    (A) narrowing of the airways.
    (B) a normal finding in a pneumonia patient.
    (C) onset of bronchitis.
    (D) mucus in the airways.

80. When using a bulb syringe device to assist in verification of proper endotracheal
    tube placement, all of the following are true except:
    (A) if the bulb syringe easily inflates, the endotracheal tube is correctly placed in the
        trachea.
    (B) if the bulb syringe does not inflate, the endotracheal tube is placed in the
        esophagus.
    (C) the cuff on the endotracheal tube must be inflated prior to using a bulb syringe
        device.
    (D) the cuff on the endotracheal tube should not be inflated prior to using a bulb
        syringe device.

Answers and Answer Explanations

1. **(B)** Total lung capacity is defined as the amount of gas contained in the lungs at the end of a maximal inspiration.

2. **(B)** Respiratory acidosis is caused by excess carbon dioxide retention.

3. **(C)** The use of end-tidal carbon dioxide detection ($ETCO_2$) is one tool to assist for proper endotracheal tube placement. The absence of carbon dioxide likely indicates that the endotracheal tube has been placed in the esophagus. Verifying correct endotracheal tube placement is absolutely essential. $ETCO_2$ is only one method to assist in verification.

4. **(D)** The endotracheal tube is likely placed in the esophagus. Your next action is to remove the endotracheal tube and provide several ventilations with supplemental oxygen prior to attempting another intubation.

5. **(A)** Anatomical dead space is defined as the volume of air in the trachea, bronchi, and air passages containing air that does not reach the alveoli during respiration.

6. **(D)** Of the choices listed, insertion of an oropharyngeal airway and ventilating with a bag-valve device is the best answer. **A** is incorrect because the oxygen flow setting is too low, it should be at least 15 LPM. **B** is incorrect because it utilizes a nonrebreather mask to assist ventilations. Nonrebreathers are not designed for or capable of assisting ventilations. **C** is incorrect because an apneic patient cannot be nasotracheally intubated.

7. **(C)** Normal intrathoracic pressure is less than atmospheric pressure. At rest (when not inhaling or exhaling), intrathoracic and atmospheric pressures are equal. On inhalation, the thoracic cavity enlarges, the pressure inside the lungs drop, and air is drawn into the lungs (thorax). The thoracic cavity is a negative pressure system.

8. **(B)** Adventitious breath sounds are considered abnormal sounds such as crackles and rhonchi.

9. **(C)** This is a simple anatomy and physiology question. The nose, nasal cavities, nasopharynx, oropharynx, laryngopharynx, larynx, and trachea correctly describe the flow of air.

10. **(D)** Breathing must be supported with a bag-valve device with supplemental high-flow oxygen. This patient's breathing is too slow and too shallow to receive enough oxygen for proper gas exchange to take place.

11. **(C)** The normal arterial pH range in the human body is: 7.35–7.45.

12. **(B)** This patient was most likely intubated in the right mainstem bronchus. Deflating the endotracheal tube cuff, withdrawing the tube slightly, reinflating the cuff, and reevaluating breath sounds is the proper procedure when a right mainstem bronchus intubation is suspected.

13. **(C)** Posterior pressure exerted on the cricoid cartilage (the Sellick maneuver) will effectively compress the esophagus, minimizing the potential for gastric distention. This maneuver will also reposition the vocal cords for clearer visualization of anatomic structures.

14. **(C)** This is a basic anatomy and physiology question. The area where the trachea divides into the right and left mainstem bronchi is known as the carina.

15. **(D)** Morphine is an opiate that can cause central nervous system depression. Administration may result in a decrease in the respiratory rate. Patients receiving morphine must be monitored closely for respiratory depression.

16. **(B)** The anatomical structure between the base of the tongue and the epiglottis into which the tip of the curved blade is placed during orotracheal intubation is the vallecula.

17. **(C)** Vesicular breath sounds are defined as normal sounds heard over most of the chest wall.

18. **(B)** Rate and depth of respiration are increased to eliminate excess CO_2 and therefore decreasing hydrogen ion concentrations. This is a normal compensatory mechanism of the body.

19. **(D)** Erythrocytes are defined as the blood component responsible for transporting oxygen from the lungs to the body tissues and transporting carbon dioxide from the tissues to the lungs.

20. **(D)** Residual volume is defined as the amount of gas that remains in the respiratory system after forced expiration.

21. **(B)** Hypoxic drive to breathe is common in patients with COPD or other degenerative respiratory disorders. Hypoxic drive is regulated by a low PaO_2 (partial pressure of oxygen). Delivering an increased concentration of oxygen may increase the PaO_2 and therefore eliminate the drive to breathe. Note: Do not withhold oxygen from a patient who needs it. If you are concerned about eliminating a patient's hypoxic drive, be prepared to manage the airway.

22. **(D)** During normal inspiration the diaphragm contracts (it drops) and becomes flatter and increases the size (volume) of the thoracic cavity. The result is air being able to enter the lungs.

23. **(A)** This is a basic airway management question. The head-tilt/chin-lift maneuver is the simplest airway management technique to open the airway when no cervical spine trauma is suspected.

24. **(C)** The proper size oropharyngeal airway (OPA) is determined by measuring from the corner of the mouth to the tip of the earlobe at the angle of the jaw. It is essential that the OPA be sized appropriately because improper sizing can lead to airway obstruction.

25. **(C)** The normal value for PCO_2 is 35 to 45 mmHg. A high PCO_2 is considered respiratory acidosis. A low PCO_2 is considered respiratory alkalosis.

26. **(A)** Respiration is defined as the exchange of gases between a living organism and its environment.

27. **(C)** Don't forget the basics! The head-tilt/chin-lift and jaw-thrust maneuver are both manual airway maneuvers that are very effective in initial management of the airway.

28. **(C)** Tidal volume is defined as the amount of gas inhaled or exhaled during a normal breath.

29. **(B)** The parietal pleura covers the thoracic cavity.

30. **(D)** The Esophageal Tracheal CombiTube is not indicated for pediatric patients due to its large diameter and the risk of perforation of the esophagus.

31. **(A)** The lungs are covered by a smooth, moist epithelial layer called the visceral pleura.

32. **(D)** Remember the basics! You must first open the airway and suction it before any other airway management.

33. **(C)** Endotracheal intubation is the only choice that is correct. **A** is incorrect because you do not ventilate through a nonrebreather mask. **B** is incorrect because the ventilation rate is too slow. **D** is incorrect because a patient must be breathing to receive oxygen through a nonrebreather mask.

34. **(A)** Minute volume is defined as the amount of gas moved in and out of the respiratory tract per minute.

35. **(A)** CO_2 is a very potent vasodilator. When a patient is hyperventilated, CO_2 is removed and the vessels will become constricted. This vasoconstriction leads to decreased cerebral pressure by decreasing cerebral blood flow.

36. **(A)** This is a trauma victim and should be managed utilizing c-spine precautions. **A** is the only correct answer. Using any other option would potentiate a cervical spine injury.

37. **(D)** Clear lung sounds do not indicate the presence of a tension pneumothorax.

38. **(D)** In a tension pneumothorax, the patient is dealing with oxygenation problems and circulation problems. The tension pneumothorax creates an intrathoracic shift, impeding venous blood return to the heart.

39. **(A)** During needle decompression, the needle is inserted on top of the third rib to ensure that the vein, artery, and nerve bundle under each rib are not damaged. Each intercostal space contains a vein, artery, and nerve, which lie underneath each rib.

40. **(B)** The phrenic nerve originates from spinal nerves C3 – C4 – C5.

41. **(B)** Pulsus paradoxus is defined as a drop in systolic blood pressure of 10 mmHg or more, or the absence of a radial pulse during inspiration.

42. **(B)** A nasal cannula will deliver 40% of oxygen at a flow rate of 6 LPM in optimal conditions.

43. **(D)** A nonrebreather mask can deliver an oxygen concentration of 90–100% at a flow rate of 15 LPM.

44. **(D)** A bag-valve-mask device with a reservoir and an adequate oxygen source (at least 15 LPM) will deliver an oxygen concentration of 100%.

45. **(B)** The minimum size bag-valve mask device used for neonates, infants, and children should be 450 ml: Although it is likely that the bag-valve-mask will not deliver 450 ml of volume, it is important to have a device capable of delivering excessive volumes because, as the bag is compressed, there is dead space, from which air cannot be fully expelled.

46. **(B)** This patient needs oxygen by nonrebreather mask. He has an increased respiratory rate and PVCs on the monitor that may indicate hypoxia. A normal pulse oximeter of 97% is an excellent finding but oxygen should not be withheld based on this reading. Always remember to treat your patient and not the pulse oximeter.

47. **(B)** Prolonged suctioning has been found to cause hypoxia; therefore, suctioning should be limited to extraction only.

48. **(B)** The nasopharyngeal airway should be measured from the tip of the nose to the earlobe.

49. **(A)** When using a straight blade to intubate an adult patient, the tip of the blade should be placed directly on or under the epiglottis.

50. **(B)** When intubating an adult patient with a curved blade, the tip of the blade should be placed in the vallecula, at the base of the tongue.

51. **(D)** Auscultating individual lung fields is of great benefit because they help to confirm tube placement. Auscultation of the epigastrium is beneficial because it will help to verify improper tube placement or problems with the cuff seal of the tube.

52. **(A)** Cheyne-Stokes respiratory pattern is characterized by a gradually increasing rate and tidal volume followed by a gradual decrease with intermittent periods of apnea. This breathing pattern is usually seen in patients with brain injury or elderly patients with terminal illness.

53. **(B)** Biot's respiratory pattern is characterized by an irregular pattern, rate, and volume with intermittent periods of apnea. This pattern is seen in patients with increased intracranial pressure.

54. **(C)** Central neurogenic hyperventilation respiratory pattern is characterized by deep, rapid respirations. This breathing pattern is usually seen in a loss of normal regulation of ventilatory control.

55. **(D)** Bradypnea respiratory pattern is characterized by slow, shallow, irregular respirations. This breathing pattern can be associated with stroke or several other nervous system diseases.

56. **(D)** Hyperthermia (fever) should not affect the accuracy of a pulse oximeter reading. Other circumstances that can affect accuracy include exposure to nail polish or acrylic nails, dark pigmentation or bruising, high bilirubin concentration.

57. **(B)** Gastric distension usually occurs with bag-valve mask ventilations prior to intubation. A correctly placed endotracheal tube should not contribute to gastric distension.

58. **(D)** Current recommendations for confirmation of endotracheal tube placement should be evaluated immediately after insertion, each time the patient is moved, and by at least two methods.

59. **(C)** Stridor is defined as a high-pitched noise associated with upper airway constriction. This can be an indication of pending complete airway obstruction when associated with conditions such as anaphylactic shock.

Questions 60 to 65 are basic life support questions. If you miss any of these questions, it is essential to review basic CPR prior to taking your exam.

60. **(C)** looking, listening, and feeling airflow through the victim's nose or mouth.

61. **(B)** Two times.

62. **(C)** On the lower half of the sternum, at the nipple line.

63. **(C)** 15 compressions to 2 ventilations.

64. **(A)** 100 times per minute.

65. **(A)** Once every 3 seconds (20 times per minute).

66. **(B)** A patient who is not able to speak in full sentences due to breathing difficulty indicates that the patient does not have an adequate tidal volume. This assessment finding can be a significant warning sign of pending respiratory failure.

67. **(D)** Pursed-lip breathing technique helps maintain pressure within the airways (even during exhalation) to support bronchial walls that have been damaged as a result of disease.

68. **(C)** Cyanosis is correct because the question asks about significant decompensation. **A,** decreased level of consciousness, is an *early* indicator of decompensation. Proper care should be instituted to hopefully prevent the development of significant decompensation. This is an example of how test-taking skills come in handy. You must understand what the question is asking in order to choose the correct answer. **B** and **D** may or may not be present depending on the cause of the respiratory difficulty.

69. **(A)** Based on the history of the patient choking, a constant cough (from broncho spasm), and diminished breath sounds (obstruction) on the right should lead you to suspect aspiration of food.

70. **(C)** A suspected basilar skull fracture is a contraindication for nasotracheal intubation because the distal tip of the endotracheal tube could enter the cranial cavity through the fracture site.

71. **(C)** Blind nasotracheal intubation requires the patient to have spontaneous respirations because the endotracheal tube is inserted as the patient inhales.

72. **(B)** Suctioning should not exceed 5 seconds in a pediatric patient and 15 seconds in an adult patient.

73. **(C)** There is no escaping the fact that the body becomes less efficient with age. Decreased chest wall compliance, loss of lung elasticity, air trapping, decreased diffusion of gases, and hypertrophy of the respiratory muscles can all contribute to a less effective respiratory system in a geriatric patient.

74. **(B)** This patient was most likely intubated in the right mainstem bronchus. Deflating the endotracheal tube cuff, withdrawing the tube slightly, reinflating the cuff, and reevaluating breath sounds is the proper procedure when a right mainstem bronchus intubation is suspected.

75. **(D)** Hyperthermia will not cause the pulse oximeter error.

76. **(A)** Field extubation is not common. If it must be performed, the patient must clearly be able to maintain and protect his or her own airway and have adequate spontaneous respirations.

77. **(C)** The endotracheal tube must be removed swiftly on a cough or expiration.

78. **(B)** A patient with a pulse oximeter reading of 86% with no significant past medical history of pulmonary disorders is considered hypoxic.

79. **(D)** Rhonchi are abnormal lung sounds heard on auscultation of airway that is obstructed by thick secretions.

80. **(C)** If the endotracheal tube has been placed in the esophagus, inflating the cuff on the endotracheal tube will hold the esophagus open and allow the bulb syringe to inflate. It is important to *not* inflate the endotracheal tube cuff prior to using any bulb syringe device.

NOTES

NOTES

CHAPTER 3

Cardiology

Cardiovascular disease is the leading cause of death in the United States. It also accounts for a large volume of EMS transports each year. It is essential for you to have a stable foundation of cardiovascular assessment, recognition, and treatment concepts.

All ECG rhythm strips used in this chapter are six-second strips.

1. Which term best describes the following definition? Disease of arterial vessels marked by thickening, hardening, and loss of elasticity in the arterial walls.
    (A) Atherosclerosis
    (B) Arterionecrosis
    (C) Arteriosclerosis
    (D) Angina

2. The innermost layer of an artery is known as the tunica _____.
    (A) adventitia.
    (B) intima.
    (C) media.
    (D) lumina.

3. The volume of blood ejected from the left ventricle into the arterial system each minute is
    (A) preload.
    (B) cardiac output.
    (C) afterload.
    (D) stroke volume.

4. The ability of certain cardiac cells to initiate impulses spontaneously is:
    (A) excitability.
    (B) ectopy.
    (C) automaticity.
    (D) conductivity.

5. The resistance against which the heart must pump is
    (A) afterload.
    (B) blood pressure.
    (C) preload.
    (D) cardiac output.

6. The amount of blood ejected from the heart in one cardiac contraction is
    (A) cardiac output.
    (B) stroke volume.
    (C) preload.
    (D) afterload.

7. The valve located between the left atrium and left ventricle is the
    (A) tricuspid valve.
    (B) mitral valve.
    (C) aortic valve.
    (D) pulmonic valve.

8. The protective sac surrounding the heart is the
    (A) myocardium.
    (B) septum.
    (C) endocardium.
    (D) pericardium.

9. Blood returning to the heart is received by the
    (A) inferior vena cava.
    (B) right and left ventricles.
    (C) right and left atria.
    (D) aorta.

10. The left ventricle pumps blood
    (A) into the aorta.
    (B) into the left atrium.
    (C) into the pulmonary arteries.
    (D) into the pulmonary veins.

11. The large artery that carries blood away from the heart is the
    (A) pulmonary artery.
    (B) coronary artery.
    (C) aorta.
    (D) inferior vena cava.

12. The right atrium and right ventricle are separated by the
    (A) tricuspid valve.
    (B) aortic valve.
    (C) semilunar valve.
    (D) mitral valve.

13. Parasympathetic stimulation of the heart causes
    (A) a decreased heart rate.
    (B) an increased force of contraction.
    (C) dilation of the coronary arteries.
    (D) No effect at all

14. The chordae tendinea connect
    (A) the papillary muscles to the outer myocardium.
    (B) the pericardium to the myocardial muscle mass.
    (C) the leaflets of the heart valves to the papillary muscles.
    (D) the intraventricular septum to the pericardium.

15. Blood is pumped into the lungs from the
    (A) right atrium to the pulmonary artery.
    (B) right ventricle to the pulmonary artery.
    (C) left atrium to the pulmonary vein.
    (D) right ventricle to the pulmonary vein.

16. The structures that prevent backflow of blood into the ventricles during diastole are the
    (A) mitral valve.
    (B) chordae tendinea.
    (C) semilunar valves.
    (D) papillary muscles.

17. The only vein of the body that carries oxygenated blood is the
    (A) coronary sinus.
    (B) pulmonary vein.
    (C) superior vena cava.
    (D) femoral vein.

18. The following correctly traces the blood through the heart and lungs:
    (A) Right atrium, mitral valve, right ventricle, pulmonary artery, lungs, pulmonary vein, left atrium, tricuspid valve, left ventricle, aorta
    (B) Right atrium, tricuspid valve, right ventricle, pulmonary vein, lungs, pulmonary artery, left atrium, mitral valve, left ventricle, aorta
    (C) Vena cava, left atrium, left ventricle, pulmonary artery, lungs, pulmonary vein, right atrium, right ventricle, aorta
    (D) Right atrium, tricuspid valve, right ventricle, pulmonary artery, lungs, pulmonary vein, left atrium, mitral valve, left ventricle, aorta

19. In Lead II, placement of the positive lead is located on the
    (A) left arm.
    (B) right shoulder.
    (C) right leg.
    (D) left leg .

20. In Lead III placement, the positive lead is located on the
    (A) left arm.
    (B) right shoulder.
    (C) right leg.
    (D) left leg.

21. _____ seconds are measured in each small square on ECG graph paper.
    (A) 0.01
    (B) 0.4
    (C) 0.04
    (D) 0.20

22. _____ seconds are measured in each large box on ECG graph paper.
    (A) 0.01
    (B) 0.4
    (C) 0.04
    (D) 0.20

23. A normal PR interval is _____ to _____ seconds.
    (A) 0.04–0.10
    (B) 0.08–0.10
    (C) 0.10–0.20
    (D) 0.12–0.20

24. The duration of a normal QRS complex is _____ seconds.
    (A) 0.12–0.20
    (B) 0.10–0.20
    (C) 0.04–0.10
    (D) 0.08–0.12

25. The intrinsic firing rate for a ventricular pacemaker is _____ beats per minute.
    (A) 20 to 40
    (B) 40 to 60
    (C) 60 to 100
    (D) 100 to 150

26. The time elapsing between the beginning of the p wave and the beginning of the QRS complex on the electrocardiogram is the
    (A) QRS complex.
    (B) first-degree heart block.
    (C) QT interval.
    (D) PR interval.

27. The return of a cardiac muscle cell to its resting state is called
    (A) synapse.
    (B) depolarization.
    (C) repolarization.
    (D) automaticity.

28. In a normal heart, the pacemaker cell is
    (A) the atrioventricular node.
    (B) Purkinje fibers.
    (C) the sinoatrial node.
    (D) the internodal pathways.

29. The SA node is located
    (A) high in the right atrium.
    (B) high in the left atrium.
    (C) in the septum.
    (D) high in the left ventricle.

30. Which of the following is not part of the heart's electrical conduction system that contains pacemaking capabilities?
    (A) Bundle of His.
    (B) Purkinje system.
    (C) SA node.
    (D) AV node.

31. The intrinsic firing rate of the AV node is
    (A) 20–40 beats per minute.
    (B) 40–60 beats per minute.
    (C) 40–80 beats per minute.
    (D) 60–100 beats per minute.

32. On an ECG tracing, the p wave indicates
    (A) depolarization of the atria.
    (B) repolarization of the atria.
    (C) depolarization of the ventricles.
    (D) repolarization of the ventricles.

33. On an ECG tracing, the QRS complex indicates
    (A) depolarization of the atria.
    (B) repolarization of the atria.
    (C) depolarization of the ventricles.
    (D) repolarization of the ventricles.

34. On an ECG tracing, the t wave indicates
    (A) depolarization of the atria.
    (B) repolarization of the atria.
    (C) depolarization of the ventricles.
    (D) repolarization of the ventricles.

35. The time for an electrical impulse to be transmitted from the atria to the ventricles
    is the
    (A) PR interval.
    (B) t wave.
    (C) QRS complex.
    (D) J point.

36. The period of the cardiac cycle when stimulation will not produce depolarization
    is the
    (A) refractory period.
    (B) decompensation period.
    (C) absolute refractory period.
    (D) relative refractory period.

37. The period of the cardiac cycle when stimulation may produce depolarization is the
    (A) refractory period.
    (B) decompensation period.
    (C) absolute refractory period.
    (D) relative refractory period.

38. Stimulation of the vagus nerve may result in
    (A) vasodilatation.
    (B) an increase in heart rate.
    (C) a decrease in heart rate.
    (D) an increase in cardiac output.

39. A rapid heart rate or irregular heartbeat may cause the patient to experience a sen-
    sation commonly known as
    (A) palpitations.
    (B) dysrhythmia.
    (C) fainting.
    (D) anxiety.

40. Cardiogenic shock can result in all of the following except
    (A) dysrhythmias.
    (B) hypertension.
    (C) respiratory failure.
    (D) an elevated heart rate.

41. The presence of pulmonary congestion indicated by abnormal lung sounds such as crackles (rales) in a patient complaining of chest pain may indicate
    (A) hypotension.
    (B) increased vagal tone.
    (C) increased stroke volume.
    (D) left ventricular failure.

42. Management of chest pain of a suspected cardiac nature includes
    (A) establishing an IV and providing a 200 cc fluid bolus.
    (B) administering Lasix 100 mg slow IV.
    (C) administering 2 liters oxygen by nasal cannula.
    (D) administering nitroglycerin gr1/150 sublingual.

43. Management of left ventricular failure in the prehospital setting may include
    (A) placing the patient supine on the cot.
    (B) increasing venous return to the heart.
    (C) administering IV furosemide and morphine.
    (D) administering 3 liters oxygen by nasal cannula.

44. Management of cardiogenic shock may include
    (A) administration of morphine.
    (B) administration of IV dopamine.
    (C) administration of nitroglycerin gr1/150 sublingual.
    (D) establishing an IV 500 cc/hr.

45. Cardiac arrest due to ventricular fibrillation requires
    (A) insertion of an ET tube.
    (B) immediate defibrillation.
    (C) administration of lidocaine.
    (D) administration of epinephrine.

46. Your patient is complaining of back and flank pain described as a tearing sensation. Inspection of the abdomen reveals a pulsatile mass. Treatment includes
    (A) palpation of the mass.
    (B) gentle handling and rapid transport.
    (C) administration of Lasix 40 mg IV.
    (D) administering lidocaine 100 mg IV.

47. Procainamide administration should be discontinued if any of the following occur except
    (A) hypotension.
    (B) widening of the QRS complex.
    (C) hypertension.
    (D) maximum dose infused.

48. Which of the following medications is not indicated in the treatment of ventricular fibrillation?
    (A) Epinephrine
    (B) Adenosine
    (C) Lidocaine
    (D) Vasopressin

49. Which of the following may require synchronized cardioversion?
    (A) Pulseless ventricular tachycardia
    (B) Pulseless electrical activity
    (C) Ventricular fibrillation
    (D) PSVT

50. Your patient in ventricular tachycardia is lethargic, diaphoretic, and pale and has vomited once. His vital signs are: BP 54/P, pulse 184, respirations 14. Describe your management of this patient.
    (A) 200 cc fluid bolus, nitroglycerin gr1/150 sublingual, lidocaine.
    (B) ABCs, high-flow oxygen, cardioversion.
    (C) ABCs, high-flow oxygen, IV, Adenocard 6 mg IV.
    (D) Intubation, IV, Dopamine infusion.

51. You respond to a 76-year-old man with syncope. He is sitting upright in the bathroom when you arrive. He is initially alert and oriented only to person but quickly regains alertness to person, place, and time. He has no complaints except an abrasion on his left knee and slight dizziness. He stated that he was having a bowel movement when he blacked out. His current vitals are BP 108/60, pulse 96 slightly irregular, and respirations of 20. ECG shows a sinus rhythm with occasional PACs. Based on the information provided, you suspect the cause of the patient's syncope is
    (A) digitalis toxicity.
    (B) an atrial dysrhythmia.
    (C) vasovagal episode.
    (D) underlying myocardial ischemia.

52. You respond to a possible drowning call. On arrival, you find bystander CPR in progress on a male patient in his thirties. Your first action should be
    (A) to take over CPR from the bystanders.
    (B) immediate defibrillation.
    (C) to stop bystander CPR to assess ABCs.
    (D) to open the airway and suction if necessary.

53. All of the following are treatable causes of pulseless electrical activity except
    (A) hypothermia, hypovolemia, cardiac tamponade, acidosis.
    (B) hypovolemia, tension pneumothorax, hyperthermia, hyperkalemia.
    (C) acidosis, coronary thrombosis, pulmonary embolism.
    (D) tension pneumothorax, hyperkalemia, coronary thrombosis.

54. You respond to a 20-year-old female complaining of dizziness and weakness. She is slow to respond to your questions but admits to taking several diet pills a day in an effort to quickly lose weight. Vitals are blood pressure 98/54, pulse 184, respirations 32; the skin is pale and moist. ECG shows the following rhythm:

   Immediate treatment should include
   (A) reassuring the patient that when the medication wears off the symptoms will go away.
   (B) IV, oxygen, continuing to monitor the patient, and transport.
   (C) IV, oxygen, adenocard 6 mg rapid IV push.
   (D) immediate cardioversion with 100 joules.

Questions 55–57 are based on the following scenario:

A 68-year-old woman is complaining of chest pain and shortness of breath. Her blood pressure is 110/64, pulse 60, respirations 32. ECG shows sinus bradycardia with a PR interval of 0.24. Lung sounds reveal crackles in the posterior bases.

55. Management should include
   (A) nitroglycerin gr1/150 mg SL.
   (B) a 200 cc fluid bolus.
   (C) Atropine 0.5 mg to 1.0 mg IVP.
   (D) preparation for immediate transcutaneous pacing.

56. The BP is now 88/50, pulse 50, respirations 40. Lung sounds reveal increased pulmonary congestion. Continued management should include
   (A) Atropine 0.5 mg to 1 mg.
   (B) administering a 200 cc fluid bolus.
   (C) administering Lasix 80 mg IVP.
   (D) immediate transcutaneous pacing.

57. The patient is experiencing severe chest pain, shortness of breath, and becomes unconscious. BP is 72/40 and the ECG now shows the following rhythm:

Treatment includes
(A) Atropine 0.5 mg IVP every five minutes to a maximum dose of 0.4 mg/kg.
(B) Dopamine infusion titrated to a systolic blood pressure >90 mmHg systolic.
(C) immediate transcutaneous pacing.
(D) 200 cc fluid bolus and rechecking vital signs.

Questions 58 and 59 are based on the following scenario:

A patient weighing 220 pounds presents in this rhythm:

58. Management should include:
(A) amiodarone 300 mg IV.
(B) lidocaine 180 mg IV.
(C) procainamide 4 mg/min IV.
(D) magnesium 1 mg IV.

59. Further management for the rhythm includes:
(A) amiodarone 150 mg IV.
(B) vasopressin 20 mg IV.
(C) procainamide 4 mg/min up to a total of 17 mg/kg IV.
(D) magnesium 1 gram IV.

---

60. How often should you provide rescue breaths for a child who is apneic?
    (A) 20 breaths per minute
    (B) 12 to 20 breaths per minute
    (C) Once every 5 seconds
    (D) Once every 10 seconds

61. What is the proper ratio of chest compressions to ventilations while performing two-person CPR on an adult?
    (A) 15 compressions to 2 ventilations
    (B) 5 compressions to 1 ventilation
    (C) 15 compressions to 1 ventilation
    (D) 5 compressions to 2 ventilations

62. Calcium chloride is indicated for a dialysis patient in
    (A) cardiac arrest with refractory v fib.
    (B) symptomatic bradycardia.
    (C) cardiac arrest with known or suspected hyperkalemia.
    (D) cardiac arrest with pulseless electrical activity.

63. The recommended dose of vasopression in ventricular fibrillation is
    (A) 40 mg IV repeated once in 10 minutes.
    (B) 20 mg IV one time only.
    (C) 40 mg IV one time only.
    (D) 40 units IV one time only.

64. The maximum amount of procainamide you should administer to a 196-pound patient is
    (A) 1,462 mcg.
    (B) 1,500 mg.
    (C) 1,514 mg.
    (D) 1,615 mg.

65. The initial dose of adenosine that should be administered is
    (A) 6 mg rapid IV push, repeated in 5 minutes if necessary.
    (B) 6 mg IV push, repeated in 10 minutes.
    (C) 6 mg rapid IV push followed by a 20 cc fluid bolus.
    (D) 12 mg IV push.

66. The recommended dose of aspirin for a patient experiencing chest pain is
    (A) 325 mg.
    (B) 162–325 mg.
    (C) 81 mg.
    (D) 650 mg.

67. Mixing 2 grams of lidocaine in 500 cc of solution will provide a mixture of
    (A) 1 mg/ml.
    (B) 2 mg/ml.
    (C) 3 mg/ml.
    (D) 4 mg/ml.

68. To administer 2 mg/min of lidocaine using the mixture of 2 grams in 500 cc and 60 gtt/ml tubing, you will administer how many drops a minute?
    (A) 15
    (B) 30
    (C) 45
    (D) 60

69. You respond to a shopping mall for a possible cardiac arrest. When you arrive, you find a male patient in his seventies in cardiac arrest. The mall security officers have an AED attached. The AED is in the process of delivering a shock. Your first response should be to
    (A) establish unresponsiveness.
    (B) open the airway and provide ventilations.
    (C) remove the AED and apply your own monitor.
    (D) allow the AED to deliver the initial shock.

70. A dissecting aortic aneurysm may produce which signs/symptoms?
    (A) A ripping or tearing pain sensation
    (B) Pain in the abdomen
    (C) The same blood pressure in each arm
    (D) Respiratory distress

71. Vasopressin is indicated for management of
    (A) any circumstance in which epinephrine 1:10,000 may be used.
    (B) ventricular fibrillation.
    (C) PEA.
    (D) ventricular tachycardia with a pulse.

72. A 78-year-old male is alert and oriented to person, place, and time and complains of chest pain and difficulty breathing. You attach him to the ECG and notice a rhythm of 42 with corresponding pulse, a P-R interval of 0.20, and normal R-R intervals. Vitals are BP 76/42, respirations 42. The patient also states that he feels nauseated and dizzy. Treatment for this patient should include
    (A) Atropine 0.5 mg.
    (B) oxygen 3 LPM nasal cannula.
    (C) immediate transvenous pacing.
    (D) Isuprel 2–10 mcg/min.

73. You encounter a patient with a P-R interval of 0.16, a QRS duration of 0.08, and a regular R-R Interval. This patient is in
    (A) atrial fibrillation.
    (B) sinus rhythm with first-degree heart block.
    (C) sinus rhythm.
    (D) supraventricular tachycardia.

74. A 14-year-old female is crying and hysterical after breaking up with her boyfriend. She had a syncopal episode prior to EMS arrival. Vitals are BP 110/68, pulse 130, and respirations 36. You place her on the cardiac monitor and interpret the following rhythm as

   (A) sinus arrest.
   (B) sinus bradycardia.
   (C) sinus dysrhythmia.
   (D) sinus tachycardia.

Question 75 and 76 are based on the following scenario:

A 62-year-old male fainted while working in the yard. His current vitals are BP 108/64, pulse 102 and irregular, and respirations 24. The ECG shows the following rhythm

75. You interpret his ECG rhythm as
   (A) second-degree heart block.
   (B) sinus rhythm.
   (C) atrial fibrillation.
   (D) sinus bradycardia.

76. The patient complains of feeling that he is going to black out again. Vitals are unchanged. Treatment for the patient should include
   (A) oxygen, monitor, IV, observation, and transport.
   (B) oxygen, monitor, IV, Atropine.
   (C) oxygen, monitor, IV, Adenocard.
   (D) oxygen, monitor, IV, synchronized cardioversion.

Questions 77 and 78 are based on the following scenario:

EMS is called to the scene of a 72-year-old male with a history of cardiac disease. He is unconscious and unresponsive. BP is not obtainable, pulse 140 and weak, respirations 6. After placing him on the monitor, you note the following rhythm:

77. You interpret the rhythm as
    (A) supraventricular tachycardia.
    (B) ventricular tachycardia.
    (C) atrial fibrillation with a rapid ventricular response.
    (D) ventricular fibrillation.

78. Initial treatment of the patient should include
    (A) synchronized cardioversion.
    (B) defibrillation.
    (C) transcutaneous pacing.
    (D) Adenocard 6 mg IVP.

---

79. A healthy female is being transported for preterm labor contractions. Per protocol, she is lying slightly tilted on her left side, is on oxygen via nonrebreather mask, and an IV is established at KVO. You place her on the monitor and notice the following rhythm.

The rhythm is
(A) sinus rhythm with PACs.
(B) sinus rhythm with PJCs.
(C) sinus dysrhythmia.
(D) sinus rhythm with PVCs.

80. A 33-year-old man has just finished playing basketball. He is complaining of chest discomfort. Physical exam shows a rapid pulse, BP 128/64, respirations 30. ECG monitor shows the following rhythm:

    Treatment includes:
    (A) Adenocard 6 mg IV.
    (B) cardioversion 100 joules.
    (C) continuing to assess and monitor the patient.
    (D) defibrillation.

81. All of the following are appropriate end points for procainamide administration except
    (A) 17 mcg/kg administered.
    (B) hypotension.
    (C) widening of the QRS complex greater than 50%.
    (D) the dysrhythmia is suppressed.

82. A patient experiencing a hypertensive crisis should receive the following medication:
    (A) nitroglycerin.
    (B) Procardia.
    (C) aspirin.
    (D) oxygen.

83. The medication treatment of choice for a narrow complex tachycardia in an unstable patient is
    (A) Adenocard.
    (B) lidocaine.
    (C) cardioversion.
    (D) Versed.

84. After defibrillating a patient with pulseless ventricular tachycardia, the first medication they should receive is
    (A) epinephrine or vasopressin
    (B) lidocaine or amiodarone
    (C) epinephrine or lidocaine
    (D) vasopressin or amiodarone

85. Vasopressin is useful in the management of
    (A) complete heart block.
    (B) PSVT.
    (C) ventricular fibrillation.
    (D) torsades v tach.

86. The recommended dose of vasopressin in v fib or pulseless v tach is
    (A) 17 mg/min IV infusion.
    (B) 2–4 mg/min IV infusion.
    (C) 40 units IV repeated once in 5 minutes.
    (D) 40 units IV in a single dose.

87. All of the following medications can be administered via endotracheal route except
    (A) lidocaine, Atropine.
    (B) epinephrine, amiodarone.
    (C) oxygen, epinephrine.
    (D) Narcan, lidocaine.

88. A second dose of amiodarone is necessary for a patient in v fib. The dose to be administered is
    (A) 300 mg IV.
    (B) 150 mg IV.
    (C) 100 mg IV.
    (D) 40 units IV.

89. You arrive on scene of a 35-year-old male who is in distress. He is grabbing his throat with both hands. What should you do first?
    (A) Get behind him and perform the Heimlich maneuver.
    (B) Give five back blows.
    (C) Ask, "Are you choking?" and look for a response.
    (D) Alternate back blows with abdominal thrusts.

90. Acute coronary syndrome is defined as
    (A) a sudden ischemic disorder of the heart.
    (B) a myocardial infarction.
    (C) congestive heart failure.
    (D) triple vessel disease.

91. All of the following are considered anginal equivalents except
    (A) diaphoresis, syncope, dizziness.
    (B) dyspnea, palpitations, syncope.
    (C) hypoglycemia, chest pain, dyspnea.
    (D) fatigue, dizziness, palpitations.

92. Which signs/symptoms are not considered atypical presentation of myocardial ischemia?
    (A) Neck pain, jaw pain, left arm pain
    (B) Lower extremity pain, shoulder pain, abdominal pain
    (C) Epigastric pain, reproducible pain, sharp or knifelike pain
    (D) Nausea, dizziness, palpitations

93. Nitroglycerin has all of the following properties except
    (A) it prevents vasospasm.
    (B) it is a vasodilator.
    (C) it decreases afterload.
    (D) it decreases preload.

Questions 94 and 95 are based on the following scenario:

You respond to a patient with shortness of breath. The patient said he was awakened from his sleep with shortness of breath. Assessment reveals vitals: BP of 188/94, pulse 116, respiration 36, and a pulse oximeter reading of 88%. Lung sound assessment reveals crackles in the posterior bases.

94. You suspect this patient to be suffering from
    (A) a myocardial infarction.
    (B) angina.
    (C) congestive heart failure.
    (D) a respiratory disorder.

95. As you continue your assessment on this patient, he becomes lethargic. BP is now 198/102, pulse 136, respirations 48, with increased pulmonary congestion. Treatment should include
    (A) preparation for intubation.
    (B) preparation for immediate transcutaneous pacing.
    (C) Adenocard 6 mg rapid IVP.
    (D) lidocaine 1.0 mg/kg IVP.

---

96. A patient is experiencing severe chest pain and dyspnea. He is nauseated and extremely diaphoretic, BP is 78/42, pulse is tachycardic, and respirations 36. The patient weighs 190 pounds. ECG shows the following rhythm:

    Initial treatment should include
    (A) lidocaine 85 to 130 mg IVP.
    (B) defibrillation.
    (C) cardioversion.
    (D) Adenocard 6 mg rapid IVP.

97. A patient is involved in a motor vehicle crash and is semiconscious. Vitals BP 92/54, pulse 110, respirations 24. ECG shows the following rhythm:

Which treatment is appropriate?
(A) Immediate cardioversion
(B) Immediate defibrillation
(C) Lidocaine 1 mg/kg
(D) Continued observation

98. You just administered Atropine 0.5 mg for a patient with a symptomatic bradycardia and multifocal PVCs. Suddenly your patient becomes unconscious and goes into ventricular fibrillation. Your next action is to
(A) administer lidocaine 1.5 mg/kg.
(B) administer another 0.5 mg of Atropine IVP.
(C) cardiovert at 100 joules.
(D) defibrillate at 200 joules.

99. You just delivered three stacked shocks to a patient in ventricular fibrillation. The monitor now shows asystole. You confirm in two leads. Your next action is to
(A) administer Atropine 1 mg IVP.
(B) consider immediate transcutaneous pacing.
(C) fluid bolus 200 cc.
(D) defibrillate at 360 joules.

100. A 22-year-old female has just finished jogging five miles. She is complaining of palpitations. Vitals are BP 112/68, pulse 148, respirations 32. She denies drug use. ECG shows the following rhythm:

Treatment should include
(A) adenosine 6 mg rapid IVP.
(B) cardioversion at 100 joules.
(C) vagal maneuver.
(D) continued observation.

101. Which of the following rhythms require immediate transcutaneous pacing?
     (A) Junctional tachycardia
     (B) Sinus bradycardia with first-degree heart block
     (C) Supraventricular tachycardia
     (D) Symptomatic third-degree AV block

102. When performing transcutaneous pacing, the paramedic should increase the
     _____delivered until mechanical capture is obtained.
     (A) joules
     (B) milliamps
     (C) rate
     (D) millivolts

103. You are called to a church where a 62-year-old male feels that his pacemaker is not
     functioning properly. He is conscious and alert but states that he is going to "pass
     out." You place him on your monitor and observe the following rhythm:

     Treatment for this patient should include
     (A) oxygen, IV, monitor, and continued observation.
     (B) oxygen, IV, monitor, and lidocaine.
     (C) oxygen, IV, monitor, nitroglycerin, and aspirin.
     (D) oxygen, IV, monitor, cardioversion.

104. You arrive on scene of a patient who has had steadily worsening chest pain for four
     hours. He has taken 12 nitroglycerin with no relief. The best description of this type
     of chest pain is
     (A) stable angina.
     (B) unstable angina.
     (C) Prinzmetal's angina.
     (D) vasospastic angina.

105. You are evaluating a male patient with complaints of a "tearing sensation" epigas-
     tric pain. He tells you that the pain began two hours ago after eating lunch. He says
     he has never experienced any pain like this. He rates the pain as a 10, and states
     that it is radiating into his back and shoulder. Based on the information provided,
     you suspect the pain may be the result of:
     (A) a myocardial infarction.
     (B) a hiatal hernia.
     (C) an aortic aneurysm.
     (D) a gastric esophageal reflux disease.

106. The effect of Dopamine administration at an infusion rate greater than 20 mcg/kg/minute includes
    (A) arterial vasoconstriction only.
    (B) venous vasoconstriction only.
    (C) both arterial and venous peripheral vasoconstriction.
    (D) improved renal blood flow.

107. The recommended dose of vasopressin in cardiac arrest due to pulseless VT or VF is:
    (A) 20 units IV bolus repeated once in 10 minutes.
    (B) a single IV bolus dose of 40 units.
    (C) 40 units IV bolus repeated once in 10 minutes.
    (D) 300 mg IV.

108. What is the initial and repeat dosing schedule for sodium bicarbonate administration?
    (A) 1 amp; the repeat dose is 1/2 amp every 10 minutes.
    (B) 1 mEq/kg; the repeat dose is 1/2 the initial dose in 10 minutes.
    (C) 1 mg/kg; the repeat dose is 1/2 the initial dose in 10 minutes.
    (D) 1 mEq/kg; the repeat dose is 1 mEq/kg in 10 minutes.

109. An unwanted side effect of Dopamine administration includes
    (A) increased myocardial oxygen demand.
    (B) respiratory depression.
    (C) ventricular dysrhythmias.
    (D) dilation of renal vessels at high doses.

110. You have administered an initial dose of amiodarone for a patient in ventricular fibrillation. The repeat dose of this medication should be
    (A) 300 mg.
    (B) 150 mg.
    (C) 0.04 mg/kg.
    (D) 1 to 1.5 mg/kg.

111. Amiodarone
    (A) should be given by rapid IV infusion only.
    (B) may produce vasodilation and hypotension.
    (C) has a maximum dose of 17 mg/kg.
    (D) is indicated only in cardiac arrest.

112. Lidocaine may be lethal if administered to a patient with which of the following dysrhythmias?
    (A) Sinus rhythm with PACs.
    (B) Second-degree AV block type I.
    (C) Accelerated junctional rhythm.
    (D) Second-degree AV block type II.

113. A 68-year-old male suffered a syncopal episode while golfing. The cardiac monitor shows a sinus tachycardia at 142 beats/minute without ectopy. His blood pressure is presently 78/42. Despite a 200 cc fluid bolus the patient remains hypotensive. He has an altered mental status with cool and diaphoretic skin. Of the following, which is not likely to be considered for administration to this patient?
    (A) Dopamine
    (B) Nitroglycerin
    (C) A second fluid bolus
    (D) High-flow oxygen

114. Sodium bicarbonate administration may be useful for treating
    (A) beta-blocker overdoses and hypocalcemia.
    (B) preexisting acidosis and hypokalemia.
    (C) tricyclic antidepressant overdoses and hyperkalemia.
    (D) calcium channel blocker overdoses and hyperkalemia.

115. Before providing rescue breathing to an unresponsive victim, you must check for breathing. You do this by
    (A) opening the airway.
    (B) shaking and shouting to stimulate him or her to breathe.
    (C) looking, listening, and feeling the airflow through the victim's nose or mouth.
    (D) establishing unresponsiveness.

116. You are performing rescue breathing. When you initially open the airway, how many initial breaths do you give?
    (A) 1
    (B) 2
    (C) 3
    (D) 4

117. Where should you place your hands on the chest of an adult victim when you are performing chest compressions?
    (A) On the top of the sternum
    (B) On the lower one third of the sternum
    (C) On the lower half of the sternum, at the nipple line
    (D) Over the very bottom of the sternum

118. What is the ratio of chest compressions to ventilations when performing one-person CPR on an adult?
    (A) 5 compressions to 1 ventilation
    (B) 15 compressions to 1 ventilation
    (C) 15 compressions to 2 ventilations
    (D) 5 compressions to 2 ventilations

119. What is the speed you should use to perform chest compressions for an adult victim of cardiac arrest?
    (A) 100 times per minute
    (B) 60 times per minute
    (C) 120 times per minute
    (D) 80 times per minute

Questions 120–122 are based on the following scenario:

You arrive on-scene of a 56-year-old male patient who developed chest pain while mowing the lawn on a hot August day. He states the pain has subsided after a few minutes of rest. Your assessment shows that he is alert and oriented, BP 148/92, pulse 48, respirations of 20. His skin is warm and moist. He has no past medical history and takes no medications. You attach the monitor and observe the following rhythm:

120. Treatment should include
    (A) Atropine 0.5 mg IVP.
    (B) Adenocard 5 mg IVP.
    (C) Transport for evaluation.
    (D) No treatment is necessary.

121. Your patient insists that he became overheated and that caused his chest pain. He is refusing any treatment. As he begins to argue with EMS, he again develops chest pain. Treatment should include
    (A) Atropine 0.5 mg IVP.
    (B) Adenocard 5 mg IV.
    (C) nitroglycerin administration.
    (D) immediate transcutaneous pacing.

122. Your patient suddenly becomes lethargic. BP is 82/40, pulse 36, respirations 10. You note the following rhythm on the monitor:

   Treatment should include
    (A) Atropine 0.5 mg IV.
    (B) Adenocard 5 mg IV.
    (C) stopping nitroglycerin administration.
    (D) immediate transcutaneous pacing.

Questions 123–125 are based on the following scenario:

You arrive on scene of a patient who presented in ventricular fibrillation. After immediately defibrillating the patient at 200, 300, and 360 joules, no vitals signs are obtainable and you note the following rhythm on the monitor:

123. Initial treatment should include:
     (A) immediate transcutaneous pacing.
     (B) Atropine 1 mg IVP.
     (C) epinephrine 1mg IVP.
     (D) vasopressin 40 units IVP.

124. There is no change in the patient's condition. Continued treatment should include
     (A) immediate transcutaneous pacing.
     (B) Atropine 1 mg IVP.
     (C) epinephrine 1 mg IVP.
     (D) vasopressin 40 units IVP.

125. Treatable causes of PEA include all of the following except
     (A) hypoxia.
     (B) hypervolemia.
     (C) acidosis.
     (D) tension pneumothorax.

Answers and Answer Explanations

1. **(C)** Arteriosclerosis is a disease of the arterial vessel marked by thickening, hardening, and loss of elasticity in the arterial walls. Atherosclerosis **(A)** is the most common form of arteriosclerosis, usually involving medium-sized and large arteries. Arteriolonecrosis, **(B)** is destruction (necrosis) of the arteriole. Choice **(D)**, angina is chest discomfort associated with a deficiency of oxygen supply to the heart muscle.

2. **(B)** The layers of an artery include the tunica intima (the innermost layer), the tunica media (the middle muscular layer), and the tunica adventitia (the outermost layer).

3. **(B)** Cardiac output is defined as the volume of blood ejected from the left ventricle into the arterial system each minute. Preload **(A)** is defined as the pressure within the ventricles at the end of diastole. Afterload **(C)** is defined as the resistance against which the heart must pump. Stroke volume **(D)** is defined as the amount of blood ejected by the heart in one cardiac contraction.

4. **(C)** Automaticity is the ability of certain cardiac cells to initiate impulses spontaneously (self-depolarization). This is a special characteristic of cardiac cells.

5. **(A)** Afterload is defined as the resistance against which the heart must pump. Blood pressure **(B)** is defined as pressure that is exerted on the walls of arteries. Preload **(C)** is defined as the pressure within the ventricles at the end of diastole. Cardiac output **(D)** is defined as the volume of blood ejected from the left ventricle into the arterial system each minute.

6. **(B)** Stroke volume is defined as the amount of blood ejected by the heart in one cardiac contraction. Cardiac output **(A)** is defined as the volume of blood ejected from the left ventricle into the arterial system each minute. Preload **(C)** is defined as the pressure within the ventricles at the end of diastole. Afterload **(D)** is defined as the resistance against which the heart must pump.

7. **(B)** The mitral valve is located between the left atrium and the left ventricle. The tricuspid valve **(A)** is located between the right atrium and right ventricle. The aortic valve, **(C)**, is located between the left ventricle and ascending aorta. The pulmonic valve, **(D)**, is located between the right ventricle and the pulmonary artery.

8. **(D)** The pericardium is the fibroserous sac enclosing the heart that is composed of two layers, the epicardium and the parietal pericardium. The myocardium **(A)** is the middle layer of the walls of the heart. The septum **(B)** is the inner walls of the heart that separate the right and left atria of the heart from the ventricles. The endocardium **(C)** is the innermost layer of the heart.

9. **(C)** Blood returning to the heart is received by the atria. Deoxygenated blood is returned to the heart via the vena cava to the right atrium. Oxygenated blood returns to the heart via the pulmonary vein to the left atrium.

10. **(A)** The left ventricle receives oxygenated blood from the left atrium and pumps blood into the aorta where it is distributed to the body.

11. **(C)** The aorta is a large artery that receives oxygenated blood from the left ventricle and carries blood away from the heart, to the body.

12. **(A)** The right atrium and right ventricle are separated by the tricuspid valve. The left atrium and left ventricle are separated by the mitral valve **(D)**. The semi-lunar valve **(C)** is a generic name given to the aortic and pulmonic valves because of its shape. The aortic valve **(B)** separates the left ventricle from the ascending aorta.

13. **(A)** The parasympathetic nervous system is a division of the autonomic nervous system that is responsible for controlling vegetative functions. When stimu-lated, a decreased heart rate is one possible response of the body.

14. **(C)** The chordae tendinea connect the leaflets of the heart valves to the papillary muscles.

15. **(B)** Deoxygenated blood is pumped into the lungs from the right ventricle to the pulmonary artery.

16. **(C)** Semilunar valves is a generic name given to the aortic and pulmonic valves because of their shape. The semilunar valves close during diastole and prevent backflow into the ventricles.

17. **(B)** Veins carry blood from the body back to the heart. The pulmonary vein is no exception but it carries oxygen-rich blood from the lungs back to the heart. Therefore, it is the only vein in the body to carry oxygenated blood.

18. **(D)** This is a basic anatomy question of blood flow: right atrium, tricuspid valve, right ventricle, pulmonary artery, lungs, pulmonary vein, left atrium, mitral valve, left ventricle, aorta.

19. **(D)** In Lead II placement, the positive electrode is located on the left leg, the nega-tive electrode on the right shoulder, and the ground on the left shoulder.

20. **(D)** In Lead III placement, the positive electrode is located on the left leg, the nega-tive electrode on the left shoulder, and the ground on the right shoulder.

21. **(C)** 0.04 seconds are measured in each small square on the ECG graph paper. Each large block is 0.20 seconds.

22. **(D)** Each large block on the ECG graph paper represents 0.20 seconds. Each small block measures 0.04 seconds.

23. **(D)** Fundamentals of ECG interpretation tell us that a normal PR interval is 0.12 to 0.20 seconds.

24. **(D)** Fundamentals of ECG interpretation tell us that the normal duration of a QRS complex is 0.08 to 0.12 seconds.

25. **(A)** The intrinsic firing rate for a ventricular pacemaker is 20 to 40 beats per minute. The intrinsic firing rate of the SA node (the primary pacemaker of the heart) is 60 to 100 **(C)**. The AV node also has pacemaker ability at a firing rate of 40 to 60 beats per minute **(B)**. There is no normal pacemake of the heart with a firing rate of 100 to 150 beats per minute.

26. **(D)** The PR interval is the time elapsing between the beginning of the P wave and the beginning of the QRS complex. The normal duration of the PR interval is 0.12 to 0.20 seconds. **(A)**, the QRS complex reflects ventricular depolarization. **(B)**, first degree heart block is an ECG rhythm with a PR interval greater than 0.20 seconds. **(C)**, the QT interval is measured from the beginning of the Q wave to the end of the T wave.

27. **(C)** The return of a cardiac muscle to its resting state is repolarization. Automaticity **(D)** is the ability for certain cardiac cells to initiate impulses spontaneously. Choice **(A)**, synapse, is the junction point of two neurons. Choice **(B)**, depolarization, is the change from the resting potential to a positive charge inside the cardiac cell.

28. **(C)** The normal pacemaker of the heart is the sinoatrial node. The normal firing rate of the SA node is 60–100 beats per minute. The AV node **(A)** is the secondary pacemaker of the heart with a firing rate of 40–60 beats per minute. The third pacemaker of the heart is the Purkinje fibers **(B)** in the ventricles with a firing rate of 20-40 beats per minute. The internodal pathways **(D)** do not have pacemaker capabilities.

29. **(A)** The SA node is located high in the right atrium.

30. **(A)** The Bundle of His does not contain pacemaker capabilities. The normal pacemaker of the heart is the SA node **(C)** with a firing rate of 60–100 beats per minute. The AV node **(D)** is the secondary pacemaker of the heart with a firing rate of 40–60 beats per minute. The third pacemaker of the heart is the Purkinje fibers **(B)** in the ventricles with a firing rate of 20–40 beats per minute.

31. **(B)** The intrinsic firing rate of the AV node is 40–60 beats per minute. The normal pacemaker of the heart is the sinoatrial node with a normal firing rate of 60–100 beats per minute. The third pacemaker of the heart is the Purkinje fibers in the ventricles with a firing rate of 20–40 beats per minute **(A)**. The internodal pathways do not have pacemaker capabilities. **(C)** is incorrect. No normal pacemaker of the heart has a firing rate of 40–80 beats per minute.

32. **(A)** The first component of the ECG is the p wave, which represents depolarization of the atria.

33. **(C)** The QRS complex reflects ventricular depolarization. The Q wave is the first negative deflection after the p wave; the r wave is the first positive deflection after the p wave; and the s wave is the first negative deflection after the r wave. All three waves are not always present.

34. **(D)** The t wave reflects repolarization of the ventricles.

35. **(A)** The PR interval is the time elapsing between the beginning of the p wave and the beginning of the QRS complex **(C)**. The normal duration of the PR interval is 0.12 to 0.20 seconds. The PR interval represents the time it takes for an electrical impulse to be transmitted from the atria to the ventricles. **(B)**, the t wave represents ventricular repolarization. **(C)**, the QRS complex reflects ventricular depolarization. **(D)**, the J point is found at the junction of the QRS complex and the ST segment.

36. **(C)** The period of the cardiac cycle when stimulation will not produce depolarization is the absolute refractory period. The refractory period **(A)** is a period of time when myocardial cells have not yet completely repolarized and cannot be stimulated again. The relative refractory period **(D)** is a period of time when a significantly strong stimulus may produce depolarization. **(B)** is not a term used in cardiology.

37. **(D)** The period of the cardiac cycle when a significantly strong stimulus may produce depolarization is the relative refractory period. **(C)**, the period of the cardiac cycle when stimulation will not produce depolarization is the absolute refractory period. The refractory period **(A)** is a period of time when myocardial cells have not yet completely repolarized and cannot be stimulated again. **(B)** is not a term used in cardiology.

38. **(C)** Stimulation of the vagus nerve can occur in many ways. When stimulated, a decrease in heart rate may be observed.

39. **(A)** A rapid heart rate or irregular heartbeat may cause a patient to experience a sensation commonly referred to as palpitations. Another common term to describe this sensation is "fluttering."

40. **(B)** Cardiogenic shock is the most severe form of pump failure that often results in dysrhythmias, hypotension, respiratory failure, and possibly organ failure. The heart rate is initially elevated as the body attempts to compensate for the shock. Hypertension will not be present in cardiogenic shock.

41. **(D)** Left ventricular failure occurs when the heart fails as an effective forward pump, which causes backpressure of blood into pulmonary circulation. When the backpressure become high enough, it forces the blood into the capillaries of the alveoli resulting in pulmonary congestion. Adventitious lung sounds such as crackles (rales) are commonly present in left ventricular failure.

42. **(D)** Administration of nitroglycerin gr1/150 sublingual is the only correct choice for this question. Establishing an IV **(A)** is warranted for a patient complaining of chest pain but the IV should be run at KVO. Administration of Lasix **(B)** may be appropriate if signs/symptoms of left ventricular failure are present but the dose of 100 mg is excessive. You certainly want to administer oxygen **(C)** but a high flow rate is recommended to increase oxygen delivery to the myocardium.

43. **(C)** Administration of IV furosemide and morphine are appropriate in the prehospital management of left ventricular failure. **(A)** is incorrect because you want to place the patient in a sitting position to facilitate breathing *not* supine. **(B)** is incorrect because increasing venous return to the heart will worsen the

condition. **(D)** is incorrect because the administration of oxygen should be at a high flow rate NOT 3 liters by nasal cannula.

44. **(B)** Management of cardiogenic shock may include the administration of IV dopamine. Dopamine is a vasopressor that increases cardiac output. You would not want to administer morphine or nitroglycerin **(A and C)** since they will further lower the blood pressure. An IV at 500 cc/hr **(D)** is not warranted because administering additional IV fluid to the patient will worsen the condition.

45. **(B)** Immediate defibrillation is required upon the diagnosis of ventricular fibrillation. Management of the airway is important, but the airway should be maintained by basic methods until defibrillation is performed. Endotracheal intubation **(A)** may be attempted after defibrillation. Administration of medications **(C and D)** is secondary treatment to defibrillation.

46. **(B)** Back and flank pain described as a tearing sensation and a pulsating abdominal mass are classic signs of an abdominal aortic aneurysm. Gentle handling and rapid transport to the hospital are essential once the diagnosis is made. Palpating the mass **(A)** is contraindicated and may worsen the condition. **(C)** and **(D)** are incorrect because there is not enough information given in the scenario to administer any medications.

47. **(C)** Procainamide should be discontinued if the QRS is widened 50% of its original width, the maximum dose is achieved, the arrhythmia is suppressed, or hypotension develops. **(A)**, **(B)**, and **(D)** are correct.

48. **(B)** Adenosine is not indicated in the treatment of ventricular fibrillation. It is useful in the treatment of narrow complex tachycardias. Epinephrine, lidocaine, and vasopressin all have indications in the treatment of ventricular fibrillation.

49. **(D)** Paroxysmal supraventricular tachycardia (PSVT) may require synchronized cardioversion, especially if the patient is hemodynamically unstable. Pulseless ventricular tachycardia **(A)** and ventricular fibrillation **(C)** require immediate defibrillation, not cardioversion. Syncrhonized cardioversion is not indicated in pulseless electrical activity, **(B)**.

50. **(B)** ABCs and high flow oxygen are indicated for this patient and cardioversion needs to be performed because the patient is in ventricular tachycardia *with a pulse*. **(A)** and **(D)** are incorrect because this patient should receive cardioversion prior to any administration of medication. **(C)** is incorrect because Adenocard is not indicated.

51. **(C)** The patient's history should lead you to the conclusion of a vasovagal episode. Having a bowel movement or bearing down to have a bowel movement can stimulate the vagus nerve and slow down the heart rate enough to cause dizziness/syncope. **(A)**, **(B)**, and **(D)** are incorrect because the scenario did not give you enough information to reach that conclusion.

52. **(C)** Bystander CPR is a courageous effort to save a life and is important in the chain of survival but there are times when bystanders perform CPR inappropriately. As an EMS provider, you must stop bystander CPR and verify a patent airway, the absence of breathing, and pulselessness when you arrive on scene.

53. **(B)** Hyperthermia is not considered a treatable cause of pulseless electrical activity. All of the following are considered treatable causes of PEA: hypovolemia, hypoxia, acidosis, hyper/hypokalemia, hypothermia, drug overdose, cardiac tamponade, tension pneumothorax, coronary thrombosis, and pulmonary embolism.

54. **(C)** IV, oxygen, and Adenocard 6 mg rapid IV push are indicated for this patient. Cardioversion **(D)** may be needed if the medication fails to convert the rhythm but is not immediately indicated since the patient lacks serious signs/symptoms of chest pain, dyspnea, or hypotension. Although the items in **(B)** are things you may do for the patient, it is not the best choice. **(A)** is incorrect since you cannot assume this.

55. **(A)** Of the choices listed, nitroglycerin is the best answer since it is indicated for the treatment of chest pain. A fluid bolus **(B)** is not indicated since the patient is not hypotensive and already has evidence of pulmonary congestion (crackles). Atropine **(C)** may be needed if the patient develops unstable signs/symptoms. Transcutaneous pacing, **(D)**, is not indicated at this point.

56. **(A)** Atropine is indicated for this patient since it appears that he is deteriorating (the BP has dropped and increased pulmonary congestion). At this point, the application of pacing pads to the patient would not be unreasonable in preparation for the possibility of future deterioration of the patient. **(B)** and **(C)** are not indicated for this patient.

57. **(C)** Immediate transcutaneous pacing is required for a hemodynamically unstable (altered LOC, chest pain, dyspnea, hypotension) bradycardic rhythm.

58. **(A)** This rhythm is ventricular fibrillation. Of the choices listed, amiodarone 300 mg is indicated. The dose of lidocaine and procainamide (**B** and **C**) are incorrect. Magnesium **(D)** is not indicated.

59. **(A)** If a second dose of amiodarone is needed in the treatment of ventricular fibrillation, the correct dose is 150 mg.

60. **(A)** This is a basic life support question to which you must know the correct answer. If you missed this question, do yourself a favor and review infant, child, and adult CPR prior to taking your certification exam.

61. **(A)** This a basic life support question to which you must know the correct answer. If you missed this question, do yourself a favor and review infant, child, and adult CPR prior to taking your certification test.

62. **(D)** Calcium chloride may be useful in a dialysis patient in cardiac arrest with PEA. Dialysis patients often suffer from hyperkalemia as a result of their disease process.

63. **(D)** Vasopressin is indicated in ventricular fibrillation at a dose of 40 *units* IV to be administered as a *one-time* dose.

64. **(C)** The maximum amount of procainamide to be administered is 17 mg/kg. The patient's weight is 89.09 kg; 89.09 × 17 equals 1,514 mg maximum dose.

65. **(C)** The initial dose of adenosine is 6 mg. Because the half-life of adenosine is so short, all doses should be administered rapid IV push, immediately followed by a 20 cc bolus of fluid.

66. **(B)** 162–325 mg is the current recommended dose of aspirin for a patient experiencing chest pain/acute coronary syndrome.

67. **(D)** This is a simple math for medication administration question. If you missed this question, a review of math is strongly recommended prior to taking your examination.

68. **(B)** Two grams of lidocaine in 500 cc of solution will provide a mixture of 4 mg/ml. To deliver 2 mg/min using 60 gtt/ml tubing, you need to administer 30 drops per minute.

69. **(D)** The best treatment for a shockable rhythm is defibrillation. If an AED is in the process of delivering a shock, allow it to do so. Removing the AED to apply your own equipment **(C)** will likely cause a delay in this essential treatment. **(A)** and **(B)** are incorrect because these steps should have already been done along with the application of the AED.

70. **(A)** The classic description of pain associated with a dissecting aortic aneurysm is a ripping or tearing sensation.

71. **(B)** Vasopressin is indicated only for the management of ventricular fibrillation and pulseless ventricular tachycardia.

72. **(A)** The only correct choice is Atropine. Atropine is indicated since the patient presents with chest pain, difficulty breathing, heart rate 42, and BP 76/42. These are considered serious signs and symptoms. A transvenous pacemaker is not utilized in EMS. Having a transcutaneous pacemaker available may be useful if the medication is ineffective, an altered LOC is observed, or the patient deteriorates. **(B)** is incorrect because the patient needs high flow oxygen. **(D)** is incorrect because the dose is wrong.

73. **(C)** Don't overlook the obvious. This question displays the normal values of sinus rhythm.

74. **(D)** This ECG demonstrates a sinus tachycardia.

75. **(C)** This ECG demonstrates atrial fibrillation

76. **(A)** Treatment for this patient would include oxygen, IV, continued monitoring and observation. Studies have shown that atrial fibrillation can decrease cardiac output as much as 33%. This patient should be transported for evaluation, especially if this rhythm is a new development for the patient. **(B)**, **(C)**, and **(D)** are not indicated in this scenario.

77. **(B)** This ECG demonstrates ventricular tachycardia

78. **(A)** Treatment of this unstable patient is synchronous cardioversion. Defibrillation **(B)** is not indicated since the patient has a pulse. If this patient were pulseless, the treatment would include defibrillation. **(C)** and **(D)** are not indicated for this patient.

79. **(A)** This ECG demonstrates a sinus rhythm with PACs.

80. **(A)** Treatment for this patient includes Adenocard 6 mg IVP since chest pain is present. This scenario does not present an unstable patient and therefore cardioversion **(B)** is not indicated. Although you will continue to assess and monitor this patient, **(C)** is not the best choice since chest pain is present and Adenocard is indicated. **(D)** is not indicated.

81. **(A)** 17 mcg/kg is incorrect because procainamide is delivered in mg/kg.

82. **(D)** Of the choices listed, oxygen is the only appropriate treatment. Nitroglycerin and aspirin **(A and C)** are not indicated since the scenario does not include a complaint of chest pain. Procardia, **(B)**, is contraindicated.

83. **(A)** Adenocard is indicated for the treatment of a narrow complex tachycardia.

84. **(A)** The first medication to be delivered after defibrillating pulseless ventricular tachycardia is epinephrine or vasopressin.

85. **(C)** Vasopressin is indicated in the management of ventricular fibrillation and pulseless ventricular tachycardia.

86. **(D)** A single dose of 40 units IV is the recommended dose of vasopressin.

87. **(B)** Amiodarone has not been approved to be administered via the endotracheal route.

88. **(B)** The correct second dose of Amiodarone for a patient in v fib is 150 mg IVP.

89. **(C)** This is a basic life support question. If you missed this question, do yourself a favor and review infant, child, and adult CPR prior to taking your certification test.

90. **(A)** Acute coronary syndrome is defined as a sudden ischemic disorder of the heart. If you are not familiar with this terminology, it is strongly recommended that you review Chapter Six of the American Heart Association ACLS Providers manual.

91. **(C)** Hypoglycemia is not considered an anginal equivalent.

92. **(A)** Neck pain, jaw pain, and left arm pain are considered a classic presentation of myocardial ischemia and not atypical.

93. **(C)** Nitroglycerin is a vasodilator, works against vasospasm, and decreases pre-load. It does not have an effect on afterload.

94. **(C)** The classic signs/symptoms in this scenario that should lead you to suspect congestive heart failure in this patient is: "He was awakened from his sleep with shortness of breath" and he has signs of pulmonary congestion (crackles) present.

95. **(A)** Of the choices listed, preparation for intubation is the only correct answer.

96. **(C)** Treatment for this unstable patient is synchronous cardioversion since the patient has a pulse. If this patient was pulseless, the treatment would include defibrillation **(B)**. Lidocaine, **(A)**, is not *initial* treatment but may be given secondary to cardioversion. **(D)** is not indicated.

97. **(C)** Lidocaine 1 mg/kg is indicated for the treatment of bigeminal PVCs.

98. **(D)** Immediate defibrillation is indicated for the treatment of ventricular fibrillation.

99. **(B)** According to the ACLS algorithm, immediate transcutaneous pacing should be considered early in asystole when the patient is witnessed going into asystole.

100. **(C)** Since the patient's presentation is considered stable, a vagal maneuver is indicated.

101. **(D)** Immediate transcutaneous pacing is indicated for type two second-degree AV block and third-degree AV block when accompanied with symptoms.

102. **(B)** Milliamps should be increased until mechanical capture is obtained.

103. **(A)** This rhythm indicates a paced rhythm with 1:1 capture. The patient should receive oxygen, IV, monitor, and continued observation. Neither lidocaine nor cardioversion **(B** and **D)** are indicated for this rhythm and nitroglycerin and ASA **(C)** are not indicated for the present complaints.

104. **(B)** Four hours of chest pain with no relief after 12 nitroglycerin is best classified as unstable angina. Stable angina **(A)** is somewhat predictable in onset, severity, character, and response to therapy. Prinzmetal's (AKA vasospastic angina) **(C** and **D)** is angina caused by decreased blood flow due to spasm of a vessel.

105. **(C)** A severe "tearing sensation" epigastric pain that radiates into the back and shoulders is the classic description of pain often associated with an aortic aneurysm.

106. **(C)** Dopamine at 1–2 mcg/kg/min administration causes renal artery dilation to occur. At 2–10 mcg/kg/min, it primarily affects beta receptors. At 10–15 mcg/kg/min, it primarily affects both alpha and beta receptors. At 15–20 mcg/kg/min it primarily affects alpha receptors.

107. **(B)** Vasopressin is indicated in ventricular fibrillation at a dose of 40 *units* IV to be administered as a *one-time* dose.

108. **(B)** Sodium bicarbonate has been in use for a long time. Current dosing instructions include 1 mEq/kg for the initial dose and half the initial dose or 0.5 mEq/kg for the second dose. It is suggested the repeat dose be given 10 minutes after the first.

109. **(A)** Dopamine is a vasopressor primarily used by EMS to improve cardiac output in cardiogenic shock. A side effect of Dopamine administration is an increased oxygen demand and workload on the heart. Therefore, Dopamine must be used with caution when cardiac ischemia is suspected.

110. **(B)** The second dose of amiodarone for the treatment of ventricular fibrillation is 150 mg.

111. **(B)** A side effect of amiodarone administration is vasodilation and hypotension. This is mainly the reason amiodarone is to be administered slow IV. Rapid IV administration of amiodarone may produce profound hypotension.

112. **(D)** Lidocaine is contraindicated in severe degrees of SA, AV, or intraventricular blocks because it may produce serious ventricular dysrhythmias or develop into complete heart block.

113. **(B)** Nitroglycerin is not indicated for this patient because of the presence of hypotension.

114. **(C)** Prehospital indications for the administration of sodium bicarbonate include tricyclic antidepressant overdose, hyperkalemia, and preexisting or suspected acidosis.

Questions 115 to 119 are basic life support questions. If you miss any of these questions, it is essential to review basic CPR prior to taking your exam.

115. **(C)** Looking, listening, and feeling the airflow through the victim's nose or mouth

116. **(B)** Two breaths

117. **(C)** On the lower half of the sternum, at the nipple line

118. **(C)** 15 compressions to 2 ventilations

119. **(A)** 100 times per minute

120. **(C)** Transport for evaluation must be considered for this patient. A bradycardic rate of 48 while mowing the lawn on a hot August day should be a concern. With the presence of chest pain, you should suspect an underlying cardiac origin and transport.

121. **(C)** With the presence of chest pain, the administration of nitroglycerin is indicated. If you selected Atropine **(A)** for your answer, this is incorrect because his blood pressure is adequate at 148/92 and no altered LOC or respiratory distress is noted. **(B)** and **(D)** are not indicated for this patient.

122. **(D)** This rhythm is complete heart block. With the presence of serious signs/symptoms, immediate transcutaneous pacing is indicated.

123. **(C)** Epinephrine is the first medication to be administered in the pulseless electrical activity algorithm.

124. **(B)** Atropine 1 mg follows the administration of epinephrine in pulseless electrical activity algorithm.

125. **(B)** Hypervolemia is not considered a treatable cause of PEA.

NOTES

CHAPTER 4

Medical Emergencies

Medical emergencies is a generic title for literally thousands of conditions. This chapter is focused on assessment, recognitions, and treatment of the more common medical emergenices encountered by EMS providers. Topics include

- Respiratory
- Neurology
- Endocrinology
- Allergies/Anaphylaxis
- Gastroenterology
- Urology
- Environmental
- Behavioral
- Toxicology

All ECG rhythm strips used in this chapter are six-second strips.

1. It's 3:00 A.M. and you receive a third-party call to the home of a 66-year-old male with a complaint of weakness. He is sitting on the couch in his living room. As you begin your assessment, the patient states, "I'm sorry you had to come here so early in the morning. There's nothing wrong with me; I'm just a little confused." The patient is cooperative but continues to ask you the same questions over and over again. His physical exam is unremarkable but you are concerned because he has developed increased confusion over the past five minutes and is now diaphoretic. You note a medical alert tag that states "Diabetic." Your next action is to
   (A) further assess for facial droop, drooling, and motor weakness.
   (B) further assess to determine if a head injury has occurred.
   (C) establish an IV and obtain a blood sample for a blood glucose test.
   (D) administer nitroglycerin and baby ASA for atypical presentation of myocardial infarction.

2. The _____ is responsible for insulin production.
   (A) adrenal
   (B) pancreas
   (C) thyroid
   (D) thymus

3. The pathophysiology of Type II diabetes mellitus includes, polydipsia, polyuria, and_____.
   (A) polyphagia
   (B) polycythemia
   (C) alkalosis
   (D) glycosuria

4. When the body is not able to use glucose as a primary source of energy
   (A) adipose cells begin breaking down resulting in hyperglycemia.
   (B) adipose cells begin breaking down resulting in hypoglycemia.
   (C) adipose cells begin breaking down resulting in hyperinsulinism.
   (D) adipose cells begin breaking down resulting in ketoacidosis.

5. Signs and symptoms of_____ include agitation, emotional changes, insomnia, heat intolerance, weight loss, and exophthalmos.
   (A) myxedema
   (B) malaise
   (C) Graves' disease
   (D) hypothyroidism

Questions 6 and 7 are based on the following scenario:

You arrive on scene of a 36-year-old male patient who has ingested thirty Levothyroxine that belonged to his mother. You recognize this medication as a thyroid replacement hormone. The ingestion occurred 60 minutes ago.

6. The patient is delirious and sweating profusely. His skin temperature is extremely hot. You suspect
   (A) Graves' syndrome.
   (B) myxedema crisis.
   (C) thyroid storm.
   (D) Addison's crisis.

7. You attach the ECG monitor and observe a sinus tachycardia of 140 with a corresponding pulse rate. Treatment would include
   (A) expedited transport for definitive care.
   (B) Adenocard 6 mg rapid IVP.
   (C) Adenocard 12 mg rapid IVP.
   (D) verapamil 2.5 mg slow IVP.

Questions 8 and 9 are based on the following scenario:

You are caring for a 78-year-old female patient who has a long history of hyperadrenalism (Cushing's syndrome). She is complaining of left side weakness. You note a flattened nasolabial fold on the left and slurring of her speech.

8. You are assigned to establish an IV line and obtain a blood sample for blood glucose testing. You should
   (A) take great care with venipuncture in this patient because hyperadrenalism leads to easy bruising and a delay in healing.
   (B) refuse to establish intravenous access because the veins are fragile and the skin is paper thin.
   (C) not bother checking a blood glucose level because Cushing's syndrome is always associated with hyperglycemia.
   (D) None of the above are correct.

9. You are concerned about this patient because you know hyperadrenalism is
   (A) associated with a high incident of atherosclerosis including hypertension and stroke.
   (B) associated with low metabolism rate and poor organ function.
   (C) associated with thyrotoxicosis.
   (D) associated with an increased insulin production.

10. A patient experiencing Addisonian crisis may display which of the following signs/symptoms?
    (A) Increased appetite, hypoglycemia, hyperthermia
    (B) Extreme hypertension, elevated temperature, vomiting
    (C) Cardiovascular collapse, hypotension, hypoglycemia
    (D) Coma secondary to hypothyroidism

11. You have a patient who presents with a whole body rash. There is no complaint of shortness of breath. Which of the following history findings lead you to conclude that the rash is the result of a delayed hypersensitivity reaction?
    (A) History of eating shellfish 30 minutes ago
    (B) History of taking a new medication for the past seven days
    (C) History of insect sting last summer
    (D) History of chlamydia

Questions 12–14 are based on the following scenario:

You are called to the local elementary school for an unknown medical problem. When you arrive, you are directed to the first-grade teacher Ms. Marsha. The first-grade class is holding a birthday party for Austin, who turned 7 today. Austin's mom baked brownies for the party that contained nuts.

12. Ms. Marsha is allergic to nuts. She states that she did not know the brownies contained nuts and ate one five minutes ago. She complains of tightness in her chest that is making it difficult to breathe. She is not able to talk in full sentences. Given this information, you suspect the patient is experiencing
    (A) a simple allergic reaction.
    (B) a severe allergic reaction.
    (C) sensitization.
    (D) delayed hypersensitivity.

13. Ms. Marsha's respiratory distress is becoming worse. Her blood pressure is 74/48, pulse 140, respirations 40. You decide to administer epinephrine. The correct dose and route are:
    (A) 0.01–0.03 mg of 1:1,000 solution SQ.
    (B) 0.3–0.5 cc of 1:10,000 solution IV.
    (C) 3–5 ml of 1:10,000 solution IV.
    (D) 0.1–0.3 mg of 1:1,000 solution SQ.

14. There is little change in the patient's condition and on-line medical control orders you to administer 100 mg of diphenhydramine (Benadryl) IV. You would
    (A) administer it slowly since hypotension and sedation may result.
    (B) administer it rapidly to prevent vomiting and headache.
    (C) ask medical control to repeat the dosage because you question 100 mg as being excessive.
    (D) administer it slowly to prevent burning at the injection site.

---

15. Maroon or tarry-colored stool indicates:
    (A) peritonitis.
    (B) bowel obstruction.
    (C) the presence of partially digested blood.
    (D) a normal finding in alcoholism.

Questions 16–18 are based on the following scenario:

You arrive on scene of a 30-year-old male lying on the ground. According to a bystander, the patient was on top of a ladder to change a light bulb. After he stuck his hand in the light fixture, he was attacked by yellow jackets that had a nest in the fixture. The patient then jumped from the top of the ladder to escape the bees. You estimate his fall to the ground to be 8 feet. He has numerous yellow jacket stings on his left arm and neck.

16. The patient is unconsciousness and unresponsive. As you assess his airway and breathing, you observe a respiratory rate of 8 per minute with deep gasping respirations, accessory muscle use, and obvious inspiratory stridor with each breath. Management of this patient's airway would include
    (A) c-spine immobilization, oral pharyngeal airway insertion, and high-flow oxygen by non-rebreather mask.
    (B) beginning bag-valve mask ventilations with supplemental oxygen.
    (C) c-spine immobilization, assist ventilations, immediate endotracheal intubation.
    (D) bag-valve mask ventilation with high-flow oxygen at a rate of 24 per minute.

17. Assessment of the chest reveals no obvious trauma. You note equal but distant lung sounds with wheezing on auscultation. You also find a medical alert necklace that states "Allergic PCN: Allergic Bee Stings" You suspect the respiratory distress to be from
    (A) tension pneumothorax.
    (B) hemothorax.
    (C) bronchial constriction secondary to anaphylactic reaction.
    (D) early pneumothorax.

18. You are unable to obtain IV access. Treatment for this patient would include
    (A) immediate chest decompression.
    (B) epinephrine 1:1,000 solution 3–5 ml SQ.
    (C) lidocaine 1 mg/kg IVP.
    (D) epinephrine 1:1,000 solution 0.3–0.5 mg SQ.

---

19. Urticaria is defined as
    (A) nausea, vomiting, and diarrhea associated with allergic reactions.
    (B) raised areas or wheals on the skin due to histamine release.
    (C) release of mast cells that cause bronchial constriction.
    (D) edema of the head, neck, and face associated with severe allergic reaction.

20. You need to administer epinephrine to a 26-year-old male who is short of breath after receiving radiologic contrast material. The subcutaneous dose is:
    (A) 0.1–0.3 mg 1:1,000 solution.
    (B) 0.1–0.3 mg 1:10,000 solution.
    (C) 0.5–1.0 mg 1:1,000 solution.
    (D) 0.3–0.5 mg 1:1,000 solution.

21. A sharp type of pain that travels along a definitive neural route is termed
    (A) peritonitis.
    (B) somatic pain.
    (C) referred pain.
    (D) visceral pain.

22. Dull, poorly localized pain that originates in the walls of the hollow organs is termed
    (A) peritonitis.
    (B) somatic pain.
    (C) referred pain.
    (D) visceral pain.

23. Pain that originates in a region other than where it is felt is known as:
    (A) peritonitis.
    (B) somatic pain.
    (C) referred pain.
    (D) visceral pain.

24. In a patient with abdominal pain, assessment of the abdomen should be performed in the following order:
    (A) Auscultate, palpate, inspect, percuss
    (B) Inspect, percuss, palpate, auscultate
    (C) Inspect, auscultate, palpate, percuss
    (D) Inspect, auscultate, percuss, palpate

Questions 25 and 26 are based on the following scenario:

You are called for a 62-year-old male with a complaint of severe abdominal pain. He is lying as still as possible in his bed.

25. Upon inspection of the abdomen, you find ecchymosis in the periumbilical area. This is known as
    (A) Cullen's sign.
    (B) Grey-Turner sign.
    (C) peritonitis.
    (D) Mallory-Weiss sign.

26. This assessment finding may indicate:
    (A) ascites.
    (B) intraabdominal hemorrhage.
    (C) dissecting aortic aneurysm.
    (D) acute appendicitis.

Questions 27–29 are based on the following scenario:

It is 11:30 A.M. and you respond to a 21-year-old male with a complaint of vomiting. His friends tell you that he was celebrating his twenty-first birthday last night and drank an excessive amount of alcohol. EMS was called because he has been vomiting for the past 45 minutes. Your patient is in the bathroom. He is conscious, alert, oriented, and experiencing excessive dry heaves at this time. He states that he drank beer most of the night and then started drinking shots of whiskey with his friends. His last drink was approximately six hours ago.

27. You note the presence of specks of blood on the toilet. He has no history of GI problems and takes no medications. You suspect the bleeding is
    (A) caused by acute gastritis.
    (B) the result of a Mallory-Weiss tear.
    (C) caused by acute peptic ulcer disease.
    (D) caused by acute duodenitis.

28. As you assess the patient, you note that the scleras of his eyes are dramatically blood red. This is most likely the result of
    (A) hyphema.
    (B) subconjunctival hemorrhage.
    (C) conjunctivitis.
    (D) the result of blunt trauma.

29. You are ordered by medical control to administer Phenergan (promethazine) to this patient. The proper dose range and route should be
    (A) 12.5 to 25 mg IV or deep IM.
    (B) 12.5 to 25 mg SQ, IV or deep IM.
    (C) 25 to 50 mg IV or deep IM.
    (D) 25 mg IV only; IM injection of this medication is not recommended.

---

30. Ecchymosis in the flank area associated with intraabdominal hemorrhage is known as
    (A) peritonitis.
    (B) Cullen's sign.
    (C) Mallory-Weiss sign.
    (D) Grey-Turner's sign.

Questions 31–34 are based on the following scenario:

You are called to the residence of a 58-year-old old male. He is vomiting over the side of the front porch when you arrive. You observe many empty bottles of whiskey and beer on the porch. You have been at this residence in the past and recall that this patient has a history of alcoholism and liver cirrhosis.

31. The patient is conscious but slow to respond and appears highly intoxicated. He asks for your help and falls to the floor. His appearance is pale and diaphoretic with a blood pressure of 90/64, pulse 144, respirations of 36. You note that the porch is covered in coffee-ground emesis. This patient is most likely suffering
    (A) Mallory-Weiss tear.
    (B) ruptured esophageal varices.
    (C) acute portal hypertension.
    (D) acute abdominal aortic aneurysm rupture.

32. His appearance and vital signs indicate
    (A) acute withdrawal from alcohol.
    (B) compensated shock.
    (C) acute alcohol intoxication.
    (D) alcohol psychosis.

33. Treatment for this patient should include
    (A) close monitoring of airway patency to prevent aspiration, administration of Phenergan to control emesis.
    (B) close monitoring of airway patency, administration of supplemental oxygen, establishing intravenous access, and treatment for shock.
    (C) administering supplemental oxygen, administration of Phenergan to control emesis, and treatment for shock.
    (D) monitoring airway, administering oxygen 3 to 6 liters nasal cannula, transport for alcohol detoxification.

34. During transport to the hospital, your patient has several additional episodes of vomiting. It starts as coffee-ground emesis that quickly changes to bright red blood. He is less responsive with intermediate periods of syncope. Blood pressure is 82/64 pulse 148, respirations 40. You know that
    (A) his change in mental status is secondary to the effects of the alcohol.
    (B) his vital signs and change in mental status indicate decompensated shock.
    (C) his condition is serious and rapid transport is necessary.
    (D) Both B and C are correct.

Questions 35 and 36 are based on the following scenario:

You respond to a local physician's office. You are instructed to transport Ms. Smith to the emergency department for acute gastroenteritis. The physician asks you to establish an IV line of normal saline and run it at 100 cc/hr and administer Compazine (prochlorperazine).

35. A proper dose of Compazine for this patient would be:
    (A) 12.5 mg IV.
    (B) 2.5 mg IV.
    (C) 10 mg IV.
    (D) 1.0 mg IV.

36. If Compazine is supplied in a 2 ml vial containing 5 mg/ml, you would administer ____ of medication.
    (A) 5 ml
    (B) 1 ml
    (C) 2 ml
    (D) 0.4 ml

---

37. _____ is an idiopathic inflammatory bowel disorder associated with the small intestine.
    (A) Inguinal hernia
    (B) Crohn's disease
    (C) Diverticulitis
    (D) Ulcerative colitis

38. Small out-pouchings of mucosal and submucosal tissue that push through the outer-most layer of the intestine is known as
    (A) Crohn's disease.
    (B) inguinal hernia.
    (C) ulcerative colitis.
    (D) diverticulitis.

Questions 39 and 40 are based on the following scenario:

You are assessing a patient with acute right lower quadrant pain. You suspect acute appendicitis.

39. A common site of pain from appendicitis located one to two inches above the anterior iliac crest in a direct line with the umbilicus is known as
    (A) the volvulus point.
    (B) McBurney's point.
    (C) Murphy's sign.
    (D) Grey-Turner's sign.

40. The presence of rebound tenderness in this patient represents:
    (A) peritoneal irritation
    (B) guarding
    (C) rupture
    (D) strangulation

Questions 41–44 are based on the following scenario:

Your uncle Ernie calls you at home on your day off. He explained that he has experienced right upper quadrant pain and right shoulder pain for the last seven days. Your uncle lives two blocks away, so you go to his house.

41. You immediately observe that Uncle Ernie is pale, diaphoretic, and in obvious discomfort. He has a bounding pulse rate of 132. After calling 911 and requesting an ambulance, you start to assess him. He states that this episode of pain began after eating fried onion rings with hot mustard sauce. You suspect his elevated heart rate is caused by
    (A) acute peritonitis.
    (B) stress response to the body and sympathetic nervous system activation.
    (C) an allergic reaction to the mustard.
    (D) acute pancreatitis.

42. As you assess Uncle Ernie's abdomen, you notice that he has pain with palpation under the right costal margin. This is known as
    (A) McBurney's point.
    (B) Murphy's sign.
    (C) Grey-Turner's sign.
    (D) Cullen's sign.

43. With all of the information gathered about your uncle's condition, you suspect
    (A) pancreatitis.
    (B) appendicitis.
    (C) cholecystitis.
    (D) diverticulitis.

44. The EMS squad arrives and they obtain a full set of vital signs. BP is 188/102, pulse 136, respirations 26. Uncle Ernie is assisted to the cot where he lies down on his left side in the fetal position. He complains of increased right upper quadrant pain and nausea. You suggest that pain medication be administered. The correct choice of medication for this patient is:
    (A) morphine 2–10 mg IV titrated for pain relief.
    (B) Demerol 25–50 mg IV titrated for pain relief.
    (C) fentanyl 25–50 mg IV one time only.
    (D) Nubain 25 mg IV with additional 12.5 mg if needed.

Questions 45 and 46 are based on the following scenario:

You respond to an unknown medical problem. When you arrive, you find a 39-year-old male patient lying on the couch, covered with several blankets. He has a garbage can next to him that has a small amount of vomitus in it. The stench of alcohol is prevalent throughout the house and you notice several empty bottles of vodka. He has a past medical history of alcoholism.

45. The patient complains of severe epigastric pain that radiates into his back and shoulders. His abdomen is softly distended and he will not allow you to palpate it due to the pain. He states that he took his temperature 30 minutes ago and it was 104.2°F. BP is 86/42, pulse 138, respirations 20. You suspect the patient is suffering from
    (A) severe peritonitis.
    (B) severe pancreatitis.
    (C) severe cholecystitis.
    (D) severe diverticulitis.

46. You suspect his vital signs are a result of
    (A) hypovolemia from excessive vomiting.
    (B) normal response to infection and hyperpyrexia.
    (C) septic shock from the disease process.
    (D) Both A and C are correct.

---

47. It is 9:15 P.M. and you arrive on scene of a 54-year-old old female patient who is unable to urinate. She states that she had surgery this afternoon to repair carpel tunnel syndrome performed through outpatient surgery in which she received anesthesia. She was unable to urinate after the procedure and was not able to be discharged until she urinated. To speed up her discharge to home, she lied to the nursing staff and told them she did urinate. She presents in severe discomfort and has a firmly distended bladder that is noticeable on inspection of the abdomen. This patient's situation is
    (A) a true medical emergency.
    (B) does not require ambulance transportation to the hospital.
    (C) requires the administration of Demerol for pain management.
    (D) Both A and C are correct.

Questions 48 and 49 are based on the following scenario:

You respond to the local college campus soccer field for a 20-year-old female patient with a complaint of severe muscle cramps. The temperature is 88°F with high humidity. The patient had just finished a strenuous workout when the cramps began. Her skin is hot to touch and she is sweating profusely.

48. You suspect this patient is suffering
    (A) heatstroke.
    (B) heat exhaustion.
    (C) heat cramps.
    (D) exercise-induced fatigue.

49. Treatment should include
    (A) oral hydration if the patient is able to take fluids.
    (B) two large-bore IVs of normal saline wide open.
    (C) initiating rapid active cooling.
    (D) Both A and C are correct.

Questions 50–53 are based on the following scenario:

Your ambulance is assigned to stand by at a building fire. The outside temperature is 103°F and the firefighters are wearing full protective clothing. Approximately 30 minutes into the incident, a firefighter has collapsed and you are assigned to care for him.

50. The patient is a 36-year-old male in good physical condition. He appears anxious and complains of nausea and a headache. He is sweating profusely with cool clammy skin. BP is 116/48, radial pulse is 150 and weak, respirations are 36 and shallow, temperature is 101.2°F. This patient's signs/symptoms indicate:
    (A) heatstroke.
    (B) heat exhaustion.
    (C) heat stress.
    (D) heat fatigue.

51. Treatment for this patient should include all of the following except
    (A) removing clothing.
    (B) establishing IV of normal saline.
    (C) placing in air conditioning.
    (D) administering salt tablets.

52. The patient is now apprehensive. Reassessment reveals a BP of 78/0, pulse 154, respirations 36 and shallow. You are unable to take another temperature because he is not cooperating. His skin is extremely hot to touch and he has stopped sweating. On-line medical control has requested that you start rapid active cooling. This can be achieved by
    (A) covering the patient in a sheet that has been soaked in tepid water.
    (B) placing several ice packs under the arms, in the groin, and on the head.
    (C) cold water immersion.
    (D) covering the patient in a sheet that has been soaked in ice water.

53. Which statement is false regarding overcooling of a heatstroke patient?
    (A) It may cause a reflex hypothermia.
    (B) Shivering may result which can lead to a rise in core temperature.
    (C) Body temperature must be lowered immediately with heatstroke and over-cooling is not a concern.
    (D) 102°F should be used as a target temperature to prevent overcooling.

54. Hypothermia is the result of
    (A) an increase in heat loss.
    (B) a decrease in heat production.
    (C) vasodilatation.
    (D) Both A and B are correct.

Questions 55–58 are based on the following scenario:

You are called by the local police department to help search for an elderly man with Alzheimer's disease who wandered away from his home. It is 11:30 P.M. and he has been missing for three hours. It is 38°F outside with a light drizzle. The man is wearing pajamas and slippers.

55. At 4:30 A.M. the patient is located lying behind a pile of wood five blocks from his home. He is unconscious, unresponsive, apneic, and pulseless. His skin is cold to the touch and his muscles are rigid. His core body temperature is 89.6°F (32°C). Initial treatment should include
    (A) CPR.
    (B) establishing intravenous access with warm normal saline.
    (C) starting passive rewarming.
    (D) placing in a Trendelenburg position.

56. You attach the ECG monitor and observe the following rhythm.

    Treatment should include
    (A) none until the core temperature is 90°F.
    (B) immediate defibrillation.
    (C) avoiding rough movement and excessive activity.
    (D) Both A and C are correct.

57. You are considering the administration of cardiac medication to this patient. Which statement is true?
    (A) IV medication may be administered, but space at longer than standard intervals.
    (B) Withhold medications until the core temperature is 90°F.
    (C) IV medications may be administered at regular intervals.
    (D) Lidocaine and procainamide will increase fibrillation threshold.

58. Care during transportation for this patient should include all of the following except
    (A) avoiding rough handling due to cardiac irritability.
    (B) protection against further heat loss.
    (C) transporting in a horizontal position.
    (D) withholding further ACLS treatment until core temperature is >90°F.

---

59. All of the following are signs and symptoms of organophosphate poisoning except
    (A) salivation.
    (B) lacrimation.
    (C) urination.
    (D) tachycardia.

60. Which of the following is true regarding frostbite?
    (A) Superficial frostbite involves freezing of the epidermal and subcutaneous tissue.
    (B) Do not thaw frozen flesh if there is any possibility of refreezing.
    (C) Massage the frozen area lightly.
    (D) Do not elevate frozen extremities.

61. Physical assessment findings, signs, or symptoms that support your suspicion that a patient is under the influence of alcohol or drugs include
    1. chest pain and dysrhythmias
    2. confusion and polyuria
    3. dilated pupils and anxiety
    4. constricted pupils and respiratory depression
    (A) 1 and 2.
    (B) 2 and 3.
    (C) 2, 3, and 4.
    (D) All of the above.

Questions 62–64 are based on the following scenario:

You are called to the scene of a 46-year-old female who is unresponsive. Her husband states that he just came home from work and found her on the floor in the bathroom. She has a history of depression for which she receives outpatient treatment. There are acetaminophen and Valium found strewn around the room. Your best assessment of the situation speculates that the patient may have ingested one hundred 500 mg acetaminophen and ten 5 mg Valium. You notice the smell of alcohol on the patient.

62. What would be considered the worst outcome of an acetaminophen overdose?
    (A) internal bleeding.
    (B) nausea and vomiting.
    (C) liver failure and death.
    (D) cardiac dysrhythmias.

63. Her vital signs are BP 72/40, pulse 128, respirations 6. What is most likely the primary cause of the hypotension, tachycardia, and respiratory depression?
    (A) Alcohol intoxication
    (B) Acetaminophen ingestion
    (C) Valium ingestion
    (D) Hypoglycemia

64. Which statement is true regarding the administration of Narcan to this patient?
    (A) Narcan will not reverse the effects of Valium.
    (B) Narcan should be administered to this patient since it is uncertain if any opiates were ingested.
    (C) A proper dose range is 1–2 mg IVP.
    (D) All of the above.

---

65. Which of the following statements about delirium tremens is false?
    (A) DTs can occur from either an abrupt discontinuation or ingestion of alcohol after prolonged use.
    (B) Withdrawal symptoms usually occur after one week of abstinence.
    (C) DTs are characterized by a decreased level of consciousness and hallucinations.
    (D) There is significant mortality associated with DTs.

66. You are called to a local restaurant for a patient exhibiting bizarre behaviors and shouting obscenities. He is pale, diaphoretic, and denies any past medical problems. Which of the following interventions would be most appropriate?
    (A) Place patient in 4 point restraints.
    (B) Administer Valium 10 mg as a sedative.
    (C) Rapid sequence intubation and hyperventilate to decrease intracranial pressure.
    (D) Fingerstick to check blood glucose.

Questions 67 and 68 are based on the following scenario:

You are called to assist a 25-year-old known Type I diabetic patient who is complaining of abdominal pain, vomiting, and lethargy. His glucometer reading is 510. Vitals include B/P 122/70, pulse 118, respirations 34.

67. The highest treatment priority for this patient is to
    (A) reverse alkalosis by hyperventilation.
    (B) administer patient's next scheduled dose of insulin intravenously.
    (C) correct fluid volume deficit.
    (D) administer morphine to provide for pain management.

68. One week later you are called to the same home. The patient's glucometer now reads 66. You may encounter all of the following symptoms of hypoglycemia except
    (A) altered mental status.
    (B) hot, dry skin.
    (C) bizarre behavior.
    (D) hunger.

Questions 69 and 70 are based on the following scenario:

A 42-year-old male presents with severe pain in the left flank area with no history or signs of trauma. The patient has excruciating colicky pain with intermittent vomiting.

69. What problem would you suspect as the cause of the patient's discomfort?
    (A) Abdominal aortic aneurysm
    (B) Appendicitis
    (C) Gallbladder attack
    (D) Renal calculi

70. Treatment for this patient would include:
    (A) IV fluids and morphine.
    (B) a nasogastric tube to decompress the stomach.
    (C) NTG and aspirin.
    (D) PASG and 2 large-bore IVs wide open.

71. When ventilating a patient via an endotracheal tube, the amount of air flowing into the lungs will be reduced if
    (A) the patient is a young adult.
    (B) there is increased airway resistance.
    (C) the bronchi are dilated.
    (D) the chest expands easily with each ventilation.

72. The chemical secreted by the lung cells that assists in keeping the alveoli open for gas exchange is
    (A) hemoglobin.
    (B) surfactant.
    (C) mucus.
    (D) pleural fluid.

73. Which of the following is often a late finding in patients with respiratory distress?
    (A) Assuming an upright, tripod position
    (B) Restlessness and agitation
    (C) Cyanosis
    (D) Diaphoresis

Questions 74–79 are based on the following scenario:

Your EMS team is called to attend to an 18-year-old male named Todd who is having a severe asthma attack in the lunchroom at his high school. He is leaning forward and bracing himself on his desk. He has accessory muscle use, is pale, and diaphoretic. He is awake and alert but appears very tired. His vital signs are as follows: blood pressure 158/90, pulse 132, respiratory rate 32 and extremely labored.

74. Upon auscultation of Todd's chest you note breath sounds heard only in the upper lobes with very little wheezing bilaterally. This is significant because it shows
    (A) bronchoconstriction with air trapping.
    (B) the lack of prominent wheezes, which rules out an asthma attack.
    (C) bronchodilation with adequate tidal volume.
    (D) the patient is not hypoxic.

75. Todd's fatigue is significant in that it tells you:
    (A) he is not in any danger of respiratory failure.
    (B) he is exchanging gases well in his lungs.
    (C) he is in danger of respiratory failure.
    (D) his condition is going to improve soon.

76. Todd is tachycardic at a rate of 132 beats per minute and has pale and diaphoretic skin. What is causing these signs?
    (A) Hypoxia.
    (B) Suppression of the sympathetic nervous system.
    (C) Release of epinephrine and norepinephrine.
    (D) Both A and C are correct.

77. Why is Todd able to talk only in short, broken phrases?
    (A) His tachycardia is impairing perfusion.
    (B) He is in left ventricular failure.
    (C) His tidal volume is inadequate for him to speak in full sentences.
    (D) He is hypoxic.

78. Which intervention will assist in dilating Todd's airways?
    (A) Supplemental oxygen via nonrebreather mask at 15 LPM.
    (B) Administration of a nebulized beta-2 agonist.
    (C) Allowing Todd to continue to sit upright.
    (D) Starting an intravenous solution.

79. What medication can be administered into the subcutaneous tissues to help alleviate Todd's respiratory distress?
    (A) Benadryl 25 mg
    (B) Epinephrine 1:10,000, 1 mg
    (C) Benadryl 5 mg
    (D) Epinephrine 1:1,000, 0.3 mg

Questions 80–84 are based on the following scenario:

Your EMS team is dispatched to care for a 39-year-old female with difficulty breathing. She is awake and appears restless and apprehensive. She tells you she had sudden onset of shortness of breath and a "sense of doom" while typing on her computer keyboard. Her vital signs are: blood pressure 148/92; radial pulse is strong at 124 beats per minute; respiratory rate is 36 per minute and shallow. Her skin is pale, cool, and dry. She denies having chest pain or any health problems.

80. Your patient's pulse oximetry reading is 89% on room air. This indicates
    (A) that she is breathing too deeply.
    (B) that her breathig is within normal limits.
    (C) that she has hypoxemia.
    (D) that she has psychogenically induced hyperventilation syndrome.

81. What is significant about her apprehension and sense of doom?
    (A) It may indicate a threat to life.
    (B) It can safely be ignored at this time.
    (C) It is not related to her shortness of breath.
    (D) These problems can be easily controlled with diazepam (Valium).

82. During your interview, you find that the patient takes birth control pills and has had left calf tenderness for two days with no history of trauma to the area. This information leads you to suspect
    (A) viral pneumonia.
    (B) pulmonary edema.
    (C) a panic attack.
    (D) a pulmonary embolus.

83. You interpret her cardiac rhythm as

    (A) junctional tachycardia.
    (B) sinus tachycardia with premature atrial contractions (PACs).
    (C) atrial fibrillation with a rapid ventricular response.
    (D) super ventricular tachycardia.

84. Management of her condition would include all of the following except:
    (A) being on alert for cardiac arrest.
    (B) administering nitroglycerin sublingually.
    (C) monitoring the cardiac rhythm.
    (D) establishing intravenous access.

85. A disease that results from the destruction of the walls of the alveoli and lessens the amount of surface area for gas exchange is termed
    (A) emphysema.
    (B) chronic bronchitis.
    (C) asthma.
    (D) pneumonia.

86. Patients with chronic obstructive pulmonary disease (COPD) often breathe through pursed lips to increase pressure in the lungs. This method of breathing helps in
    (A) decreasing the blood carbon dioxide levels.
    (B) preventing alveolar collapse.
    (C) preventing the loss of elasticity in the lungs.
    (D) reversing peripheral vasoconstriction.

87. In COPD, changes in the bronchioles that can result in significant air trapping include
    (A) inflammation.
    (B) bronchospasm.
    (C) increased mucus production.
    (D) all of the above are correct.

Questions 88–92 are based on the following scenario:

A 64-year-old male presents with increased dyspnea. He has a barrel chest, is thin, and pink in color. Clubbing of the fingers is present. Wheezes and rhonchi are present bilaterally in all lobes, and pursed lip breathing is noted. Vital signs are: blood pressure 162/92; pulse 118 beats per minute; respiratory rate 22.

88. This patient's appearance suggests that he most likely is suffering from
    (A) pneumonia.
    (B) COPD.
    (C) asthma.
    (D) spontaneous pneumothorax.

89. The wheezes auscultated bilaterally indicate
    (A) narrowing of the airways.
    (B) partial obstruction by the tongue.
    (C) fluid in the smaller airways.
    (D) pleural inflammation.

90. The rhonchi auscultated bilaterally indicate
    (A) partial obstruction by the tongue.
    (B) fluid in the smaller airways.
    (C) excessive mucus in the larger airways.
    (D) a pleural friction rub.

91. The clubbing of the fingers is associated with
    (A) pulsus paradoxus.
    (B) respiratory disease.
    (C) an excess of red blood cells.
    (D) chronic dilation of the bronchioles.

92. The "pink" color of this patient's skin is a result of
    (A) an excess of circulating red blood cells.
    (B) high oxygen blood levels.
    (C) chronic dilation of the bronchioles.
    (D) wheezing.

Questions 93–95 are based on the following scenario:

Eric, a 19-year-old male, is found breathing very rapidly. His roommate tells you Eric has been having a stressful time lately and recently lost his job. Eric is awake, alert, and very anxious. You note that he has spasms of his fingers and feet. Vital signs are: blood pressure 130/78, pulse rate is 116, respiratory rate is 44 and regular. He takes no medications and has no past medical problems.

93. Hyperventilation resulting from pure anxiety leads to
    (A) respiratory acidosis.
    (B) respiratory alkalosis.
    (C) A decreasing blood pH.
    (D) hepatic failure.

94. Spasms of the hands and feet is termed
    (A) hypercalcemic contractions.
    (B) bronchospasm.
    (C) proximal extremity spasms.
    (D) carpopedal spasms.

95. In this situation, it is important to
    (A) withhold oxygen.
    (B) have Eric breathe into a paper bag as a rebreathing technique.
    (C) consider that Eric has a serious medical problem.
    (D) offer reassurance to Eric.

---

96. A medication that can assist in reversing bronchospasm is
    (A) albuterol.
    (B) nitroglycerin.
    (C) Benadryl.
    (D) Both A and B.

97. Upper respiratory infections (URI) are more severe in which of the following patients?
    (A) Patients with asthma or COPD
    (B) Patients with HIV infection
    (C) Patients with mild hypertension
    (D) Both A and B.

98. Which of the following is not a known risk factor for developing lung cancer?
    (A) Cigarette smoking
    (B) Asbestos exposure
    (C) Carbon monoxide poisoning
    (D) Hydrocarbons

Questions 99–101 are based on the following scenario:

You are called to attend to a 61-year-old female complaining of headache, vomiting, abdominal pain, and loss of coordination. She has recently been using a gas home-heating device to warm up her bedroom. Her sister lives next door and they always eat every meal together. The patient cannot get out of bed saying she is too tired. She appears to be sleeping now.

99. Upon assessing the patient, you note that she can speak clearly, slowly moves all extremities, and has a blood pressure of 164/86, pulse regular at 104, respiratory rate at 18 with normal effort. She has not eaten since last evening when she ate dinner with her sister. Her sister, however, feels fine. The patient's condition suggests
    (A) food poisoning.
    (B) carbon monoxide poisoning.
    (C) a cardiac disorder.
    (D) transient ischemic attack (TIA).

100. Her pulse oximetry is 99%. This can be misleading because
    (A) pulse oximetry is inaccurate in certain cases of poisoning.
    (B) the hemoglobin is fully saturated with oxygen.
    (C) the carbon dioxide blood level is dangerously low.
    (D) the carbon dioxide level is normal.

101. Which of the following is most important?
    (A) Provide high-flow oxygen
    (B) Apply a nonrebreather mask
    (C) Obtain a detailed history from the sister
    (D) Continue reassessment for acute CVA

---

102. A diagnostic device for measuring forced exhalation is:

    (A) pulse oximeter.
    (B) capnometer.
    (C) peak flow meter.
    (D) end-tidal CO_2 detector.

103. Which device listed below would be most effective in determining if an endotracheal tube is placed in the stomach?
    (A) Pulse oximeter.
    (B) CPAP device.
    (C) Peak flow meter.
    (D) End-tidal CO_2 detector.

104. A peak flow value of 100 (liters/min) shows
    (A) normal value.
    (B) mild severity.
    (C) moderate severity.
    (D) severe respiratory compromise.

105. The process of gas exchange between the alveoli and the pulmonary capillary bed is termed
    (A) ventilation.
    (B) diffusion.
    (C) perfusion.
    (D) osmosis.

106. Side effects of albuterol (Proventil, Ventolin) administration include
    (A) hypotension and bradycardia.
    (B) pallor and sedation.
    (C) tachycardia and tremor.
    (D) respiratory depression.

107. Of the following choices, which is not a predisposing factor contributing to the development of pneumonia?
    (A) Alcoholism
    (B) Cigarette smoking
    (C) Extremes of age
    (D) Chest pain

108. A patient is anxious and has been breathing rapidly and deeply for the past 45 minutes. You can expect his blood carbon dioxide level to be
    (A) elevated.
    (B) decreased.
    (C) normal.
    (D) acidotic.

109. When the entire lobe of a lung is filled with infection and cellular debris, it is termed
    (A) pleuritic disease.
    (B) mild aspiration.
    (C) consolidation.
    (D) hemoptysis.

110. An antiinflammatory medication that can be used to treat asthma or chronic obstructive pulmonary disease (COPD) is
    (A) Proventil.
    (B) Alupent.
    (C) Solu-Medrol.
    (D) Benadryl.

111. Which medication and dosage is correct for a person with a long history of COPD and cardiac disease that presents with sudden onset of dyspnea who you believe is suffering acute pulmonary edema?
    (A) Nitroglycerin 4.0 mg.
    (B) Furosemide (Lasix) 40 mg IV.
    (C) Morphine sulfate 20 mg IV.
    (D) Epinephrine (adrenalin) 1:1,000 0.3 SQ.

112. A syndrome that develops as a complication of an illness such as multi-system trauma, severe sepsis, or toxic inhalation is termed
    (A) adult respiratory syndrome (ARDS).
    (B) pneumonia syndrome (PS).
    (C) chronic obstructive pulmonary disease (COPD).
    (D) congestive heart failure (CHF).

113. An expression of uncontrolled growth of abnormal lung cells is best termed
    (A) pulmonary disease.
    (B) chronic bronchitis.
    (C) lung cancer.
    (D) viral pneumonia.

114. A 49-year-old male with COPD is tired, confused, and in severe respiratory distress. His altered mental status is most likely caused by
    (A) carbon dioxide excretion.
    (B) hypoxia.
    (C) tachypnea.
    (D) Both A and B.

115. The body's respiratory center is located in the
    (A) aortic arch.
    (B) medulla and pons.
    (C) baroreceptors in the carotids.
    (D) cerebellum.

116. Why is it important to limit the time for suctioning a patient's airway?
    (A) The blood carbon dioxide will decrease.
    (B) The blood oxygen level will decrease.
    (C) Bradycardia can develop.
    (D) Both B and C are correct.

117. You are called to attend to a patient who fell seven feet from a porch and landed on his head. He is unresponsive, has erratic respirations, and is bleeding from a head wound. Your first action to manage the airway would be
    (A) nasotracheal intubation.
    (B) head-tilt, chin-lift.
    (C) a modified jaw thrust.
    (D) to initiate in-line traction with intubation.

118. A 58-year-old female has a history of smoking two packs of cigarettes per day. She suffers from frequent upper respiratory infections with a productive cough and expectorates white, thick phlegm. She most likely is suffering from
    (A) asthma.
    (B) congestive heart failure.
    (C) chronic bronchitis.
    (D) bronchiolitis.

119. Minute respiratory volume is best described as
    (A) the volume of air exhaled during the first minute of forced exhalation.
    (B) the volume of air moving through the alveoli in one minute.
    (C) a small amount of air being exchanged in the alveoli over one minute.
    (D) the amount of air moved in and out of the lungs during one minute.

120. The term orthopnea refers to
    (A) dyspnea while lying in the supine position.
    (B) shortness of breath while standing upright.
    (C) dyspnea while lying in the prone position.
    (D) shortness of breath while sitting upright in bed.

121. A 23-year-old healthy male who has been threatened by another person has a pulse rate of 146 and a respiratory rate of 32. These vital signs indicate that his
    (A) sympathetic nervous system is activated.
    (B) parasympathetic nervous system is activated.
    (C) sympathetic nervous system is blocked.
    (D) somatic nervous system is activated.

Questions 122–127 are based on the following scenario:

Elly, a 66-year-old female, is unable to get out of bed and her son has called EMS. She responds to verbal stimuli with clear speech, her smile is asymmetrical, she cannot move her left leg, and weakly moves her left arm. Her skin is warm but pale. Vital signs are: BP 162/88, pulse 110 beats per minute and irregular, respiratory rate 22 per minute with lung sounds clear bilaterally. A blood glucose reading is 130 mg/dl. The cardiac monitor shows a very irregular, narrow complex tachycardia with no identifiable p waves.

122. Damage to what body system is affecting movement of the left side of her body?
    (A) Cardiovascular system.
    (B) Central nervous system.
    (C) Pulmonary system.
    (D) Endocrine system.

123. The patient's asymmetrical smile is most likely a direct result of
    (A) damage to cranial nerve VII.
    (B) injury to the medulla oblongata.
    (C) damage to cranial nerve III.
    (D) cardiac disease.

124. Why was it important to obtain a blood glucose reading on this patient?
     (A) Blood glucose readings can help determine if the patient is an alcoholic.
     (B) Dextrose 50% in water can often reverse the effects of stroke.
     (C) Diabetics are less prone to stroke than healthy individuals.
     (D) Hypoglycemia can mimic stroke.

125. Elly's cardiac rhythm is
     (A) first-degree AV block.
     (B) atrial fibrillation.
     (C) sinus tachycardia.
     (D) second-degree AV block.

126. This cardiac rhythm makes Elly more prone to the development of:
     (A) diabetes.
     (B) emboli.
     (C) brain tumors.
     (D) cardiogenic shock.

127. Elly's son states that his mother was fine one hour ago when he talked to her on the telephone. This is important information because
     (A) there is a six-hour window for treating occlusive strokes with thrombolytics.
     (B) it rules out a problem affecting her cerebral hemispheres.
     (C) it establishes a reference point for the onset of symptoms.
     (D) it clearly proves that Elly has an intracranial hemorrhage.

---

128. Stroke, or brain attack, can be compared to a heart attack in that:
     (A) both have the same signs and symptoms.
     (B) in both cases, oxygen deprivation causes tissue damage.
     (C) thrombolytics can be beneficial in treating certain heart and brain attacks.
     (D) Both B and C are correct.

129. Chemicals that are released from the axon terminal and cross over the synaptic cleft are called
     (A) dendrites.
     (B) polyneuropathies.
     (C) neoplasms.
     (D) neurotransmitters.

Questions 130–133 are based on the following scenario:

John, a healthy 30-year-old, suddenly developed a two- to three-minute grand mal seizure while reading a book. On scene you find an unconscious and unresponsive patient with the following vital signs: BP 178/100, pulse 50 and regular, respiratory rate 32 and irregular. He has no history of substance abuse but has complained of headaches for the past two weeks. His blood glucose registers 110.

130. You suspect that his problem is most likely the result of
    (A) hypoglycemia.
    (B) a structural lesion.
    (C) hyperglycemia.
    (D) atrial fibrillation.

131. Two minutes after the insertion of an oropharyngeal airway, applying high-flow oxygen, and assisting John's ventilations with a bag-valve mask, the patient's pulse oximetry reading is 90%. His skin is pale and moist. It is important to consider
    (A) starting two large-bore IVs.
    (B) immediate transport to a hospital.
    (C) immediate endotracheal intubation.
    (D) immediate placement of a nasopharyngeal airway.

132. It is important to avoid excessively hyperventilating John because it can
    (A) increase the blood $PaCO_2$ to dangerously high levels.
    (B) decrease the blood $PaCO_2$ to dangerously low levels.
    (C) cause jugular vein distention.
    (D) vasodilate the brain's vasculature.

133. John is now exhibiting decorticate posturing to painful stimuli. These are signs that indicate
    (A) decreased peripheral perfusion.
    (B) a lesion of the spinal cord.
    (C) decreased $PaCO_2$ blood levels.
    (D) a lesion at or above the upper brainstem.

Questions 134 and 135 are based on the following scenario:

You are called to attend to a 51-year-old male who fell in his living room. His wife states that he has been very depressed and has not eaten or drunk anything for the past 24 hours. You notice that the patient has a stonelike face, muscular rigidity, and is exhibiting "pill-rolling" movements.

134. These are all signs of
    (A) multiple sclerosis.
    (B) Bell's palsy.
    (C) Parkinson's disease.
    (D) vertebral disc disease.

135. In managing this patient, it is important to
     (A) start an intravenous line.
     (B) determine a blood glucose level.
     (C) apply a cardiac monitor.
     (D) All of the above are correct.

---

136. In differentiating between syncope and a grand mal seizure, you know that syncope
     (A) often begins in a standing position.
     (B) presents with jerking motions during unconsciousness.
     (C) causes the patient to remain drowsy following the event.
     (D) is often preceded by an aura.

Questions 137 and 138 are based on the following scenario:

A 27-year-old patient is complaining of persistent headache, fatigue, and pain upon flexion of his neck. He has had a chronic fever of 100°F for the past two days.

137. His complaints lead you to suspect
     (A) Reye's syndrome.
     (B) meningitis.
     (C) transient ischemic attack.
     (D) a mental disorder.

138. In treating this patient, you would
     (A) wear gloves and place a mask on yourself and the patient.
     (B) wear gloves only.
     (C) transport the patient to a hospital that can administer thrombolytics.
     (D) arrange for a psychiatric consult to meet you at the hospital.

---

139. A seizure characterized by a rapid mood change or auras that include unusual smells, tastes, or sounds is termed
     (A) simple partial seizure disorder.
     (B) petit mal seizure disorder.
     (C) pseudoseizure disorder.
     (D) complex partial seizure disorder.

140. You are having lunch with your nephew Josh and his friend Sam. You notice that Sam appears to have periods of inattentiveness and daydreaming. During these spells, his eyelids flutter and he appears to be unaware of his surroundings. You ask Josh if he has ever noticed this before. Josh says he has been "goofing around" like this for a week now. These signs indicate Sam may have
     (A) simple partial seizure disorder.
     (B) petit mal seizure disorder.
     (C) pseudoseizure disorder.
     (D) complex partial seizure disorder.

Questions 141–144 are based on the following scenario:

Your EMS team is called to attend to a patient in her mid-thirties who is having a generalized motor seizure. Bystanders inform you that she has been seizing continually for the past 10 minutes. You note that the patient is shaking violently, is diaphoretic, and slightly cyanotic.

141. This prolonged seizure is specifically termed
    (A) petit mal seizure disorder.
    (B) grand mal seizure disorder.
    (C) complex seizure disorder.
    (D) status epilepticus.

142. The most valuable early intervention is to
    (A) force an oropharyngeal airway between the teeth.
    (B) start an IV of crystalloid solution.
    (C) use bag-valve mask assistance with 100% oxygen.
    (D) give dextrose 50% and water IVP.

143. An IV is started and blood glucose reading is 120 mg/dl. A medication and correct dose range that you could administer to her is
    (A) Valium (diazepam) 5–10 mg IVP.
    (B) Dextrose 50% in water 5–10 grams.
    (C) Valium (diazepam) 5–10 mcg IVP.
    (D) Versed (midazolam) 10–25 mg IVP.

144. Administration of the medication terminated her seizure activity. Now you should be alert for which of the following side effects?
    (A) Respiratory depression.
    (B) Hyperglycemia.
    (C) Hypertension.
    (D) Fever.

145. Your EMS unit is called to attend to a 79-year-old female who experienced an abrupt onset of facial drooping, dysphasia, and marked hemiparesis. Upon examiantion, she is now alert and oriented, speech clear, and moves all extremities well. Vital signs are normal. Your assessment findings lead you to suspect
    (A) stroke.
    (B) transient ischemic attack.
    (C) Alzheimer's disease.
    (D) amyotrophic lateral sclerosis.

146. Intracranial hemorrhage can cause vital sign changes characterized by an increasing systolic blood pressure and widening pulse pressure, bradycardia, and irregular respiratory rate. These changes are collectively termed
    (A) Cheyne-Stokes respiration.
    (B) Cushing's reflex.
    (C) Wernicke's syndrome.
    (D) hypertensive crisis.

147. One area that the Glasgow Coma Scale measures is
    (A) pupillary response and size.
    (B) respiratory rate.
    (C) heart rate.
    (D) motor response.

148. _____ injuries are tissue disruptions that occur directly at the point of impact.
    (A) concussion
    (B) contrecoup
    (C) coup
    (D) epidural

149. You have a patient with metastatic brain cancer. He opens his eyes to pain, and answers questions with incomprehensible sounds. When you start an IV in his left arm, he withdraws from the IV needle piercing the skin. You would calculate his Glasgow Coma Scale to be
    (A) 9.
    (B) 11.
    (C) 7.
    (D) 4.

150. Which of the following are signs/symptoms of an acute cerebral vascular accident?
    (A) Slurring of the speech.
    (B) Facial droop.
    (C) Drooling.
    (D) Weak motor response on the affected side.

Answers and Answer Explanations

1. **(C)** This question is an example of a long scenario that results in a simple answer. With a presentation of confusion, diaphoresis, and a medical alert tag stating "Diabetic," you should be thinking hypoglycemia. Of the choices listed, establishing an IV and obtaining a blood sample for a blood glucose test is the best answer. Choices **(A)** and **(B)** may need to be further evaluated, especially if the blood glucose test is within normal limits. **(D)** is not correct because you were not given enough information in the scenario to determine a cardiac origin.

2. **(B)** Pancreas. This is basic anatomy and physiology information that becomes important when you are faced with complex medical conditions such as pancreatitis.

3. **(A)** Polydipsia (excessive thirst), polyuria (excessive urination), and polyphagia (excessive hunger) are just a few symptoms of untreated diabetes mellitus.

4. **(D)** When the body is not able to use glucose as a primary source of energy, the body starts to break down adipose (fat) tissue as a source of energy. This fat-based metabolism results in a rise of blood ketones, which can lead to ketoacidosis.

5. **(C)** You must be familiar with signs and symptoms of the most common endocrine disorders. Agitation, emotional changes, insomnia, heat intolerance, weight loss, and exophthalmos are all common in Graves' disease. Graves' disease is the result of thyrotoxicosis (excessive thyroid hormones).

6. **(C)** Based on the history of ingestion of 30 thyroid replacement hormone pills and his presentation of an extreme metabolic state, you should suspect thyroid storm.

7. **(A)** Thyroid storm is a true medical emergency that requires expedited transport to definitive care. Drug therapy that will block the effects of the toxic level of thyroid hormone is required. If you chose Adenocard or verapamil for your answer, this is incorrect because these medications are not indicated for sinus tachycardia and you simply do not have enough information in this scenario to warrant its use.

8. **(A)** Long-term effects of hyperadrenalism lead to paper thin (almost transparent) skin that can be easily bruised or torn. The disease process also results in delayed healing, so great care with venipuncture is required. **(B)** is incorrect because IV therapy is *not* contraindicated. **(C)** is incorrect because you should never make an assumption about a patient's blood glucose level.

9. **(A)** Left side weakness, flattened nasolabial fold on the left, and slurring of her speech may indicate CVA. Hyperadrenalism is associated with high incidents of atherosclerosis, hypertension, and diabetes, which are all risk factors for stroke.

10. **(C)** Presentation of adrenal insufficiency (Addisonian crisis) may include cardiovascular collapse, hypotension, and hypoglycemia. These serious signs/symptoms are attributed to major disturbances in the water and electrolyte balance within the body.

11. **(B)** A delayed hypersensitivity reaction may occur several hours or even days after exposure. Common causes are medications and chemicals. A patient may very well present with the signs/symptoms of allergic reaction several days after starting a new medication.

12. **(B)** Ms. Marsha is experiencing a severe allergic (anaphylactic) reaction as evidenced by chest tightness, dyspnea, and inability to talk in complete sentences within five minutes of exposure.

13. **(C)** Because this patient is demonstrating pending cardiovascular and respiratory collapse, the administration of intravenous epinephrine is indicated. The correct dose range is 3 to 5 ml of 1:10,000 solution IV.

14. **(C)** The normal dose range of Benadryl is 25 to 50 mg. While there is no doubt this patient is in critical condition, the on-line medical control order to administer such a large dose of Benadryl should be questioned.

15. **(C)** Melena is dark, tarry, foul-smelling stool that indicates the presence of partially digested blood.

16. **(C)** A patient who is unconscious and unresponsive with deep gasping respirations of eight per minute and inspiratory stridor requires assisted ventilations and endotracheal intubation. With the possibility of c-spine injury, proper precautions must be taken. **(D)** is incorrect because a rate of 24 ventilations per minute is too fast. **(A)** is incorrect because the respiratory rate is too slow to apply a nonrebreather mask. **(B)** is not a bettter answer than **(C)**.

17. **(C)** Based on the medical alert necklace, the presence of bee stings, and the absence of obvious chest trauma causing the respiratory distress, you should suspect severe bronchial constriction secondary to anaphylactic reaction.

18. **(D)** Epinephrine 1:1,000 solution 0.3–0.5mg SQ.

19. **(B)** Raised areas or wheals on the skin associated with allergic reaction and histamine release are known as urticaria (hives).

20. **(D)** The standard adult dose of subcutaneous epinephrine in the treatment of allergic reaction is 0.3–0.5 mg of 1:1,000 solution.

21. **(B)** Somatic pain is a sharp type of pain that travels along a definitive neural route. Visceral pain **(D)** is dull, poorly localized pain that originates in the walls of the hollow organs. Referred pain **(C)** is pain that originates in a region other than where it is felt. Peritonitis, **(A)**, is inflammation of the peritoneum.

22. **(D)** Visceral pain is dull, poorly localized pain that originates in the walls of the hollow organs. Somatic pain **(B)** is a sharp type of pain that travels along a definitive neural route. Referred pain **(C)** is pain that originates in a region other than where it is felt. Peritonitis, **(A)**, is inflammation of the peritoneum.

23. **(C)** Referred pain is pain that originates in a region other than where it is felt. Somatic pain **(B)** is a sharp type of pain that travels along a definitive neural route. Visceral pain **(D)** is dull, poorly localized pain that originates in the walls of the hollow organs. Peritonitis, **(A)**, is inflammation of the peritoneum.

24. **(C)** The correct assessment order of the abdomen is inspect, auscultate, palpate, percuss. Inspection is the obvious first step since you are going to look before you do anything. Auscultation may not provide much useful information but if you are going to auscultate, it must be performed before palpation. Palpation is the third step. You can gain a lot of information through palpation. Percussion (if performed) is the last assessment step.

25. **(A)** Ecchymosis in the periumbilical area in known as Cullen's sign. Grey-Turner's sign **(B)** is ecchymosis in the flank area. Both may indicate intraabdominal hemorrhage. Mallory-Weiss sign **(D)** is associated with an esophageal tear or laceration that results from excessive vomiting. Peritonitis, **(C)**, is inflammation of the peritoneum.

26. **(B)** The presence of Cullen's sign may indicate intraabdominal hemorrhage.

27. **(B)** An esophageal tear or laceration that results from excessive vomiting is known as a Mallory-Weiss tear. While you may suspect this type of injury, it is difficult to be 100% certain. Do not rule out more serious causes of upper GI bleeding.

28. **(B)** A subconjunctival hemorrhage involves rupture of small blood vessels in the subconjunctival space resulting in the "white" of the eye becoming blood red. This may occur after a strong sneeze or excessive vomiting. While it looks dramatic, this type of hemorrhage usually clears without intervention and rarely causes any residual problems.

29. **(A)** The usual dose range of Phenergan is 12.5 to 25 mg. It can be administered slow IVP or by deep IM injection. SQ administration is not indicated.

30. **(D)** Ecchymosis in the flank area associated with intraabdominal hemorrhage is known as Grey-Turner's sign. Ecchymosis in the periumbilical area in known as Cullen's sign **(B)**. Mallory-Weiss sign **(C)** is associated with an esophageal tear or laceration that results from excessive vomiting. Peritonitis, **(A)**, is inflammation of the peritoneum.

31. **(B)** The patient's past medical history and presentation should lead you to the conclusion of ruptured esophageal varices. **(A)** is incorrect because a Mallory-Weiss tear is usually not associated with significant blood loss. **(C)** and **(D)** are incorrect. You do not have enough information in the scenario to determine this.

32. **(B)** This patient is experiencing compensated shock as evidenced by his elevated pulse rate (144), evidence of vasoconstriction (pale moist skin), and his ability to maintain his blood pressure.

33. **(B)** As always, the airway is your priority. You must protect the airway and prevent aspiration of emesis. Supplemental oxygen, establishing intravenous access, and treating this patient for shock are required. **(A)** and **(C)** are incorrect because Phenergan potentiates the effects of alcohol. **(D)** is incorrect because this patient needs supplemental oxygen and transport to an acute care hospital.

34. **(D)** Choice **(D)** is "Both **(B)** and **(C)** are correct." His vital signs indicate decompensated shock and rapid transport is necessary. While it is true alcohol is a CNS depressant and can alter mental status, you cannot assume this is the cause of his change in mental status since decompensated shock is present; therefore **(A)** is incorrect.

35. **(C)** The usual dose range of Compazine is 5–10 mg. It can be administered IV or IM.

36. **(C)** If Compazine is supplied in a 2 ml vial containing 5 mg/ml, you would administer 2 ml of medication to deliver a 10 mg dose. This is a simple math question. If you answered incorrectly, you must review math for medication administration.

37. **(B)** Crohn's disease is an idiopathic inflammatory bowel disorder involving the small intestine.

38. **(D)** Diverticulitis is small out-pouchings of mucosal and submucosal tissue that push through the outermost layer of the intestine.

39. **(B)** McBurney's point is a common site of pain from appendicitis and is located one to two inches above the anterior iliac crest in a direct line with the umbilicus.

40. **(A)** Rebound tenderness is pain on release of the examiner's hand, allowing the patient's abdominal wall to return to its normal position and is usually associated with peritoneal irritation. This assessment finding can be present in other abdominal conditions and is not specific to appendicitis.

41. **(B)** Pain and discomfort to the body can activate the sympathetic nervous system.

42. **(B)** Murphy's sign is pain caused when an inflamed gallbladder is palpated by pressing under the right costal margin. McBurney's point **(A)** is a common site of pain from appendicitis located one to two inches above the anterior iliac crest in a direct line with the umbilicus. Grey-Turner's sign **(C)** is ecchymosis in the flank area. Cullen's sign **(D)** is ecchymosis in the periumbilical area.

43. **(C)** All of the information presented in this scenario should have led you to the conclusion of cholecystitis (inflammation of the gallbladder).

44. **(B)** Demerol 25–50 mg IV is titrated for pain relief. **(A)** is incorrect, as morphine is contraindicated because it is believed to cause spasm of the cystic duct in the gallbladder. **(C)** and **(D)** are incorrect because the dosages listed are wrong. Note: While there might be concern about use of pain medication in "undiagnosed"

abdominal pain or the administration of pain medication may mask symptoms and make in-hospital assessment more difficult, the use of Demerol is not contraindicated in cholecystitis.

45. **(B)** His history of alcoholism and presentation should lead you to suspect severe pancreatitis. Eighty percent of all cases of pancreatitis are associated with alcoholism.

46. **(C)** His BP of 86/42 and pulse of 138 lead you to believe a shock state is present. His temperature of 104.2°F may indicate sepsis. Severe pancreatitis is associated with septic shock, and when present it has a high mortality rate. **(A)** is incorrect because this scenario did not give you enough information to conclude that excessive vomiting caused hypovolemia. **(B)** is incorrect because these vital signs indicate shock and not a normal response to an infection.

47. **(A)** The inability to urinate is a true medical emergency because a full, distended bladder is extremely painful for the patient. Definitive care usually requires insertion of a urethral catheter, which is not common in the prehospital setting. EMS treatment is primarily supportive. **(C)** is incorrect because Demerol may cause urethral constriction and further complicate the problem. **(B)** is incorrect, the patient should be transported to the hospital by ambulance.

48. **(C)** Heat cramps are acute painful spasms of the voluntary muscles following strenuous activities in a hot environment.

49. **(A)** Treatment for heat cramps include removing the patient from the hot environment and administration of oral saline solution or sport drinks for hydration. If oral fluids cannot be administered because of nausea, an IV line of normal saline may be needed. **(C)** and **(B)** are incorrect because rapid cooling is indicated for heat stroke *not* heat cramps and two large-bore IVs are not indicated.

50. **(B)** Profuse sweating with *cool* and clammy skin, tachycardia, rapid shallow respiration, and a body temperature over 100°F indicates heat exhaustion.

51. **(D)** Treatment for heat exhaustion includes removal of clothing **(A)**, removal of the patient from the hot environment **(C)**, establishing an IV of normal saline **(B)**, and oral hydration if the patient is able to take fluids. The administration of salt tablets is *not* indicated because they are not readily absorbed through the stomach and can lead to hypernatremia.

52. **(A)** This patient has progressed from heat exhaustion to heatstroke as indicated by severe apprehension, hypotension, hot skin, and the cessation of sweating. Treatment for heatstroke includes removal of clothing, removal of the patient from the hot environment, establishing large-bore IVs of normal saline to run wide open, and rapid active cooling. One method of rapid active cooling is covering the patient in a sheet that has been soaked in *tepid* water. Using ice or cold water may cause a reflex hypothermia and cause the patient to shiver, which will raise the body temperature again.

53. **(C)** This choice is incorrect because overcooling of a heatstroke patient will produce a reflex hypothermia and cause the patient to shiver, which will raise the body temperature again. All of the other statements are true regarding overcooling of a heatstroke patient.

54. **(D)** Hypothermia can result from an increase in heat loss, a decrease in heat production, or a combination of these two factors.

55. **(A)** CPR is indicated even if signs of death are present. Hypothermic patients cannot be presumed dead until a core body temperature of 94–95°F has been achieved and resuscitation efforts are still unsuccessful.

56. **(B)** Immediate defibrillation is required for this patient. A series of stacked shocks, 200j, 200–300j, and 360j should be delivered.

57. **(A)** IV medication may be administered, but spaced at longer than standard intervals, therefore **(C)** is incorrect. Drug metabolism is reduced so administered medication such as epinephrine and lidocaine may accumulate to toxic levels. In addition, administered drugs may remain in the peripheral circulation. When the patient is rewarmed and peripheral circulation resumes, a large toxic bolus of medication may be delivered to the central circulation. **(D)** is incorrect because lidocaine and procainamide will actually lower fibrillation threshold in a severely hypothermic patient. **(B)** is incorrect because medications should be withheld when the core temperature is below 86°F.

58. **(D)** If the hypothermic cardiac arrest patient fails to respond to initial defibrillation attempts and drug therapy, subsequent ACLS care should be held until the core temperature is 86°F. **(D)** is incorrect because it states "90°F." **(A)**, **(B)**, and **(C)** are all true.

59. **(D)** SLUDGE is a helpful mnemonic to remember signs of poisoning—S = salivation, L = lacrimation, U = urination, D = defecation, G = GI upset, E = emesis. Other symptoms of organophosphate poisoning include, bronchoconstriction, bradycardia, anxiety, and visual disturbances.

60. **(B)** A golden rule for the treatment of frozen flesh is to never thaw it if there is any possibility of refreezing. **(A)** is incorrect because deep frostbite involves freezing of the epidermal and subcutaneous tissue. **(C)** is incorrect because massaging frozen flesh may further damage the tissue

61. **(D)** While I'm not a fan of multiple-multiple guess questions such as this one, there is a possibility you may see this type of question format on a certification exam. The correct answer is All of the above. Chest pain and dysrhythmias are a typical sign/symptom of cocaine abuse. Confusion and polyuria represent alcohol use. Dilated pupils and anxiety represent evidence of hallucinogens. Constricted pupils and respiratory depression are the result of opiates.

62. **(C)** This patient may have ingested 50,000 mg of acetaminophen. A dose of 150 mg/kg of acetaminophen is considered toxic. Unless this patient weighed approximately 334 kg (734 lbs) this is likely to be a toxic dose. Severe acetaminophen toxicity will often result in death within three to six days due to acute liver failure.

63. **(C)** Side effects of Valium or benzodiazepine ingestion include hypotension, respiratory depression, drowsiness, headache, blurred vision, nausea, and vomiting. Tachycardia is a compensatory mechanism of the body in response to the hypotension.

64. **(D)** Narcan is primarily used for complete or partial reversal of opiates. Valium is a benzodiazepine; therefore, Narcan will not reverse its effects. Romazicon is used to reverse effects of benzodiazepines. The administration of Narcan to this patient would not be unreasonable since it is unclear if the patient ingested opiates. A normal dose range of Narcan is 1–2 mg.

65. **(B)** This is false because DTs can occur several hours after sudden abstinence from alcohol and can last up to seven days.

66. **(D)** A glucose fingerstick is a quick tool to rule out hypoglycemia, which could be the cause of this patient's behavior. Any patient with an altered level of consciousness should be tested for hypoglycemia.

67. **(C)** This patient has diabetic ketoacidosis and is likely to be profoundly dehydrated because excess glucose acts as an osmotic diuretic. Fluid replacement with normal saline should be started immediately.

68. **(B)** The signs and symptoms of hypoglycemia are many and varied. Altered mental state including irritability, bizarre behavior, or agitation is often the most important and early indicator of a problem. Other signs/symptoms may include diaphoresis, tachycardia, weakness, and headache. Coma may be present in severe cases.

69. **(D)** Sudden onset of flank pain, excruciating colicky pain, and vomiting are considered classic signs and symptoms of renal calculi (kidney stones).

70. **(A)** Prehospital care should be focused on comfort and support. Give nothing by mouth and establish an IV line for medication administration. An antiemetic may be indicated, and pain management is important. Note: While there may be concern about the use of pain medication in "undiagnosed" abdominal pain or that administration of pain medication may mask symptoms and make in-hospital assessment more difficult, the use of morphine is not contraindicated in renal calculi.

71. **(B)** Airway resistance resulting from edema, bronchoconstriction, or increased mucus production can cause increased airway resistance, resulting in a decrease in the amount of air flowing into the lungs.

72. **(B)** Surfactant is secreted by cells in the lungs. It increases the surface tension of the alveoli and assists in keeping them open for gas exchange.

73. **(C)** Cyanosis is a late finding and may not be present even when the patient is severely hypoxic.

74. **(A)** This assessment finding indicates that there is bronchoconstriction and air trapping. This serious condition results in decreased air exchange in the lungs and can lead to profound hypoxia.

75. **(C)** Fatigue in this situation indicates that the patient is becoming tired. This is an ominous sign of pending respiratory failure and the development of respiratory arrest.

76. **(D)** Both hypoxia and anxiety cause activation of the sympathetic nervous system and the release of epinephrine and norepinephrine, which causes diaphoresis, elevation of the heart rate (tachycardia), and peripheral vasoconstriction (pale skin).

77. **(C)** Because of the air trapping, he does not have enough air (tidal volume) available to speak.

78. **(B)** A nebulized beta-2 agonist (such as albuterol) delivered by mask or hand-held device using 5–10 LPM of oxygen can assist in bronchodilation.

79. **(D)** Subcutaneous epinephrine is an option to treat cases of severe asthma because of its beta-2 agonist properties.

80. **(C)** A pulse oximeter is used as an assessment tool. A patient with a pulse oximetry value of less than 90% with no apparent cause or past medical history is considered to be moderately hypoxic and needs high-flow oxygen administration.

81. **(A)** A patient who alerts you to his or her "sense of doom" should be taken very seriously. There are numerous reports of patients who have "sensed" a problem and later suffered a catastrophic event including a threat to life.

82. **(D)** A history of taking birth control pills combined with signs and symptoms that include a painful and inflamed lower extremity suggest deep vein thrombosis. This predisposes the patient to developing pulmonary embolus.

83. **(C)** This rhythm indicates atrial fibrillation with a rapid ventricular response.

84. **(B)** Nitroglycerin administration is inappropriate for this patient because the scenario did not give you enough information to warrant its use.

85. **(A)** Emphysema results from the destruction of the walls of the alveoli and lessens the amount of surface area for gas exchange. Chronic bronchitis **(B)** is the result of an increased number of mucus-secreting cells in the respiratory tree. Asthma **(C)** is a chronic inflammation disorder. Pneumonia **(D)** is an infection of the lung.

86. **(B)** Pursed-lip breathing technique helps maintain pressure within the airways (even during exhalation) to support bronchial walls that have been damaged as a result of disease.

87. **(D)** All of these pathologies impair the flow of air through the bronchial tree.

88. **(B)** A barrel chest, clubbing of the fingers, and dyspnea are all classic signs of COPD.

89. **(A)** Wheezes indicate narrowing of the airways. Edema and bronchoconstriction are examples of problems that can narrow the airway.

90. **(C)** Rhonchi are rattling sounds with a low pitch and "snoring quality" that is usually associated with excessive mucus or other material in the larger airways.

91. **(B)** Clubbing is a deformity produced by the growth of soft tissue about the fingers or toes. It is associated with chronic cardiac or respiratory disease.

92. **(A)** As part of the body's own compensatory mechanism, a chronic state of low blood oxygen levels will cause an increased production of red blood cells (polycythemia) that give the patient's skin a pink color.

93. **(B)** Hyperventilation can result in an excess elimination of carbon dioxide leading to respiratory alkalosis.

94. **(D)** Alkalosis decreases blood calcium levels, which leads to hypocalcemia. This results in cramping and spasms of the feet and hands.

95. **(C)** Since hyperventilation can mask a true medical emergency such as a pulmonary embolism, it is important to consider that this patient has a serious medical problem.

96. **(A)** Albuterol is a beta-2 agonist that dilates the bronchial tree.

97. **(D)** Patients with preexisting respiratory disease or who are immunocompromised are more prone to developing URI.

98. **(C)** Carbon monoxide has not been identified as a link to cancer.

99. **(B)** The home-heating device in the bedroom, the patient's signs and symptoms, and the fact that her sister is not sick should lead you to suspect carbon monoxide poisoning.

100. **(A)** Because carbon monoxide binds readily with the hemoglobin molecule, the pulse oximetry reading can read normal even though the patient may be hypoxic.

101. **(A)** Providing high flow oxygen is essential for a patient with carbon monoxide poisoning.

102. **(C)** The peak expiratory flow meter measures the amount of air a patient can forcefully exhale with one breath.

103. **(D)** This instrument measures the presence or absence of carbon dioxide in the sampled gas at the tip of the endotracheal tube. It can be used as an assessment tool to help determine proper endotracheal tube placement.

104. **(D)** A peak flow of 100 liters/min is very low; 400–650 liters/min is the normal range.

105. **(B)** Diffusion is the process of gas molecules moving across a cell membrane from a higher concentration of molecules to a lower concentration.

106. **(C)** Administration of albuterol can stimulate the sympathetic nervous system resulting in an increased heart rate and tremors.

107. **(D)** Chest pain may be a symptom of a problem but it is not a predisposing factor in itself. The very young and old, cigarette smokers, and alcoholism are all predisposing factors to the development of pneumonia.

108. **(B)** Rapid, deep breathing can result in excess elimination of carbon dioxide leading to respiratory alkalosis.

109. **(C)** The infection, debris, and fluid can fill up the lung creating consolidation.

110. **(C)** Solu-Medrol is a corticosteroid that can act as an antiinflammatory agent. It is commonly used in the treatment of COPD

111. **(B)** Lasix is indicated for the treatment of acute pulmonary edema. **(A)** and **(C)** are incorrect because the dose is wrong. **(D)** is not indicated.

112. **(A)** ARDS is a form of pulmonary edema that occurs as a response to a wide variety of lung injury insults.

113. **(C)** Lung cancer is an excessive and uncontrolled growth of abnormal (cancerous) cells.

114. **(B)** Hypoxia can affect the brain at the cellular level resulting in a decreased mental status.

115. **(B)** The body's respiratory control center is in the medulla and the pons.

116. **(D)** Suctioning removes oxygen from the airway and can cause vagal stimulation resulting in bradycardia. Adults should not be suctioned for longer than 10–15 seconds. Pediatric patients should not be suctioned for longer than 5 seconds.

117. **(C)** From the choices listed, the modified jaw thrust is the easiest and safest method to manage the airway immediately.

118. **(C)** Years of exposure to toxic irritation, (i.e., cigarettes) can result in an increase in the number of goblet cells in the bronchial system with an increased production of mucus.

119. **(D)** Minute volume is the amount of air moved in and out of the lungs in one minute.

120. **(A)** Dyspnea while lying supine best describes orthopnea.

121. **(A)** Sympathetic nervous system stimulation causes pupillary dilation, and will increase the pulse and respiratory rates.

122. **(B)** An asymmetrical smile in conjunction with the inability to move her left leg and weakness of the left arm indicate injury to the patient's central nervous system (CNS).

123. **(A)** A patient's ability to smile, frown, lift eyebrows, and wrinkle the forehead is controlled by cranial nerve VII.

124. **(D)** Patients who are hypoglycemic can exhibit sign and symptoms similar to a stroke.

125. **(B)** Atrial fibrillation is an irregular, narrow complex rhythm with nondiscernible p waves.

126. **(B)** As the atria fibrillate, they also dilate. This allows for blood to stagnate in the atria and can lead to clot formation.

127. **(C)** Studies suggest that there is a three-hour window between the time of onset of symptoms and time of thrombolytic intervention for treatment to be effective. Establishing a reference point for the onset of symptoms is critical.

128. **(D)** Both heart attack and brain attack cause organ tissue damage due to the interruption of blood flow. Studies show that thrombolytic agents used to treat heart attack patients can be effective in treating occlusive strokes.

129. **(D)** Neurotransmitters are chemicals that travel across the synaptic cleft to act on the target cell to either excite or inhibit it.

130. **(B)** Structural lesions, such as brain tumors and intracerebral bleeds, can press on and destroy brain tissue. This can cause seizures and a number of other illnesses.

131. **(C)** A pulse oximetry reading of 90% in a person who is on high-flow oxygen indicates moderate hypoxia. Intubation should be considered.

132. **(B)** Excessive hyperventilation of a patient with increasing intracranial pressure can decrease the blood arterial carbon dioxide to dangerous levels.

133. **(D)** Decorticate posturing (flexion) indicates a lesion at or above the brainstem. Decerebrate posturing (extension), however, results from a lesion within the brainstem.

134. **(C)** Parkinson's disease is characterized by tremor, rigidity of muscles, bradykinesia, and impaired balance. It affects 500,000 Americans.

135. **(D)** Starting an intravenous line will allow access for medications if necessary, determining the blood glucose level will show if the altered mental status is due to hypoglycemia, and applying a cardiac monitor will determine if there is a rhythm disturbance.

136. **(A)** Syncope usually occurs when the person is in the standing position. It can begin with dizziness or feeling light-headed, or can occur without warning.

137. **(B)** Headache with fever, fatigue, and pain upon flexion of the neck are all suspicious signs and symptoms of meningitis.

138. **(A)** Universal precautions include use of gloves and a mask by the care provider as well as putting a mask on the patient, which significantly reduces the chance of exposure to the pathogen.

139. **(D)** A complex partial seizure disorder can present in many ways since they usually originate in the temporal lobe of the brain. They are usually of short duration and while patients experience a loss of contact with their surroundings, they do not lose motor tone.

140. **(B)** Petit mal, or absence, seizure is characterized by a brief loss of awareness for 10–30 seconds. This type of seizure occurs in childhood and usually disappears after 20 years of age.

141. **(D)** Status epilepticus is two or more generalized motor seizures occurring in succession and is a life-threatening emergency situation.

142. **(C)** Air exchange is poor during a generalized motor seizure. It is extremely important to protect the airway from obstruction and deliver 100% oxygen using a bag-valve mask for respiratory assistance.

143. **(A)** Valium (diazepam) is a sedative and anticonvulsant that depresses seizure activity in the brain. **(C)** and **(D)** are incorrect because the dose is wrong. **(B)** is not indicated with a blood glucose reading of 120 mg/dl.

144. **(A)** A side effect of Valium is respiratory depression.

145. **(B)** Since her signs and symptoms disappeared rapidly, and she has no neurological deficits, she most likely suffered a transient ischemic attack. TIA is considered a significant warning sign for the development of a stroke.

146. **(B)** Change in vital signs that are associated with increased intracranial pressure is termed Cushing's reflex.

147. **(D)** The Glasgow Coma Scale measures eye opening, and verbal response, and motor response.

148. **(C)** Coup injuries are tissue disruptions that occur directly at the point of impact. Contrecoup injuries **(B)** produce tissue damage away from (the opposite side) of the impact. Concussion, **(A)**, is a transient period of unconsciousness usually followed by a complete return of function. Epidural, **(D)**, is a location over or on the dura.

149. **(A)** You should always have a Glasgow Coma Scale chart available to reference in your EMS practice. Unfortunately, you may not have a chart to reference on a certification exam; therefore, you must be familiar with its contents. This patient has a GCS score of 9—eye opening = 2, verbal response = 3, motor response = 4.

150. **(A) (B) (C) (D)** All of these signs/symptoms may be present with an acute cerebrovascular accident. How long did you spend on this question? This is an example of a question with no obvious correct answer. You may experience this type of question on a certification exam. When this happens, keep cool and remember the advice on test taking that is found in chapter one of this book.

NOTES

NOTES

CHAPTER 5

Trauma

This chapter contains questions on assessment, recognition, and treatment of various traumatic injuries.

All ECG rhythm strips used in this chapter are six-second strips.

1. You are caring for a victim of a motor vehicle collision who has sustained multiple traumatic injuries. It has taken 15 minutes on the scene to secure your patient's airway, immobilize him on a backboard, and place him in the back of the ambulance. You are in a region in which the trauma care system consists of a Level I trauma center 50 minutes away and a Level III trauma center 10 minutes away. What is your choice of treatment facilities and why?
   (A) Level I trauma center because it is the only true center that is capable of handling trauma cases
   (B) Level I trauma center because you may be held liable if you take the patient to a facility of lesser capability.
   (C) Level III trauma center because it is capable of handling all types of specialty trauma
   (D) Level III trauma center because it will stabilize and transfer serious patients as needed as part of a trauma system

Questions 2–4 are based on the following scenario:

You are called to a scene of a motor vehicle collision (MVC). During your initial assessment, you find an unresponsive 32-year-old male with multiple contusions to his face and head. He has snoring respirations and a weak, thready peripheral pulse.

2. Your first action would be
   (A) to control major bleeding.
   (B) rapid extrication.
   (C) to open the airway with a modified jaw thrust and immobilize the cervical spine.
   (D) endotracheal intubation and start two large-bore intravenous lines with normal saline and run at "wide open" rate.

3. Your partner performs a rapid trauma survey and finds him lethargic and very pale, with cool and clammy skin. He has contusions, crepitus, and diminished breath sounds on the right side of the chest. BP 74/50, pulse of 140 centrally, no peripheral pulse found at this time, and respirations 32 and shallow. What is the most likely cause of these findings?
   (A) Beck's triad
   (B) Hemopneumothorax
   (C) Cushing's syndrome
   (D) Ruptured liver

4. These critical findings should have been found in what length of time?
   (A) Five minutes
   (B) Ten minutes
   (C) Less than two minutes
   (D) Three to six minutes

5. You are called to the scene of a mass casualty incident where you are responsible for the triage transportation decisions. Which of the following patients would be the first to be transported to the local trauma center.
   (A) a 50-year-old man complaining of knee and ankle pain.
   (B) an 18-year-old female with a five-minute lapse of consciousness after being struck in the head
   (C) a 25-year-old female, eight months pregnant with partial thickness burns on her arms and legs covering 5% of her BSA
   (D) a 32-year-old male with a large piece of metal impaled in his left foot.

Questions 6–9 are based on the following scenario:

A 42-year-old male is the victim of a house fire. He has reddened and blistered areas over most of his anterior chest, abdomen, and anterior surfaces of both arms.

6. Using the rule of nines, estimate what percent of BSA he has burned.
   (A) 45%.
   (B) 36%.
   (C) 22.5%.
   (D) 27%.

7. Initial treatment for this burn patient would include which of the following?
   (A) Debridement of the blistered skin and antibiotic ointment
   (B) Covering the burn area with gauze and cooling with iced saline
   (C) Administering morphine and then cleaning the burn area with an iodine solution
   (D) Covering the burn area with dry bulky dressings and keeping the patient warm

8. Medical control has asked that you initiate fluid therapy enroute to the hospital. Which of the following statements regarding fluid resuscitation for this burn patient is true?
   (A) The Parkland Formula directs the fluid amount needed for the burn patient. It can be initiated only after a Foley catheter is in place so that accurate intake and output measurements can be monitored.
   (B) Two large-bore catheters are introduced and a bolus of 0.5 ml of normal saline (NS) for every kilogram of the patient's weight multiplied by the percentage of BSA is initiated.
   (C) Two large-bore IVs should run wide open for the length of the transport. Do not infuse more than 8,500 ml's.
   (D) An IV is not attainable due to the location of the burns

9. While transporting your burn patient to the burn center, you notice that his voice now sounds hoarse and he is making a "crowing" sound on inspiration. What is the most likely cause?
   (A) Screaming for help while standing inside the burning house
   (B) Fluid overload precipitating pulmonary edema
   (C) Allergic reaction to the by-products of the burning materials
   (D) Anxiety reaction to the traumatic event of being burned

10. A burn victim with suspected thermal or chemical airway burns needs close monitoring for signs of respiratory compromise. Appropriate management would include
    (A) immediate intubation using RSI upon all inhalation injuries.
    (B) using cool nebulized oxygen in a blow-by manner with a simple pocket mask to prevent further mucosal tissue damage.
    (C) providing high-flow oxygen by nonrebreather mask at 15 liters per minute once the airway has been secured.
    (D) suspecting cyanide toxicity and administering the sulfur-containing antidote.

11. Which one of the following statements is not true regarding electrical injuries?
    (A) Until the power is off, nobody should be allowed to approach the electrical burn patient.
    (B) The rescuer must be grounded to prevent electrical shock when treating a victim of a recent lightning strike.
    (C) Patients in cardiac arrest because of electrocution have a high survival rate if prehospital intervention is prompt.
    (D) Consider the use of 1 mEq/kg of sodium bicarbonate to prevent the complications of rhabdomyolyses.

12. Which of the following statements is true regarding chemical burns?
    (A) Always use antidotes or neutralizing agents.
    (B) Acid burns are typically more serious than alkali burns.
    (C) Both acids and alkalis cause burns by disrupting cell membranes and damaging tissues on contact.
    (D) Always approach a chemical spill from downwind.

Questions 13–15 are based on the following scenario:

You have arrived on scene where you find a 50-year-old male who has a large jagged laceration from a chain saw on his medial left upper thigh. Bright red blood is spurting from the wound despite pressure being applied by a bystander with a wadded-up T-shirt. Your patient is alert, oriented, and anxious, with pale, diaphoretic skin.

13. What is the priority of care for this patient?
    (A) Two large-bore IVs wide open
    (B) Immobilize the c-spine and prepare to intubate
    (C) Tourniquet the upper right leg
    (D) Apply a pressure dressing while elevating the left leg

14. Your rapid trauma assessment reveals an isolated upper leg laceration that is seven inches in length and pumping bright red blood freely. His BP is 110/60, peripheral pulse 128, respiratory rate 24, and his GCS is 15. Several components of the circulatory system are essential for adequate profusion. Which of the following is not a component of the circulatory system?
    (A) Stroke volume and the Frank-Starlings mechanism
    (B) Positive end expiratory pressure
    (C) Preload and afterload
    (D) The pump, the fluid, and the container

15. Bleeding has been controlled and your patient is enroute to the trauma center. You instruct your partner to establish IV access and deliver fluid resuscitation. Pick the most appropriate treatment.
    (A) A bolus of normal saline or Ringer's lactate solution
    (B) Normal saline at "keep open" rate
    (C) Ringer's lactate at a "keep open" rate
    (D) Hold IV fluid infusion because your patient has a peripheral pulse

---

Questions 16–19 are based on the following scenario:

You are on duty at your EMS service when you are called to respond to a car that struck a light pole. As you arrive on scene you notice that power lines are down on top of the car. The driver is hanging halfway out of the driver's side window, unconscious, with slow, snoring-type respirations.

16. What is your first priority?
    (A) In-line stabilization of the c-spine and modified jaw thrust
    (B) Removing the wire from the top of the car and proceeding with caution
    (C) C-spine stabilization and oral pharyngeal airway with BVM ventilations
    (D) Calling the power company for assistance prior to starting patient care

17. After the patient is removed from the car, a rapid trauma survey shows a GCS of 9, BP 178/100, pulse 56, and respirations 34 and irregular. What is your differential diagnosis from this assessment?
    (A) Hypoglycemia
    (B) Hyperglycemia
    (C) Cushing's syndrome
    (D) CVA

18. To manage the airway of this patient appropriately you would:
    (A) administer 100% O_2 by BVM at 30 breaths per minute.
    (B) use a nonrebreather mask on 10 liters of O_2.
    (C) use a nasal cannula on 10 liters of O_2.
    (D) intubate and hyperoxygenate with BVM at a rate of 24 breaths per minute

19. You have established two large-bore IVs of normal saline. Choose the appropriate rate.
    (A) Enough fluid to maintain stable vital signs
    (B) Both lines wide open
    (C) TKO
    (D) 500 cc bolus

---

20. Please choose the best clue for determining possible injuries that may be sustained in an MVC.

    (A) Length of skidmarks
    (B) Debris at the scene
    (C) Patient symptoms
    (D) Mechanism of injury

21. Which of the following would you expect to cause the greatest cavitation?
    (A) a hunting knife
    (B) a bullet from a handgun
    (C) a bullet from a rifle
    (D) an arrow

Questions 22–24 are based on the following scenario:

You are called to the scene of a 60-year-old woman who fell down a flight of stairs. The patient is found to be alert and oriented, with warm, dry, and pink skin. She is complaining of a headache and upper back pain. Her vital signs are BP 90/62, pulse 60, and respiratory rate 20.

22. Which of the following would be your initial impression?
    (A) Neurogenic or distributive shock
    (B) No significant injury
    (C) The patient is taking beta-blockers
    (D) Mechanical shock

23. During your rapid trauma survey you find that the patient has no sensation below the border of the rib cage. This would suggest spinal pathology between which vertebral areas?
    (A) C1-C4
    (B) T4-T10
    (C) T10-S1
    (D) Below S1

24. You have started a large-bore IV or normal saline on this patient. Choose the appropriate solution and rate.
    (A) two large-bore IVs of normal saline wide open
    (B) Normal saline at a rate to maintain a systolic BP of 90
    (C) D5W TKO
    (D) 1,000 cc bolus of Ringer's lactate

Questions 25 and 26 are based on the following scenario:

You are called to the scene of a 22-year-old man who was playing in a softball tournament. He was hit in the eye with a hard-hit line-drive softball. According to his teammates he was knocked to the ground and had a brief loss of consciousness that lasted approximately seven seconds.

25. While assessing the injured eye you notice a collection of blood in front of the patient's pupil and iris. What is your differential diagnosis?
    (A) Raccoon's eye
    (B) Retinal detachment
    (C) Hyphema
    (D) Corneal laceration

26. How would you transport this patient to the hospital?
    (A) Recovery position
    (B) Sitting up at a 90 degree angle
    (C) Trendelenburg
    (D) Immobilized on a backboard with the head of backboard elevated

---

Questions 27 and 28 are based on the following scenario:

You are called to the scene of a patient who was involved in an altercation at the local pool hall. You find one victim in the back alley anxious and screaming for your assistance. You notice immediately that he has clammy skin and a dusky appearance. He has a respiratory rate of 40 and his breathing is shallow. He tells you that he has been hit multiple times in the chest, abdomen, and back with a pool stick by "two big guys." While assessing his chest you notice multiple contusions to the right side with diminished respirations on the right.

27. What would you suspect?
    (A) Cardiac tamponade
    (B) Hemothorax
    (C) Ruptured diaphragm
    (D) Pneumothorax

28. While enroute to the local trauma center with this patient, you notice that his level of consciousness has decreased and his color has not improved despite 100% O_2 by nonrebreather mask. He is becoming hypotensive and his pulse rate is 140. Respiratory rate remains at 40 and his breathing is still shallow. Ongoing assessment reveals distended neck veins and hyperresonant percussion on the right chest. Your next course of action would be
    (A) oropharyngeal intubation with RSI.
    (B) positive pressure ventilation with BVM.
    (C) needle decompression between the second and third intercostal space anterior chest.
    (D) to stabilize flail segment with a bulky dressing.

Questions 29 and 30 are based on the following scenario:

You are called to the scene of a stabbing. You find one victim lying supine on the ground in a large pool of blood with multiple lacerations to the abdomen. The scene is secure. Your initial assessment finds a patient responding only to pain with no peripheral pulse and respiratory rate of 8.

29. Priority care of this patient would be
    (A) MAST trousers and IV wide open.
    (B) BVM ventilations and moist saline dressings to the abdomen.
    (C) intubation and fluid resuscitation.
    (D) peritoneal lavage.

30. While transporting this patient to the hospital, a large section of bowel protrudes through one of the lacerations. Your management would be
    (A) to increase pressure in the abdominal compartment of MAST trousers.
    (B) to replace protruding bowel and apply a pressure dressing.
    (C) to make a note, no treatment necessary except to notify medical control.
    (D) to gently cover the area with moistened gauze and nonadherent material as a dressing.

Questions 31–33 are based on the following scenario:

You are called to the scene of an assault on a 75-year-old woman in a bank parking lot. Bystanders report that she was found lying between two cars, unresponsive, with blood coming from the back of her head and multiple contusions and skin tears to her knees and arms. The bank teller states that she had just withdrawn a large sum of money. Your rapid trauma assessment reveals an elderly female responsive to pain only, snoring respirations, a strong radial pulse of 60 beats per minute, and a moderate amount of bright red blood from a large laceration and hematoma on her occipital region.

31. What is your first priority?
    (A) Move the patient to an area for privacy.
    (B) Immediately stabilize the c-spine and open the airway.
    (C) Control bleeding with a pressure dressing to the head laceration.
    (D) Immediately load and go.

32. Why would this patient be more susceptible to severe head trauma?
    (A) a history of Alzheimer's disease
    (B) Dehydration
    (C) Pickwickian syndrome
    (D) Decreased size of the brain

33. After completing your rapid trauma assessment on your patient, you find a blood pressure of 96/54, heart rate of 50, and respiratory rate of 14 and regular. What is your priority of care?
    (A) Hyperventilation at a rate of 30 with 100% O_2
    (B) Two large-bore IVs at a wide-open rate
    (C) Careful fluid resuscitation
    (D) Atropine 0.5 mg IVP

---

34. You are called to the scene of a single-car MVC involving a 25-year-old female who is 30 weeks pregnant. What normal physiological alterations take place during pregnancy that may affect your assessment of this patient?
    (A) Increased blood pressure and increased pulse
    (B) Increased blood pressure and decreased pulse
    (C) Decreased blood pressure and decreased pulse
    (D) Decreased blood pressure and increased pulse

35. You ascertain that this patient needs to be transported to the local trauma center for evaluation. What would be the best technique for the transport?
    (A) Properly secured to backboard and tilted to left side
    (B) Properly secured to backboard and tilted to right side
    (C) Position of comfort
    (D) Lithotomy position

36. During what month of gestation does the uterus rise out of the pelvic cavity and become more susceptible to blunt trauma?
    (A) Third month
    (B) Seventh month
    (C) Fifth month
    (D) Second month

Questions 37 and 38 are based on the following scenario:

A 5-year-old boy fell 10 feet from a jungle gym at school. Bystanders state that the child lost his balance and fell, striking his left leg on the bars and hitting his head on the ground. Your initial evaluation reveals a child who is lethargic and does not respond appropriately to commands. His respirations are shallow at a rate of 40 with a rapid and weak radial pulse.

37. What is your first priority?
    (A) Splinting the deformed left leg
    (B) Wait for consent from the mother before giving definitive treatment
    (C) Application of c-collar and secure to backboard for immediate transport.
    (D) Rapid c-spine control and airway assistance with BVM and high-flow O_2

38. Which of the following is one of the most important indicators of potential CNS injury?
    (A) Ipsilateral pupil dilatation
    (B) History of loss of consciousness
    (C) Lethargy
    (D) Elevated heart rate.

39. Which of these should not be included in the documentation of baseline neurologic status?
    (A) Pulse oximetry
    (B) Response to sensory stimulation
    (C) Pupillary reaction
    (D) Motor function

40. Which of the following describes the most definitive treatment of a patient with a flail chest injury?
    (A) Position of comfort with O_2 per NRB mask
    (B) Intubation and positive pressure ventilation
    (C) Stabilization of the flail segment with a sandbag
    (D) Needle decompression

Questions 41 and 42 are based on the following scenario:

You arrive on scene to find a pickup truck that struck a utility pole head on. The patient is ambulatory on-scene. He has a large amount of blood on his face and down the front of his shirt. He is alert and oriented to person and place but slow to respond. You note the smell of alcohol on the patient as you speak with him. He denies any loss of consciousness. He states that he was traveling 40 MPH and was not wearing a seat belt.

41. You are sent to evaluate the damage to the truck. Which finding would lead you to believe the patient may have a life-threatening injury?
    (A) a deformed dashboard
    (B) a deformed steering wheel
    (C) the airbag did not deploy
    (D) significant front end damage

42. It is important to remember that when dealing with an intoxicated patient, your assessment must be thorough because:
    (A) alcohol increases pain tolerance.
    (B) alcohol decreases the patient's judgment.
    (C) alcohol is a CNS stimulant.
    (D) alcohol can mask signs and symptoms of injury.

---

43. One of the most common mechanisms of injury in the geriatric population is falls. Which statement is true regarding the force required to break a bone in a geriatric patient?
    (A) The same force is required as in other patients.
    (B) Less of a force is required than in other patients.
    (C) Slightly greater force is required than in other patients.
    (D) None of these statements are correct.

Questions 44 and 45 are based on the following scenario:

You arrive on the scene of a trench collapse. There are three trapped victims who are buried to the mid-chest. The rescue will take several hours because they will need to be dug out by hand.

44. Crushing syndrome is a significant concern because crush injuries release toxins into the central circulation that can cause
    (A) alkalosis.
    (B) increased renal function.
    (C) cardiac dysrhythmias.
    (D) dyspnea.

45. Which medications would be given to a patient to combat the effects of Crushing syndrome?
    (A) Narcan
    (B) Oxygen
    (C) Atropine
    (D) Sodium bicarbonate

---

46. You are caring for a 24-year-old male who wrecked his 4-wheeler. He states that his handlebar struck him in the stomach. He has bruising and tenderness in the abdomen and you suspect bowel rupture. This condition can lead to _____ and the development of serious complications.
    (A) peritonitis
    (B) diaphragm dysfunction
    (C) gastric distention
    (D) herniated bowel

Questions 47–50 are based on the following scenario:

You respond to a 25-year-old male involved in an industrial accident. Upon arrival, you see that your patient is trapped in a machine. He has suffered a partial amputation of the right leg just above the knee that is bleeding profusely.

47. Your first action is to
    (A) control bleeding.
    (B) stabilize the machinery.
    (C) do a rapid trauma assessment.
    (D) establish two large-bore IVs.

48. The patient remains trapped in the machine. He is awake, alert, and anxious. His blood pressure is 96/44, pulse 142, respiration 26. His skin is pale and moist. He is in what state of shock?
    (A) Decompensated
    (B) Compensated
    (C) Irreversible
    (D) Pneumatic

49. The patient has been freed from the machinery. Direct pressure and elevation do not stop the hemorrhage. The next step would be to apply
    (A) a tourniquet.
    (B) pressure at an arterial point proximal to the injury.
    (C) application of additional trauma dressings.
    (D) a vacuum splint.

50. Despite all efforts to control the bleeding, you are not successful. His pulse is now 52 and very weak. His respirations are 6 and labored. Blood pressure is 78/30. This shock state signifies
    (A) decompensated shock.
    (B) compensated shock.
    (C) irreversible shock.
    (D) pneumatic shock.

Questions 51 to 54 are based on the following scenario:

You are dispatched to a 77-year-old male patient who has fallen from a ladder while cleaning the gutters. He fell approximately 14 feet and struck the ground. He is awake and very anxious. He is having obvious trouble breathing. His pulse is 104, respirations 34, and blood pressure is 122/76. His wife tells you that he struck his back on the riding lawn mower as he fell.

51. In your assessment, you find crepitus and instability to the left rib cage. Lung sounds are present and equal. Closer assessment reveals paradoxical movement. You suspect a
    (A) tension pneumothorax.
    (B) massive hemothorax.
    (C) flail chest.
    (D) abdominal aneurysm.

52. Paradoxical movement is best described as chest wall movement that is
    (A) inward with both inspiration and expiration.
    (B) inward with expiration and outward with inspiration.
    (C) inward with inspiration and outward with expiration.
    (D) outward with both inspiration and expiration.

53. Prehospital management for this patient includes
    (A) a needle decompression mid-clavicular line.
    (B) positive pressure ventilation.
    (C) an occlusive dressing.
    (D) chest decompression mid-axillary line.

54. Your patient is in severe respiratory distress. Reassessment reveals absent lung sounds on the left, tracheal deviation to the right, and a SpO$_2$ reading of 82%. Immediate treatment must include
    (A) intubation.
    (B) right side chest decompression.
    (C) left side chest decompression.
    (D) oxygen administration.

Questions 55 to 57 are based on the following scenario:

Your patient rolled a farm tractor over a hill. He has a large puncture wound to his right neck, above the clavicle. It appears that the wound is from a tree branch. Moderate bleeding is present.

55. Care for the puncture wound would include
    (A) application of direct pressure with a bulky trauma dressing.
    (B) application of an occlusive dressing.
    (C) application of a sterile dressing.
    (D) needle decompression.

56. Which transport position would be appropriate for this patient?
    (A) Trendelenburg position
    (B) Left lateral recumbent
    (C) Right lateral recumbent
    (D) Prone

57. A major concern with this type of injury is
    (A) rib fracture.
    (B) clavicle fracture.
    (C) flail chest.
    (D) edema.

---

58. Your patient is a 44-year-old female who was burned when a high-temperature water
    pipe exploded. She has blisters to the chest, abdomen, entire right arm, and front of
    the right leg. According to the rule of nines, this patient has sustained _____ percent
    burns.
    (A) 40.5%
    (B) 36%
    (C) 45%
    (D) 31.5%

59. On the first day of summer vacation, you are called to a rooftop for a 17-year-old
    female who was sunbathing. She is alert and oriented and states she was using
    lotion without any SPF protection to "speed up her tan." She was in the sun from
    9:00 A.M. to 2:00 P.M. She is in significant pain and requests that you help her off the
    rooftop. She has blisters covering the entire front of her body. You should consider
    this patient to have
    (A) first-degree burns.
    (B) minor burns.
    (C) nothing to worry about.
    (D) critical burns.

Questions 60 and 61 are based on the following scenario:

You respond to a "man down" call. When you arrive, you find a 52-year-old male lying on
the ground next to a ladder. It is unclear if he was placing the ladder against the house
when it came into contact with power lines or if he fell from the top of the ladder.

60. Examination shows the patient to be unresponsive. He has a rapid irregular pulse
    and snoring respirations of 8, BP is 88/42. Treatment should include
    (A) assisted ventilation with a bag-valve device at 6–10 L/min.
    (B) assisted ventilation with a nonrebreather mask at 10–15 L/min.
    (C) opening the airway with a jaw thrust maneuver and ventilation with a bag-valve
        device.
    (D) insertion of an oropharyngeal airway and oxygen by nonrebreather mask at
        10–15 L/min.

61. You apply a cardiac monitor and note the following rhythm.

Treatment includes
(A) immediate cardioversion.
(B) immediate defibrillation.
(C) lidocaine 1 mg/kg.
(D) continued observation.

---

62. Which of the following facial injuries involves a fracture of both the maxillary and nasal bone?
(A) Mandibular fracture
(B) LeFort I
(C) LeFort II
(D) LeFort III

63. Cushing's reflex includes a sudden increase in systolic pressure, bradycardia, and
(A) erratic respirations.
(B) irregular pulse.
(C) increased respirations.
(D) pupil dilation.

64. Which head injury will likely result in *immediate* neurological signs/symptoms with rapid deterioration?
(A) Concussion
(B) Contusion
(C) Subdural hematoma
(D) Epidural hematoma

65. You arrive on the scene of a patient who has been stabbed with a knife in the right side of the back. The patient presents with left-sided hemiparalysis and sensory loss. Despite another stab wound to the right abdomen, the patient denies pain. What type of spinal cord injuries do you suspect?
(A) Compression
(B) Transection
(C) Neurogenic shock
(D) Brown-Sequard's syndrome

66. Which of the following best describes the effects of pericardial tamponade?
    (A) Cardiac output increases, and central venous pressure falls.
    (B) Cardiac output is reduced, and central venous pressure rises.
    (C) Cardiac output increases, and venous pressure is not affected.
    (D) Cardiac output is not affected, and central venous pressure falls.

67. Beck's triad is often associated with pericardial tamponade. It includes distant heart tones, JVD (jugular venous distension), and
    (A) pulse paradoxus.
    (B) hypotension.
    (C) wheezing.
    (D) delayed capillary refill.

68. A stab wound to the stomach or small intestine would cause gastric contents to enter the peritoneal cavity. Presentation would include
    (A) a rapid onset of cramping pain.
    (B) referred pain to the left shoulder.
    (C) a gradual onset of pain throughout the abdomen.
    (D) a rapid onset of sharp pain, diffuse throughout the abdomen.

69. Your patient was struck in the head with a six-inch-diameter tree branch while trimming a tree. He complained of dizziness immediately after the incident but states he "feels fine" now. The next day, he complains of dizziness and vomiting. You suspect:
    (A) epidural hematoma.
    (B) subdural hematoma.
    (C) concussion.
    (D) contusion.

Questions 70 to 73 are based on the following scenario:

You respond to an explosion at a local fireworks production factory. The explosion rocked the ground several blocks away. There are multiple patients.

70. The mechanism of injury from a blast or explosion can be from three factors; primary, secondary, and tertiary. The mechanism of injury of a patient who suffers injuries from being struck by material propelled by the blast force is considered
    (A) a primary mechanism of injury.
    (B) a secondary mechanism of injury.
    (C) a tertiary mechanism of injury.
    (D) All of the above.

71. The mechanism of injury of a patient being thrown and impacting the ground or other object is considered
    (A) a primary mechanism of injury.
    (B) a secondary mechanism of injury.
    (C) a tertiary mechanism of injury.
    (D) All of the above.

72. Your first patient is a 43-year-old male with burns over the front of his right arm, upper chest, and the front of his right leg. Using the rule of nines, what percent of burns does this patient have?
    (A) 27%
    (B) 22.5%
    (C) 18%
    (D) 35%

73. This patient is hoarse, has singed nasal hair, is coughing up charcoal-colored sputum, and has developed inspiratory stridor. Treatment should include
    (A) high-flow oxygen via a simple mask.
    (B) immediate endotracheal intubation.
    (C) continued monitoring for complications.
    (D) humidified oxygen via nasal cannula.

---

74. Which of the following statements is correct regarding a Glasgow Coma Scale score of seven?
    (A) A perfect GCS score is ten and a score of seven represents minor injuries.
    (B) A perfect GCS score is twelve and a score of seven represents moderate injuries.
    (C) A perfect GCS score is fifteen and a score of seven represents moderate injuries.
    (D) A perfect GCS score is fifteen and a score of seven represents serious injuries.

Questions 75 and 76 are based on the following scenario:

You arrive on scene of a 34-year-old male who was struck by a car. Bystanders tell you the patient was standing on the sidewalk when his neighbor, who was backing out of the driveway, struck him. The speed of impact is estimated at less than 5 miles per hour. Your patient is sitting in the yard with an obvious open tibia/fibula fracture of the right leg. He is alert and oriented and denies any loss of consciousness. He states that he was struck in the abdomen and lower legs and thrown onto the trunk of the car and then rolled into the yard. He complains of right leg pain and right shoulder pain.

75. As you auscultate his right upper chest, you notice the patient guarding his shoulder. Closer exam reveals a fractured clavicle. Complications associated with a fractured clavicle include injury to the
    (A) carotid artery.
    (B) subclavian vein.
    (C) descending aorta.
    (D) inferior vena cava.

76. Physical exam concludes that the right clavicle fracture and open right tibia/fibula fracture are his only obvious injuries but you are concerned because his level of consciousness is deteriorating and his heart rate has increased 30 beats per minute. Although his abdomen was unremarkable upon examination, you know that an indicator of severe abdominal trauma is the presence of
    (A) absent bowel sounds.
    (B) back pain.
    (C) referred pain to the clavicle.
    (D) unexplained shock.

---

77. There are anatomical differences in pediatric patients compared to adults. When using the rule of nines for calculating burns, which of the following is a correct modification for a child?

    (A) The front of each arm for a child is 7% compared to 4½% on an adult.
    (B) The front of each leg for a child is 4½% compared to 9% on an adult.
    (C) The head of a child is 18% compared to 9% on an adult.
    (D) The entire leg of a child is 9% compared to 18% on an adult.

Questions 78–80 are based on the following scenario:

A 22-year-old male is found in an alley with multiple stab wounds to the extremities, abdomen, and chest. BP is 82/40, pulse 142 weak, respirations 10.

78. Your exam reveals distended neck veins, equal breath sounds, and a radial pulse that disappears during inspiration. You suspect
    (A) a hemothorax.
    (B) a tension pneumothorax.
    (C) a sucking chest wound.
    (D) cardiac tamponade.

79. As you logroll the patient to place him on the long spine board, you inspect his back and discover another stab wound just below the right scapula. You observe blood bubbling out of the wound with each breath. You suspect
    (A) a massive hemothorax.
    (B) a tension pneumothorax.
    (C) an open pneumothorax.
    (D) a hematoma formation.

80. Priority care for this patient would include
    (A) IV fluids to stabilize vital signs
    (B) closure of the chest wall with an occlusive dressing taped on three sides
    (C) immediate chest decompression of the right chest
    (D) rapid transport to a trauma center

Answers and Answer Explanations

1. **(D)** Level III trauma center because it will stabilize and transfer serious patients as needed as part of a trauma system. Transport decisions will be dependent on many factors, one of those being transport time.

2. **(C)** Open the airway with a modified jaw thrust and immobilize the cervical spine. Always remember the ABCs.

3. **(B)** With the information given, hypotension, absent peripheral pulses, diminished breath sounds on the right with chest trauma on the right, a hemopneumothorax is likely.

4. **(C)** This patient received an initial assessment and rapid trauma survey to identify all life threats. It is recommended that these assessment steps be performed in two minutes or less.

5. **(B)** Of the choices listed, the patient with a possible head injury should be transported first. **(A)**, **(C)**, and **(D)** are all isolated injuries that do not pose an immediate life threat that a head injury is capable of.

6. **(D)** 27%—chest = 9%, abdomen = 9%, anterior surface of both arms = 9%.

7. **(D)** Manage the burns by covering them with a dry bulky dressing. A dressing reduces air movement past sensitive partial thickness burns, thus reducing pain. Damaged skin loses temperature regulation capacity so it is important to keep the patient covered, even if the environment is not cold. **(B)** is incorrect because the use of ice in any form can worsen the injury as it causes vasoconstriction and reduces blood flow to the already damaged area. **(A)** and **(C)** are incorrect because debridement or cleaning of a burn with iodine are not indicated.

8. **(B)** Current fluid resuscitation recommends that two large-bore catheters be introduced. When EMS transport time is less than one hour, a bolus of 0.5 ml of normal saline (NS) for every kilogram of the patient's weight multiplied by the percentage of BSA should be initiated.

9. **(A)** Risk factors for inhalation injuries associated with burns include standing in the burn environment (hot gases rise), screaming or yelling in the hot environment (the open glottis allows toxic gases to enter the lower airway), and being trapped in a closed burn environment.

10. **(C)** Of the choices listed, provide high-flow oxygen by nonrebreather mask at 15 liters per minute once the airway has been assured is correct. **(A)** is incorrect because it states "all" inhalation injury. **(B)** is incorrect because the patient requires high-flow oxygen. **(D)** is incorrect because the scenario does not give you engough information to conclude cyanide toxicity.

11. **(B)** By the time the victim of a lightning strike is reached, the electricity will have dissipated. While you may be concerned as long as the storm remains nearby, there is no danger of electrical shock from touching the victim of a lightning strike.

12. **(C)** Both acids and alkalis cause burns by disrupting cell membranes and damaging tissues on contact. **(A)** is incorrect because antidotes and neutralizing agents should never be used as they may cause a violent reaction with the contaminant. **(B)** is incorrect because alkali burns are typically more severe because of their liquefaction necrosis process. **(C)** is incorrect because you should approach from up wind.

13. **(D)** This patient is alert and oriented, so he has an intact airway and is breathing. Your priority for this patient is "circulation," which includes stopping major hemorrhage. Applying a pressure dressing and elevation are necessary. **(A)** is incorrect because it is not a higher priority than controlling hemorrhage. **(B)** is not indicated for this patient. **(C)** is incorrect because it states right leg.

14. **(B)** How well do you know your medical terminology and definitions? If you know your medical terminology you answered this question correctly because positive end expiratory pressure is not a component of essential perfusion.

15. **(A)** Once external hemorrhage has been controlled, start fluid resuscitation with normal saline (NS) or Ringer's lactate solution.

16. **(D)** Your safety is the first priority. Do not approach the car until you are notified by the proper officials that the power has been turned off.

17. **(C)** Cushing's or Herniation syndrome is manifested by hypertension, bradycardia, and erratic respirations. This patient has a GCS score of 9, hypertension (178/100), bradycardia (56), and irregular respirations that indicate head injury with Cushing's syndrome.

18. **(D)** Intubation and supplemental oxygen are essential. You would hyperventilate this patient because he exhibits signs/symptoms of increased intracranial pressure (Cushing's syndrome).

19. **(A)** The objective of prehospital fluid resuscitation is to stabilize vital signs until the patient arrives at the hospital.

20. **(D)** Mechanism of injury can provide clues for determining possible injuries.

21. **(C)** Ballistics is the study of projectiles in motion. Studies suggest that wounds from rifle bullets are two to four times more lethal than handgun bullets due to mass energy and velocity.

22. **(A)** Neurogenic or distributive shock is recognized by hypotension, bradycardia, and a normal initial appearance. **(C)** is something to consider but should not be part of your initial impression. **(B)** is clearly wrong. **(D)** is incorrect because this is distributive shock not mechanical shock.

23. **(B)** You would suspect injury at the thoracic level between T4 and T11. Memorization of all of the dermatomes is difficult and really not necessary. However, you should have a general knowledge of associated injuries to the spinal nerve plexuses.

24. **(B)** The objective of prehospital fluid resuscitation is to stabilize vital signs until the patient arrives at the hospital. This patient requires close observation since neurogenic shock does not allow the body's normal compensatory mechanisms to work.

25. **(C)** Hyphema is a collection of blood in the anterior chamber of the eye due to trauma. This type of injury is a potential threat to the patient's vision and requires evaluation by an ophthalmologist.

26. **(D)** A c-spine injury should be suspected with any injury to the head. Treatment for this patient would include full body immobilization. The preferred position of transport of a hyphema is with the head elevated; therefore, you should elevate the head of the backboard.

27. **(D)** With a history of chest trauma, diminished breath sounds, agitation, increased respiratory rate, along with dusky color, you should suspect pneumothorax.

28. **(C)** The above symptoms are classic for tension pneumothorax, which is a serious and immediate life threat that requires immediate chest decompression.

29. **(C)** Priority for this patient who presents with respiratory compromise and hypovolemia is airway support and fluid resuscitation.

30. **(D)** Intestines should never be pushed back into the abdominal compartment. A moist nonadherent dressing should be gently placed over the bowel to prevent it from "drying out" because of the risk of irreversible damage.

31. **(B)** Airway and c-spine are always a priority before other treatments.

32. **(D)** As part of the normal physiologic changes with aging, a decrease occurs in brain weight and size. By the age of 80, the brain loses approximately 3.5 ounces in weight.

33. **(C)** Fluid resuscitation needs to be carefully administered due to the decreased response of the cardiovascular system with age. Reduced circulation, loss of circulatory defense responses, coupled with increased presence of ventricular dysfunction produces a significant challenge in managing shock in the elderly.

34. **(D)** Normal physiological changes to vital signs during the second trimester of pregnancy include a drop in blood pressure 10–15 mmHg due to a reduction in peripheral vascular resistance. The heart rate will increase 10–20 beats per minute due to an increased maternal blood volume. Note: The blood pressure will rise back to baseline in the third trimester. Keep these normal changes in mind when assessing a pregnant trauma patient.

35. **(A)** The backboard must be tilted on its left side 10–15 degrees to prevent supine hypotension syndrome. Tilting the board will allow the uterus to displace to the left and prevent compression of the inferior vena cava

36. **(C)** After the third month of gestation the fetus and uterus grow rapidly. After the fifth month of pregnancy, the uterus rises out of the pelvis and is more prone to injury.

37. **(D)** Injured children can rapidly transition from a state of rapid and labored breathing to a state of total exhaustion resulting in respiratory arrest. Airway management is essential.

38. **(B)** A history of loss of consciousness is one of the most important prognostic indicators of potential CNS injury.

39. **(A)** Contrary to popular belief, pulse oximetry is not the "fifth vital sign." Complete documentation of baseline neurological status includes response to sensory stimulation, pupillary reaction, and motor function.

40. **(B)** Positive pressure ventilation of the patient with a flail chest injury reverses the mechanism that causes the paradoxical chest wall movement, restores tidal volume, and reduces pain of chest wall movement.

41. **(B)** The amount of energy required to deform a steering wheel is significant. Possible life-threatening injuries from the body striking a steering wheel include: flail chest, myocardial contusion, aortic tear, tracheal or vascular injuries, pulmonary contusion, pneumothorax, solid and hollow organ injury. Bilateral femur fractures may result if an "up-and-over" path occurred.

42. **(D)** Alcohol is a central nervous system depressant. Because of this, alcohol can mask signs and symptoms of injury. It is important to assess all trauma patients thoroughly, but be especially meticulous when you suspect drug/alcohol use.

43. **(B)** Osteoporosis is common in the geriatric population. This disease process makes bones much more susceptible to hip and other fractures. In severe cases, a simple action such as sneezing may result in a fracture.

44. **(C)** Crushing syndrome is a complex process. Part of this process causes toxin production including an increased potassium level. One of the major concerns with releasing a body part that has been crushed for several hours is the release of toxins into the circulating blood volume, which can lead to cardiac arrhythmia and immediate death.

45. **(D)** Crushing syndrome creates lactic acid due to anaerobic metabolism that takes place within the crushed body part. One of the major concerns with releasing a body part that has been crushed for several hours is the release of the lactic acid and other toxins into the circulating blood volume that can lead to profound metabolic acidosis. Sodium bicarbonate is indicated in the treatment of Crushing syndrome.

46. **(A)** Rupture of the stomach or small bowel that allows digestive enzymes to enter the peritoneal cavity can cause peritonitis, which can lead to infection and serious complications.

47. **(B)** Stabilizing the machinery serves two purposes. First, it assures your safety, and second it will prevent additional injury to the patient. If you choose "control bleeding" for your answer **(C)**, this is important but it does not supersede *your* safety. **(C)** and **(D)** will both be done, but *after* the machinery is stablized.

48. **(B)** This patient is in compensated shock. His elevated pulse rate (142) and evidence of vasoconstriction (pale, moist skin) is able to maintain his blood pressure despite continued blood loss.

49. **(B)** If bleeding still persists after direct pressure and elevation, the next step is to find an arterial pulse point proximal to the wound and apply firm pressure.

50. **(A)** Decompensated shock is when the body can no longer respond to the continued blood loss. This is evident in the scenario by a decreased pulse rate, respirations, and blood pressure.

51. **(C)** Flail chest is three or more adjacent ribs that are fractured in two or more places. This segment of the chest is free to move with the pressure changes of respirations.

52. **(C)** Paradoxical chest wall movement associated with flail chest is defined as the motion of a flail segment opposite to the normal motion of the chest wall.

53. **(B)** Positive pressure ventilation of the patient with a flail chest reverses the mechanism that causes the paradoxical chest wall movement, restores tidal volume, and reduces the pain of chest wall movement.

54. **(C)** The signs and symptoms displayed by this patient are consistent with a left side tension pneumothorax and immediate chest decompression is required.

55. **(B)** Application of an occlusive dressing is necessary because this is a highly vascular area. An occlusive dressing will prevent air from entering an injured vessel and the development of an air embolism.

56. **(A)** The Trendelenburg position would be appropriate to decrease the potential for air aspiration into an injured vessel.

57. **(D)** Edema is a serious concern because injury to this highly vascular area of the neck can lead to a rapidly expanding hematoma. This hematoma can put pressure on other blood vessels resulting in decreased blood flow to the brain or put pressure on nearby airway structures resulting in an airway management nightmare!

58. **(B)** 36%—chest = 9%, abdomen = 9%, entire arm 9%, front of the leg = 9%.

59. **(D)** This should be classified as a critical burn with over 50% body surface area containing second-degree burns.

60. **(C)** It is unclear if this patient fell, so you must suspect trauma and c-spine injury. A jaw thrust maneuver and bag-valve mask ventilation is the best choice. **(A)** is incorrect because the oxygen flow setting is too low; it should be at least 15 L/min. **(B)** is incorrect because it utilizes a nonrebreather mask to assist ventilations. Nonrebreathers are not designed for or capable of assisting ventilations. **(D)** is incorrect because the patient needs his ventilations assisted.

61. **(C)** Treatment for this rhythm includes lidocaine 1 mg/kg IVP.

62. **(C)** This is a difficult question. If you knew this answer, pat yourself on the back. A LeFort II fracture involves both the maxillary and nasal bones.

63. **(A)** Cushing's reflex includes an increase in systolic blood pressure, bradycardia, and erratic (usually slow) respirations.

64. **(D)** An epidural hematoma involves arterial vessels. Because the bleeding is arterial, intracranial pressure builds rapidly, compressing the cerebrum and increasing pressure within the skull. As the pressure rapidly builds, the patient will immediately display neurological signs/symptoms.

65. **(D)** This is another difficult question. If you knew this answer, pat yourself on the back. Brown-Sequard's syndrome is caused by a penetrating injury that affects one side of the spinal cord. The damage to the one side results in sensory and motor loss to that side of the body. Pain and temperature perception are lost on the opposite side of the body because of the switching of the associated nerves as they enter the spinal cord.

66. **(B)** In pericardial tamponade, the pericardial sac fills with fluid and compresses the heart. This impairs ventricular filling. The result is a decrease in cardiac output (the left ventricle cannot effectively fill and pump) and an increase in central venous pressure (venous blood returning to the heart is impaired and the right ventricle cannot fill or pump effectively).

67. **(B)** Beck's triad includes hypotension, distant heart tones, and JVD. This triad of symptoms can aid in the diagnosis of cardiac tamponade.

68. **(D)** Injury to the stomach or small bowel that allows digestive enzymes to enter the peritoneal cavity can cause a rapid development of sharp pain throughout the abdomen. This is a serious concern because peritonitis can develop and lead to serious complications.

69. **(B)** A subdural hematoma is usually due to rupture of small venous vessels. This type of bleeding is slow and the onset of symptoms may take several hours to develop after the injury.

70. **(B)** A secondary mechanism of injury from a blast or explosion is defined as any injury sustained from being struck by material propelled by the blast force.

71. **(C)** A tertiary mechanism of injury from a blast or explosion is defined as any injury sustained from being thrown and impacting the ground or other objects.

72. **(B)** 22.5%—front of right arm = 4.5%, upper chest = 9%, front of right leg = 9%.

73. **(B)** Your concern with this patient is complete airway obstruction secondary to swelling of the airway. Immediate endotracheal intubation is indicated.

74. **(D)** A perfect GCS score is 15. A score between 9 and 12 indicates moderate injury, while a score of 8 or below represents severe head injury.

75. **(B)** Complications associated with a fracture of the clavicle include injury to the subclavian vein.

76. **(D)** When assessment of a trauma patient does not reveal significant injury, the presence of unexplained shock should lead you to suspect serious abdominal/thorax trauma.

77. **(C)** When using the rule of nines, the head of a child is assigned 18% BSA compared to 9% BSA on an adult. There are several other "rule of nine" modifications for children and infants you should be familiar with before taking your certification exam.

78. **(D)** The diagnosis of cardiac tamponade often relies upon symptoms. Hypotension, distended neck veins, and muffled heart sounds are classic symptoms of cardiac tamponade and are know as Beck's triad. If the patient loses his or her peripheral pulse during inspiration, it is suggestive of pulsus paradoxus and the presence of cardiac tamponade.

79. **(C)** An open pneumothorax (sucking chest wound) includes a sucking or bubbling sound as air moves in and out of the chest wall. Bleeding is usually present and frothing of the blood may occur as the air and blood combine.

80. **(B)** Treatment of an open pneumothorax includes closing the chest wall by application of an occlusive dressing that is taped on three sides. **(A)** may be necessary, but it is not a more important priority than sealing the chest. **(D)** is necessary for this patient but sealing the chest should be performed on-scene, prior to rapid transport to a trauma center. **(C)** is incorrect because this patient does not have a tension pneumothorax although he will need to be monitored closely because an open pneumothorax can rapidly transition into a tension pneumothorax.

NOTES

CHAPTER 6

Obstetrics/Gynecology/
Pediatrics

This chapter has 45 questions devoted to obstetrics and gynecology, with the remaining 75 questions devoted to pediatric emergencies.

It is essential that you know pediatric drug dosages. If you are guessing the answers for these questions, STOP!! While you have the luxury of thinking about (and guessing) the answer to these questions as you go through this chapter, you will not have that luxury when you have a patient in front of you. You *must* know the correct dosage!

All ECG rhythm strips used in this chapter are six-second strips.

1. Supine hypotension syndrome occurs from
   (A) reduction of cardiac output due to compression of the aorta.
   (B) reduction of cardiac output due to compression of the inferior vena cava.
   (C) reduction of cardiac output due to compression of the superior vena cava.
   (D) the uterus pushing up on the diaphragm.

2. You are caring for a female patient who is at 35 weeks gestation. She was involved in a car accident and complains of neck pain. You suspect spinal injury and fully immobilize her on a long spine board. You would then
   (A) carefully tilt the board on its left side 10–15 degrees.
   (B) carefully tilt the board on its right side 10–15 degrees.
   (C) manually displace the uterus to the right.
   (D) allow the patient to roll onto her side.

3. The major concern with a prolapsed cord is that it
   (A) will dry, become contaminated, and infection may result.
   (B) will delay delivery.
   (C) will be compressed and reduce blood flow to the infant, resulting in hypoxia.
   (D) will lower the temperature of the blood going to the infant, when exposed to room temperature.

4. Abdominal pain in the region of the ovary during ovulation is known as
   (A) Braxton-Hicks contractions.
   (B) cystitis.
   (C) mittelschmerz.
   (D) endometritis.

5. In obstetrics, a woman's parity refers to her number of
   (A) pregnancies.
   (B) viable deliveries.
   (C) cesarean sections.
   (D) spontaneous abortions.

Questions 6–8 are based on the following scenario:

Your patient is 26 years old and 30 weeks pregnant. She is multigravida but nullipara. She complains of sudden severe tearing abdominal pain with some minor vaginal bleeding. Upon careful palpation, her abdomen is very tender and her uterus seems to be tightly contracted.

6. You suspect
   (A) abruptio placenta.
   (B) an ectopic pregnancy.
   (C) a miscarriage.
   (D) placenta previa.

7. This medical emergency is caused by
   (A) implantation of the fertilized ovum in a fallopian tube.
   (B) the uterus covering the cervical opening.
   (C) premature separation of the placenta from the uterine wall.
   (D) spontaneous abortion.

8. The patient's pregnancy history includes
   (A) one pregnancy and one birth.
   (B) many pregnancies and one birth.
   (C) one pregnancy and no births.
   (D) many pregnancies and no births.

---

9. Which of the following best states the normal physiological changes to vital signs during the second trimester of pregnancy?

   (A) Blood pressure rises, pulse rate rises
   (B) Blood pressure rises, pulse rate falls
   (C) Blood pressure falls, pulse rate rises
   (D) Blood pressure falls, pulse rate falls

10. Signs and symptoms of a pregnant patient with preeclampsia include
    (A) elevated BP, increased weight gain, facial edema, and seizures.
    (B) elevated BP, abdominal rigidity, and bright red vaginal bleeding.
    (C) elevated BP, normal respirations, and normal pulse rate.
    (D) elevated BP, visual disturbance, headache, and edema.

Questions 11–14 are based on the following scenario:

You are called to the scene of a 26-year-old female patient who is 27 weeks pregnant and in active labor. The patient states, "The baby is coming." You perform a visual examination of the perineum and notice a prolapsed cord.

11. You would immediately place the patient in which position?
    (A) Hips elevated as much as possible
    (B) Knee-chest position
    (C) Left lateral recumbent position
    (D) Both A and B are correct

12. You would instruct the patient to
    (A) push with each contraction.
    (B) pant with each contraction.
    (C) bear down.
    (D) hold her breath.

13. Additional treatment would include
    (A) providing oxygen and preparing to assist the mother for a normal delivery.
    (B) with a gloved hand, attempting to push the cord back into the vagina, and transporting with lights and siren.
    (C) with a gloved hand, placing two fingers into the vagina to raise the fetus off the cord, providing oxygen and transport.
    (D) attempting to reposition the cord laterally by gently pulling on it.

14. Care for the prolapsed cord would include
    (A) application of a sterile dressing.
    (B) attempting to reposition the cord.
    (C) doing nothing.
    (D) packing in ice to prevent it from drying.

---

15. The hormone secreted by the pituitary gland that stimulates the uterus to produce stronger contractions is
    (A) estrogen.
    (B) actin.
    (C) progesterone.
    (D) oxytocin.

16. The most common sexually transmitted disease is
    (A) chlamydia.
    (B) gonorrhea.
    (C) syphilis.
    (D) herpes.

17. You are treating a 20-year-old female complaining of abdominal pain that becomes more intense when walking. She states that if she shuffles her feet when she walks, the pain isn't as intense. Other signs and symptoms include fever, chills, and nausea. This patient is most likely suffering from
    (A) endometritis.
    (B) pelvic inflammatory disease.
    (C) ruptured ovarian cyst.
    (D) mittelschmerz cystitis.

Questions 18–20 are based on the following scenario:

You are called to a 32-year-old female who is in her twenty-eighth week of pregnancy. She complains of dizziness, blurred vision, and a feeling that she is going to pass out. She is emotionally upset and crying. She explains that at her doctor's appointment last week, her doctor scolded her for gaining too much weight. Her hands and ankles are edematous and her face is puffy. Vitals are BP 178/108, pulse 104, respirations 24.

18. You suspect that this patient
    (A) is emotionally upset.
    (B) has preeclampsia.
    (C) has borderline hypotension.
    (D) has postpartum depression.

19. Treatment for this patient would include
    (A) rapid transport with lights and siren.
    (B) administering nitroglycerin to lower the blood pressure.
    (C) transporting for psychiatric evaluation.
    (D) keeping the patient calm, and transporting without lights and siren.

20. You are enroute to the hospital when the patient has a grand mal seizure. Treatment for this patient includes
    (A) administering high-flow oxygen, magnesium sulfate 2–5 mg.
    (B) administering oxygen, magnesium sulfate 2–5 g, placing her in right lateral recumbent position.
    (C) maintaining an airway, administering oxygen, administering magnesium sulfate 2–5 g, monitoring vital signs.
    (D) maintaining an airway, administering magnesium sulfate 6–8 g, monitoring vital signs, placing her in left lateral recumbent position.

Questions 21 and 22 are based on the following scenario:

Your patient is a 38-year-old multigravida in her thirtieth week of gestation. She presents with bright red vaginal bleeding but denies abdominal pain. Her uterus is soft and feels "out of place." Her problem began following sexual intercourse.

21. You suspect
    (A) a uterine rupture.
    (B) placenta previa.
    (C) an ectopic pregnancy.
    (D) abruptio placenta.

22. Management of this patient includes all of the following except
    (A) IV fluids.
    (B) high-flow oxygen.
    (C) a vaginal examination.
    (D) transport for evaluation.

---

23. APGAR assessment of the newborn should be performed
    (A) only in the ambulance during transport.
    (B) at one and five minutes after birth.
    (C) at five-minute intervals after birth.
    (D) immediately after delivery and then every two minutes.

24. If the amniotic sac has not ruptured and the baby's head emerges, you should
    (A) use a sterile scalpel to carefully open the sac and provide suction before the baby takes a breath.
    (B) delay further delivery and transport immediately for an emergency cesarean section.
    (C) use your fingers to pinch and puncture the sac, then push the sac away from the nose and mouth.
    (D) continue with the delivery; the sac will break on its own once the baby's head is delivered.

25. Suctioning of the infant's mouth and nose should be performed after
    (A) the cord is clamped and cut.
    (B) the infant begins to cry.
    (C) the chest has been delivered.
    (D) the head has been delivered.

26. Chest compressions should be performed on any newborn with a heart rate less than ___ beats per minute.
    (A) 60
    (B) 40
    (C) 100
    (D) 120

27. Your 26-year-old female patient complains of nausea, dizziness, sudden onset of sharp left lower quadrant pain, and shoulder pain. You suspect
    (A) a ruptured appendix.
    (B) an ectopic pregnancy.
    (C) cholecystitis.
    (D) kidney stones.

28. The function of the placenta includes all of the following except
    (A) the transfer of antibodies.
    (B) the transfer of oxygen and nutrients.
    (C) the production of hormones.
    (D) the excretion of CO_2 and waste products.

29. Which of the following is the most appropriate care for a suspected sexual assault patient?
    (A) Perform a limited physical examination and care for injuries requiring immediate treatment.
    (B) Conduct a SAMPLE history and have the patient bathe prior to transporting to the hospital.
    (C) Prior to transport examine the genitalia for signs of injury.
    (D) Have the patient remove all clothing and place all clothing in a plastic bag.

Questions 30 and 31 are based on the following scenario:

You arrive on the scene of a 25-year-old female who states she is 9 months pregnant and is in apparent labor. The patient states she is gravida 3, para 2. She states that her "water broke" about 15 minutes ago and the baby is coming. Vital signs are: BP 152/86, pulse 96, respirations 24.

30. The term "gravida" means
    (A) number of live children.
    (B) number of pregnancies.
    (C) number of miscarriages.
    (D) time period for intrauterine fetal development.

31. Upon visual examination, you notice that crowning is present. You should
    (A) place the patient in the right lateral recumbent position and transport.
    (B) prepare for delivery because the birth of the baby is imminent.
    (C) place the patient in the knee to chest position and transport with lights and siren.
    (D) place the patient on her left side; birth of the baby will be delayed.

Questions 32 and 33 are based on the following scenario:
You arrive on the scene of a motor vehicle crash and notice that a car has struck a telephone pole. There is extensive damage to the vehicle. You find a confused female in her mid-twenties complaining of neck, chest, and abdominal pain. She keeps asking if her baby is going to be okay. You find out that she is eight months pregnant. Assessment reveals a large laceration to the forehead with active bleeding, BP 96/54, pulse 142, with pale cool skin, respirations 24 and shallow.

32. Treatment includes
    (A) placing the patient on 100% oxygen, continuing your assessment, immobilizing to the KED, transporting.
    (B) immediately removing the patient onto a backboard, administering 100% oxygen, starting two large-bore IVs, placing her on a backboard 30 degrees on the left side, and transporting.
    (C) administering 100% oxygen, rapid extrication from the vehicle with c-spine immobilization onto a backboard, placing her on a backboard on the left side, starting two large-bore IVs while enroute to the hospital.
    (D) removing the patient from the vehicle while protecting the c-spine, immobilizing the patient on the backboard and placing her in the right lateral recumbent position, administering high-flow oxygen, gaining IV access enroute to the hospital.

33. During transport, she suddenly goes into cardiac arrest. The patient is apneic and pulseless and the cardiac monitor shows ventricular fibrillation. What should be your next action?
    (A) intubate the trachea and confirm tube placement, chest compressions, administer epinephrine 1 mg every 3 to 5 minutes, rapid transport to the hospital.
    (B) defibrillate at 200, 200–300, 360 joules, begin CPR and intubate, administer epinephrine 1 mg IVP.
    (C) defibrillate at 200, 200–300, 360 joules, begin CPR, administer amiodarone 150 mg IVP.
    (D) stop resuscitative measures since this was blunt trauma and there is no chance of survival.

---

34. You are treating a 22-year-old female complaining of severe abdominal pain and left shoulder pain. Vital signs are BP 88/64, pulse 128 and regular, respirations of 22, skin is cool and wet. She states that she has a small amount of pink vaginal discharge. This patient is most likely experiencing
    (A) a ruptured ectopic pregnancy.
    (B) endometriosis.
    (C) pelvic inflammatory disease.
    (D) amenorrhea.

35. You are providing positive-pressure ventilation to a newborn. Which of the following statements is correct regarding oxygen administration to a newborn?
    (A) An anesthesia bag provides the best ventilation and is easiest to use.
    (B) A large bag-valve is needed to provide adequate tidal volume.
    (C) Never deprive a newborn of oxygen for fear of oxygen toxicity.
    (D) Positive pressure ventilations are often required in newborn resuscitation.

36. To prevent over- or undertransfusion of blood from the umbilical cord to the newborn, correct positioning of the newborn until the umbilical cord is clamped should be
    (A) at the level of the vagina.
    (B) at a higher level than the placenta.
    (C) at a level lower than the vagina.
    (D) placed in the left lateral recumbent position.

37. The umbilical vein
    (A) carries fetal blood to the placenta.
    (B) carries oxygenated blood from the placenta to the fetus.
    (C) returns oxygenated blood from the fetus to the placenta.
    (D) produces testosterone for male newborns and estrogen for female infants.

38. Four assessment maneuvers used to determine fetal position is called
    (A) the Leopold maneuver.
    (B) passive movement.
    (C) the Lewis manipulation.
    (D) the Patterson maneuver.

Questions 39–41 are based on the following scenario:

You have a female patient at 39 weeks gestation. She has regular contractions lasting 45–60 seconds at one to two minute intervals and is crowning.

39. Contraction intervals are correctly measured
    (A) from the beginning of one contraction to the end.
    (B) from the end of one contraction to the end of the next.
    (C) from the beginning of one contraction to the beginning of the next.
    (D) from the end of one contraction to the beginning of the next.

40. Contraction length is correctly measured
    (A) from the beginning of one contraction to the end.
    (B) from the end of one contraction to the end of the next.
    (C) from the beginning of one contraction to the beginning of the next.
    (D) from the end of one contraction to the beginning of the next.

41. Treatment for this patient should include
    (A) transport since delivery will not occur immediately.
    (B) preparing for delivery.
    (C) starting immediate transport to the hospital.
    (D) placing the patient on her left side and administering oxygen.

---

42. You are delivering a child when you observe the umbilical cord wrapped around the neck. Your first action should be
    (A) to stop delivery and delay as long as possible.
    (B) to gently remove the cord from around the neck.
    (C) to immediately cut the cord and remove it from around the neck.
    (D) rapid transport to the delivery room.

43. You are delivering a child in a breech presentation. You have delivered the feet and chest. You note that the chest of the child is moving and suspect the child is attempting to breathe. You should
    (A) guide the body toward the floor to assist in delivering the head.
    (B) gently pull on the torso to allow the head to be delivered.
    (C) insert two fingers in the vagina to form an airway around the infant's nose and mouth.
    (D) instruct the mother to pant with her next contraction.

44. Applying gentle countertraction to the infant's head to prevent explosive delivery is essential because
    (A) fetal hypoxia can result from rapid delivery.
    (B) if a nuchal cord is present, rapid delivery will make it worse.
    (C) this will allow the perineum to stretch and reduce the chance of tearing.
    (D) the placenta will detach too soon in rapid delivery.

45. Meconium-stained amniotic fluid indicates
    (A) a fetal hypoxic incident.
    (B) that the infant is full term.
    (C) no concern.
    (D) low birth weight.

Questions 46 and 47 are based on the following scenario:

You are sent to a private residence for a 13-month-old child with a barky cough. On arrival, you find the child being held in his mother's arms. He is awake, slow to respond, and visibly uncomfortable. Initial vital signs reveal a pulse of 170, respiratory rate of 46, and a blood pressure of 90/52. The barky cough is audible without a stethoscope but lung sounds reveal inspiratory stridor at rest. There is use of accessory muscles and you note nasal flaring.

46. From the information given in the scenario, you would suspect the child to be suffering from
    (A) epiglottitis.
    (B) croup.
    (C) bronchiolitis.
    (D) a common cold.

47. This child can be categorized as a child who is experiencing
    (A) respiratory arrest.
    (B) respiratory insufficiency.
    (C) prerespiratory arrest.
    (D) respiratory failure.

---

48. You are treating a 50-kg child who was found to be unconscious. The cardiac monitor attached to the patient shows a heart rate of 200 beats per minute with narrow QRS complexes. You palpate a weak pulse; blood pressure is 60/32. Oxygen is being delivered and an IV line has been established. Initial management of this patient would include
    (A) giving Adenocard 6 mg IVP.
    (B) synchronizing cardioversion at 25 joules.
    (C) synchronizing cardioversion at 100 joules.
    (D) transporting with continued assessment.

49. The most common use for naloxone in the prehospital setting is to reverse the effects of overdose with an abused drug such as heroin. The recommended pediatric dose of naloxone for infants and children from birth to five years is
    (A) 20 mg.
    (B) 2.0 mg.
    (C) 0.01 mg/kg.
    (D) 0.1 mg/kg.

50. During transport of a seven-year-old male who has sustained multisystem trauma, you determine the need for fluid resuscitation. Appropriate administration of fluid would be to
    (A) rapidly infuse 250–300 cc of dextrose 5% in water.
    (B) rapidly infuse 350 cc of dextrose 5% in water.
    (C) determine the child's weight in kilograms and administer a 20 cc/kg bolus of an isotonic crystalloid.
    (D) give an immediate rapid infusion of normal saline, reassess, and then give additional boluses as needed.

51. You have been called to treat a five-year-old child previously diagnosed with an upper respiratory infection. She now presents with increased work of breathing, fever, and increased cough. The child appears pale, is lying on the couch, and slow to respond. She has obvious nasal flaring with a respiratory rate of eight per minute. Further history given by the mother reveals that the child has been drinking very little and not eating. In addition, the child has complained of her "tummy" hurting. From the information in the scenario, this child is most likely in
    (A) respiratory distress with impending respiratory failure.
    (B) no acute distress.
    (C) respiratory insufficiency easily corrected with oxygen.
    (D) cardiogenic shock.

52. After bag-valve mask ventilation is performed on a two-year-old patient with impending respiratory failure, the child fails to improve. You determine that the best course of action would be to intubate. However, the patient is awake with an intact gag reflex. Rapid sequence intubation is preferred in this setting. Using Atropine, midazolam, and succinylcholine as the medications of choice for RSI, the correct dosage of succinylcholine for this two-year-old would be
    (A) 0.01 mg/kg.
    (B) 0.1 mg/kg.
    (C) 1.0 mg/kg.
    (D) None of the above are the correct dosage.

53. Signs and symptoms associated with Shaken Baby Syndrome may be difficult to assess in the prehospital setting. Injury resulting from violent shaking might include
(A) contusions or abrasions visible on the knees of children three to five years old.
(B) an intracranial hemorrhage resulting from torn veins between the brain and skull in children under the age of 24 months.
(C) a red rash visible on the child's chest and back.
(D) a spiral fracture of the wrist.

54. You respond to a call for a two-month-old female who is reported by the mother to be seizing. Upon arrival, you find the infant lying in a crib motionless; no seizure activity is evident. The mother reports that the episode began approximately 10 minutes ago when she went to the baby's room to wake her from her nap. Your assessment reveals a flaccid infant with slow respirations of 10 per minute; bulging anterior fontanel, and several areas of bruising on the extremities in various stages of healing. From the information given and the general appearance of the infant, you suspect
(A) child abuse, most probably Shaken Baby Syndrome.
(B) respiratory insufficiency with shock.
(C) cardiovascular compromise with impending arrest.
(D) a postictal state.

55. You are assessing a newborn infant who presents with respiratory distress. Physical findings reveal that the patient has a low birth weight, a small head, and small eye openings. Besides the obvious respiratory distress initially described, you might suspect the infant to be suffering from
(A) a heroin overdose.
(B) crack cocaine ingestion.
(C) fetal alcohol syndrome.
(D) apnea of infancy.

56. You are assessing a 1½-year-old male who presents with obvious breathing difficulty. Inspiratory stridor is heard with evident use of all accessory muscles. The trouble breathing is worse at night. No other significant findings are visible. The child is on no medications and has otherwise been well. You suspect
(A) epiglottitis.
(B) asthma.
(C) bronchiolitis.
(D) croup.

57. Intraosseous access allows for the administration of fluids, medications, and blood products into the bone marrow. Possible complications of intraosseous infusion include all of the following except
(A) osteomyelitis.
(B) improvement in vascular volume and/or condition.
(C) fractures.
(D) compartment syndrome.

58. When caring for a pediatric patient, the standard dose of epinephrine for pulseless arrest or symptomatic bradycardia is
    (A) 0.1 mg/kg IV/IO of 1:1,000.
    (B) 0.01 mg/kg IV/IO of 1:10,000.
    (C) 0.01 mg/kg IV/IO of 1:1,000.
    (D) 0.1 mg/kg IV/IO of 1:10,000.

59. Amiodarone is indicated for the treatment of a variety of cardiac arrhythmias. The recommended dose of amiodarone in a pediatric patient with ventricular fibrillation is
    (A) 5 mg.
    (B) 150 mg.
    (C) 0.5 mg/kg.
    (D) 5 mg/kg.

60. Croup, bronchiolitis, epiglottitis, and asthma are all examples of pediatric respiratory problems. From the selection below, identify the statement that best describes or defines bronchiolitis.
    (A) A viral disease caused by RSV that affects children between the ages of 6–18 months
    (B) A viral infection of the upper airway affecting children between the ages of 3 months and 1 year
    (C) A bacterial infection from an unknown cause
    (D) An inflammatory disease causing restrictive airway compromise

61. You have been summoned to a local residence for a child who fell. On arrival, you find a seven-year-old boy supporting his left arm with his right hand. You note that the boy also has what appears to be some swelling around his right eye. You also note bruises in various stages of healing on his chest and lower back. His parents are upstairs, providing no comfort or support to the boy. Given this information, you suspect
    (A) "coining."
    (B) "rubbing."
    (C) child abuse.
    (D) Shaken Baby Syndrome.

62. During your assessment of a five-year-old child, you discover a heart rate of 200 beats per minute. The rhythm strip reveals narrow QRS complexes corresponding to the patient's pulse rate. The rhythm most probably represents
    (A) ventricular tachycardia.
    (B) rapid atrial fibrillation.
    (C) supraventricular tachycardia.
    (D) sinus tachycardia.

63. Management of pediatric bradycardia with significant signs and symptoms related to cardiac or respiratory compromise should be treated with
    (A) Atropine.
    (B) lidocaine.
    (C) sodium bicarbonate.
    (D) epinephrine.

64. You respond to a bee sting call and find a six-year-old with a full body rash. He has no respiratory difficulty at this time. You are going to administer Benadryl. The correct dose is
    (A) 25 mg.
    (B) 50 mg.
    (C) 1 mg/kg.
    (D) 0.5 mg/kg.

65. A 16-month-old child presents with seizures. Airway assessment reveals copious secretions. Breath sounds are present and coarse bilaterally. Heart rate is regular with weak pulses. After suctioning the airway and assisting ventilations, you are able to establish IV access. Identify, from the choices below, those that can cause seizures in this age group.
    (A) Bronchiolitis, croup, fever
    (B) Drug overdose, hyperglycemia, pneumonia
    (C) Hypoglycemia, fever, drug overdose
    (D) Hyperglycemia, pneumonia, fever

66. The pediatric dose of lorazepam in the treatment of seizures is
    (A) 0.5–1.0 mg/kg IV/IO.
    (B) 0.05–0.1 mg/kg IV/IO.
    (C) 0.05–0.01 mg/kg IV/IO.
    (D) 5–10 mg IV/IO.

67. The recommended dose of lidocaine in the pediatric cardiac arrest patient presenting in ventricular fibrillation is
    (A) 0.001 mg/kg.
    (B) 0.01–0.02 mg/kg.
    (C) 0.1–0.2 mg/kg.
    (D) 1 mg/kg.

68. You are treating a six-month-old infant who presents as "fussy." The infant is crying and has a respiratory rate of 40 per minute. She has pink skin with a capillary refill of 2 seconds. The cardiac monitor shows a narrow complex tachycardia of 260 beats per minute. Based on this assessment, the correct pharmacological intervention to control the rate would be
    (A) adenosine 0.1 mg/kg IV.
    (B) amiodarone 5 mg/kg IV over 20 minutes.
    (C) procainamide 15 mg/kg IV over 30 minutes.
    (D) lidocaine 1 mg/kg IV bolus.

69. You are dispatched to a private residence for an eight-year-old boy complaining of trouble breathing. On arrival, you find the patient lethargic with blue lips and rapid labored respirations. He is able to answer questions with only one- or two-word sentences. Physical examination reveals a respiratory rate of 50 per minute; diminished breath sounds and crackles are heard over the right lung field with dullness to percussion. He also has a temperature of 104°F. Based on your assessment, this patient may be experiencing
    (A) cardiogenic shock.
    (B) a drug overdose.
    (C) respiratory distress.
    (D) respiratory failure, most probably due to pneumonia.

70. While treating a three-year-old child for amitriptyline ingestion, he suddenly begins to have seizure activity. You decide that administration of diazepam is appropriate. The recommended dose range for this age group is
    (A) 0.01–0.02 mg/kg.
    (B) 0.05–0.1 mg.
    (C) 0.1–0.3 mg/kg.
    (D) 5–10 mg.

71. You are caring for a lethargic two-year-old. Her blood glucose test confirms hypo-glycemia. You are able to establish IV access. What is the appropriate drug to admin-ister?
    (A) 50% dextrose
    (B) 10 mg glucagon
    (C) Instant glucose
    (D) 25% dextrose

72. You are caring for a 13-year-old tricyclic antidepressant overdose. What cardiac arrhythmia is likely to develop as a result of this type of overdose?
    (A) Tall, peaked t waves
    (B) SVT
    (C) Wide QRS complex and prolonged QT interval
    (D) Narrow QRS complexes with normal PR interval

73. While enjoying an "off" day from work, you hear your neighbor screaming. You rush outside to see her pulling her four-year-old child from the swimming pool. The child is limp, blue, and not responsive to any stimulus. What should you do?
    (A) Perform the Heimlich maneuver in an attempt to eliminate water from the lungs.
    (B) Begin chest compressions.
    (C) Send the mother to call 911; open the airway and initiate rescue breathing.
    (D) Go to your car and get your AED and attach it as soon as possible.

74. A small child has been struck by a car traveling approximately 25 MPH. The child is unresponsive. The airway maneuver of choice for this patient is
    (A) jaw-thrust with c-spine stabilization.
    (B) head-tilt/chin-lift.
    (C) hyperextension with jaw-thrust.
    (D) hyperflexing the head to the "sniffing" position.

75. You are called to the scene of a two-year-old child with a three-day history of diar-rhea. The child appears to be in no respiratory distress with good breath sounds bilaterally. The heart rate is 140 per minute and the BP is 86/60. Capillary refill is delayed at about four seconds. The peripheral pulses are weak. After obtaining vascular access, which of the following would be the next intervention?
    (A) Get a chest X-ray.
    (B) Initiate a Dopamine infusion at 2–5 mcg/kg/minute.
    (C) Start oral hydration.
    (D) Administer a 20 cc/kg bolus of normal saline.

76. You have initiated an IO line in a pediatric patient suffering from severe dehydration. What is the most reliable indicator of successful placement of the IO needle?
    (A) Take an X-ray.
    (B) The ability to draw arterial blood through the IO.
    (C) Aspiration of bone marrow.
    (D) No evidence of fractures after insertion.

77. You have just delivered a full-term baby in the back of your ambulance. The initial APGAR score is 5. Treatment should consist of
    (A) CPR.
    (B) effective ventilation.
    (C) vascular access.
    (D) administration of epinephrine.

78. External signs that may indicate an intraabdominal injury in a pediatric patient may include
    (A) a contusion to the forehead, deformity of the right wrist.
    (B) pale skin, abdominal contusion, seat belt abrasions across the abdomen.
    (C) dilated pupils, bradycardia, poor peripheral pulses.
    (D) tracheal deviation, JVD.

79. Which of the following assessment finding would indicate that a pediatric patient is progressing from respiratory distress to respiratory failure?
    (A) Nasal flaring
    (B) Respiratory rate over 32
    (C) Poor muscle tone
    (D) Grunting/head bobbing

80. Identify the anatomical differences in the pediatric airway compared to the adult airway.
    (A) The airway diameter is larger, the larynx is more anterior, the tongue is proportionally smaller.
    (B) The airway diameter is larger, the larynx is more posterior, the tongue is proportionally smaller.
    (C) The airway diameter is smaller, the larynx is more anterior, the tongue is proportionally larger.
    (D) The airway diameter is smaller, the larynx is more posterior, the tongue is proportionally larger.

81. The pediatric assessment triangle provides a systematic approach to the assessment of the pediatric patient. It is based on three parameters, which are
    (A) airway, breathing, circulation.
    (B) appearance, breathing, circulation.
    (C) airway, respiratory rate, pulses.
    (D) appearance, lung sounds, skin color.

82. It is important to compare central and peripheral pulses in the pediatric patient to determine
    (A) the presence of shock.
    (B) skin color.
    (C) mental status.
    (D) airway patency.

83. Establishing the care and transport priorities for the pediatric patient can be determined by utilizing the "CUPS" assessment. "CUPS" stands for
    (A) critical, unstable, perfect, stable.
    (B) coma, unresponsive, potentially unstable, stable.
    (C) coma, unresponsive, potentially unstable, seizures.
    (D) critical, unstable, potentially unstable, stable.

84. Of the following choices below, which is most likely to result from Shaken Baby Syndrome?
    (A) Hypoglycemia
    (B) Abdominal bruising
    (C) Subdural hematoma
    (D) Lower extremity fracture

85. You have administered _____ to an eight-year-old. Drowsiness, decreased mental status, muscle twitching, and seizures are side effects that may result from its administration.
    (A) Atropine
    (B) lidocaine
    (C) calcium chloride
    (D) adenosine

86. Your squad is dispatched to the scene of a six-year-old child with an elevated temperature. The mother tells you that the child was fine last night and got up this morning complaining of a sore throat and trouble swallowing. The initial assessment reveals a sick-looking child who is leaning forward in the tripod position. He is obviously drooling. From this information, you suspect
    (A) bronchiolitis.
    (B) croup.
    (C) epiglottitis.
    (D) meningitis.

87. During transport of a child with epiglottitis, he becomes unresponsive and apneic. You are still able to palpate a weak pulse at a rate of 64 per minute. Your immediate action should be to
    (A) apply a nonrebreather mask with 10–15 liters per minute of oxygen.
    (B) insert an OPA and administer bag-valve mask ventilations.
    (C) position the child's head and provide bag-valve mask ventilation with 100% oxygen.
    (D) immediately intubate the child.

88. Your patient is an ill-appearing four-month-old lying in his mother's arms. The mother tells you that the infant won't take a bottle and cries whenever he moves. Your exam reveals a lethargic infant, warm to touch, with fine pinpoint petechia on the abdomen, chest, and face. The infant's fontanelle appears to be bulging. The information gained on exam should lead you to suspect
    (A) bronchiolitis.
    (B) meningitis.
    (C) croup.
    (D) epiglottitis.

89. Select the statement that correctly relates to pediatric seizures.
    (A) Febrile seizures correlate to the speed in which the temperature rises, not to the degree of the fever.
    (B) Always suspect a fever to be the cause of a seizure if the temperature is more than 101°F.
    (C) Infants and children between the ages of four months and eight years commonly suffer from febrile seizures.
    (D) Febrile seizures do not require transport if the patient can be cooled.

Questions 90–92 are based on the following scenario:

You are dispatched to a local department store when a concerned customer notices an infant left unattended in a car. It is bitterly cold outside. Once you gain entry into the car, you find the infant to be dusky in color with no activity or movement. The respiratory rate is 12 per minute and irregular with grunting and short sighs. The heart rate is 64 per minute with weak central pulses. The infant's hands and feet are cold to touch. Capillary refill is 5 seconds.

90. Your immediate action would be to
    (A) start CPR.
    (B) ventilate with a bag-valve mask device and 100% oxygen.
    (C) give oxygen by blow-by.
    (D) intubate the infant.

91. After the above treatment is given, the infant does not improve. The ECG shows narrow complexes with p waves. The rate is 64 per minute. Your next action would be to
    (A) obtain IV/IO access and give Atropine for the bradycardia.
    (B) obtain IV/IO access and give Atropine 0.01–0.02 mg/kg.
    (C) obtain IV/IO access and give 0.01 mg/kg of 1:1,000 epinephrine.
    (D) obtain IV/IO access and give 0.01 mg/kg of 1:10,000 epinephrine.

92. After obtaining venous access and delivering the pharmacological intervention, the patient's heart rate increases to 130 per minute with strong central pulses but no peripheral pulses. To further stabilize the infant, the next course of action should be to
    (A) repeat the Atropine dose.
    (B) repeat the epinephrine dose.
    (C) continue CPR.
    (D) begin rewarming the patient.

93. A seven-year-old child has been struck by a car and is lying motionless in the street. He has obvious head trauma. Identify the signs of Cushing's triad.

    (A) Increased BP, bradycardia, abnormal respirations
    (B) Decreased BP, tachycardia, increased respirations
    (C) Increased BP, tachycardia, increased respirations
    (D) Decreased BP, bradycardia, abnormal respirations

94. From the following list, identify an example of distributive shock.
    (A) Hypovolemic shock
    (B) Anaphylactic shock
    (C) Cardiogenic shock
    (D) Psychogenic shock

95. Seizure-like activity triggered by stimuli other than cerebral electrical discharges, such as major mood disorders or severe environmental stress, is defined as
    (A) partial seizure.
    (B) partial complex seizure.
    (C) generalized seizure.
    (D) pseudo-seizure.

96. You are caring for a child with respiratory distress. You note a harsh high-pitched sound with each breath. You suspect this is indicative of
    (A) stridor.
    (B) wheezing.
    (C) crackles.
    (D) rhonchi.

97. Which of the following vital signs is most likely present in a 13-year-old with spinal shock?
    (A) BP 64/30; pulse 56 per minute
    (B) BP 64/30; pulse 150 per minute
    (C) BP 160/100; pulse 56 per minute
    (D) BP 160/100; pulse 150 per minute

98. You have been called to the home of a three-year-old child. You are told by the mother that he is not eating well, "acting funny," and is not playful. You find a frail-looking small child who is lethargic on examination. Vital signs reveal a respiratory rate of 46 per minute; heart rate is 190 per minute, BP is not obtainable. The patient is given oxygen by nonrebreather mask at 15 LPM and you determine that an IV line is necessary. After three attempts at a peripheral line, you are not able to establish venous access. Of the choices below, select the most appropriate intervention.
    (A) Initiate an IO in the proximal femur and infuse a 20 cc/kg bolus of D5W.
    (B) Initiate an IO in the distal humerus and infuse fluid at a KVO rate.
    (C) Initiate an IO in the proximal tibia and give a 20 cc/kg bolus of normal saline.
    (D) Initiate an IO in the distal radius and infuse fluid wide open to maintain blood pressure.

99. You respond to a MVC involving a young child. The child is found apneic but still has a palpable pulse. You immediately begin positive pressure ventilation with a bag-valve mask device. You note that the left side of the chest moves, but the right does not. Lung sounds are absent on the right side and the trachea is deviated to the left. Your immediate action is to
    (A) increase the tidal volume with each ventilation.
    (B) perform a needle decompression on the left side.
    (C) give a 20 cc/kg bolus of IV fluids.
    (D) perform a needle decompression on the right side.

100. Your patient has injured his right arm in a bicycle accident. When assessing the injured extremity, which of the following is most important?
    (A) Check for compartment syndrome.
    (B) Check deep tendon reflexes.
    (C) Do a good neurovascular exam.
    (D) Check for position sense (proprioception).

101. Sudden Infant Death Syndrome (SIDS) is defined as death of an infant
    (A) due to trauma.
    (B) within the first 24 months of life.
    (C) from child abuse.
    (D) within the first year of life that is unexplained.

102. A small child has fallen through the ice while skating. After 30 minutes, the child is pulled from the icy water apneic and pulseless. Your first action in the management of this child should be to
    (A) keep the child cool to maintain the mammalian dive reflex.
    (B) defibrillate the child immediately.
    (C) pronounce the child dead at the scene.
    (D) secure the child's airway and control the cervical spine.

103. You have intubated a six-week-old infant found in respiratory arrest. While performing ventilations, the child becomes blue and the pulse rate drops into the lower 50s. Your next step should be to
    (A) check the pulse oximeter reading.
    (B) administer epinephrine down the endotracheal tube to correct the bradycardia.
    (C) auscultate the chest.
    (D) administer Atropine.

104. A child has suffered multisystem trauma and IV access cannot be obtained. You determine the best course of action would be to establish an IO. A contraindication for IO insertion is
    (A) a child is under one year old.
    (B) a child who is apneic and pulseless.
    (C) a fracture of the lower extremity.
    (D) a previous attempt in the opposite leg.

105. Abdominal trauma is a serious injury in the pediatric patient. An injury to which abdominal organ is most likely to cause death in the pediatric patient?
(A) Pancreas
(B) Liver
(C) Spleen
(D) Kidney

106. You have performed a Rapid Trauma Survey on a child and are prepared to transport. In which situation is it appropriate to perform the detailed exam enroute to the hospital?
(A) Fracture of the humerus
(B) Amputated thumb
(C) Mottled skin with tachycardia
(D) Fractured tibia with numbness in the foot

107. You are treating a child with a tension pneumothorax. Needle decompression is needed. The correct site for insertion of the needle is
(A) below the third rib in the mid-clavicular line.
(B) below the second rib in the mid-axillary line.
(C) top of the second rib in the mid-axillary line.
(D) top of the third rib in the mid-clavicular line.

108. Of the statements below, identify that which is true concerning pediatric airway management.
(A) The Sellick maneuver is not appropriate for use in the child.
(B) Nasotracheal intubation is the preferred method of intubation.
(C) Cuffed endotracheal tubes can be used in children.
(D) Bradycardia can result from suctioning a child.

109. Which of the following is most likely to cause shock in a child?
(A) Laceration to the face
(B) a fractured radius
(C) Cerebral edema
(D) a splenic injury

110. Which action is most important when treating an unresponsive child?
(A) Performing chest compressions
(B) Checking for a pulse
(C) Administering supplemental oxygen
(D) Manually opening the airway

111. The minimum chest compression rate for a two-year-old in cardiac arrest is
(A) 80/minute.
(B) 100/minute.
(C) 110/minute.
(D) 120/minute.

112. The compression-ventilation ratio for a newborn in cardiac arrest is
    (A) 5:1.
    (B) 3:1.
    (C) 15:2.
    (D) 5:2.

113. What is the first pharmacological agent to be administered in a pediatric cardiac arrest?
    (A) Atropine 1.0 mg
    (B) Epinephrine 1:10,000
    (C) Lidocaine 1 mg/kg
    (D) Epinephrine 1:1,000

114. In a pediatric patient, initial defibrillation should be performed at
    (A) 0.5 J/kg.
    (B) 4 J/kg.
    (C) 2 J/kg.
    (D) 100 J.

115. In a pediatric patient, initial cardioversion should be performed at
    (A) 0.5–1.0 J/kg.
    (B) 4 J/kg.
    (C) 2 J/kg.
    (D) 100 J.

116. You need to administer diazepam for a three-year-old in status epilepticus. He weighs 15 kg. An acceptable dose range is
    (A) 1.5–4.5 mg.
    (B) 1.0–3.5 mg.
    (C) 2.0–5 mg.
    (D) 0.01 mg/kg.

117. In caring for an infant burn patient, the rule of nines assigns _____ percent of the body surface area to the head.
    (A) 9%
    (B) 4½%
    (C) 18%
    (D) 36%

118. You respond to the local high school football practice field for a sports injury. The coach tells you that the patient made a tackle and after the play did not get up. Your patient is supine on the ground with all of his equipment on. He is awake but slow to answer questions. You should remove the football helmet if
    (A) a c-spine injury is suspected.
    (B) you do not have easy access to the airway.
    (C) you suspect the patient had a loss of consciousness.
    (D) the patient has numbness in his hands.

119. A priority in evaluating a two-year-old with diarrhea and vomiting includes determining
    (A) temperature elevation.
    (B) a viral infection.
    (C) a respiratory infection.
    (D) adequate hydration.

120. Cuffed endotracheal tubes are usually not indicated in children under what age?
    (A) Five
    (B) Eight
    (C) Three
    (D) Ten

Answers and Answer Explanations

1. **(B)** Supine hypotension syndrome (or vena cava syndrome) occurs when the pregnant uterus compresses the inferior vena cava when the patient is in a supine position. This results in a decrease in blood return back to the heart and a reduction of cardiac output. This syndrome can occur as early as the third month of gestation.

2. **(A)** The backboard must be tilted on its left side 10–15 degrees to prevent supine hypotension syndrome. Tilting the board will allow the uterus to displace to the left and prevent compression of the inferior vena cava.

3. **(C)** The major concern with a prolapsed cord is compression of the cord by the head of the infant. This can result in a reduced blood flow to the infant and lead to fetal hypoxia.

4. **(C)** Mittelschmerz is German for "middle pain" and is defined as abdominal pain in the region of the ovary during ovulation.

5. **(B)** Parity refers to the number of viable deliveries. This is common obstetric medical terminology you must be familiar with.

6. **(A)** Abruptio placenta is premature separation of the placenta from the uterus. There are different presentations that can occur depending on the severity of the abruption. Classic presentation includes a sudden, sharp, tearing pain and the development of a stiff boardlike abdomen. Bleeding can be severe or not present depending on many factors.

7. **(C)** Abruptio placenta is premature separation of the placenta from the uterus and is a true medical emergency because it poses a life threat to the mother and fetus.

8. **(D)** Multigravida is when a woman has been pregnant more than once. Nullipara is a woman who has not yet delivered her first child. If you did not know this common terminology, you must review obstetric medical terminology.

9. **(C)** Normal physiological changes to vital signs during the second trimester of pregnancy include a drop in blood pressure 10–15 mmHg due to a reduction in peripheral vascular resistance. The heart rate will increase 10–20 beats per minute due to an increased maternal blood volume. Note: The blood pressure will rise back to baseline in the third trimester.

10. **(D)** Common signs and symptoms of preeclampsia include headache, dizziness, confusion, blurred vision, nausea, vomiting, proteinuria, hypertension, and edema.

11. **(D)** Position the mother with the hips elevated as much as possible or in the knee-chest position in an attempt to relieve pressure on the cord.

12. **(B)** You would instruct the patient to pant with each contraction to prevent bearing down and applying pressure on the cord.

13. **(C)** With a gloved hand, place two fingers into the vagina to elevate the presenting part to relieve pressure on the cord. Provide oxygen and rapid transport to a hospital that can perform a cesarean delivery.

14. **(A)** Applying a sterile dressing to the exposed cord will minimize temperature change. If the cord is exposed to room temperature, the temperature of blood flowing to the infant will decrease. This can cause hypothermia. Additionally, a temperature change of the blood may cause the umbilical vessels to spasm resulting in decreased blood flow to the infant.

15. **(D)** Oxytocin is a hormone secreted by the pituitary gland that stimulates the uterus to produce stronger contractions. The medication Pitocin (oxytocin) is used to induce labor or control postpartum hemorrhage.

16. **(A)** Chlamydia Trachomatis is the most common sexually transmitted disease in the United States. Gonorrhea, syphilis, and herpesvirus are also sexually transmitted diseases.

17. **(B)** Pelvic inflammatory disease is often accompanied by increased pain when walking. The patient will bend forward and take short, slow steps. Guarding of the abdomen and nausea are also common with PID.

18. **(B)** Common signs and symptoms of preeclampsia include headache, dizziness, confusion, blurred vision, nausea, vomiting, proteinuria, hypertension, and edema.

19. **(D)** If you suspect preeclampsia, you should take precautions to prevent seizures, which include keeping the patient calm, and transporting without lights and sirens.

20. **(C)** Treatment of seizure activity in eclampsia includes placing the patient in the left lateral recumbent position, maintaining the airway, administering high-flow oxygen, establishing IV access, and the administration of 2–5 grams of magnesium sulfate IV. If seizures cannot be controlled, sedatives may be required.

21. **(B)** Placenta previa is usually in a multigravida in her third trimester of pregnancy. A recent history of sexual intercourse or vaginal examination just before the onset of vaginal bleeding is not uncommon. The onset of painless bright red vaginal bleeding or spotting is considered the hallmark sign of placenta previa.

22. **(C)** A vaginal exam should not be attempted when placenta previa is suspected. The exam may puncture the placenta and cause a severe hemorrhage.

23. **(B)** It is important to wait one full minute to perform the first APGAR assessment. A second APGAR should be performed at five minutes.

24. **(C)** If the amniotic sac is present around the baby's head, use your fingers to pinch the sac and then push it away from the nose and mouth. Using a scalpel or scissors is *not* recommended.

25. **(D)** This is one of the most basic OB questions you can be asked. If you missed this question, you need to review childbirth.

26. **(A)** If a newborn's heart rate is 60–80 and does not increase despite stimulation and ventilation, it is necessary to start chest compressions.

27. **(B)** An ectopic pregnancy should be suspected when abdominal pain is present in women of childbearing age who are sexually active. An ectopic pregnancy can be difficult to distinguish from other conditions. The classic triad of symptoms includes abdominal pain, vaginal bleeding, and amenorrhea. Other symptoms include referred pain to the shoulder, nausea, vomiting, or syncope. Signs of shock may be present if the ectopic ruptures.

28. **(C)** The placenta has many functions including the transport of oxygen, nutrients, and other substances to the fetus and the excretion of CO_2 and other waste products. Production of hormones is not a function of the placenta.

29. **(A)** EMS providers should limit the patient's history to the elements necessary to provide care. Patient contact should be nonjudgmental and supportive.

30. **(B)** Gravida or gravidity refers to the number of times a women has been pregnant. If you did not know this common terminology, you must review obstetric medical terminology.

31. **(B)** Preparation for delivery is necessary. The information presented in this scenario should lead you to believe that delivery of the baby is imminent.

32. **(C)** This is a trauma patient who requires 100% oxygen, rapid extrication from the vehicle with c-spine immobilization onto a backboard, placing the backboard on the left side (to prevent supine hypotension syndrome), and establishing two large-bore IVs while enroute to the hospital.

33. **(B)** Treatment for a pregnant patient in cardiac arrest would include defibrillation, CPR, intubation, and administration of appropriate medications.

34. **(A)** An ectopic pregnancy should be suspected when abdominal pain is present in women of childbearing age who are sexually active, an ectopic pregnancy can be difficult to distinguish from other conditions. The classic triad of symptoms includes abdominal pain, vaginal bleeding, and amenorrhea. Other symptoms include referred pain to the shoulder, nausea, vomiting, or syncope. Signs of shock may be present if the ectopic ruptures.

35. **(C)** If central cyanosis is present, or you are unsure about the adequacy of ventilation, the administration of supplemental oxygen is necessary. Never deprive a newborn of oxygen for fear of oxygen toxicity.

36. **(A)** Keep the newborn at the same level of the vagina with the head slightly lower than the rest of the body. This will prevent over- or undertransfusion of blood from the umbilical cord to the newborn and facilitate drainage of secretions from the nose and mouth to help prevent aspiration.

37. **(B)** The umbilical cord consists of one vein and two arteries. The umbilical vein carries oxygenated blood from the placenta to the fetus. The umbilical arteries transport waste products from the fetus to the placenta.

38. **(A)** The Leopold maneuver is palpation of the abdomen in four different assessment steps. This is used to identify the number of fetuses, the fetal presentation, presenting part, degree of descent, point of maximum intensity of fetal heart tones, and internal rotation of the fetus.

39. **(C)** Contraction intervals are correctly measured from the beginning of one contraction to the beginning of the next. Many health care providers incorrectly measure intervals from the end of one contraction to the beginning of the next.

40. **(A)** Contraction length is correctly measured from the beginning of the contraction to the end of that contraction.

41. **(B)** Regular contractions lasting 45–60 seconds at one- to two-minute intervals and crowning indicate delivery is imminent.

42. **(B)** Initial care for nuchal cord (cord around the neck) is to first try to gently remove the cord from around the neck. If this is not successful and the cord is so tight that it is inhibiting labor, it will be necessary to clamp the cord in two places and cut between the clamps.

43. **(C)** If the infant starts to breathe with its face pressed against the vaginal wall, it is necessary to insert two fingers in the vagina to form an airway around the infant's nose and mouth.

44. **(C)** Applying gentle countertraction to the infant's head to prevent explosive delivery is essential to decrease the likelihood of tearing of the perineum and decreases the potential for rapid expulsion of the baby's skull through the birth canal, which may cause intracranial injury.

45. **(A)** Meconium-stained amniotic fluid indicates a fetal hypoxic incident. Hypoxia causes an increase in digestive activity along with the relaxation of the anal sphincter, which allows meconium to pass into the amniotic fluid.

46. **(B)** Croup is a viral infection of the upper airway that causes inflammation of the subglottic region that can lead to airway obstruction. Inspiratory stridor is often present. Other assessment findings include nasal flaring, tracheal tugging or retractions. The vital signs of this patient are compensatory to the airway obstruction.

47. **(D)** Respiratory failure is evident for the following reasons: tachypnea, tachycardia, nasal flaring, retractions, audible airway noises (stridor/barky) cough, and slowness to respond, which indicates a decreased level of consciousness.

48. **(B)** The child is unstable (decreased LOC, rapid heart rate, and hypotension). Synchronized cardioversion should be provided at 0.5–1.0 joules per kilogram.

49. **(D)** Naloxone is used to reverse the effects of opiate toxicity. The recommended dose in pediatrics is 0.1 mg/kg.

50. **(C)** Fluid resuscitation for multisystem trauma in the pediatric patient includes a bolus of an isotonic crystalloid at 20 cc/kg. Reassess and repeat as needed.

51. **(A)** Respiratory distress is defined as the inability to maintain gaseous exchange sufficient to meet the needs of the body. Evidence of abnormal respirations (tachypnea or bradypnea) or increased work of breathing; use of accessory muscles, nasal flaring, grunting, and decreased mentation can also signal respiratory distress in the pediatric patient.

52. **(C)** 1.0 mg/kg of succinylcholine is the recommended dose for this patient. There are no contraindications to its use in this scenario.

53. **(B)** The result of violent shaking in a baby less that 24 months old may include damage to nerve tissues deep within the brain and torn veins between the brain and the skull, which can cause severe bleeding.

54. **(A)** You may suspect Shaken Baby Syndrome based on bulging of the anterior fontanelle without fever or overhydration as a cause. In addition, the multiple areas of bruising provide information that may indicate child abuse.

55. **(C)** Characteristics of a newborn with fetal alcohol syndrome include low birth weight, a small head, and small eye openings.

56. **(D)** Inspiratory stridor, absence of drooling, trouble swallowing, and symptoms persistently worse at night leads to the conclusion of the croup.

57. **(B)** IO infusions will generally improve the patient's condition or improve his or her vascular volume, thereby increasing the BP and cardiac output. Osteomyelitis **(A)** can occur if the needle is left in place for longer than 24 hours; fractures **(C)** can occur when the extremity is not well stabilized or an attempt was made at a improper site where the bone is weaker; compartment syndrome **(D)** occurs when extravasation is not detected.

58. **(B)** 0.01 mg/kg IV/IO of 1:10,000 solution is the recommended dose of epinephrine for pediatric cardiac arrest and/or symptoms of bradycardia.

59. **(D)** 5 mg/kg of amiodarone is the recommended dose for the treatment of pulseless v tach or v fib in a pediatric patient.

60. **(A)** The pathology of bronchiolitis is closely matched with that of respiratory syncytial virus (RSV). Any number of viruses including parainfluenza, adenovirus, and rhinovirus may also be a cause.

61. **(C)** Child abuse is prevalent in all socioeconomic groups. With the parents at home, yet away from the child, offering no consolation is a standard "red flag" signal to child abuse. The swelling around the right eye and the evidence of unexplained bruises might also indicate child abuse. Since the child is seven years old, Shaken Baby Syndrome **(D)** is not correct. "Rubbing" **(B)** and "coining" **(A)** are characteristic cultural differences that must be recognized and documented but not suspected child abuse.

62. **(C)** Heart rates ranging from 180–220 beats per minute in a child is considered SVT if the QRS complexes remain narrow. V tach **(A)** presents with a wide QRS; sinus tachycardia **(D)** usually shows waves and, rapid atrial fibrillation **(B)** will be irregularly irregular.

63. **(D)** Epinephrine is the drug of choice for symptomatic bradycardia in the pediatric patient. Atropine **(A)** is effective in the *adult* bradycardic patient since bradycardia is often a result of parasympathetic stimulation; Lidocaine **(B)** is contraindicated in bradycardia. **(C)** is not indicated.

64. **(C)** The recommended dose of Benadryl for a pediatric patient with an allergic reaction is 1 mg/kg.

65. **(C)** Hypoglycemia, fever, drug overdoses, or hypoxia are common causes of seizures in an infant.

66. **(B)** Pediatric administration of lorazepam is 0.05–0.1 mg/kg with repeated doses of 0.05–0.1 mg/kg for persistent seizures.

67. **(D)** The pediatric dose of lidocaine is 1 mg/kg bolus given IV/IO in cardiac arrest with a presenting rhythm of ventricular fibrillation or pulseless ventricular tachycardia.

68. **(A)** In a pediatric patient, adenosine given at 0.1 mg/kg IV is indicated to correct a stable tachycardia.

69. **(D)** The patient may be experiencing respiratory failure, most probably due to pneumonia based on tachypnea, increased work of breathing, diminished breath sounds, dullness to percussions, and elevated temperature.

70. **(C)** The recommended pediatric dose of diazepam is 0.1–0.3 mg/kg for the treatment of seizures.

71. **(D)** A 25% dextrose solution is recommended for pediatric patients because it is less viscous than 50% dextrose. This will allow easier administration through a smaller diameter IV catheter and reduce the occurrence of sclerosis to small peripheral veins.

72. **(C)** TCA overdose produces a prolonged QT interval along with widening of the QRS complex. Tall, peaked t waves are most commonly associated with hyperkalemia.

73. **(C)** The lone rescuer should initially provide rescue breathing to the child while someone is sent to call 911. AEDs are not currently recommended for infants and children under 25 kg or less than eight years old. This is basic life support material you must be familiar with before taking your certification exam.

74. **(A)** With the probability of significant trauma and c-spine injury, the child's airway should be assessed using a jaw-thrust maneuver while stabilizing the cervical spine. Head-tilt/chin-lift hyperextension and hyperflexion **(B, C, and D)** cause manipulation of the cervical spine and are not indicated when cervical spine injury is suspected.

75. **(D)** With the vital signs given in the scenario, the child is displaying signs and symptoms consistent with compensated shock. The shock is most probably related to diarrhea. A 20 cc/kg bolus of normal saline or an isotonic crystalloid fluid is recommended.

76. **(C)** One of the ways to determine successful placement of the IO needle is by aspiration of bone marrow. Additionally, an unobstructed infusion of fluid without evidence of infiltration can also be used. X-rays are not needed to confirm placement. You should not be able to aspirate arterial blood from a properly placed IO needle.

77. **(B)** Most newborn infants respond quite favorably to warming, drying, suctioning, and stimulation. Occasionally, administration of oxygen with assisted ventilations may be necessary. Vascular access and CPR are utilized only after the infant fails to respond effectively to ventilatory assistance.

78. **(B)** Pale skin, abdominal contusion, seat belt abrasions, or unexplained shock may suggest the possibility of intraabdominal injury with a probability of abdominal hemorrhage.

79. **(C)** Nasal flaring, elevated respiratory rate, grunting, and head bobbing all indicate respiratory distress. The development of poor muscle tone indicates the patient is tiring and is an ominous sign of respiratory failure.

80. **(C)** The airway diameter in children is smaller than an adult airway; the larynx is more anterior making visualization difficult; the tongue is proportionally larger to the jaw.

81. **(B)** The pediatric assessment triangle is based on appearance, which includes mental status, body position and muscle tone; breathing, which includes visible movement, effort and audible sounds, and circulation, which includes skin color. All are obtained as part of the initial assessment to formulate a rapid determination of the child's stability.

82. **(A)** The presence or absence of shock may be indicated by a difference between the central and peripheral pulses. Pulse differences or deficit may be a sign of poor peripheral perfusion.

83. **(D)** After completing the initial assessment and providing appropriate treatment for life-threatening emergencies, the "CUPS" assessment can help determine the severity of the patient's condition: "CUPS" stands for: Critical, Unstable, Potentially unstable, Stable.

84. **(C)** Head injury (including the possibility of a subdural hematoma) is a common finding in Shaken Baby Syndrome.

85. **(B)** Lidocaine has central nervous system properties that cause drowsiness, decreased mental status, muscle twitching, and the possibility of seizures.

86. **(C)** Epiglottitis is a bacterial infection causing the acute swelling of the epiglottis and the soft tissues above the glottic opening. Clinical findings include but are not limited to sudden onset high fever (102–105°F), pain on swallowing, typically sitting in tripod position, and drooling.

87. **(C)** Any external manipulation of the epiglottis (i.e., intubation or OPA insertion) can cause complete airway obstruction in the child with epiglottitis. Carefully position the child's head and provide positive pressure ventilation with 100% oxygen.

88. **(B)** Recognize the syndrome of fever and petechia as a medical emergency. Inflammation of the meninges will cause the fontanelle to bulge and appear full. Meningitis should be suspected in this patient.

89. **(A)** How fast the temperature of the child rises will increase a child's risk for developing a seizure. For example, a child who transitions from a temperature of 100.2 to 104.5°F in 30 minutes is more likely to suffer a febrile seizure than a child who develops a 104.5°F temperature over several hours.

90. **(B)** Recognize that the infant has inadequate oxygenation (dusky color) and immediately begin bag-valve mask ventilation with 100% oxygen.

91. **(D)** Epinephrine 1:10,000 solution should be given at 0.01 mg/kg IV/IO for persistent bradycardia unresponsive to ventilation.

92. **(D)** Considering the ambient temperature to be very cold in this scenario, hypothermia is a significant cause of the patient's presentation. Begin rewarming the patient.

93. **(A)** Cushing's triad (sometimes referred to as Cushing's reflex or response) characteristically presents with an elevated blood pressure, bradycardia, and abnormal (usually slow) respirations.

94. **(B)** Distributive shock is a shock state that exists when there is no loss of body fluid, but the fluid distribution is altered from an increase in the vascular space or leaking of fluid from the vascular space. This results in an insufficiency of fluid relative to the vascular space. Types of distributive shock include anaphylactic, septic, and neurogenic.

95. **(D)** Pseudo-seizures are triggered by any mechanism other than cerebral electrical discharge.

96. **(A)** Stridor is a harsh high or low-pitched sound caused by breathing through a partially blocked airway; wheezing **(B)** is a high or low-pitched whistling sound; crackles/rhonchi (**C** and **D**) represent fluid in the larger bronchial airways.

97. **(A)** Spinal shock (neurogenic) is a distributive shock producing hypotension relative to an increase in the vascular space in the absence of a loss of body fluids. A spinal cord injury results in a "lack of communication" between the brain and the body so there is no response to catecholamine release resulting in bradycardia and hypotension.

98. **(C)** Initiation of an IO line is appropriate after three unsuccessful attempts at a standard peripheral IV line. The best site for placement of the IO line is in proximal tibia. Because of the clinical presentation of the child in this scenario, a 20 cc/kg bolus of normal saline is appropriate.

99. **(D)** The signs and symptoms are consistent with a tension pneumothorax (absent breath sounds, tracheal deviation, no or little chest movement on the affected side). Immediate needle decompression is warranted.

100. **(C)** It is important to check for pulses, motor, and sensory functions distal to any injury in an extremity. Assessment and documentation of the neurovascular status is required before and after splinting.

101. **(D)** SIDS is the leading cause of death in American infants under one year of age. The technical definition is the sudden death of an apparently healthy infant that remains unexplained by history and through autopsy.

102. **(D)** Since it is unknown if there are any c-spine injuries from the fall through the ice, you must secure the airway and control the cervical spine during resuscitation.

103. **(C)** Auscultation of the chest for proper endotracheal tube placement is necessary. If lung sounds are diminished or absent, it may be necessary to extubate, ventilate, reassess, and then reintubate.

104. **(C)** A fracture of the lower extremity is a contraindication to an IO insertion.

105. **(B)** The liver is a solid, vascular organ in the right upper quadrant. Rupture or laceration of the liver can cause severe hemorrhage. Injury to the liver is the most common abdominal injury that leads to death in the pediatric patient.

106. **(C)** A sign of poor perfusion includes mottled skin and tachycardia. This is indicative of shock and a detailed exam should be performed enroute to the hospital. Other indicators of shock include weak peripheral pulses and prolonged capillary refill time.

107. **(D)** Inserting the needle over (on top of) the second or third rib avoids inadvertent puncturing or laceration of the adjoining vessels and nerves located at the inferior border of the ribs.

108. **(D)** Suctioning may result in bradycardia from stimulation of the vagus nerve, particularly in children less than six months old. Do not use prolonged suction attempts.

109. **(D)** The spleen is a blood-filled organ located in the left upper quadrant. Blunt trauma can cause injury to the spleen resulting in blood loss and shock. The spleen is the most injured organ resulting in *shock*, while the liver is the most injured organ resulting in *death* of a pediatric patient.

110. **(D)** Establishing a patent airway is the most important treatment step in providing care for an unresponsive patient. This is basic life support material you must be familiar with before taking your certification exam.

111. **(B)** The answer is a minimum of 100 chest compressions per minute. This is basic life support material you must be familiar with before taking your certification exam.

112. **(A)** Five compressions to one ventilation. This is basic life support material you must be familiar with before taking your certification exam.

113. **(B)** Epinephrine 0.01 mg/kg of 1:10,000 solution is the recommended dose for pediatric cardiac arrest and/or symptoms of bradycardia

114. **(C)** The recommended energy setting when defibrillation is necessary is 2 joules/kg. Repeat defibrillation is recommended at 4 joules/kg.

115. **(A)** The recommended energy setting when cardioversion is necessary is 0.5–1.0 joules/kg. Repeat cardioversion can be increased to 2 joules/kg.

116. **(A)** The dose range for diazepam is 0.1–0.3 mg/kg. A 15 kg patient would receive 1.5 to 4.5 mg of medication.

117. **(C)** Using the rule of nines, the head of an infant is assigned 18% body surface area.

118. **(B)** Unless special circumstances exist such as respiratory distress or airway compromise, the helmet should not be removed by EMS. This question asks when you *should* remove the helmet. Not having easy access to the airway is the best choice.

119. **(D)** Of the choices listed, evaluating the patient for adequate hydration is the top priority. Evaluating the patient's temperature (**A**) and the presence of infection (**B** and **C**) are necessary but secondary to determining adequate hydration.

120. **(B)** Cuffed endotracheal tubes are not indicated for children under the age of eight. In a child less than eight, the normal anatomic narrowing at the level of the cricoid cartilage provides a "functional cuff," and eliminates the need for a cuffed tracheal tube under most circumstances.

NOTES

CHAPTER 7

Operations

This chapter covers a variety of topics including scene safety, legal considerations, vehicle operations, communications, documentation, infection control, quality improvement, DNR, basic patient assessment, basic physiology, hazardous materials, mass casualty incidents, and scene management.

1. A properly written patient care report (PCR) is important because
   (A) the PCR relays the paramedic's true opinion of the patient.
   (B) the PCR provides the receiving hospital with important billing information.
   (C) the PCR may be the only source for pertinent information for receiving health-care professionals.
   (D) the PCR links traits of the paramedic with documentation abilities.

2. The PCR is a legal document making it necessary to record accurate
   (A) incident times.
   (B) paramedic certifications.
   (C) names of nearest relatives.
   (D) personal opinions.

3. Findings that require no medical intervention, but require documentation as evidence of a thorough history and exam are termed
   (A) negative responses.
   (B) positive therapeutics.
   (C) noteworthy responses.
   (D) pertinent negatives.

4. The proper way to correct a written error on the PCR is to
   (A) use white-out to cover the error.
   (B) draw a single line through the error, initial, and date the area.
   (C) scribble through the error completely and sign your name next to the error.
   (D) use a black marker to eliminate the error from the PCR, initial, and date the area.

5. An incomplete or illegible patient care report
   (A) may be acceptable in some areas.
   (B) may cause subsequent caregivers to provide inappropriate treatment based on the report.
   (C) is of no use.
   (D) is useful in the ongoing care and treatment of the patient.

6. Documentation of a patient's refusal for care or transport should include all of the following except
   (A) the patient's insurance information.
   (B) the paramedic's advice to the patient.
   (C) on-line medical control's advice.
   (D) a complete narrative of the event.

7. Revisions to the original patient care report
   (A) should be added on the original document.
   (B) are never appropriate.
   (C) are done on a separate report form and then attached to the original.
   (D) can easily be done with a different color ink.

8. Appropriate professional language on a PCR includes
   (A) medical terminology.
   (B) slang.
   (C) personal opinion.
   (D) personally acceptable abbreviations.

9. A telephone is an example of a _____ communication system:
   (A) simplex
   (B) duplex
   (C) multiplex
   (D) trunked

10. For communication to be effective, the receiver must give appropriate _____ to the sender:
    (A) ideas
    (B) encodings
    (C) decodings
    (D) feedback

11. When communicating medical information, using proper terminology can
    (A) shorten transmission and provide an unambiguous form of communication.
    (B) serve no vital importance.
    (C) alter the interpretation of the nature of the incident if heard by several different people.
    (D) reflect upon the EMS professional negatively.

12. Disadvantages of a simplex system may include that
    (A) the process is slower and more formal.
    (B) either party can interrupt the other party as necessary.
    (C) voice transmission may interfere with data transmission.
    (D) simplex system facilitates discussion.

13. Disadvantages of using a cellular telephone for EMS communications include that
    (A) the conversation is less formal.
    (B) the system promotes discussion.
    (C) the system reduces on-line time.
    (D) geography can interfere with the system or signs.

14. The federal agency that regulates telecommunications in the United States is the
    (A) FBI.
    (B) FDIC.
    (C) FCC.
    (D) FACEP.

15. Functions of an EMS dispatcher include all of the following except
    (A) call taking.
    (B) proper diagnosis of the caller's illness.
    (C) alerting and directing the EMS response.
    (D) giving prearrival instructions to the caller.

16. Communication from the EMS dispatcher that provides the caller with emotional support, may be life sustaining to the patient during a critical event, provides immediate assistance to the caller as well as ongoing information to responding units is
    (A) incident data collection.
    (B) predispatch education.
    (C) prearrival instructions.
    (D) incident referral data.

17. Bacteria, viruses, and fungi are all examples of
    (A) pathogenetic hosts.
    (B) nonspecific inflammatory agents.
    (C) disease processes.
    (D) infectious agents.

18. The body's first line of defense against infection is
    (A) the skin.
    (B) the respiratory system.
    (C) the G.I. system.
    (D) humoral response.

19. You respond to the home of a patient with an unknown illness for two days. You
    approach the call suspecting an infectious or communicable disease. Which action is
    not appropriate for this patient's care?
    (A) Gloves and protective eye goggles are worn.
    (B) A full history and detailed physical exam is obtained.
    (C) Make the patient a "load and go" due to the potential for paramedic exposure.
    (D) Dispose of supplies and sharps appropriately on disposition of patient.

20. Proper care of the patient with known HIV includes all of the following except
    (A) isolation of the patient.
    (B) effective handwashing.
    (C) use of eye protection and gowns where exposure to bodily fluids in large
        quantities is possible.
    (D) BSI, based on task performed.

21. Of the following hepatitis groups, which is not transmitted via blood?
    (A) Hepatitis A
    (B) Hepatitis B
    (C) Hepatitis C
    (D) Hepatitis D

Questions 22 and 23 are based on the following scenario:

You are called to a local homeless shelter for a gentleman with complaint of a cough for
two to three weeks, night sweats, and weight loss.

22. You suspect
    (A) hepatitis A.
    (B) HIV.
    (C) TB (tuberculosis).
    (D) meningitis.

23. You diagnose the above illness appropriately and know the disease is spread
    through
    (A) exposure to blood.
    (B) exposure through airborne droplets.
    (C) exposure to body fluids.
    (D) direct physical contact.

---

24. You respond to a home of a patient with complaint of sudden onset of fever/chills, joint pain, neck stiffness, and severe headache. Upon examination the medics note a petechial rash. You suspect
    (A) rabies.
    (B) influenza.
    (C) hepatitis A.
    (D) meningitis.

25. The causative organism of chicken pox is the varicella zoster virus, which is a member of the
    (A) varicella virus group.
    (B) zoster virus group.
    (C) herpesvirus group.
    (D) rubivirus group.

26. Reportable infectious/communicable disease exposures include
    (A) contact of infectious materials with eye, mouth, or mucous membrane.
    (B) working with a partner with a URI.
    (C) contact with blood and body fluids on intact gloves.
    (D) spill of infectious material in the EMS unit with no contact.

27. Legislation that governs the practice of medicine and may prescribe a physician's ability to delegate authority to perform medical acts by the paramedic is
    (A) licensure.
    (B) medical direction.
    (C) standard of care.
    (D) medical practice act.

28. Exercising the degree of care, skill, and judgment that would be expected under like or similar circumstances by a similarly trained, reasonable paramedic in a similar community or location is the definition of
    (A) duty to act.
    (B) standard of care.
    (C) malfeasance.
    (D) proximate cause.

29. The elements of a negligence claim include all of the following except
    (A) duty to act.
    (B) breach of duty.
    (C) code of conduct.
    (D) proximate cause.

30. You arrive on the scene of a two-car MVC. The driver of the first vehicle is unconscious. Consent for this patient is said to be
    (A) informed.
    (B) implied.
    (C) expressed.
    (D) involuntary.

31. You and your partner are treating a 16-year-old female with lower abdominal pain. The patient's husband arrives and informs you his wife may be pregnant. You can treat this patient without parental consent based on
    (A) the nonurgent doctrine.
    (B) an emancipated minor is considered an adult.
    (C) the fact that she is mentally competent.
    (D) the fact that the consent is involuntary.

32. You are called to the middle of a bridge to transport a violent patient who is suicidal. Per local police, the patient threatened to jump from the bridge and needs a psychiatric evaluation. The patient refuses transport threatening to sue anyone who touches him. You transport this patient against his will based on
    (A) informed consent.
    (B) implied consent.
    (C) expressed consent.
    (D) involuntary consent.

33. You and your partner are treating a patient who needs to be transported to the hospital for chest pain. You have established an IV, placed the patient on the monitor, administered oxygen and aspirin. Your partner checks his watch and notes that his shift is over. You remove the monitor and politely tell the patient the oncoming crew will come and transport him to the hospital shortly. Leaving this patient is an example of
    (A) false imprisonment.
    (B) assault.
    (C) battery.
    (D) abandonment.

34. Unlawful touching of an individual without his or her consent could leave the paramedic open to allegations of
    (A) assault.
    (B) battery.
    (C) abandonment.
    (D) false imprisonment.

35. Advance directives are documents that express the patient's wishes in the event that he or she is unconscious or otherwise unable to express his or her choice for care. These include living wills, do not resuscitate orders, and
    (A) slow code requests.
    (B) durable power of attorney for health care.
    (C) artificial care order.
    (D) health care denial form.

36. The paramedic's primary responsibility at a crime scene or accident scene is
    (A) quality patient care.
    (B) quality documentation.
    (C) thorough knowledge of the event.
    (D) to protect self and other EMS personnel.

37. Laws that protect a paramedic if he or she acts in good faith, is not negligent, acts within his or her scope of practice, and does not accept payment for service constitutes the
    (A) implied consent laws.
    (B) Good Samaritan laws.
    (C) malfeasance laws.
    (D) absolute immunity laws.

38. Commonly mandated injuries that are reportable to local authorities include all of the following except
    (A) falls greater than 10 feet.
    (B) child abuse or neglect.
    (C) animal bites.
    (D) gunshot/stab wounds.

39. You and your partner are overheard in the elevator discussing a patient's injuries from a motor vehicle crash. Your conversation included pertinent personal and medical information about the patient. A call was placed to your supervisor because
    (A) you failed to keep patient confidentiality.
    (B) you failed to discuss the appropriate medical care.
    (C) you failed to speak loud enough.
    (D) you failed to recall the injuries correctly.

40. Intentional false communication that injures another person's reputation or good name is a definition of
    (A) invasion of privacy.
    (B) breach of confidentiality.
    (C) informed slander.
    (D) defamation.

41. Personal protective equipment used to operate safely in the rescue environment includes all of the following except
    (A) head protection.
    (B) eye protection.
    (C) hand protection.
    (D) throat and neck protection.

42. It is generally considered unsafe to walk in fast-moving water _____ deep.
    (A) ankle
    (B) knee
    (C) waist
    (D) chest

43. _____ (is) are considered "drowning machines" due to recirculating currents created by water moving over a uniform obstruction.
    (A) Low-head dams
    (B) Current-generated dams
    (C) Rapid-moving water
    (D) White water

44. The body responds to cold water by rapidly losing heat. Protective measures exist within the body, which stimulates a parasympathetic response, decreasing heart rate, causing peripheral vasoconstriction, and shunting blood to the core. This cold protective response is known as the
    (A) mammalian dive reflex.
    (B) core shunt mechanism.
    (C) cold survival mechanism.
    (D) physiologic shunt response.

45. Of the following, which is not considered an oxygen-deficient environment or confined space?
    (A) Basement
    (B) Storage tanks
    (C) Silos
    (D) Underground vaults

46. You are the first unit on the scene of a multiple-vehicle crash. Upon arrival, each of the following actions would be appropriate except
    (A) to establish scene command.
    (B) to treat and transport the most critically ill patient.
    (C) the scene sizeup.
    (D) control scene hazards.

47. Which of the following definitions best describes a disaster?
    (A) Motor vehicle collision with two to three patients
    (B) An everyday incident that generates three or more patients
    (C) A bus or train collision with 25–30 injured
    (D) An incident that overwhelms resources and may damage the infrastructure of a region

48. You are assigned the duties of safety officer under the incident command of a local mass casualty incident. You understand the responsibilities of this position to
    (A) monitor all on-scene actions to ensure no potentially harmful situations are created.
    (B) coordinate all operations of this incident that involves outside agencies.
    (C) collect data regarding the incident and relay information to the press or media.
    (D) act as an officer who supervises a specific safety unit or area.

49. The "S" in the acronym START stands for
    (A) suitable.
    (B) simple.
    (C) salvageable.
    (D) sorting.

50. You are the triage officer at a car versus bus collision. Your first victim is approximately 30 years old, awake, alert, and oriented. He is the driver of the car that collided with the bus head on. He complains of lower abdominal pain and has obvious deformity to both femurs. Respirations 24, pulse 140, BP 80/palpated, capillary refill >2 sec. How would you triage the following patient?
    (A) Green
    (B) Yellow
    (C) Red
    (D) Black

51. You are assessing a patient involved in a two-car MVC with severe blunt trauma to the abdomen. You suspect internal hemorrhage. The patient's BP is 100/52 with a pulse rate of 130. You know the elevation in the heart rate is the body's attempt to maintain
    (A) metabolism.
    (B) system integration.
    (C) homeostasis.
    (D) end-organ damage.

52. The movement of water across a cell membrane is known as
    (A) oncotic pressure.
    (B) osmosis.
    (C) diffusion.
    (D) osmolarity.

53. You are treating a patient with diabetic ketoacidosis. The patient is tachycardic and has deep, rapid respirations. The most likely cause for the deep, rapid respirations is that
    (A) the body is compensating for a low pH by increasing respirations.
    (B) the body is compensating for a high pH by increasing respirations.
    (C) the body is compensating for an excess of HCO_3 by increasing respirations.
    (D) the body is compensating for a decrease in H+ ions by increasing respirations.

54. You are treating a patient with hyperventilation syndrome due to an anxiety attack. Which acid-base derangement will hyperventilation produce?
    (A) Respiratory acidosis
    (B) Metabolic acidosis
    (C) Respiratory alkalosis
    (D) Metabolic alkalosis

55. _____ are the primary solutions used for intravenous therapy in the prehospital setting:
    (A) Colloids
    (B) Blood products
    (C) Hypotonic solutions
    (D) Crystalloids

56. The Controlled Substance Act of 1970 created five schedules of controlled substances. Schedule 1 drugs are those drugs with
    (A) accepted medical indications, low potential for abuse and dependence.
    (B) accepted medical indications, high potential for abuse or dependence.
    (C) no accepted medical indications, high potential for abuse and dependence.
    (D) accepted medical indications, less abuse potential and low to moderate physical dependence potential.

57. You are administering amiodarone 300 mg to a patient in full cardiac arrest with a rhythm of ventricular fibrillation. As you start to administer the drug through the endotracheal tube, your partner stops you. Which of the six rights of medication administration were you about to violate?
    (A) Right dose
    (B) Right medication
    (C) Right patient
    (D) Right route

58. Parenteral routes of drug administration include all of the following except
    (A) sublingual.
    (B) intravenous.
    (C) intramuscular.
    (D) topical.

59. A 53-year-old female who is being treated for chronic pain with morphine sulfate continues to complain of pain despite taking her medications as prescribed. The patient is most likely experiencing what response to this medication?
    (A) Allergic reaction
    (B) Tolerance
    (C) Dependence
    (D) Antagonism

60. The desired effects of bronchodilation from the administration of albuterol is the result of stimulation of the_____ receptors in the sympathetic nervous system:
    (A) Alpha 1
    (B) Alpha 2
    (C) Beta 1
    (D) Beta 2

61. The standards known as _____ are a major influence on safety standards, standardizing the look and manufacturing designs of ambulances.
    (A) medical equipment standards
    (B) essential equipment standards
    (C) DOT KKK 1822 D specs
    (D) gold standard

62. The type of ambulance that is a standard van with forward control integral cab body is a
    (A) Type I ambulance.
    (B) Type II ambulance.
    (C) Type III ambulance.
    (D) medium-duty ambulance.

63. This agency is involved in the protection of safety for workers including ensuring ambulances are disinfected properly, have sharps containers, and red trash bags.
    (A) OSHA
    (B) FCC
    (C) SOP
    (D) NHTSA

64. At the scene of an MVC your ambulance should be parked at least 100 feet from the accident, uphill and upwind to ensure
    (A) the safety of the vehicle.
    (B) the safety of your crew.
    (C) that the crime scene is not violated.
    (D) clear distance for secondary units to arrive.

65. The following statements regarding scene safety with regard to helicopter and air medical transport are all true except:
    (A) Generally a helicopter requires a landing zone of approximately 100 feet by 100 feet.
    (B) Approach a helicopter from the rear, nearest the tail rotor for safe loading and unloading.
    (C) Ensure that the landing zone is clear of wires, loose debris, towers, or vehicles.
    (D) Mark the landing zone with a single flare and do not shine lights directly into the pilot's eyes.

66. Promptly recognizing the need for emergency management, assessing the scene for danger, contacting Dispatch to mobilize other units for care and transportation of the patient, establishing rapport with the patient and other paramedics on the scene represent the paramedic's_____.
    (A) ethical responsibility
    (B) roles
    (C) triage criteria
    (D) care responsibility

67. In the mnemonic C-FLOP, when describing the practices of the Incident Management System, the "O" stands for
    (A) operations.
    (B) ongoing assessment.
    (C) order of command.
    (D) officer in charge.

Questions 68–70 are based on the following scenario:

You are assigned to triage patients at the scene of an explosion in a park. You are using the METTAG system of triage.

68. The first victim you come in contact with has no palpable pulse and no respiratory effort. The patient has a major laceration of the scalp with an open skull fracture. You would tag this person as
    (A) Green.
    (B) Yellow.
    (C) Red.
    (D) Black.

69. The next patient with whom you come into contact is a 34-year-old female who is wandering around the incident looking for her three-year-old daughter. The patient has multiple abrasions to her face and arms. You would most likely triage this patient
    (A) Green.
    (B) Yellow.
    (C) Red.
    (D) Black.

70. The third patient you find is awake, alert, and oriented. The patient has tachypnea with shallow respirations. Your assessment reveals a sucking chest wound on the right side of the chest, a fracture of the right femur, and a large laceration on the forehead. You will most likely triage this patient
    (A) Green.
    (B) Yellow.
    (C) Red.
    (D) Black.

---

71. You and your partner are the first EMS units to arrive on the scene of a single-car MVC, car versus pole. Electrical lines are down across the car. One victim is trapped inside the vehicle. Which action would be most correct?
    (A) Immobilize the patient's cervical spine and do a rapid extrication ensuring that the patient does not touch the downed wires.
    (B) Control the airway and cervical spine manually while awaiting other units to arrive for proper extrication.
    (C) Contact Dispatch and have the power company turn the power off to the lines prior to attempting rescue of this patient.
    (D) Ask the patient to slide himself out of the vehicle through a window, being careful not to touch anything metal while exiting.

72. You are the paramedic in charge of a single patient entrapped in a vehicle that was involved in a head-on crash. The extrication of this patient will require a lengthy period of time. Your responsibility during the time of disentanglement will be that
    (A) no treatment is necessary during extrication.
    (B) management of this patient will remain the same as for other emergency patients. Initiation of assessment and care should be started as soon as possible.
    (C) you should initiate only treatment that will assist in the disentanglement.
    (D) treatment should be limited only to identification of injuries.

73. You are transporting a patient who has been exposed to a hazardous material. You have come into contact with this patient with Level D hazmat protection equipment on. You have most likely experienced
    (A) a secondary exposure.
    (B) a primary contamination.
    (C) a tertiary contamination.
    (D) no contamination; this level of hazmat protection is sufficient.

74. The paramedic faces many stress-inducing situations. All of the following are phases of the stress response except
    (A) alarm reaction.
    (B) resistance.
    (C) exhaustion.
    (D) acceptance.

75. While eating lunch at a local eatery, you and your partner are discussing a call you had just completed. The patient's relative who is sitting at the next table overhears your partner talking about the patient's condition. Your partner has violated the patient's
    (A) right to consent.
    (B) right to confidentiality.
    (C) right of refusal of treatment.
    (D) character by defamation.

76. While assessing a patient complaining of abdominal pain, you should first
    _____ then _____ the abdomen.
    (A) palpate/auscultate
    (B) inspect/percuss
    (C) inspect/ausculate
    (D) palpate/percuss

77. A 50-year-old male is experiencing an acute exacerbation of asthma. Your partner establishes an IV and you prepare to administer albuterol via a hand-held nebulizer. Your actions are in direct accordance with your local protocol. This type of standing order is considered
    (A) on-line medical direction.
    (B) off-line medical direction.
    (C) closed-control medical direction.
    (D) proactive medical command.

78. You and your partner respond to the home of an elderly gentleman who is unresponsive. Your assessment reveals no respiratory effort, skin that is cool and mottled with obvious pooling, and no palpable pulse. The patient's wife presents a valid Do Not Resuscitate order. All of the actions below would be correct except to
    (A) address the wife using gentle eye contact and choosing appropriate words.
    (B) begin to resuscitate this patient without delay.
    (C) explain to the wife that her loved one has died; do not use terms that can be misinterpreted.
    (D) offer assistance to the survivor(s) if necessary.

79. You are one of many local EMS workers who just completed working the scene of a devastating plane crash that left several hundred people dead or injured. You and your crew are called in for CISD (Critical Incident Stress Debriefing). You understand this to be
    (A) a technique for reducing stress on scene that includes fluid replacement, food services, and change of assignments.
    (B) a formal, structured, planned intervention done by a trained team within 24–72 hours of a posttraumatic event. The team includes mental health workers and peers.
    (C) a spontaneous post-call discussion of the events.
    (D) a short informal meeting that gives the crew a chance to vent and verbalize their feelings about this incident.

80. Your crew is dispatched to the home of an obese woman who has fallen. The general rules for lifting and moving this patient include all the following except to
    (A) anticipate a lengthy time for backup units to arrive; so move this patient to the best of your ability.
    (B) position the load as close to your body as possible.
    (C) bend your knees; let the large muscles of the legs do the work of lifting.
    (D) take your time; do not hurry, and maintain a wide base of support.

Answers and Answer Explanations

1. **(C)** The patient care report may be the only accurate account available to healthcare professionals, as well as other people interested in the event.

2. **(A)** All incident times are to be recorded accurately for legal purposes including time of call, time of dispatch, time of arrival, time of medication administration, etc.

3. **(D)** Pertinent negatives are findings that require no medical treatment but help to show the completeness of the paramedic's history and exam on the PCR.

4. **(B)** To correct an error on a PCR, a single line should be struck through the error with the EMT-Paramedic's initials next to the error and dated.

5. **(B)** The accuracy and completeness of the patient care report may have a significant impact on ongoing care and treatment of the patient.

6. **(A)** The patient's insurance information is not a necessary part of documentation included in a patient care refusal.

7. **(C)** Revisions are acceptable and must be done on a separate form and then attached to the original document.

8. **(A)** Medical terminology is an integral part of good documentation on a PCR.

9. **(B)** A duplex communication system allows the user to both listen and speak at the same time. A simplex system **(A)** allows a person to listen or speak at one time. A multiplex system **(C)** allows a person to listen and speak, as well as transmit data. A trunked system **(D)** pools all frequencies and routes transmissions to the next available frequency.

10. **(D)** Feedback is a vital part of communication, allowing the sender to know that the receiver understands the message.

11. **(A)** Proper terminology helps to make communication clear, concise, and unambiguous.

12. **(A)** In a simplex system the user is able only to listen or speak. The major disadvantages include the fact that the process is slower, more formal, and not facilitating discussion.

13. **(D)** An advantage of cellular telephones include promoting a less formal, shorter discussion of EMS events. Disadvantages include lost or broken signals due to geographical area or cell sites.

14. **(C)** FCC stands for the Federal Communications Commission, which regulates telecommunications in the United States. Functions include licensing, frequency allocation, technical standards, and rule making/enforcement.

15. **(B)** It is not the role of the EMS dispatcher to diagnose the nature of the illness. EMS dispatchers serve by receiving the call, taking information regarding the nature of the event, and providing prearrival instructions to assist prior to the EMS unit's arrival.

16. **(C)** Prearrival instructions provide immediate instructions and assistance to patients prior to arrival of EMS units.

17. **(D)** Bacteria, viruses, and fungi are all examples of infectious agents, which have the potential of causing an infection.

18. **(A)** The skin is the body's first line of defense against infectious agents.

19. **(C)** Making this patient a load and go patient based on the information provided is an inappropriate action.

20. **(A)** Isolation of the HIV patient is an inappropriate action. Care includes being supportive, using appropriate BSI based on the task being performed, effective handwashing, disinfection of equipment, and care in use of equipment, especially sharps.

21. **(A)** Hepatitis A is transmitted via the oral/fecal route.

22. **(C)** Tuberculosis presents with a chronic cough persistent for two to three weeks, low-grade fever, and night sweats. Certain populations are at a higher risk of developing TB including children less than 3 years old and geriatric patients.

23. **(B)** Tuberculosis is transmitted through exposure to airborne droplets, and prolonged close exposure to a person with active TB.

24. **(D)** Meningitis signs and symptoms include a severe headache, vomiting, fever, and chills of sudden onset. The patient may have a petechial rash and usually has muscle rigidity.

25. **(C)** Chicken pox/varicella zoster virus is a member of the herpesvirus group. The herpesvirus group also contains a virus responsible for genital herpes and the common cold sore.

26. **(A)** Exposure includes contact of infectious material with eyes, mouth, exposed mucous membranes, or nonintact skin.

27. **(D)** The Medical Practice Act is legislation that governs the practice of medicine to include rules governing the physician's ability to delegate authority to perform medical acts by the paramedic. This legislation varies from one state to another.

28. **(B)** Standard of care can be established by court testimony, reference to published codes, standard criteria, and standards appropriate for the situation.

29. **(C)** Code of conduct. The four elements of a negligence claim include the duty to act, breach of duty, actual damages, and proximate cause.

30. **(B)** Consent is assumed (implied) from any patient requiring emergency intervention who is physically, mentally, or emotionally unable to provide expressed consent.

31. **(B)** Care for this patient would not require parental consent because the patient is married and therefore an emancipated minor.

32. **(D)** This patient can be treated and transported against his will under involuntary consent. Law enforcement personnel can direct transport and treatment of a patient who is a threat to himself or others.

33. **(D)** Abandonment is the termination of the paramedic-patient relationship without ensuring appropriate care for the patient.

34. **(B)** Battery is the unlawful touching of someone without his or her consent.

35. **(B)** Durable power of attorney for health care or health care proxy, once signed and witnessed are effective until the patient revokes them.

36. **(D)** The primary responsibility of the paramedic at all scenes is the protection of himself or herself and other EMS personnel.

37. **(B)** Good Samaritan laws protect a paramedic if he or she acts in good faith and is not negligent, acts within his or her scope of practice, and does not accept payment for service.

38. **(A)** Falls of greater than 10 feet are not reportable injuries. Injuries reportable to local authorities include spousal abuse, child abuse or neglect, elder abuse, sexual assault, gunshot/stab wounds, animal bites, and communicable diseases.

39. **(A)** Breach of confidentiality. Any medical or personal information about a patient should not be discussed in public or released without the patient's consent.

40. **(D)** Defamation is intentional false communication that injures another person's reputation or good name. Defamation includes slander, which is verbal, and libel, which is written.

41. **(D)** No specific equipment is designed for throat and neck protection. PPE used to safely operate in rescue operations includes eye protection, head protection, hand protection, personal flotation devices, thermal protection, high visibility clothing, and specialized footwear.

42. **(B)** Knee deep. Walking in fast-moving water places the person at risk of having an extremity pinned and then being pulled under by the current.

43. **(A)** Low-head dams create a recirculating current, which can repeatedly pull the victim under the water, making escape difficult. These dams also make rescue operations hazardous.

44. **(A)** The mammalian dive reflex is a protective physiologic response, which increases survivability by shunting blood to the core, decreasing heart rate and dropping blood pressure. These factors are affected by the person's age and health status and the water temperature.

45. **(A)** A basement is not an oxygen-deficient environment. Oxygen-deficient/confined spaces include storage tanks, grain bins or silos, wells, manholes, and underground vaults.

46. **(B)** The first unit to arrive on the scene should begin the scene sizeup, which includes establishing command, calling for back-up units, controlling any hazards, and locating any triage patients. It would not be appropriate for the primary unit to locate and transport the most critically injured patient.

47. **(D)** A disaster is an incident that may generate hundreds of patients, may overwhelm the existing resources, and may damage the infrastructure of the region shutting down railroads, hospitals, and other normal operations.

48. **(A)** The safety officer monitors all on-scene actions to ensure that no potentially harmful situations are created.

49. **(B)** "Simple." START stands for simple triage and rapid transport. This system focuses on four easily identifiable findings: 1) ability to walk, 2) respiratory effort, 3) pulses/perfusion, 4) neurological status.

50. **(C)** This patient should be tagged Red with immediate life threats including the possibility of bilateral femur fractures and intraabdominal bleeding.

51. **(C)** Homeostasis is the natural tendency of the body to maintain a steady state of equilibrium within the body's internal environment.

52. **(B)** Osmosis is the movement of any solvent (usually water) across a cell membrane.

53. **(A)** The brain recognizes a decrease in pH or excess of $H+$ ions and attempts to compensate by increasing the respiratory effort.

54. **(C)** Respiratory alkalosis results from an increase in respirations and an excessive elimination of CO_2.

55. **(D)** Crystalloids are the primary solutions used for intravenous fluid therapies in the prehospital setting.

56. **(C)** Schedule 1 drugs include heroin, LSD, and mescaline. Schedule 1 drugs pose a high abuse potential and may lead to severe dependence.

57. **(D)** Right route. Amiodarone cannot be given via the endotracheal route. The six rights of medication administration include: right medication, right dose, right time, right route, right patient, and right documentation.

58. **(A)** Parenteral routes for delivery of medication include all those areas outside the gastrointestinal tract. Parenteral routes include intravenous, endotracheal, intramuscular, subcutaneous, topical, and inhalation. The sublingual route administers the drug through the enteral route, or through the gastrointestinal tract.

59. **(B)** Tolerance is a decreased response to the same amount of a drug after taking the drug over a period of time.

60. **(D)** The stimulation of Beta 2 receptors causes bronchodilation, dilatation of arterioles, inhibition of uterine contractions, and skeletal muscle tremors.

61. **(C)** The DOT KKK 1822 D specs outline the design and manufacturing specifications produced by the Federal General Services Administrative Automotive Commodity Center.

62. **(B)** Type II is a standard van-type ambulance. The Type I ambulance is the design of a conventional truck cab chassis with a modular ambulance body. Type III is a specialty van with the larger cab body ambulance. The medium-duty ambulance is a larger vehicle designed to handle heavier loads.

63. **(A)** OSHA stands for Occupational Safety and Health Administration. This agency is charged with protecting worker safety.

64. **(B)** The number one priority of every EMS call is assurance of your personal safety.

65. **(B)** The helicopter should cautiously be approached in a crouched position away from the tail rotor. Approach a helicopter that is on a slight incline from the downhill side.

66. **(B)** Roles: Recognizing an emergency exists, assessing the situation, managing the emergency care, coordinating efforts of your team as well as other agencies involved in the care and transportation of the patient, and establishing rapport with the patient and other EMS crew are all examples of a paramedic's roles.

67. **(A)** The mnemonic C-FLOP stands for: C—command; F—finance/administration; L—logistics; O—operations; P—planning.

68. **(D)** Black. The designation of this patient would be black due to the absence of signs of life and injuries that were possibly incompatible with life. The morgue area should be a triage area away from other treatment areas.

69. **(A)** Green. This patient can be triaged to the green treatment area. The green treatment area is the area where patients require little or no care in preparation for transport.

70. **(C)** Red. This patient has critical injuries that require immediate attention. The red treatment area has the equipment and skilled providers to best care for, stabilize, and transport this patient.

71. **(C)** The rescuer's top priority is the safety of himself or herself and other rescuers. Attempting any rescue prior to cutting power to the downed lines would jeopardize the safety of the rescuers and the patient.

72. **(B)** Keep in mind that rapid extrication and transport may not be possible. Management of this patient should remain the same as similar emergency patients. You must initiate assessment and care as soon as possible.

73. **(A)** For a secondary contamination Level D hazmat protection equipment is the lowest level of protection. Level D equipment consists of structural firefighting, or turn-out gear. Secondary contamination **(A)** occurs when an uncontaminated person comes in contact with a contaminated person.

74. **(D)** The three phases of the body's response to stress are alarm reaction (or the fight or flight response). **(A)** resistance, as the body sustains increasing stress **(B)**, the level of resistance to stress rises; therefore, higher levels of stress must occur for the alarm reaction to occur; exhaustion **(C)**, as stress continues, coping mechanisms begin to fail.

75. **(B)** Information related to the patient's condition or treatment is considered confidential information.

76. **(C)** Inspection is the visual assessment of the patient. Inspection can reveal many important aspects of the patient. Auscultation of abdominal sounds should precede palpation and percussion.

77. **(B)** Off-line medical direction includes the authority of a medical director or advisory group to establish treatment protocols or standing orders.

78. **(B)** This patient has a valid DNR (Do Not Resuscitate) order and no obvious signs of life. The correct actions would be to address the survivor in terms that leave no doubt about the outcome of the deceased. Use gentle reassuring eye contact and offer any assistance that may be needed to the survivor.

79. **(B)** CISD is a formal, structured, planned intervention performed by a CISM (critical incident stress management) team, which includes mental health workers and peers. The intervention should take place within 24–72 hours after a posttraumatic event.

80. **(A)** Proper lifting techniques should be utilized during all patient encounters. Ask for assistance if needed; do not jeopardize the rescuer or patient's safety.

NOTES

CHAPTER 8

Practice Test 1

Now that you have reviewed the questions and "brushed up" on any material you may have found difficult, you can take the practice tests. This will be a helpful assessment of how well you know the material. This test is not divided into individual sections or chapters. The questions are in random order and consist of questions from each chapter in the following breakdown:

• Airway and Breathing	26–34 questions
• Cardiology	29–37 questions
• Trauma	26–34 questions
• Medical Emergenices	26–34 questions
• Obstetrics/Pediatrics	24–32 questions
• Operations	25–33 questions
Total	**180 questions**

You should allow yourself 180 minutes to take the test. This will give you a realistic idea of how you will need to pace yourself come test day.

Hold yourself to a high standard for this practice test by scoring 85% or better. This is achievable by correctly answering 153 questions.

All ECG rhythm strips used in this test are six-second strips.

1. You arrive on the scene of a two-car MVC. The driver of the first vehicle is unconscious. Consent for this patient is said to be
    (A) informed.
    (B) implied.
    (C) expressed.
    (D) involuntary.

2. When using a straight blade (Miller blade) to intubate an adult patient, the tip of the blade should be placed
    (A) directly on or under the epiglottis.
    (B) above the epiglottis.
    (C) in the vallecula.
    (D) past the epiglottis at the vocal cords.

3. You are caring for a victim of a motor vehicle collision who has sustained multiple traumatic injuries. It has taken 15 minutes on the scene to secure your patient's airway, immobilize him on a backboard, and place him in the back of the ambulance. You are in a region in which the trauma care system consists of a Level I trauma center 50 minutes away and a Level III trauma center 10 minutes away. What is your choice of treatment facilities and why?
    (A) Level I trauma center because it is the only true center that is capable of handling trauma cases
    (B) Level I trauma center because you may be held liable if you take the patient to a facility of lesser capability.
    (C) Level III trauma center because it is capable of handling all types of specialty trauma
    (D) Level III trauma center because it will stabilize and transfer serious patients as needed as part of a trauma system

4. Of the following choices below, which is most likely to result from Shaken Baby Syndrome?
    (A) Hypoglycemia
    (B) Abdominal bruising
    (C) Subdural hematoma
    (D) Lower extremity fracture

5. The anatomical structure between the base of the tongue and the epiglottis into which the tip of the curved blade (Macintosh blade) is placed during orotracheal intubation is the
    (A) carina.
    (B) vallecula.
    (C) glottis.
    (D) esophagus.

6. Laws that protect a paramedic if he or she acts in good faith, is not negligent, acts within his or her scope of practice, and does not accept payment for service are the
    (A) implied consent laws.
    (B) Good Samaritan laws.
    (C) malfeasance laws.
    (D) absolute immunity laws.

7. Vasopressin is indicated for management of
    (A) any circumstance in which epinephrine 1:10,000 may be used.
    (B) ventricular fibrillation.
    (C) PEA.
    (D) ventricular tachycardia with a pulse.

8. What is the first pharmacological agent to be administered in a pediatric cardiac arrest?
    (A) Atropine 1.0 mg
    (B) Epinephrine 1:10,000
    (C) Lidocaine 1 mg/kg
    (D) Epinephrine 1:1,000

9. You have a patient who presents with a whole body rash. There is no complaint of shortness of breath. Which of the following history findings lead you to conclude that the rash is the result of a delayed hypersensitivity reaction?
    (A) History of eating shellfish 30 minutes before
    (B) History of taking a new medication for the past seven days
    (C) History of insect sting last summer
    (D) History of chlamydia

Questions 10–12 are based on the following scenario:

You have arrived on scene where you find a 50-year-old male who has a large jagged laceration from a chain saw on his medial left upper thigh. Bright red blood is spurting from the wound despite pressure being applied by a bystander with a wadded-up T-shirt. Your patient is alert, oriented, and anxious, with pale, diaphoretic skin.

10. What is the priority of care for this patient?
    (A) Two large-bore IVs wide open
    (B) Immobilization of the c-spine and preparation to intubate
    (C) Tourniquet of the upper right leg
    (D) Application of a pressure dressing while elevating the left leg

11. Your rapid trauma assessment reveals an isolated upper leg laceration that is seven inches in length and pumping bright red blood freely. His BP 110/60, peripheral pulse 128, respiratory rate 24, and his GCS is 15. Several components of the circulatory system are essential for adequate profusion. Which of the following is not a component of the circulatory system?
    (A) Stroke volume and the Frank-Starlings mechanism
    (B) Positive end expiratory pressure
    (C) Preload and afterload
    (D) The pump, the fluid, and the container

12. Bleeding has been controlled and your patient is enroute to the trauma center. You instruct your partner to establish IV access and deliver fluid resuscitation. Pick the most appropriate treatment:
    (A) A bolus of normal saline or Ringer's lactate solution
    (B) Normal saline at "keep open" rate
    (C) Ringer's lactate at a "keep open" rate
    (D) Holding IV fluid infusion because your patient has a peripheral pulse

13. _____ seconds are measured in each large box on ECG graph paper.
    (A) 0.01
    (B) 0.4
    (C) 0.04
    (D) 0.20

14. A rapid heart rate or irregular heartbeat may cause the patient to experience a sensation commonly known as
    (A) palpitations.
    (B) dysrhythmia.
    (C) fainting.
    (D) anxiety.

15. The federal agency that regulates telecommunications in the United States is known as the
    (A) FBI.
    (B) FDIC.
    (C) FCC.
    (D) FACEP.

16. The minimum chest compression rate for a two-year-old in cardiac arrest is
    (A) 80/minute.
    (B) 100/minute.
    (C) 110/minute.
    (D) 120/minute.

17. A bag-valve mask device with a reservoir and an adequate oxygen source (at least 15 LPM) will deliver an oxygen concentration of
    (A) 21%.
    (B) 40% to 60%.
    (C) 80%.
    (D) 100%.

Questions 18–21 are based on the following scenario:

John, a healthy 30-year-old, suddenly developed a two- to three-minute grand mal seizure while reading a book. On scene you find an unconscious and unresponsive patient with the following vital signs: BP 178/100; pulse 50 and regular; respiratory rate 32 and irregular. He has no history of substance abuse but has complained of headaches for the past two weeks. His blood glucose registers 110.

18. You suspect that his problem is most likely the result of
    (A) hypoglycemia.
    (B) a structural lesion.
    (C) hyperglycemia.
    (D) atrial fibrillation.

19. Two minutes after the insertion of an oropharyngeal airway, applying high-flow oxygen and assisting John's ventilations with a bag-valve mask, the patient's pulse oximetry reading is 90%. His skin is pale and moist. It is important to consider
    (A) starting two large-bore IVs.
    (B) immediate transport to a hospital.
    (C) immediate endotracheal intubation.
    (D) immediate placement of a nasopharyngeal airway.

20. It is important to avoid *excessively* hyperventilating John because it can
    (A) increase the blood $PaCO_2$ to dangerously high levels.
    (B) decrease the blood $PaCO_2$ to dangerously low levels.
    (C) cause jugular vein distention.
    (D) vasodilate the brain's vasculature.

21. John is now exhibiting decorticate posturing to painful stimuli. These are signs that indicate
    (A) decreased peripheral perfusion.
    (B) a lesion of the spinal cord.
    (C) decreased $PaCO_2$ blood levels.
    (D) a lesion at or above the upper brain stem.

---

22. Amiodarone is indicated for the treatment of a variety of cardiac arrhythmias. The recommended dose of amiodarone in a pediatric patient with ventricular fibrillation is
    (A) 5 mg.
    (B) 150 mg.
    (C) 0.5 mg/kg.
    (D) 5 mg/kg.

23. The desired effects of bronchodilation from the administration of albuterol is the result of stimulation of the_____ receptors in the sympathetic nervous system.
    (A) Alpha 1
    (B) Alpha 2
    (C) Beta 1
    (D) Beta 2

24. A patient is experiencing severe chest pain and dyspnea. He is nauseated and extremely diaphoretic, BP is 78/42, pulse is tachycardic, respirations are 36. The patient weighs 190 pounds. ECG shows the following rhythm:

Initial treatment should include
(A) lidocaine 85 to 130 mg IVP.
(B) defibrillation.
(C) cardioversion.
(D) Adenocard 6 mg rapid IVP.

Questions 25–27 are based on the following scenario:

Eric, a 19-year-old male is found breathing very rapidly. His roommate tells you Eric has been having a stressful time lately and recently lost his job. Eric is awake, alert, and very anxious. You note that he has spasms of his fingers and feet. Vital signs are: BP 130/78, pulse 116, respirations 44 and regular. He takes no medications and has no past medical problems.

25. Hyperventilation resulting from pure anxiety leads to
(A) respiratory acidosis.
(B) respiratory alkalosis.
(C) a decreasing blood pH.
(D) hepatic failure.

26. Spasms of the hands and feet are termed
(A) hypercalcemic contractions.
(B) bronchospasms.
(C) proximal extremity spasms.
(D) carpopedal spasms.

27. In this situation, it is important to
(A) withhold oxygen.
(B) have Eric breathe into a paper bag as a rebreathing technique.
(C) consider that Eric has a serious medical problem.
(D) offer reassurance to Eric.

28. Beck's triad is often associated with pericardial tamponade. It includes distant heart tones, JVD, and
    (A) pulse paradoxus.
    (B) hypotension.
    (C) wheezing.
    (D) delayed capillary refill.

29. During inspiration
    (A) the diaphragm contracts and the intercostal muscles relax.
    (B) the diaphragm relaxes and the intercostal muscles contract.
    (C) the diaphragm relaxes and the intercostal muscles relax.
    (D) the diaphragm contracts and the intercostal muscles relax.

30. The intrinsic firing rate for a ventricular pacemaker is _____ beats per minute.
    (A) 20 to 40
    (B) 40 to 60
    (C) 60 to 100
    (D) 100 to 150

31. You are caring for a child with respiratory distress. You note a harsh high-pitched sound with each breath. You suspect this is indicative of
    (A) stridor.
    (B) wheezing.
    (C) crackles.
    (D) rhonchi.

32. In Lead II, placement of the positive lead is located on the
    (A) left arm.
    (B) right shoulder.
    (C) right leg.
    (D) left leg.

Questions 33–35 are based on the following scenario:

Your Uncle Ernie calls you at home on your day off. He explained that he has experienced right upper quadrant pain and right shoulder pain for the last seven days. Your uncle lives two blocks away, so you go to his house.

33. You immediately observe that Uncle Ernie is pale, diaphoretic, and in obvious discomfort. He has a bounding pulse of 132. After calling 911 and requesting an ambulance, you start to assess him. He states that this episode of pain started after eating fried onion rings with hot mustard sauce. You suspect his elevated heart rate is caused by
    (A) acute peritonitis.
    (B) stress response to the body and sympathetic nervous system activation.
    (C) an allergic reaction to the mustard.
    (D) acute pancreatitis.

34. As you assess Uncle Ernie's abdomen, you note that he has pain with palpation under the right costal margin. This is known as
    (A) McBurney's point.
    (B) Murphy's sign.
    (C) Grey-Turner's sign.
    (D) Cullen's sign.

35. With all of the information gathered about your uncle's condition, you suspect
    (A) pancreatitis.
    (B) appendicitis.
    (C) cholecystitis.
    (D) diverticulitis.

36. The EMS squad arrives and they obtain a full set of vital signs. BP is 188/102, pulse 136, respirations 26. Uncle Ernie is assisted to the cot where he lies down on his left side in the fetal position. He complains of increased right upper quadrant pain and nausea. You suggest that pain medication be administered. The correct choice of medication for this patient is
    (A) morphine 2–10 mg IV titrated for pain relief.
    (B) Demerol 25–50 mg IV titrated for pain relief.
    (C) fentanyl 25–50 mg IV one time only.
    (D) Nubain 25 mg IV with additional 12.5 mg if needed.

37. Minute volume is
    (A) the amount of gas moved in and out of the respiratory tract per minute.
    (B) the amount of gas contained in the lungs at the end of a maximal inspiration.
    (C) the amount of gas inhaled or exhaled during a normal breath.
    (D) the amount of gas that remains in the respiratory system after forced expiration.

38. This agency is involved in the protection of safety for workers including ensuring ambulances are disinfected properly, have sharps containers, and red bag trash.
    (A) OSHA
    (B) FCC
    (C) SOP
    (D) NHTSA

39. Cushing's reflex includes a sudden increase in systolic pressure, bradycardia, and
    (A) erratic respirations.
    (B) irregular pulse.
    (C) increased respirations.
    (D) pupil dilation.

40. Lidocaine may be lethal if administered to a patient with which of the following dysrhythmias?
    (A) Sinus rhythm with PACs
    (B) Second-degree AV block type I
    (C) Accelerated junctional rhythm
    (D) Second-degree AV block type II

41. What is the ratio of chest compressions to ventilations when performing one-person CPR on an adult?
    (A) 5 compressions to 1 ventilation
    (B) 15 compressions to 1 ventilation
    (C) 15 compressions to 2 ventilations
    (D) 5 compressions to 2 ventilations

42. Field extubation is indicated if the patient
    (A) is awake and able to maintain his or her own airway.
    (B) is unconscious and continually bites the endotracheal tube.
    (C) is not suspected of alcohol intoxication.
    (D) becomes combative and starts to delay additional treatment.

43. You have just delivered a full-term baby in the back of your ambulance. The initial APGAR score is 5. Treatment should consist of
    (A) CPR.
    (B) effective ventilation.
    (C) vascular access.
    (D) administration of epinephrine.

44. The paramedic faces many stress-inducing situations. All of the following are phases of the stress response EXCEPT
    (A) alarm reaction.
    (B) resistance.
    (C) exhaustion.
    (D) acceptance.

45. The return of a cardiac muscle cell to its resting state is called
    (A) synapse.
    (B) depolarization.
    (C) repolarization.
    (D) automaticity.

Questions 46–50 are based on the following scenario:

Your EMS team is dispatched to care for a 39-year-old female with difficulty breathing. She is awake and appears restless and apprehensive. She tells you she had sudden onset of shortness of breath and a "sense of doom" while typing on her computer keyboard. Her vital signs are: BP 148/92; radial pulse is strong at 124; respirations 36 and shallow. Her skin is pale, cool, and dry. She denies having chest pain or any health problems.

46. Your patient's pulse oximetry reading is 89% on room air. This indicate that
    (A) she is breathing too deeply.
    (B) she is breathing within normal limits.
    (C) she has hypoxemia.
    (D) she has psychogenically induced hyperventilation syndrome.

47. What is significant about her apprehension and sense of doom?
    (A) It may indicate a threat to life.
    (B) It can safely be ignored at this time.
    (C) It is not related to her shortness of breath.
    (D) These problems can be easily controlled with diazepam (Valium).

48. During your interview, you find that the patient takes birth control pills and has had left calf tenderness for two days with no history of trauma to the area. This information leads you to suspect
    (A) viral pneumonia.
    (B) pulmonary edema.
    (C) a panic attack.
    (D) a pulmonary embolus.

49. You interpret her cardiac rhythm as

    (A) junctional tachycardia.
    (B) sinus tachycardia with premature atrial contractions (PACs).
    (C) atrial fibrillation with a rapid ventricular response.
    (D) superventricular tachycardia.

50. Management of her condition would include all of the following EXCEPT
    (A) being on alert for cardiac arrest.
    (B) administering nitroglycerin sublingually.
    (C) monitoring the cardiac rhythm.
    (D) establishing intravenous access.

___

51. What is the correct speed you should perform chest compressions on an adult victim of cardiac arrest?
    (A) 100 times per minute
    (B) 60 times per minute
    (C) 120 times per minute
    (D) 80 times per minute

Questions 52 and 53 are based on the following scenario:

You respond to a "man down" call. When you arrive, you find a 52-year-old male patient lying on the ground next to a ladder. It is unclear if he was placing the ladder against the house when it came into contact with power lines or if he fell from the top of the ladder.

52. Examination shows the patient to be unresponsive. He has a rapid irregular pulse and snoring respirations at 8, BP is 88/42. Treatment should include
    (A) assisted ventilation with a bag-valve device at 6–10 LPM.
    (B) assisted ventilation with a nonrebreather mask at 10–15 LPM.
    (C) opening the airway with a jaw-thrust maneuver and ventilation with a bag-valve device.
    (D) insertion of an oropharyngeal airway and oxygen by nonrebreather mask at 10–15 LPM.

53. You apply a cardiac monitor and note the following rhythm:

    Treatment includes
    (A) immediate cardioversion.
    (B) immediate defibrillation.
    (C) lidocaine 1 mg/kg.
    (D) continued observation.

54. Communication from the EMS dispatcher that provides the caller with emotional support, may be life sustaining to the patient during a critical event, provides immediate assistance to the caller as well as ongoing information to responding units is
    (A) incident data collection.
    (B) predispatch education.
    (C) prearrival instructions.
    (D) incident referral data.

55. For communication to be effective, the receiver must give appropriate _____ to the sender.
    (A) ideas
    (B) encodings
    (C) decodings
    (D) feedback

56. The movement of water across a cell membrane is known as
    (A) oncotic pressure.
    (B) osmosis.
    (C) diffusion.
    (D) osmolarity.

57. Physical assessment findings, signs, or symptoms that support your suspicion that a
    patient is under the influence of alcohol *or* drugs include

        1. chest pain and dysrhythmias

        2. confusion and polyuria

        3. dilated pupils and anxiety

        4. constricted pupils and respiratory depression

    (A) 1 and 2
    (B) 2 and 3
    (C) 2, 3, and 4
    (D) All of the above

58. After defibrillating a patient with pulseless ventricular tachycardia, the first medica-
    tion you should give is
    (A) epinephrine or vasopressin.
    (B) lidocaine or amiodarone.
    (C) epinephrine or lidocaine.
    (D) vasopressin or amiodarone.

59. In a pediatric patient, initial cardioversion should be performed at
    (A) 0.5–1.0 J/kg.
    (B) 4 J/kg.
    (C) 2 J/kg.
    (D) 100 J.

60. Manual maneuvers used to open a patient's airway
    (A) are contraindicated in most patients.
    (B) are difficult to perform.
    (C) include head-tilt/chin-lift and jaw thrust.
    (D) do not usually work without more extensive intervention.

61. Your patient was struck in the head with a six-inch-diameter tree branch while trim-
    ming a tree. He complained of dizziness immediately after the incident but states he
    "feels fine" now. The next day, he complains of dizziness and vomiting. You suspect
    (A) an epidural hematoma.
    (B) a subdural hematoma.
    (C) a concussion.
    (D) a contusion.

62. Management of chest pain of a suspected cardiac nature includes
    (A) establishing an IV and providing a 200 cc fluid bolus.
    (B) administering Lasix 100 mg slow IV.
    (C) administering 2 liters oxygen by nasal cannula.
    (D) administering nitroglycerin gr1/150 sublingual.

63. The administration of which of the following may result in a decrease in the respiratory rate?
    (A) Nubain
    (B) Diltiazem
    (C) Cordarone
    (D) Morphine sulphate

64. The paramedic's primary responsibility at a crime scene or accident scene is
    (A) quality patient care.
    (B) quality documentation.
    (C) thorough knowledge of the event.
    (D) to protect self and other EMS personnel.

65. The causative organism of chicken pox is the varicella zoster virus, which is a member of the
    (A) varicella virus group.
    (B) zoster virus group.
    (C) herpesvirus group.
    (D) rubivirus group.

66. Supine hypotension syndrome occurs from
    (A) reduction of cardiac output due to compression of the aorta.
    (B) reduction of cardiac output due to compression of the inferior vena cava.
    (C) reduction of cardiac output due to compression of the superior vena cava.
    (D) the uterus pushing up on the diaphragm.

67. A properly written patient care report is important because
    (A) the PCR relays the paramedic's true opinion of the patient.
    (B) the PCR provides the receiving hospital with important billing information.
    (C) the PCR may be the only source for pertinent information for receiving healthcare professionals.
    (D) the PCR links traits of the paramedic with documentation abilities.

68. The simplest airway management technique in a patient *without* suspected cervical spine injury is
    (A) the head-tilt/chin-lift maneuver.
    (B) the modified jaw-thrust maneuver.
    (C) endotracheal intubation.
    (D) nasotracheal intubation.

69. Which of these should not be included in the documentation of baseline neurologic status?
    (A) Pulse oximetry
    (B) Response to sensory stimulation
    (C) Pupillary reaction
    (D) Motor function

70. The thoracic cavity is covered by a smooth, moist epithelial layer called the
    (A) visceral pleura.
    (B) parietal pleura.
    (C) visceral peritoneum.
    (D) parietal peritoneum.

71. A dissecting aortic aneurysm may produce the following signs/symptoms:
    (A) a ripping or tearing pain sensation
    (B) pain in the abdomen
    (C) the same blood pressure in each arm
    (D) respiratory distress

72. Revisions to the original patient care report
    (A) should be added on the original document.
    (B) are never appropriate.
    (C) are done on a separate report form and then attached to the original.
    (D) can easily be done with a different color ink.

Questions 73–75 are based on the following scenario:

You arrive on scene of a 56-year-old male patient who developed chest pain while mowing the lawn on a hot August day. He states that the pain has subsided after a few minutes of rest. Your assessment shows that he is alert and oriented, BP 148/92, pulse 48, respirations 20. His skin is warm and moist. He has no past medical history and takes no medications. You attach the monitor and observe the following rhythm:

73. Treatment should include
    (A) Atropine 0.5 mg IVP.
    (B) Adenocard 5 mg IVP.
    (C) transport for evaluation.
    (D) No treatment is necessary.

74. Your patient insists that he became overheated and that caused his chest pain. He is refusing any treatment. As he begins to argue with EMS, he again develops chest pain. Treatment should include
    (A) Atropine 0.5 mg IVP.
    (B) Adenocard 5 mg IV.
    (C) nitroglycerin administration.
    (D) immediate transcutaneous pacing.

75. Your patient suddenly becomes lethargic. BP is 82/40, pulse 36, respirations 10. You note the following rhythm on the monitor:

Treatment should include
(A) Atropine 0.5 mg IV.
(B) Adenocard 5 mg IV.
(C) stopping nitroglycerin administration.
(D) immediate transcutaneous pacing.

Questions 76–78 are based on the following scenario:

You are called to a 32-year-old female who is in her twenty-eighth week of pregnancy. She complains of dizziness, blurred vision, and a feeling that she is going to pass out. She is emotionally upset and crying. She explains that at her doctor's appointment last week, her doctor scolded her for gaining too much weight. Her hands and ankles are edematous and her face is puffy. Vitals are BP 178/108, pulse 104, respirations 24.

76. You suspect that this patient
(A) is emotionally upset.
(B) has preeclampsia.
(C) has borderline hypotension.
(D) has postpartum depression.

77. Treatment for this patient would include
(A) rapid transport with lights and siren.
(B) administering nitroglycerin to lower the blood pressure.
(C) transport for psychiatric evaluation.
(D) keeping the patient calm; transport without lights and siren.

78. You are enroute to the hospital when the patient has a grand mal seizure. Treatment for this patient includes
(A) administering high-flow oxygen, magnesium sulfate 2–5 mg.
(B) administering oxygen, magnesium sulfate 2–5 grams, placing in right lateral recumbent position.
(C) maintaining airway, administering oxygen, administering magnesium sulfate 2–5 grams, monitoring vital signs.
(D) maintaining airway, administering magnesium sulfate 6–8 grams, monitoring vital signs, placing in left lateral recumbent position.

79. You and your partner are the first EMS units to arrive on the scene of a single-car MVC, car versus pole. Electrical lines are down across the car. One victim is trapped inside the vehicle. Which action would be most correct?
    (A) Immobilize the patient's cervical spine and do a rapid extrication ensuring that the patient does not touch the downed wires.
    (B) Control the airway and cervical spine manually while awaiting other units to arrive for proper extrication.
    (C) Contact Dispatch and have the power company turn power off to the lines prior to attempting rescue of this patient.
    (D) Ask the patient to slide himself out of the vehicle through a window, being careful not to touch anything metal while exiting.

80. You and your partner are treating a patient who needs to be transported to the hospital for chest pain. You have established an IV, placed the patient on the monitor, administered oxygen and aspirin. Your partner checks his watch and notes that his shift is over. You remove the monitor and politely tell the patient the oncoming crew will come and transport him to the hospital shortly. Leaving this patient is an example of
    (A) false imprisonment.
    (B) assault.
    (C) battery.
    (D) abandonment.

81. After decompressing the chest of the victim with a tension pneumorthorax, you determine your intervention was successful by observing for
    (A) air rushing from the catheter.
    (B) a decrease in the patient's cyanosis.
    (C) an improvement in the patient's level of consciousness.
    (D) an improvement in the patient's ventilatory and circulatory status.

82. Which of the following statements is true regarding chemical burns?
    (A) Always use antidotes or neutralizing agents.
    (B) Acid burns are typically more serious than alkali burns.
    (C) Both acids and alkalis cause burns by disrupting cell membranes and damaging tissues on contact.
    (D) Always approach a chemical spill from downwind.

83. Procainamide administration should be discontinued if any of the following occur EXCEPT
    (A) hypotension.
    (B) widening of the QRS complex.
    (C) hypertension.
    (D) maximum dose infused.

220 Chapter 8

Questions 84 and 85 are based on the following scenario:

You are called to the scene of a 22-year-old man who was playing in a softball game. He was hit in the eye with a hard-hit line-drive softball. According to his teammates he was knocked to the ground and had a brief loss of consciousness that lasted approximately seven seconds.

84. While assessing the injured eye, you notice a collection of blood in front of the patient's pupil and iris. What is your differential diagnosis?
(A) Raccoon's eye
(B) Retinal detachment
(C) Hyphema
(D) Corneal laceration

85. How would you transport this patient to the hospital?
(A) Recovery position
(B) Sitting up at a 90 degree angle
(C) Trendelenburg
(D) Immobilized on a backboard with the head of the backboard elevated

86. You are administering amiodarone 300 mg to a patient in full cardiac arrest with a rhythm of ventricular fibrillation. As you start to administer the drug through the endotracheal tube, your partner stops you. Which of the six rights of medication administration were you about to violate?
(A) Right dose
(B) Right medication
(C) Right patient
(D) Right route

87. All of the following can affect the accuracy reading of a pulse oximeter EXCEPT
(A) hypoperfusion.
(B) anemia.
(C) carbon monoxide poisoning.
(D) hyperthermia.

88. Sodium bicarbonate administration may be useful for treating
(A) beta-blocker overdoses and hypocalcemia.
(B) preexisting acidosis and hypokalemia.
(C) tricyclic antidepressant overdoses and hyperkalemia.
(D) calcium channel blocker overdoses and hyperkalemia.

89. The most common use for naloxone in the prehospital setting is to reverse the effects of overdose with an abused drug such as heroin. The recommended pediatric dose of naloxone for infants and children from birth to five years is
(A) 20 mg.
(B) 2.0 mg.
(C) 0.01 mg/kg.
(D) 0.1 mg/kg.

90. Applying gentle countertraction to the infant's head to prevent explosive delivery is essential because
    (A) fetal hypoxia can result from rapid delivery.
    (B) if a nuchal cord is present, rapid delivery will make it worse.
    (C) this will allow the perineum to stretch and reduce the chance of tearing.
    (D) the placenta will detach too soon in rapid delivery.

91. The medication treatment of choice for a narrow complex tachycardia in an unstable patient is
    (A) Adenocard.
    (B) lidocaine.
    (C) cardioversion.
    (D) Versed.

92. Reportable infectious/communicable disease exposures include
    (A) contact of infectious materials with eye, mouth, or mucous membrane.
    (B) working with a partner with a URI.
    (C) contact with blood and body fluids on intact gloves.
    (D) spill of infectious material in the EMS unit with no contact.

93. You are performing rescue breathing with a bag-mask device for an apneic child. How often should you provide rescue breaths?
    (A) Once every 3 seconds
    (B) Once every 4 seconds
    (C) Once every 5 seconds
    (D) Once every 6 seconds

94. A 14-year-old female is crying and hysterical after breaking up with her boyfriend. She had a syncopal episode prior to EMS arrival. Vitals are BP 110/68, pulse 130, and respirations 36. You place her on the cardiac monitor and interpret the following rhythm as

    (A) sinus arrest.
    (B) sinus bradycardia.
    (C) sinus dysrhythmia.
    (D) sinus tachycardia.

95. Please choose the best clue for determining possible injuries that may be sustained in an MVC.
   (A) Length of skidmarks
   (B) Debris at the scene
   (C) Patient symptoms
   (D) Mechanism of injury

Questions 96–99 are based on the following scenario:

You are called by the local police department to help search for an elderly man with Alzheimer's disease who wandered from his home. It is 11:30 P.M. and he has been missing for three hours. It is 38°F outside with a light drizzle. The man is wearing pajamas and slippers.

96. At 4:30 A.M. the patient is located lying behind a pile of wood five blocks from his home. He is unconscious, unresponsive, apneic, and pulseless. His skin is cold to the touch and his muscles are rigid. His core body temperature is 89.6°F. Initial treatment should include
   (A) CPR.
   (B) establishing intravenous access with warm normal saline.
   (C) starting passive rewarming.
   (D) placing in a Trendelenburg position.

97. You attach the ECG monitor and observe the following rhythm:

   Treatment should include
   (A) this rhythm should not be treated until the core temperature is 90°F.
   (B) immediate defibrillation.
   (C) avoiding rough movement and excessive activity.
   (D) Both A and C are correct.

98. You are considering the administration of cardiac medication to this patient. Which statement is true?
   (A) IV medication may be administered, but spaced at longer than standard intervals.
   (B) Withhold medications until the core temperature is 90°F.
   (C) IV medications may be administered at regular intervals.
   (D) Lidocaine and procainamide will increase the fibrillation threshold.

99. Care during transportation for this patient should include all of the following EXCEPT
    (A) avoiding rough handling due to cardiac irritability.
    (B) protection against further heat loss.
    (C) transporting in a horizontal position.
    (D) withholding further ACLS treatment until core temperature is more than 90°F.

---

100. Abdominal trauma is a serious injury in the pediatric patient. Injury to which abdominal organ is most likely to cause death in the pediatric patient?
    (A) Pancreas
    (B) Liver
    (C) Spleen
    (D) Kidney

101. The blood component responsible for transporting oxygen from the lungs to the body tissues and transporting carbon dioxide from the body tissues to the lungs is the
    (A) plasma.
    (B) platelets.
    (C) leukocytes.
    (D) erythrocytes.

Questions 102 and 103 are based on the following scenario:

You arrive on scene to find a pickup truck that struck a utility pole head on. The patient is ambulatory on scene. He has a large amount of blood on his face and down the front of his shirt. He is alert and oriented to person and place but slow to respond. You note the smell of alcohol on the patient as you speak with him. He denies any loss of consciousness. He states he was traveling 40 MPH and did not have on a seat belt.

102. You are sent to evaluate the damage to the truck. Which finding would lead you to believe the patient may have a life-threatening injury?
    (A) a deformed dashboard
    (B) a deformed steering wheel
    (C) the airbag did not deploy
    (D) significant front end damage

103. It is important to remember that when dealing with an intoxicated patient your assessment must be thorough because
    (A) alcohol increases pain tolerance.
    (B) alcohol decreases the patient's judgment.
    (C) alcohol is a CNS stimulant.
    (D) alcohol can mask signs and symptoms of injury.

---

104. _____ (is) are considered "drowning machines" due to recirculating currents created by water moving over a uniform obstruction.
    (A) Low-head dams
    (B) Current-generated dams
    (C) Rapid-moving water
    (D) White water

105. You respond to the home of a patient who has had an unknown illness for two days. You approach the call suspecting an infectious or communicable disease. Which action is not appropriate for this patient's care?
    (A) Gloves and protective eye goggles are worn.
    (B) A full history and detailed physical exam is obtained.
    (C) Make the patient a "load and go" due to the potential for paramedic exposure.
    (D) Disposal of supplies, sharps, appropriately on disposition of the patient.

106. You are assessing a 1½-year-old male with breathing trouble. Inspiratory stridor is heard with evident use of all accessory muscles. The trouble breathing is worse at night. No other significant findings are visible. The child is on no medications and has otherwise been well. You suspect
    (A) epiglottitis.
    (B) asthma.
    (C) bronchiolitis.
    (D) croup.

107. Residual volume is
    (A) the amount of gas moved in and out of the respiratory tract each minute.
    (B) the amount of gas contained in the lungs at the end of a maximal inspiration.
    (C) the amount of gas inhaled or exhaled during a normal breath.
    (D) the amount of gas that remains in the respiratory system after forced expiration.

108. You are treating a 22-year-old female complaining of severe abdominal pain and left shoulder pain. Vital signs are BP 88/64, pulse 128 and regular, respirations of 22, skin is cool and wet. She states that she has small amount of pink vaginal discharge. This patient is most likely experiencing
    (A) a ruptured ectopic pregnancy.
    (B) endometriosis.
    (C) pelvic inflammatory disease.
    (D) amenorrhea.

109. You are treating a child with a tension pneumothorax. Needle decompression is needed. The correct site for insertion of the needle is
    (A) below the third rib in the mid-clavicular line.
    (B) below the second rib in the mid-axillary line.
    (C) top of the second rib in the mid-axillary line.
    (D) top of the third rib in the mid-clavicular line.

110. Which of the following rhythms requires immediate transcutaneous pacing?
    (A) Junctional tachycardia
    (B) Sinus bradycardia with first-degree heart block
    (C) Supraventricular tachycardia
    (D) Symptomatic third-degree AV block

111. Which of the following may require synchronized cardioversion?
    (A) Pulseless ventricular tachycardia
    (B) Pulseless electrical activity
    (C) Ventricular fibrillation
    (D) PSVT

112. The proper way to correct a written error on the PCR is to
    (A) use white-out to cover the error.
    (B) draw a single line through the error, initial, and date the area.
    (C) scribble through the error completely and sign your name next to the error.
    (D) use a black marker to eliminate the error from the PCR, initial, and date the area.

113. A patient experiencing a hypertensive crisis should receive which medication?
    (A) Nitroglycerin
    (B) Procardia
    (C) Aspirin
    (D) Oxygen

Questions 114 and 115 are based on the following scenario:

You are caring for a 78-year-old female patient who has a long history of hyperadrenalism (Cushing's syndrome). She is complaining of left side weakness. You note a flattened nasolabial fold on the left and slurring of her speech.

114. You are assigned to establish an IV line and obtain a blood sample for blood glucose testing. You should
    (A) take great care with venipuncture in this patient because hyperadrenalism leads to easy bruising and a delay in healing.
    (B) refuse to establish intravenous access because the veins are fragile and the skin is paper thin.
    (C) not bother checking a blood glucose level because Cushing's syndrome is always associated with hyperglycemia.
    (D) None of the above are correct.

115. You are concerned about this patient because you know hyperadrenalism is
    (A) associated with a high incident of atherosclerosis including hypertension and stroke.
    (B) associated with low metabolism rate and poor organ function.
    (C) associated with thyrotoxicosis.
    (D) associated with an increased insulin production.

---

116. While eating lunch at a local eatery, you and your partner are discussing a call you had just completed. The patient's relative who is sitting at the next table overhears your partner talking about the patient's condition. Your partner has violated the patient's
    (A) right to consent.
    (B) right to confidentiality.
    (C) right of refusal of treatment.
    (D) character by defamation.

Questions 117 and 118 are based on the following scenario:

You arrive on scene of a 34-year-old male who was struck by a car. Bystanders tell you the patient was standing on the sidewalk when his neighbor, who was backing out of the driveway, struck him. The speed of impact is estimated at less than 5 MPH. Your patient is sitting in the yard with an obvious open tibia/fibula fracture of the right leg. He is alert and oriented and denies any loss of consciousness. He states that he was struck in the abdomen and lower legs and thrown onto the trunk of the car and then rolled into the yard. He complains of right leg pain and right shoulder pain.

117. As you auscultate his right upper chest, you notice the patient guarding his shoulder. Closer exam reveals a fractured clavicle. Complications associated with a fractured clavicle include injury to the
    (A) carotid artery.
    (B) subclavian vein.
    (C) descending aorta.
    (D) inferior vena cava.

118. Physical exam concludes that the right clavicle fracture and open right tibia/fibula fracture are his only obvious injuries but you are concerned because his level of consciousness is deteriorating and his heart rate has increased 30 beats per minute. Although his abdomen was unremarkable upon examination, you know that an indicator of severe abdominal trauma is the presence of
    (A) absent bowel sounds.
    (B) back pain.
    (C) referred pain to the clavicle.
    (D) unexplained shock.

---

119. You are dispatched to a private residence for an eight-year-old boy complaining of trouble breathing. On arrival, you find the patient lethargic with blue lips and rapid labored respirations. He is able to answer questions with only one- or two-word sentences. Physical exam reveals a respiratory rate of 50 per minute; diminished breath sounds and crackles are heard over the right lung field with dullness to percussion. He also has a temperature of 104°F. Based on your assessment, this patient may be experiencing
    (A) cardiogenic shock.
    (B) a drug overdose.
    (C) respiratory distress.
    (D) respiratory failure, most probably due to pneumonia.

120. You and your partner respond to the home of an elderly gentleman who is unresponsive. Your assessment reveals no respiratory effort, skin that is cool and mottled with obvious pooling and no palpable pulse. The patient's wife presents a valid Do Not Resuscitate order. All of the actions would be correct except to
    (A) address the wife using gentle eye contact and choosing appropriate words.
    (B) begin to resuscitate this patient without delay.
    (C) explain to the wife that her loved one has died; do not use terms that can be misinterpreted.
    (D) offer assistance to the survivor(s) if necessary.

121. The nasopharyngeal airway should be measured
    (A) from the corner of the mouth to the earlobe.
    (B) from the tip of the nose to the earlobe.
    (C) from the tip of the nose to the corner of the mouth.
    (D) from the tip of the nose to the chin.

122. During your assessment of a five-year-old child, you discover a heart rate of 200 beats per minute. The rhythm strip reveals narrow QRS complexes corresponding to the patient's pulse rate. The rhythm most probably represents
    (A) ventricular tachycardia.
    (B) rapid atrial fibrillation.
    (C) supraventricular tachycardia.
    (D) sinus tachycardia.

123. During needle decompression, the needle is inserted on the top of the rib for what purpose?
    (A) To ensure that the vein, artery, and nerve bundle under each rib are not damaged
    (B) To ensure proper placement
    (C) To ensure that the catheter enters the pleural space at the correct angle
    (D) To ensure that the site does not become a sucking chest wound

124. You respond to a 76-year-old man with syncope. He is sitting upright in the bathroom when you arrive. He is initially alert and oriented only to person but quickly regains alertness to person, place, and time. He has no complaints except an abrasion on his left knee and slight dizziness. He stated that he was having a bowel movement when he blacked out. His current vitals are BP 108/60, pulse 96 slightly irregular, and respirations 20. ECG shows a sinus rhythm with occasional PACs. Based on the information provided, you suspect the cause of the patient's syncope is
    (A) digitalis toxicity.
    (B) an atrial dysrhythmia.
    (C) a vasovagal episode.
    (D) underlying myocardial ischemia.

125. The chordae tendinea connect
    (A) the papillary muscles to the outer myocardium.
    (B) the pericardium to the myocardial muscle mass.
    (C) the leaflets of the heart valves to the papillary muscles.
    (D) the intraventricular septum to the pericardium.

126. All of the following are considered anginal equivalents EXCEPT
    (A) diaphoresis, syncope, dizziness.
    (B) dyspnea, palpitations, syncope.
    (C) hypoglycemia, chest pain, dyspnea.
    (D) fatigue, dizziness, palpitations.

127. Intentional false communication that injures another person's reputation or good name is a definition of
    (A) invasion of privacy.
    (B) breach of confidentiality.
    (C) informed slander.
    (D) defamation.

128. A small child has been struck by a car traveling approximately 25 MPH. The child is unresponsive. The airway maneuver of choice for this patient is
    (A) jaw-thrust with c-spine stabilization.
    (B) head-tilt/chin-lift.
    (C) hyperextension with jaw-thrust.
    (D) hyperflexion of the head to the "sniffing" position.

129. You arrive on the scene of a patient who has been stabbed with a knife in the right side of the back. The patient presents with left-sided hemiparalysis and sensory loss. Despite another stab wound to the right abdomen, the patient denies pain. What type of spinal cord injuries do you suspect?
    (A) Compression
    (B) Transection
    (C) Neurogenic shock
    (D) Brown-Sequard's syndrome

130. Tidal volume is
    (A) the amount of gas moved in and out of the respiratory tract per minute.
    (B) the amount of gas contained in the lungs at the end of a maximal inspiration.
    (C) the amount of gas inhaled and exhaled during a normal breath.
    (D) the amount of gas that remains in the respiratory system after forced expiration.

131. The valve located between the left atrium and left ventricle is the
    (A) tricuspid valve.
    (B) mitral valve.
    (C) aortic valve.
    (D) pulmonic valve.

Questions 132–134 are based on the following scenario:

You arrive on scene of a 30-year-old male lying on the ground. According to a bystander, the patient was on top of a ladder to change a lightbulb. After he stuck his hand in the light fixture, he was attacked by yellow jackets that had a nest in the fixture. The patient then jumped from the top of the ladder to escape the bees. You estimate his fall to the ground to be 8 feet. He has numerous yellow jacket stings on his left arm and neck.

132. The patient is unconsciousness and unresponsive. As you assess his airway and breathing, you observe a respiratory rate of 8 per minute with deep gasping respirations, accessory muscle use, and obvious inspiratory stridor with each breath. Management of this patient's airway would include
    (A) c-spine immobilization, oral pharyngeal airway insertion, and high-flow oxygen by nonrebreather mask.
    (B) beginning bag-valve mask ventilations with supplemental oxygen.
    (C) c-spine immobilization, assisting ventilations, immediate endotracheal intubation.
    (D) bag-valve mask ventilation with high-flow oxygen at a rate of 24 per minute.

133. Assessment of the chest reveals no obvious trauma. You note equal but distant lung sounds with wheezing on auscultation. You also find a medical alert necklace that states "Allergic PCN: Allergic Bee Stings" You suspect the respiratory distress to be from
    (A) a tension pneumothorax.
    (B) a hemothorax.
    (C) a bronchial constriction secondary to anaphylactic reaction.
    (D) an early pneumothorax.

134. You are unable to obtain IV access. Treatment for this patient would include
    (A) immediate chest decompression.
    (B) epinephrine 1:1,000 solution 3–5 ml SQ.
    (C) lidocaine 1 mg/kg IVP.
    (D) epinephrine 1:1,000 solution 0.3–0.5 mg SQ.

135. The Sellick maneuver
    (A) is used to clear a foreign body airway obstruction in an infant or child.
    (B) is used to clear blood or mucus from an endotracheal tube or the nasopharynx.
    (C) may be used to minimize gastric distention and facilitate placement of an endotracheal tube into the glottic opening.
    (D) is the preferred method for opening the airway of an unconscious patient when cervical spine injury is suspected.

136. Croup, bronchiolitis, epiglottitis, and asthma are all examples of pediatric respiratory problems. From the selection below, identify the statement that best describes or defines bronchiolitis?
    (A) A viral disease caused by RSV that affects children between the ages of 6–18 months
    (B) A viral infection of the upper airway affecting children between the ages of three months and one year
    (C) A bacterial infection from an unknown cause
    (D) An inflammatory disease causing restrictive airway compromise

137. You have administered an initial dose of amiodarone for a patient in ventricular fibrillation. The repeat dose of this medication should be
    (A) 300 mg.
    (B) 150 mg.
    (C) 0.04 mg/kg.
    (D) 1 to 1.5 mg/kg.

138. The maximum amount of procainamide you should administer to a 196-pound patient is
    (A) 1,462 mcg.
    (B) 1,500 mg.
    (C) 1,514 mg.
    (D) 1,615 mg.

139. In the mnemonic C-FLOP, when describing the practices of the Incident Management System, the "O" stands for
    (A) operations.
    (B) ongoing assessment.
    (C) order of command.
    (D) officer in charge.

140. A small child has fallen through the ice while skating. After 30 minutes, the child is pulled from the icy water apneic and pulseless. Your first action in the management of this child should be to
    (A) keep the child cool to maintain the mammalian dive reflex.
    (B) defibrillate the child immediately.
    (C) pronounce the child dead at the scene.
    (D) secure the child's airway and control the cervical spine.

141. The pediatric assessment triangle provides a systematic approach to the assessment of the pediatric patient. It is based on three parameters, which are
    (A) airway, breathing, circulation.
    (B) appearance, breathing, circulation.
    (C) airway, respiratory rate, pulses.
    (D) appearance, lung sounds, skin color.

142. Nitroglycerin has all of the following properties EXCEPT that it
    (A) prevents vasospasm.
    (B) is a vasodilator.
    (C) decreases afterload.
    (D) decreases preload.

143. When intubating an adult patient with a curved blade (Macintosh blade), the tip of the blade should be placed
    (A) under the epiglottis.
    (B) in the vallecula, at the base of the tongue.
    (C) in the vallecula, at the opening of the vocal cords.
    (D) to the right of the epiglottis.

144. Promptly recognize the need for emergency management, assessing the scene for danger, contacting Dispatch to mobilize other units for care and transportation of the patient, establishing rapport with the patient and other paramedics on the scene represent the paramedic's _____:
    (A) ethical responsibility
    (B) roles
    (C) triage criteria
    (D) care responsibility

145. You are the first unit on the scene of a multiple-vehicle crash. Upon arrival, each of the following actions would be appropriate EXCEPT to
    (A) establish scene command.
    (B) treat and transport the most critically ill patient.
    (C) perform a scene sizeup.
    (D) control scene hazards.

146. All of the following are signs and symptoms of organophosphate poisoning EXCEPT
    (A) salivation.
    (B) lacrimation.
    (C) urination.
    (D) tachycardia.

147. You have initiated an IO line in a pediatric patient suffering from severe dehydration. What is the most reliable indicator of successful placement of the IO needle?
    (A) Take an X-ray
    (B) The ability to draw arterial blood through the IO
    (C) Aspiration of bone marrow
    (D) No evidence of fractures after insertion

148. The only vein of the body that carries oxygenated blood is the
    (A) coronary sinus.
    (B) pulmonary vein.
    (C) superior vena cava.
    (D) femoral vein.

149. You are assigned the duties of safety officer under the incident command of a mass casualty incident. You understand the responsibilities of this position to be to
    (A) monitor all on-scene actions to ensure that no potentially harmful situations are created.
    (B) coordinate all operations of this incident, which involves outside agencies.
    (C) collect data regarding the incident and relay information to the press or media.
    (D) supervise a specific safety unit or area.

150. Where should you place your hands on the chest of an adult victim when you are performing chest compressions?
    (A) On the top of the sternum
    (B) On the lower one-third of the sternum
    (C) On the lower half of the sternum, at the nipple line
    (D) Over the very bottom of the sternum

151. Which one of the following statements is not true regarding electrical injuries?
    (A) Until the power is off, nobody should be allowed to approach the electrical burn patient.
    (B) The rescuer must be grounded to prevent electrical shock when treating a victim of a recent lightning strike.
    (C) Patients in cardiac arrest because of electrocution have a high survival rate if prehospital intervention is prompt.
    (D) Consider the use of 1 mEq/kg of sodium bicarbonate to prevent the complications of rhabdomyolyses.

152. While treating a three-year-old child for amitriptyline ingestion, he suddenly begins to have seizure activity. You decide that administration of diazepam is appropriate. The recommended dose range for this age group is
    (A) 0.01–0.02 mg/kg.
    (B) 0.05–0.1 mg.
    (C) 0.1–0.3 mg/kg.
    (D) 5–10 mg.

Questions 153 to 156 are based on the following scenario:

You are dispatched to a 77-year-old male patient who has fallen from a ladder while cleaning the gutters. He fell approximately 14 feet and struck his back on the riding lawn mower as he fell. He is awake and very anxious. He is having obvious trouble breathing. His pulse is 104, respirations 34, and blood pressure is 122/76.

153. In your assessment, you find crepitus and instability to the left rib cage. Lung sounds are present and equal. Closer assessment reveals paradoxical chest movement. You suspect
    (A) a tension pneumothorax.
    (B) a massive hemothorax.
    (C) a flail chest.
    (D) an abdominal aneurysm.

154. Paradoxical movement is best described as chest wall movement that is
    (A) inward with both inspiration and expiration.
    (B) inward with expiration and outward with inspiration.
    (C) inward with inspiration and outward with expiration.
    (D) outward with both inspiration and expiration.

155. Prehospital management for this patient includes
    (A) needle decompression mid-clavicular line.
    (B) positive pressure ventilation.
    (C) an occlusive dressing.
    (D) chest decompression mid-axillary line.

156. Your patient is in severe respiratory distress. Reassessment reveals absent lung sounds on the left, tracheal deviation to the right, and a SpO_2 reading of 82%. Immediate treatment must include
    (A) intubation.
    (B) right side chest decompression.
    (C) left side chest decompression.
    (D) oxygen administration.

---

157. The volume of blood ejected from the left ventricle into the arterial system each minute is
    (A) preload.
    (B) cardiac output.
    (C) afterload.
    (D) stroke volume.

158. A high-pitched noise associated with upper airway constriction is known as
    (A) wheezes.
    (B) rhonchi.
    (C) stridor.
    (D) rales.

Questions 159 and 160 are based on the following scenario:

You respond to a local physician's office. You are instructed to transport Ms. Smith to the emergency department for acute gastroenteritis. The physician asks you to establish an IV line of normal saline and run it at 100 cc/hr and administer Compazine (prochlorperazine).

159. A proper dose of Compazine for this patient would be
    (A) 12.5 mg IV.
    (B) 2.5 mg IV.
    (C) 10 mg IV.
    (D) 1.0 mg IV.

160. If Compazine is supplied in a 2 ml vial containing 5 mg/ml, you would administer ____ ml of medication.
    (A) 5 ml
    (B) 2 ml
    (C) 4 ml
    (D) 0.4 ml

---

161. You respond to a cafeteria for a 16-year-old patient who is choking. Your patient is conscious and coughing forcefully. He appears anxious and is difficult to communicate with due to the coughing but is able to follow commands. Assessment reveals a respiratory rate of 28 and shallow, diminished breath sounds on the right side, and a SpO$_2$ reading of 96%. Based on the history and assessment findings, you suspect
    (A) aspiration of food into the right mainstem bronchus causing obstruction.
    (B) a spontaneous pneumothorax on the left side secondary to the forceful coughing.
    (C) the choking episode has subsided and the patient is recovering.
    (D) a spontaneous pneumothorax on the right side secondary to the forceful coughing.

162. You respond to an MVC involving a young child. The child is found apneic but still has a palpable pulse. You immediately begin positive pressure ventilation with a bag-valve mask device. You note that the left side of the chest moves, but the right does not. Lung sounds are absent on the right side and the trachea is deviated to the left. Your immediate action is to
    (A) increase the tidal volume with each ventilation.
    (B) perform a needle decompression on the left side.
    (C) give a 20 cc/kg bolus of IV fluids.
    (D) perform a needle decompression on the right side.

163. Select the statement that correctly relates to pediatric seizures.
    (A) Febrile seizures correlate to the speed in which the temperature rises, not to the degree of the fever.
    (B) Always suspect a fever to be the cause of a seizure if the temperature is more than 101°F.
    (C) Infants and children between the ages of four months and eight years commonly suffer from febrile seizures.
    (D) Febrile seizures do not require transport if the patient can be cooled.

164. You have orally intubated a patient. While your partner ventilates the patient with a bag-valve device, you evaluate placement. Auscultation reveals sounds heard over the right chest and an absence of breath sounds over the left chest. Your best course of action would be to
    (A) hyperventilate the patient and prepare the equipment necessary for a surgical cricothyrotomy.
    (B) deflate the endotracheal tube cuff, withdraw the tube 2 cm, reinflate the cuff, and reevaluate breath sounds.
    (C) deflate the endotracheal tube cuff, remove the endotracheal tube, and hyper-ventilate the patient with a bag-valve device.
    (D) insert a large diameter needle into the fourth or fifth intercostal space, mid-axillary line.

165. Your patient is a 44-year-old female who was burned when a high-temperature water pipe exploded. She has blisters to the chest, abdomen, entire right arm, and front of the right leg. According to the rule of nines, this patient has sustained _____ percent burns.
    (A) 40.5%
    (B) 36%
    (C) 45%
    (D) 31.5%

166. The recommended dose of vasopressin in cardiac arrest due to pulseless VT or VF is
    (A) 20 units IV bolus repeated once in 10 minutes.
    (B) a single IV bolus dose of 40 units.
    (C) 40 units IV bolus repeated once in 10 minutes.
    (D) 300 mg IV.

Questions 167–169 are based on the following scenario:

Your patient is 26 years old and 30 weeks pregnant. She is multigravida but nullipara. She complains of sudden severe tearing abdominal pain with some minor vaginal bleeding. Upon careful palpation, her abdomen is very tender and her uterus seems to be tightly contracted.

167. You suspect
    (A) abruptio placenta.
    (B) an ectopic pregnancy.
    (C) a miscarriage.
    (D) placenta previa.

168. This medical emergency is caused by
    (A) implantation of the fertilized ovum in a fallopian tube.
    (B) the uterus covering the cervical opening.
    (C) premature separation of the placenta from the uterine wall.
    (D) a spontaneous abortion.

169. The patient's pregnancy history includes
    (A) one pregnancy and one birth.
    (B) many pregnancies and one birth.
    (C) one pregnancy and no births.
    (D) many pregnancies and no births.

170. Which of the following is NOT part of the heart's electrical conduction system that contain pacemaking capabilities?
    (A) Bundle of His
    (B) Purkinje system
    (C) SA node
    (D) AV node

Questions 171–174 are based on the following scenario:

Your EMS team is called to attend to a patient in her mid-thirties who is having a generalized motor seizure. Bystanders inform you that she has been seizing continually for the past 10 minutes. You note that the patient is shaking violently, is diaphoretic, and slightly cyanotic.

171. This prolonged seizure is specifically termed
    (A) petit mal seizure disorder.
    (B) grand mal seizure disorder.
    (C) complex seizure disorder.
    (D) status epilepticus.

172. The most valuable *early* intervention is to
    (A) force an oropharyngeal airway between the teeth.
    (B) start an IV of crystalloid solution.
    (C) use bag-valve mask assistance with 100% oxygen.
    (D) give dextrose 50% and water IVP.

173. An IV is started and the blood glucose reading is 120 mg/dl. A medication and correct dose range that you could administer to her is
    (A) Valium (diazepam) 5–10 mg IVP.
    (B) dextrose 50% in water 5–10 grams.
    (C) Valium (diazepam) 5–10 mcg IVP.
    (D) Versed (midazolam) 10–25 mg IVP.

174. Administration of the medication terminated her seizure activity. Now you should be alert for which of the following side effects?
    (A) Respiratory depression
    (B) Hyperglycemia
    (C) Hypertension
    (D) Fever

175. You are called to the scene of a two-year-old child with a three-day history of diarrhea. The child appears to be in no respiratory distress with good breath sounds bilaterally. The heart rate is 140 per minute and the BP is 86/60. Capillary refill is delayed at about 4 seconds. The peripheral pulses are weak. After obtaining vascular access, which of the following would be the next intervention?
    (A) Get a chest X-ray
    (B) Initiate a Dopamine infusion at 2–5 mcg/kg/minute
    (C) Start oral hydration
    (D) Administer a 20 cc/kg bolus of normal saline

Questions 176 and 177 are based on the following scenario:

You are using an end-tidal carbon dioxide detector as a tool to assist for proper endotracheal intubation placement.

176. The absence of carbon dioxide in exhaled air indicates that the endotracheal tube has been
    (A) placed in the right mainstem bronchus.
    (B) correctly placed in the trachea.
    (C) placed in the esophagus.
    (D) placed in the left mainstem bronchus.

177. Your next action is to
    (A) deflate the cuff, pull the endotracheal tube back 2 cm, and reassess placement.
    (B) secure the endotracheal tube and confirm correct placement by auscultation.
    (C) inflate the distal cuff with 7–10 cc of air and secure the endotracheal tube.
    (D) remove the endotracheal tube and provide several ventilations prior to attempting intubation again.

178. There are anatomical differences in pediatric patients compared to adults. When using the rule of nines for calculating burns, which of the following is a correct modification for a child?
    (A) The front of each arm for a child is 7% compared to 4½% on an adult.
    (B) The front of each leg for a child is 4½% compared to 9% on an adult.
    (C) The head of a child is 18% compared to 9% on an adult.
    (D) The entire leg of a child is 9% compared to 18% on an adult.

179. Your squad is dispatched to the scene of a six-year-old child with an elevated temperature. The mother tells you that the child was fine last night and got up this morning complaining of a sore throat and trouble swallowing. The initial assessment reveals a sick-looking child who is leaning forward in the tripod position. He is obviously drooling. From this information, you suspect
    (A) bronchiolitis.
    (B) croup.
    (C) epiglottitis.
    (D) meningitis.

180. A 22-year-old female has just finished jogging five miles. She is complaining of palpitations. Vitals are blood pressure, 112/68; pulse, 148; and respirations, 32. She denies drug use. ECG shows the following rhythm:

Treatment should include
(A) adenosine 6 mg rapid IVP.
(B) cardioversion at 100 joules.
(C) vagal maneuvers.
(D) continued observation.

Answer Key

1. B	46. C	91. A	136. A
2. A	47. A	92. A	137. B
3. D	48. D	93. A	138. C
4. C	49. C	94. D	139. A
5. B	50. B	95. D	140. D
6. B	51. A	96. A	141. B
7. B	52. C	97. B	142. C
8. B	53. C	98. A	143. B
9. B	54. C	99. D	144. B
10. D	55. D	100. B	145. B
11. B	56. B	101. D	146. D
12. A	57. D	102. B	147. C
13. D	58. A	103. D	148. B
14. A	59. A	104. A	149. A
15. C	60. C	105. C	150. C
16. B	61. B	106. D	151. B
17. D	62. D	107. D	152. C
18. B	63. D	108. A	153. C
19. C	64. D	109. D	154. C
20. B	65. C	110. D	155. B
21. D	66. B	111. D	156. C
22. D	67. C	112. B	157. B
23. D	68. A	113. D	158. C
24. C	69. A	114. A	159. C
25. B	70. B	115. A	160. C
26. D	71. A	116. B	161. A
27. C	72. C	117. B	162. D
28. B	73. C	118. D	163. A
29. D	74. C	119. D	164. B
30. A	75. D	120. B	165. B
31. A	76. B	121. B	166. B
32. D	77. D	122. C	167. A
33. B	78. C	123. A	168. C
34. B	79. C	124. C	169. D
35. C	80. D	125. C	170. A
36. B	81. D	126. C	171. D
37. A	82. C	127. D	172. C
38. A	83. C	128. A	173. A
39. A	84. C	129. D	174. A
40. D	85. D	130. C	175. D
41. C	86. D	131. B	176. C
42. A	87. D	132. C	177. D
43. B	88. C	133. C	178. C
44. D	89. D	134. D	179. C
45. C	90. C	135. C	180. C

Answer Explanations

1. **(B)** Consent is assumed from any patient requiring emergency intervention who is physically, mentally, or emotionally unable to provide expressed consent.

2. **(A)** When using a straight blade to intubate an adult patient, the tip of the blade should be placed directly on or under the epiglottis.

3. **(D)** Level III trauma center is the choice because it will stabilize and transfer serious patients as needed as part of a trauma system. Transport decisions will be dependent on many factors, one of those being transport time.

4. **(C)** Head injury (including the possibility of a subdural hematoma) is a common finding in Shaken Baby Syndrome.

5. **(B)** The anatomical structure between the base of the tongue and the epiglottis into which the tip of the curved blade is placed during orotracheal intubation is the vallecula.

6. **(B)** Good Samaritan laws protect a paramedic if he or she acts in good faith and is not negligent, acts within his or her scope of practice, and does not accept payment for service.

7. **(B)** Vasopressin is indicated only for the management of ventricular fibrillation and pulseless ventricular tachycardia.

8. **(B)** Epinephrine 0.01 mg/kg of 1:10,000 solution is the recommended dose for pediatric cardiac arrest.

9. **(B)** A delayed hypersensitivity reaction may occur several hours or even days after exposure. Common causes are medications and chemicals. A patient may very well present with the signs/symptoms of allergic reaction several days after starting a new medication.

10. **(D)** This patient is alert and oriented, so he has an intact airway and is breathing. Your priority for this patient is "circulation," which includes stopping major hemorrhage. Applying a pressure dressing and elevation are necessary. **(A)** is incorrect because it is not a higher priority than controlling hemorrhage. **(B)** is not indicated for this patient. **(C)** is incorrect because it states right leg.

11. **(B)** How well do you know your medical terminology and definitions? If you know your medical terminology you answered this question correctly because positive end expiratory pressure is not a component of perfusion.

12. **(A)** Once external hemorrhage has been controlled, start fluid resuscitation with normal saline or Ringer's lactate solution.

13. **(D)** Each large block on the ECG graph paper represents 0.20 seconds. Each small block measures 0.04 seconds.

14. **(A)** A rapid heart rate or irregular heartbeat may cause a patient to experience a sensation commonly referred to as palpitations. Another common term to describe this sensation is "fluttering."

15. **(C)** FCC stands for the Federal Communications Commission, which regulates telecommunications in the United States. Functions include licensing, frequency allocation, technical standards, and rule making/enforcement.

16. **(B)** A minimum of 100 compressions per minute. This is basic life support material you must be familiar with before taking your certification exam.

17. **(D)** A bag-valve mask device with a reservoir and an adequate oxygen source (at least 15 LPM) will deliver an oxygen concentration of 100%.

18. **(B)** Structural lesions, such as brain tumors and intracerebral bleeds, can press on and destroy brain tissue. This can cause seizures and a number of other illnesses.

19. **(C)** A pulse oximetry reading of 90% in a person who is on high-flow oxygen indicates moderate hypoxia. Intubation should be considered.

20. **(B)** Excessive hyperventilation of a patient with increasing intracranial pressure can decrease the blood arterial carbon dioxide to dangerous levels.

21. **(D)** Decorticate posturing (flexion) indicates a lesion at or above the brain stem. Decerebrate posturing (extension) results from a lesion within the brain stem.

22. **(D)** 5 mg/kg of amiodarone is the recommended dose for the treatment of pulseless v tach or v fib in pediatric patients.

23. **(D)** The stimulation of Beta 2 receptors causes bronchodilation, dilatation of arterioles, inhibition of uterine contractions and skeletal muscle tremors.

24. **(C)** Treatment for this unstable patient is synchronous cardioversion (since the patient has a pulse). If this patient was pulseless, the treatment would include defibrillation.

25. **(B)** Hyperventilation can result in an excess elimination of carbon dioxide leading to respiratory alkalosis.

26. **(D)** Alkalosis decreases blood calcium levels, which leads to hypocalcemia. This results in cramping and spasms of the feet and hands.

27. **(C)** Since hyperventilation can mask a true medical emergency such as a pulmonary embolism, it is important to consider that this patient has a serious medical problem.

28. **(B)** Beck's triad includes hypotension, distant heart tones, and JVD. This triad of symptoms can aid in the diagnosis of cardiac tamponade.

29. **(D)** During normal inspiration the diaphragm contracts (it drops) and becomes flatter and increases the size (volume) of the thoracic cavity. The result is air being able to enter the lungs.

30. **(A)** The intrinsic firing rate for a ventricular pacemaker is 20 to 40 beats per minute. The Intrinsic firing rate of the SA Node (the primary pacemaker of the heart) is 60–100. The AV Node also has pacemaker ability at a firing rate of 40–60 beats per minute.

31. **(A)** Stridor is a harsh, high- or low-pitched sound caused by breathing through a partially blocked airway; wheezing **(B)** is a high- or low-pitched whistling sound; crackles/rhonchi **(C and D)** represent fluid/mucus in the larger bronchial airways.

32. **(D)** Lead II placement of the positive electrode is located on the left leg, the negative electrode on the right shoulder, and the ground on the left shoulder.

33. **(B)** Remember that lecture on the autonomic nervous system? Pain and discomfort to the body can activate the sympathetic nervous system.

34. **(B)** Murphy's sign is pain caused when an inflamed gallbladder is palpated by pressing under the right costal margin. McBurney's point **(A)** is a common site of pain from appendicitis located one to two inches above the anterior iliac crest in a direct line with the umbilicus. Grey-Turner's sign **(C)** is ecchymosis in the flank area. Cullen's sign **(D)** is ecchymosis in the periumbilical area.

35. **(C)** All of the information presented in this scenario should have led you to the conclusion of cholecystitis (inflammation of the gallbladder).

36. **(B)** Demerol 25–50 mg IV titrated for pain relief. **(A)** is incorrect; morphine is contraindicated because it is believed to cause spasm of the cystic duct in the gallbladder. **(C)** and **(D)** are incorrect because the dosages listed are wrong. Note: While there might be concern about use of pain medication in "undiagnosed" abdominal pain or the administration of pain medication may mask symptoms and make in-hospital assessment more difficult, the use of Demerol is not contraindicated in cholecystitis.

37. **(A)** Minute volume is defined as the amount of gas moved in and out of the respiratory tract per minute.

38. **(A)** OSHA stands for Occupational Safety and Health Administration. This agency is charged with protecting worker safety.

39. **(A)** Cushing's reflex includes an increase in systolic blood pressure, bradycardia, and erratic (usually slow) respirations.

40. **(D)** Lidocaine is contraindicated in severe degrees of SA, AV, or intraventricular blocks because it may produce serious ventricular dysrhythmias or develop into complete heart block.

41. **(C)** 15 compressions to 2 ventilations.

42. **(A)** Field extubation is not common. If it must be performed, the patient must clearly be able to maintain and protect his or her own airway and have adequate spontaneous respirations.

43. **(B)** Most newborn infants respond quite favorably to warming, drying, suctioning, and stimulation. Occasionally, administration of oxygen with assisted ventilations may be necessary. Vascular access and CPR are utilized only after the infant fails to respond effectively to ventilatory assistance.

44. **(D)** The three phases of the body's response to stress are alarm reaction (or the fight on flight response); resistance—as the body sustains increasing stress, the level of resistance to stress raises; therefore, higher levels of stress must occur for the alarm reaction to occur; exhaustion—as stress continues, coping mechanisms begin to fail.

45. **(C)** The return of a cardiac muscle to its resting state is repolarization. Automaticity **(D)** is the ability for certain cardiac cells to initiate impulses spontaneously. **(A)**, synapse is the junction point of two neurons. **(B)**, depolarization is the change from the resting potential to a positive charge inside the cardiac cell.

46. **(C)** A pulse oximeter is used as an assessment tool. A patient with a pulse oximeter value of less than 90% with no apparent cause or past medical history is considered to be moderately hypoxic and needs high-flow oxygen administration.

47. **(A)** A patient who alerts you to his or her "sense of doom" should be taken very seriously. There are numerous reports of patients who have "sensed" a problem and later suffered a catastrophic event including a threat to life.

48. **(D)** A history of taking birth control pills combined with signs and symptoms that include a painful and inflamed lower extremity suggest deep vein thrombosis. This predisposes the patient to developing a pulmonary embolus.

49. **(C)** This rhythm indicates atrial fibrillation with a rapid ventricular response.

50. **(B)** Nitroglycerin administration is inappropriate for this patient because the scenario did not give you enough information to warrant its use.

51. **(A)** 100 times per minute.

52. **(C)** It is unclear if this patient fell, so you must suspect trauma and c-spine injury. A jaw-thrust maneuver and bag-valve mask ventilation is the best choice. **(A)** is incorrect because the oxygen flow setting is too low; it should be at least 15 LPM. **(B)** is incorrect because it utilizes a nonrebreather mask to assist ventilations; nonrebreathers are not designed for or capable of assisting ventilations. **(D)** is incorrect because the patient needs his ventilations assisted.

53. **(C)** Treatment for this rhythm includes lidocaine 1 mg/kg IVP.

54. **(C)** Prearrival instructions provide immediate instructions and assistance to the caller prior to arrival of EMS units.

55. **(D)** Feedback is a vital part of communication, allowing the sender to know that the receiver understands the message.

56. **(B)** Osmosis is the movement of any solvent (usually water) across a cell membrane.

57. **(D)** The correct answer is all of the above. Chest pain and dysrhythmias are a typical sign/symptom of cocaine abuse. Confusion and polyuria represent alcohol use. Dilated pupils and anxiety are hallucinogens. Constricted pupils and respiratory depression are the result of opiates.

58. **(A)** The first medication to be delivered after defibrillating pulseless ventricular tachycardia is epinephrine or vasopressin.

59. **(A)** 0.5–1.0 joules/kg is the recommended energy setting when cardioversion is necessary. Repeat cardioversion can be increased to 2 joules/kg.

60. **(C)** Don't forget the basics! The head-tilt/chin-lift and jaw-thrust maneuver are both manual airway maneuvers that are very effective in initial management of the airway.

61. **(B)** A subdural hematoma is usually due to rupture of small venous vessels. This type of bleeding is slow and the onset of symptoms may take several hours to develop after the injury.

62. **(D)** Administration of nitroglycerin gr1/150 sublingual is the only correct choice for this question. Establishing an IV **(A)** is warranted for a patient complaining of chest pain but the IV should be run at KVO. Administration of Lasix **(B)** may be appropriate if signs/symptoms of left ventricular failure are present but the dose of 100 mg is excessive. You certainly want to administer oxygen **(C)** but a high-flow rate is recommended to increase oxygen delivery to the myocardium.

63. **(D)** Morphine is an opiate that can cause central nervous system depression. Administration may result in a decrease in the respiratory rate. Patients receiving morphine must be monitored closely for respiratory depression.

64. **(D)** The primary responsibility of the paramedic at all scenes is the protection of himself or herself and other EMS personnel.

65. **(C)** Chicken pox/varicella zoster virus is a member of the herpesvirus group. The herpesvirus group also contains the virus responsible for genital herpes and the common cold sore.

66. **(B)** Supine hypotension syndrome (or vena cava syndrome) occurs when the pregnant uterus compresses the inferior vena cava when the patient is in a supine position. This results in a decrease in blood return back to the heart and a reduction of cardiac output. This syndrome can occur as early as the third month of gestation.

67. **(C)** The patient care report may be the only accurate account available to healthcare professionals, as well as other people interested in the event.

68. **(A)** This is a basic airway management question. The head-tilt/chin-lift maneuver is the simplest airway management technique to open the airway when no cervical spine trauma is suspected.

69. **(A)** Contrary to popular belief, pulse oximetry is NOT the "fifth vital sign." Complete documentation of baseline neurological status includes response to sensory stimulation, pupillary reaction, and motor function.

70. **(B)** The parietal pleura covers the thoracic cavity.

71. **(A)** The classic description of pain associated with a dissecting aortic aneurysm is a ripping or tearing sensation.

72. **(C)** Revisions are acceptable and must be done on a separate form and then attached to the original document.

73. **(C)** Transport for evaluation must be considered for this patient. A bradycardic rate of 48 while mowing the lawn on a hot August day should be a concern. With the presence of chest pain, you should suspect an underlying cardiac origin and transport.

74. **(C)** With the presence of chest pain, the administration of nitroglycerin is indicated. If you selected Atropine for your answer **(A)**, this is incorrect because his blood pressure is adequate at 148/92 and no altered LOC or respiratory distress is noted. **(B)** and **(D)** are not indicated for this patient.

75. **(D)** This rhythm is complete heart block. With the presence of serious signs/symptoms, immediate transcutaneous pacing is indicated.

76. **(B)** Common signs and symptoms of preeclampsia include headache, dizziness, confusion, blurred vision, nausea, vomiting, proteinuria, hypertension, and edema.

77. **(D)** If you suspect preeclampsia, you should take precautions to prevent seizures, which include keeping the patient calm and transporting without lights and sirens.

78. **(C)** Treatment of seizure activity in eclampsia includes placing the patient in the left lateral recumbent position, maintaining the airway, administering high-flow oxygen, establishing IV access, and the administration of 2–5 grams of magnesium sulfate IV. If seizures cannot be controlled, sedatives may be required.

79. **(C)** The rescuer's top priority is the safety of himself of herself and other rescuers. Attempting any rescue prior to cutting power to the downed lines would jeopardize the safety of the rescuers and the patient.

80. **(D)** Abandonment is the termination of the paramedic-patient relationship without ensuring appropriate care for the patient.

81. **(D)** In a tension pneumothorax, the patient is dealing with oxygenation problems and circulation problems. The tension pneumothorax creates an intrathoracic shift, impeding venous blood return to the heart.

82. **(C)** Both acids and alkalis cause burns by disrupting cell membranes and damaging tissues on contact. **(A)** is incorrect because antidotes and neutralizing agents

should never be used as they may cause a violent reaction with the contaminant. (**B**) is incorrect because alkali burns are typically more severe because of their liquefaction necrosis process. (**D**) is incorrect because you should always approach from upwind.

83. (**C**) Procainamide should be discontinued if the QRS is widened 50% of its original width, the maximum dose is achieved, the arrhythmia is suppressed, or hypotension develops.

84. (**C**) Hyphema is a collection of blood in the anterior chamber of the eye due to trauma. This type of injury is a potential threat to the patient's vision and requires evaluation by an ophthalmologist.

85. (**D**) C-spine injury should be suspected with any injury to the head. Treatment for this patient would include full body immobilization. The preferred position of transport of a hyphema is with the head elevated; therefore, you should elevate the head of the backboard.

86. (**D**) Right route. Amiodarone cannot be given via the endotracheal route. The six rights of medication administration include: right medication, right dose, right time, right route, right patient, and right documentation.

87. (**D**) Hyperthermia (fever) should not affect the accuracy of a pulse oximeter reading. Some circumstances that can affect accuracy include nail polish, acrylic nails, dark pigmentation or bruising, high bilirubin concentration.

88. (**C**) Prehospital indications for the administration of sodium bicarbonate include tricyclic antidepressant overdoses, hyperkalemia, and preexisting or suspected acidosis.

89. (**D**) Naloxone is used to reverse the effects of opiate toxicity. The recommended dose in pediatrics is 0.1 mg/kg.

90. (**C**) Applying gentle countertraction to the infant's head to prevent explosive delivery is essential to decrease the likelihood of tearing of the perineum and to decrease the potential for rapid expulsion of the baby's skull through the birth canal, which may cause intracranial injury.

91. (**A**) Adenocard is indicated for the treatment of a narrow complex tachycardia.

92. (**A**) Exposure includes contact of infectious material with eyes, mouth, exposed mucous membranes, or nonintact skin.

93. (**A**) Once every 3 seconds (20 times per minute).

94. (**D**) This ECG demonstrates a sinus tachycardia.

95. (**D**) Mechanism of injury can provide clues for determining possible injuries.

96. (**A**) CPR is indicated even if signs of death are present. A hypothermic patient cannot be presumed dead until a core body temperature of 94–95°F has been achieved and resuscitation efforts are still unsuccessful.

97. **(B)** Immediate defibrillation is required for this patient. A series of stacked shocks, 200j, 200-300j, and 360j, should be delivered.

98. **(A)** IV medication may be administered, but spaced at longer than standard intervals; therefore **(C)** is incorrect. Drug metabolism is reduced so administered medication such as epinephrine and lidocaine may accumulate to toxic levels. In addition, administered drugs may remain in the peripheral circulation. When the patient is rewarmed and peripheral circulation resumes, a large toxic bolus of medication may be delivered to the central circulation. **(D)** is incorrect because lidocaine and procainamide will actually lower fibrillation threshold in a severely hypothermic patient. **(B)** is incorrect because medication should not be withheld unless the core temperature is below 86°F.

99. **(D)** If the hypothermic cardiac arrest patient fails to respond to initial defibrillation attempts and drug therapy, subsequent ACLS care should be held until the core temperature is 86°F. **(D)** is incorrect because it states "90°F."

100. **(B)** The liver is a solid, vascular organ in the right upper quadrant. Rupture or laceration of the liver can cause severe hemorrhage. Injury to the liver is the most common abdominal injury that leads to *death* in the pediatric patient.

101. **(D)** Erythrocytes are defined as the blood component responsible for transporting oxygen from the lungs to the body tissues and transporting carbon dioxide from the tissues to the lungs.

102. **(B)** The amount of energy required to deform a steering wheel is significant. Possible life-threatening injuries from the body striking a steering wheel include: flail chest, myocardial contusion, aortic tear, tracheal or vascular injuries, pulmonary contusion, pneumothorax, solid and hollow organ injury. Bilateral femur fractures may result if an "up-and-over" path occurred.

103. **(D)** Alcohol is a central nervous system depressant. Because of this, alcohol can mask signs and symptoms of injury. It is important to assess all trauma patients thoroughly, but be especially meticulous when you suspect drug/alcohol use.

104. **(A)** "Low-head" dams create a recirculating current, which can repeatedly pull the victim under the water, making escape difficult. These dams also make rescue operations hazardous.

105. **(C)** Making this patient a "load and go" patient based on the information provided is an inappropriate action.

106. **(D)** Inspiratory stridor, absence of drooling or trouble swallowing, and symptoms persistently worse at night, leads to the conclusion of the croup.

107. **(D)** Residual volume is defined as the amount of gas that remains in the respiratory system after forced expiration.

108. **(A)** An ectopic pregnancy should be suspected when abdominal pain is present in women of childbearing age who are sexually active. An ectopic pregnancy can be difficult to distinguish from other conditions. The classic triad of symptoms

includes abdominal pain, vaginal bleeding, and amenorrhea. Other symptoms include referred pain to the shoulder, nausea, vomiting, or syncope. Signs of shock may be present if the ectopic ruptures.

109. **(D)** Inserting the needle over (on top of) the second or third rib avoids inadvertent puncturing or laceration of the adjoining vessels and nerves located at the inferior border of the ribs.

110. **(D)** Immediate transcutaneous pacing is indicated for Type Two second-degree AV block and third-degree AV block when accompanied with symptoms.

111. **(D)** Paroxysmal supraventricular tachycardia (PSVT) may require synchronized cardioversion, especially if the patient is hemodynamically unstable. Pulseless ventricular tachycardia and ventricular fibrillation require immediate defibrillation, not cardioversion.

112. **(B)** To correct an error on a PCR, a single line should be struck through the error with the EMT-Paramedic's initials and date next to the error.

113. **(D)** Of the choices listed, oxygen is the only appropriate treatment. Nitroglycerin and aspirin are not indicated since the scenario does not include a complaint of chest pain.

114. **(A)** Long-term effects of hyperadrenalism lead to paper thin (almost transparent) skin that can be easily bruised or torn. The disease process also results in delayed healing, so great care with venipuncture is required. **(B)** is incorrect because IV therapy is *not* contraindicated. **(C)** is incorrect because you should never make an assumption about a patient's blood glucose level.

115. **(A)** Left side weakness, flattened nasolabial fold on the left, and slurring of her speech may indicate CVA. Hyperadrenalism is associated with high incidents of atherosclerosis, hypertension, and diabetes, which are all risk factors for stroke.

116. **(B)** Information related to the patient's condition or treatment is considered confidential information.

117. **(B)** Complications associated with a fracture of the clavicle include injury to the subclavian vein.

118. **(D)** When assessment of a trauma patient does not reveal significant injury, the presence of unexplained shock should lead you to suspect serious abdominal/thorax trauma.

119. **(D)** Respiratory failure, most probably due to pneumonia. This is based on tachypnea, increased work of breathing, diminished breath sounds, dullness to percussions, and elevated temperature.

120. **(B)** This patient has a valid DNR (Do Not Resuscitate) order and no obvious signs of life. The correct actions would be to address the survivor in terms that leave no doubt about the outcome of the deceased. Use gentle reassuring eye contact and offer any assistance that may be needed to the survivor.

121. **(B)** The nasopharyngeal airway should be measured from the tip of the nose to the earlobe.

122. **(C)** Heart rates ranging from 180–220 beats per minute in a child are considered SVT if the QRS complexes remain narrow. V tach presents with a wide QRS; sinus tachycardia usually shows p waves, and rapid atrial fibrillation will be irregularly irregular.

123. **(A)** During needle decompression, the needle is inserted on top of the third rib to ensure that the vein, artery, and nerve bundle under each rib are not damaged. Each intercostal space contains a vein, artery, and nerve, which lie *underneath* each rib.

124. **(C)** The patient's history should lead you to believe a vasovagal episode. Having a bowel movement or bearing down to have a bowel movement can stimulate the vagus nerve and slow down the heart rate enough to cause dizziness/syncope.

125. **(C)** The chordae tendinea connect the leaflets of the heart valves to the papillary muscles.

126. **(C)** Hypoglycemia is not considered an anginal equivalent.

127. **(D)** Defamation is intentional false communication that injures another person's reputation or good name. Defamation includes slander, which is verbal, and libel, which is written.

128. **(A)** With the probability of significant trauma and c-spine injury, the child's airway should be assessed using a jaw-thrust maneuver while stabilizing the cervical spine. Head-tilt/chin-lift hyperextension and hyperflexion (**B**, **C**, and **D**) cause manipulation of the cervical spine and are not indicated when cervical spine injury is suspected.

129. **(D)** This is a difficult question. If you knew this answer, pat yourself on the back. Brown-Sequard's syndrome is caused by a penetrating injury that affects one side of the spinal cord. The damage to the one side results in sensory and motor loss to that side of the body. Pain and temperature perception are lost on the opposite side of the body because of the switching of the associated nerves as they enter the spinal cord.

130. **(C)** Tidal volume is defined as the amount of gas inhaled or exhaled during a normal breath.

131. **(B)** The mitral valve is located between the left atrium and the left ventricle. The tricuspid valve is located between the right atrium and right ventricle.

132. **(C)** A patient who is unconscious and unresponsive with deep gasping respirations of 8 per minute, and inspiratory stridor requires assisted ventilations and endotracheal intubation. With the possibility of c-spine injury, proper precautions must be taken. **(D)** is incorrect because a rate of 24 ventilations per minute is too fast. **(A)** is incorrect because the patient needs assisted ventilations. **(B)** is not the best choice listed.

133. **(C)** Based on the medical alert necklace, the presence of bee stings, and the absence of obvious chest trauma causing the respiratory distress, you should suspect severe bronchial constriction secondary to anaphylactic reaction.

134. **(D)** Epinephrine 1:1,000 solution 0.3–0.5mg SQ.

135. **(C)** Posterior pressure exerted on the cricoid cartilage (the Sellick maneuver) will effectively compress the esophagus, minimizing the potential for gastric distention. This maneuver will also reposition the vocal cords for clearer visualization of anatomic structures.

136. **(A)** The pathology of bronchiolitis is closely matched with that of Respiratory Syncytial Virus (RSV). Any number of viruses including parainfluenza, adenovirus, and rhinovirus may also be a cause.

137. **(B)** The second dose of amiodarone for the treatment of ventricular fibrillation is 150 mg.

138. **(C)** The maximum amount of procainamide to be administered is 17 mg/kg. The patient's weight is 89.09 kg; 89.09×17 equals 1,514 mg maximum dose.

139. **(A)** The mnemonic C-FLOP stands for: C—Command; F—Finance/administration; L—logistics; O—operations; P—planning.

140. **(D)** Since it is unknown if there are any c-spine injuries from the fall through the ice, you must secure the airway and control the cervical spine during resuscitation.

141. **(B)** The pediatric assessment triangle is based on appearance, which includes mental status, body position, and muscle tone; breathing, which includes visible movement, effort, and audible sounds; and circulation, which includes skin color. All are obtained as part of the initial assessment to formulate a rapid determination of the child's stability.

142. **(C)** Nitroglycerin is a vasodilator; it works against vasospasm and decreases preload. It does not have an effect on afterload.

143. **(B)** When intubating an adult patient with a curved blade, the tip of the blade should be placed in the vallecula, at the base of the tongue.

144. **(B)** Roles. Recognizing an emergency exists, assessing the situation, managing the emergency care, coordinating efforts of your team as well as other agencies involved in the care and transportation of the patient and establishing rapport with the patient and other EMS crew are all examples of a paramedic's roles.

145. **(B)** The first unit to arrive on the scene should begin the scene sizeup which includes establishing command, calling for back-up units, controlling any hazards and locating and triaging patients. It would not be appropriate for the primary unit to locate and transport the most critically injured patient.

146. **(D)** SLUDGE is a helpful mnemonic to remember signs of poisoning—S = salivation, L = lacrimation, U = urination, D = defecation, G = GI upset, E = emesis. Other symptoms of organophosphate poisoning include, bronchoconstriction, bradycardia, anxiety, and visual disturbances.

147. **(C)** One of the ways to determine successful placement of the IO needle is by aspiration of the bone marrow. Additionally, an unobstructed infusion of fluid without evidence of infiltration can also be used. X-rays are not needed to confirm placement. You should not be able to aspirate arterial blood from a properly placed IO needle.

148. **(B)** Veins carry blood from the body back to the heart. The pulmonary vein is no exception but it carries oxygen-rich blood from the lungs back to the heart. Therefore, it is the only vein in the body to carry oxygenated blood.

149. **(A)** The safety officer monitors all on-scene actions to ensure that no potentially harmful situations are created.

150. **(C)** Place your hands on the lower half of the sternum at the nipple line

151. **(B)** By the time the victim of a lightning strike is reached, the electricity will have dissipated. While you may be concerned as long as the storm remains nearby, there is no danger of electrical shock from touching the victim of a lightning strike.

152. **(C)** The recommended pediatric dose of diazepam is 0.1–0.3 mg/kg for the treatment of seizures.

153. **(C)** A flail chest is three or more adjacent ribs that are fractured in two or more places. This segment of the chest is free to move with the pressure changes of respirations.

154. **(C)** Paradoxical chest wall movement associated with flail chest is defined as the motion of a flail segment opposite to the normal motion of the chest wall.

155. **(B)** Positive pressure ventilation of the patient with a flail chest reverses the mechanism that causes the paradoxical chest wall movement, restores tidal volume, and reduces the pain of chest wall movement.

156. **(C)** The signs and symptoms displayed by this patient are consistent with a left side tension pneumothorax and immediate chest decompression is required.

157. **(B)** Cardiac output is defined as the volume of blood ejected from the left ventricle into the arterial system each minute. Preload **(A)** is defined as the pressure within the ventricles at the end of diastole. Afterload **(C)** is defined as the resistance against which the heart must pump. Stroke volume **(D)** is defined as the amount of blood ejected by the heart in one cardiac contraction.

158. **(C)** Stridor is defined as a high-pitched or low-pitched sound associated with upper airway constriction. This can be an indication of pending complete airway obstruction when associated with conditions such as anaphylactic shock.

159. **(C)** The usual dose range of Compazine is 5–10 mg. It can be administered IV or IM.

160. **(B)** If Compazine is supplied in a 2 ml vial containing 5 mg/ml, you would administer 2 ml of medication to deliver a 10 mg dose. This is a simple math question. If you answered incorrectly, you must review math for medication administration.

161. **(A)** Based on the history of the patient choking, a constant cough (from bronchospasm), and diminished breath sounds (obstruction) on the right should lead you to suspect aspiration of food.

162. **(D)** The signs and symptoms are consistent with a tension pneumothorax (absent breath sounds, tracheal deviation, no or little chest movement on the affected side). Immediate needle decompression is warranted.

163. **(A)** How fast the temperature of the child rises will increase a child's risk for developing a seizure. For example, a child who transitions from a temperature of 100.2 to 104.5°F in 30 minutes is more likely to suffer a febrile seizure than a child who develops a 104.5°F temperature over several hours.

164. **(B)** This patient was most likely intubated in the right mainstem bronchus. Deflating the endotracheal tube cuff, withdrawing the endotracheal tube slightly, reinflating the cuff, and reevaluating breath sounds is the proper procedure when a right mainstem bronchus intubation is suspected.

165. **(B)** 36% (chest = 9%, abdomen = 9%, entire arm 9%, front of the leg = 9%)

166. **(B)** Vasopressin is indicated in ventricular fibrillation at a dose of 40 units IV to be administered as a *one-time* dose.

167. **(A)** Abruptio placenta is premature separation of the placenta from the uterus. There are different presentations that can occur depending on the severity of the abruption. Classic presentation includes a sudden, sharp, tearing pain and the development of a stiff boardlike abdomen. Bleeding can be severe or not present depending on many factors.

168. **(C)** Abruptio placenta is premature separation of the placenta from the uterus and is a true medical emergency because it poses a life threat to the mother and fetus.

169. **(D)** Multigravida is when a woman has been pregnant more than once. Nullipara is a woman who has not yet delivered her first child. If you did not know this common terminology, you must review obstetric medical terminology.

170. **(A)** The Bundle of His does not possess pacemaker capabilities. The normal pacemaker of the heart is the sinoatrial node with a firing rate of 60–100 beats per minute. The atrioventricular node is secondary pacemaker of the heart with a firing rate of 40–60 beats per minute. The third pacemaker of the heart is the Purkinje fibers in the ventricles with a firing rate of 20–40 beats per minute.

171. **(D)** Status epilepticus is two or more generalized motor seizures occurring in succession and is a life-threatening emergency situation.

172. **(C)** Air exchange is poor during a generalized motor seizure. It is extremely important to protect the airway from obstruction and deliver 100% oxygen using a bag-valve mask for respiratory assistance.

173. **(A)** Valium (diazepam) is a sedative and anticonvulsant that depresses seizure activity in the brain. **(C)** and **(D)** are incorrect because the dose is wrong. **(B)** is not indicated with a blood glucose reading of 120 mg/dl.

174. **(A)** A side-effect of Valium is respiratory depression.

175. **(D)** With the vital signs given in the scenario, the child is displaying signs and symptoms consistent with compensated shock. The shock is most probably related to diarrhea. A 20 cc/kg bolus of normal saline or an isotonic crystalloid fluid is recommended.

176. **(C)** The use of end-tidal carbon dioxide detection ($ETCO_2$) is one tool to assess for proper endotracheal tube placement. The absence of carbon dioxide likely indicates that the endotracheal tube has been placed in the esophagus. Verifying correct endotracheal tube placement is absolutely essential. $ETCO_2$ is only one method to assist in verification of proper placement.

177. **(D)** The endotracheal tube is likely placed in the esophagus. Your next action is to remove the endotracheal tube and provide several ventilations with supplemental oxygen prior to attempting another intubation.

178. **(C)** When using the rule of nines, the head of a child is assigned 18% BSA compared to 9% BSA on an adult. There are several other "rule of nine" modifications for children and infants you should be familiar with before taking your certification exam.

179. **(C)** Epiglottitis is a bacterial infection causing the acute swelling of the epiglottis and the soft tissues above the glottic opening. Clinical findings include but are not limited to: sudden onset high fever (102–105°F), pain on swallowing, typically sitting in tripod position, and drooling.

180. **(C)** Since the patient's presentation is considered stable, a vagal maneuver is indicated.

NOTES

NOTES

CHAPTER 9

Practice Test 2

Practice Test 2 follows the same format as Practice Test 1 and consists of questions from each chapter in the following breakdown:

• Airway and Breathing	26–34 questions
• Cardiology	29–37 questions
• Trauma	26–34 questions
• Medical Emergencies	26–34 questions
• Obstetrics/Pediatrics	24–32 questions
• Operations	25–33 questions
Total	**180 questions**

Allow yourself 180 minutes to take the test and again hold yourself to a high standard for this practice test by scoring 85% or better. This is achievable by answering 153 questions correctly.

All ECG rhythm strips used in this test are six-second strips.

1. When communicating medical information, using proper terminology can
   (A) shorten transmission and provide an unambiguous form of communication.
   (B) serve no vital importance.
   (C) alter the interpretation of the nature of the incident if heard by several people.
   (D) reflect upon the EMS professional negatively.

2. You are called to the middle of a bridge to transport a violent patient who is suicidal. Per local police, the patient threatened to jump from the bridge and needs a psychiatric evaluation. The patient refuses transport threatening to sue anyone who touches him. You transport this patient against his will based on
   (A) informed consent.
   (B) implied consent.
   (C) expressed consent.
   (D) involuntary consent.

3. Legislation that governs the practice of medicine and may prescribe a physician's ability to delegate authority to perform medical acts by the paramedic is
   (A) licensure.
   (B) medical direction.
   (C) standard of care.
   (D) medical practice act.

4. Complications of endotracheal intubation include all of the following EXCEPT
   (A) trauma to the teeth.
   (B) gastric distension.
   (C) esophageal intubation.
   (D) laryngospasm.

5. Which of the following is NOT considered a sign or symptom indicating a tension pneumothorax?
   (A) Dyspnea
   (B) Hyperresonance to percussion
   (C) Distended jugular veins
   (D) Clear lung sounds

6. What is the ratio of compressions to ventilations when performing one-person CPR on an adult?
   (A) 5 compressions to 1 ventilation
   (B) 15 compressions to 1 ventilation
   (C) 15 compressions to 2 ventilations
   (D) 5 compressions to 2 ventilations

7. Stimulation of the vagus nerve may result in
   (A) vasodilatation.
   (B) an increase in heart rate.
   (C) a decrease in heart rate.
   (D) an increase in cardiac output.

8. The time for an electrical impulse to be transmitted from the atria to the ventricles is
   (A) PR interval.
   (B) t wave.
   (C) QRS complex.
   (D) J point.

Questions 9 and 10 are based on the following scenario:

You are called for a 62-year-old male with a complaint of severe abdominal pain. He is lying as still as possible in his bed.

9. Upon inspection of the abdomen, you find ecchymosis in the periumbilical area. This is known as
   (A) Cullen's sign.
   (B) Grey-Turner sign.
   (C) peritonitis.
   (D) Mallory-Weiss sign.

10. This assessment finding may indicate
    (A) ascites.
    (B) an intraabdominal hemorrhage.
    (C) a dissecting aortic aneurysm.
    (D) acute appendicitis.

Questions 11–13 are based on the following scenario:

You are called to the scene of a 60-year-old woman who fell down a flight of stairs. The patient is found to be alert and oriented, with warm, dry, and pink skin. She is complaining of a headache and upper back pain. Her vital signs are BP 90/62, pulse 60, and respiratory rate 20.

11. Which of the following would be your initial impression?
    (A) Neurogenic or distributive shock.
    (B) No significant injury.
    (C) The patient is taking beta-blockers.
    (D) Mechanical shock.

12. During your rapid trauma survey you find that the patient has no sensation below the border of the rib cage. This would suggest spinal pathology between which vertebral areas?
    (A) C1–C4
    (B) T4–T10
    (C) T10–S1
    (D) Below S1

13. You have started a large-bore IV of normal saline on this patient. Choose the appropriate solution and rate.
    (A) Two large-bore IVs of normal saline wide open
    (B) Normal saline at a rate to maintain a systolic BP of 90
    (C) D5W TKO
    (D) 1,000 cc bolus of Ringer's lactate

14. Intraosseous access allows for the administration of fluids, medications, and blood products into the bone marrow. Possible complications of intraosseous infusion include all of the following EXCEPT
    (A) osteomyelitis.
    (B) improvement in vascular volume and/or condition.
    (C) fractures.
    (D) compartment syndrome.

15. You are caring for a lethargic two-year-old. A blood glucose test confirms hypoglycemia. You are able to establish IV access. What is the appropriate drug to administer?
    (A) 50% dextrose
    (B) 10 mg glucagon
    (C) instant glucose
    (D) 25% dextrose

16. A nonrebreather mask can deliver an oxygen concentration of _____% at a flow rate of 15 LPM.
    (A) 40 to 60%
    (B) 60 to 80%
    (C) 80 to 95%
    (D) 90 to 100%

17. A drop in systolic blood pressure of 10 mmHg or more or the absence of a radial pulse during inspiration is known as
    (A) pericardial tamponade.
    (B) pulsus paradoxus.
    (C) orthostatic change.
    (D) pulse pressure change.

18. It is generally considered unsafe to walk in fast-moving water _____ deep.
    (A) ankle
    (B) knee
    (C) waist
    (D) chest

19. Amiodarone
    (A) should be given by rapid IV infusion only.
    (B) may produce vasodilation and hypotension.
    (C) has a maximum dose of 17 mg/kg.
    (D) is not indicated in cardiac arrest.

20. You arrive on scene of a 35-year-old male who is in distress. He is grabbing his throat with both hands. What should you do first?
    (A) Get behind him and perform the Heimlich maneuver.
    (B) Give five back blows.
    (C) Ask "Are you choking" and look for a response.
    (D) Alternate back blows with abdominal thrusts.

21. You respond to a home of a patient with complaints of sudden onset of fever/chills, joint pain, neck stiffness, and severe headache. Upon examination the medics note a petechial rash. You suspect
    (A) rabies.
    (B) influenza.
    (C) hepatitis A.
    (D) meningitis.

22. Which of the following medications and dosages are correct for a person with a long history of COPD and cardiac disease that presents with sudden onset of dyspnea who you believe is suffering acute pulmonary edema?
    (A) Nitroglycerin 4.0 mg
    (B) Furosemide (Lasix) 40 mg IV
    (C) Morphine sulfate 20 mg IV
    (D) Epinephrine (adrenalin) 1:1,000 0.3 SQ

23. Sudden Infant Death Syndrome (SIDS) is defined as death of an infant
    (A) due to trauma.
    (B) within the first 24 months of life.
    (C) from child abuse.
    (D) within the first year of life that is unexplained.

Questions 24–26 are based on the following scenario:

You are assigned to triage patients at the scene of an explosion in a park. You are using the METTAG system of triage.

24. The first victim you come in contact with has no palpable pulse and no respiratory effort. The patient has a major laceration of the scalp with an open skull fracture. You would tag this person as
    (A) Green.
    (B) Yellow.
    (C) Red.
    (D) Black.

25. The next patient with whom you come into contact is a 34-year-old female who is wandering around the incident looking for her 3-year-old daughter. The patient has multiple abrasions to her face and arms. You would most likely triage this patient
    (A) Green.
    (B) Yellow.
    (C) Red.
    (D) Black.

26. The third patient you find is awake, alert, and oriented. The patient has tachypnea with shallow respirations. Your assessment reveals a sucking chest wound on the right side of the chest, a fracture of the right femur, and a large laceration on the forehead. You will most likely triage this patient
    (A) Green.
    (B) Yellow.
    (C) Red.
    (D) Black.

Questions 27 and 28 are based on the following scenario:

You respond to an unknown medical problem. When you arrive, you find a 39-year-old male patient lying on the couch, covered up with several blankets. He has a garbage can next to him that has a small amount of vomitus in it. The stench of alcohol is prevalent throughout the house and you notice several empty bottles of vodka. He has a past medical history of alcoholism.

27. The patient complains of severe epigastric pain that radiates into his back and shoulders. His abdomen is softly distended and he will not allow you to palpate it due to the pain. He states that he took his temperature 30 minutes ago and it was 104.2°F. BP is 86/42, pulse 138, respirations 20. You suspect the patient is suffering from
    (A) severe peritonitis.
    (B) severe pancreatitis.
    (C) severe cholecystitis.
    (D) severe diverticulitis.

28. You suspect his vital signs are a result of
    (A) hypovolemia from excessive vomiting.
    (B) a normal response to infection and hyperpyrexia.
    (C) septic shock from the disease process.
    (D) Both A and C are correct.

---

29. The duration of a normal QRS complex is _____ seconds.
    (A) 0.12–0.20
    (B) 0.10–0.20
    (C) 0.04–0.10
    (D) 0.08–0.12

30. The intrinsic firing rate of the AV node is
    (A) 20–40 beats per minute.
    (B) 40–60 beats per minute.
    (C) 40–80 beats per minute.
    (D) 60–100 beats per minute.

31. You are caring for a female patient who is at 35 weeks gestation. She was involved in a car accident and complains of neck pain. You suspect spinal injury and fully immobilize her on a long spine board. You would then
    (A) carefully tilt the board on its left side 10–15 degrees.
    (B) carefully tilt the board on its right side 10–15 degrees.
    (C) manually displace the uterus to the right.
    (D) allow the patient to roll onto her side.

32. The pediatric dose of lorazepam in the treatment of seizures is
    (A) 0.5–1.0 mg/kg IV/IO.
    (B) 0.05–0.1 mg/kg IV/IO.
    (C) 0.05–0.01 mg/kg IV/IO.
    (D) 5–10 mg IV/IO.

33. What effects does hyperventilation have on cerebral circulation and intracranial pressure?
    (A) More pronounced decrease in circulation than decrease in intracranial pressure
    (B) Vasoconstriction and increased intracranial pressure
    (C) Vasodilation and decreased intracranial pressure
    (D) Little or no effect on cerebral circulation or intracranial pressure

34. Which of the following statements is correct regarding a Glasgow Coma Scale score of seven?
    (A) A perfect GCS score is 10 and a score of 7 represents minor injuries.
    (B) A perfect GCS score is 12 and a score of 7 represents moderate injuries.
    (C) A perfect GCS score is 15 and a score of 7 represents moderate injuries.
    (D) A perfect GCS score is 15 and a score of 7 represents serious injuries.

Questions 35–37 are based on the following scenario:

You are called to the scene of a 46-year-old female who is unresponsive. Her husband states that he just came home from work and found her on the floor in the bathroom. She has a history of depression for which she receives outpatient treatment. There are acetaminophen and Valium found strewn around the room. Your best assessment of the situation speculates that the patient may have ingested one hundred 500 mg acetaminophen and ten 5 mg Valium. You notice the smell of alcohol on the patient.

35. What would be considered he worst outcome of an acetaminophen overdose?
    (A) Internal bleeding
    (B) Nausea and vomiting
    (C) Liver failure and death
    (D) Cardiac dysrhythmias

36. Her vital signs are BP 72/40, pulse 128, respirations 6. What is most likely the primary cause of the hypotension, tachycardia, and respiratory depression?
    (A) Alcohol intoxication
    (B) Acetaminophen ingestion
    (C) Valium ingestion
    (D) Hypoglycemia

37. Which statement is true regarding the administration of Narcan to this patient?
    (A) Narcan will not reverse the effects of Valium.
    (B) Narcan should be administered to this patient since it is uncertain if any opiates were ingested.
    (C) A proper dose range is 1–2 mg IVP.
    (D) All of the above.

---

38. The PCR is a legal document making it necessary to record accurate
    (A) incident times.
    (B) paramedic certifications.
    (C) names of nearest relatives.
    (D) personal opinions.

39. Disadvantages of using a cellular telephone for EMS communications include the fact that
    (A) the conversation is less formal.
    (B) the system promotes discussion.
    (C) the system reduces on-line time.
    (D) geography can interfere with the system or signs.

40. Bacteria, viruses, and fungi are all examples of
    (A) pathogenetic hosts.
    (B) nonspecific inflammatory agents.
    (C) disease processes.
    (D) infectious agents.

41. A nasal cannula will deliver ___ % of oxygen at a flow rate of 6 LPM in optimal conditions.
    (A) 30%
    (B) 40%
    (C) 50%
    (D) 65%

42. Before providing rescue breathing to an unresponsive victim, you must check for breathing. You do this by
    (A) opening the airway.
    (B) shaking and shouting to stimulate them to breathe.
    (C) looking, listening, and feeling airflow through the victim's nose or mouth.
    (D) establishing unresponsiveness.

43. Respiration is
    (A) the exchange of gases between a living organism and its environment.
    (B) the process that moves air into and out of the lungs.
    (C) inadequate oxygenation at the cellular level.
    (D) a respiratory rate greater than that metabolically necessary for gas exchange.

Questions 44–46 are based on the following scenario:

You are called to the scene of an assault on a 75-year-old woman in a bank parking lot. Bystanders report that she was found lying between two cars, unresponsive, with blood coming from the back of her head and multiple contusions and skin tears to her knees and arms. The bank teller states that she had just withdrawn a large sum of money. Your rapid trauma assessment reveals an elderly female responsive to pain only, snoring respirations, a strong radial pulse of 60 beats per minute, and a moderate amount of bright red blood from a large laceration and hematoma on her occipital region.

44. What is your first priority?
    (A) Move the patient to an area for privacy.
    (B) Immediate management of the c-spine and open airway.
    (C) Bleeding control with pressure dressing to head laceration.
    (D) Immediately load and go.

45. Why would this patient be more susceptible to severe head trauma?
    (A) A history of Alzheimer's disease
    (B) Dehydration
    (C) Pickwickian syndrome
    (D) Decreased size of the brain

46. After completing your rapid trauma assessment on the patient, you find a blood pressure of 96/54, heart rate of 50, and respiratory rate of 14 and regular. What is your priority of care?
    (A) Hyperventilate at a rate of 30 with 100% O_2.
    (B) Establish two large-bore IVs at a wide open rate.
    (C) Provide careful fluid resuscitation.
    (D) Give Atropine 0.5 mg IVP.

47. Which of the following describes the most definitive treatment of a patient with a flail chest injury?
    (A) Position of comfort with O_2 per NRB mask
    (B) Intubation and positive pressure ventilation
    (C) Stabilization of the flail segment with a sandbag
    (D) Needle decompression

48. One of the most common mechanisms of injury in the geriatric population is falls. Which statement is true regarding the force required to break a bone in a geriatric patient?
    (A) The same force is required as in other patients.
    (B) Less of a force is required than in other patients.
    (C) Slightly greater force is required than in other patients.
    (D) None of these statements are correct.

49. Your 26-year-old female patient complains of nausea, dizziness, sudden onset of sharp left lower quadrant pain, and shoulder pain. You suspect
    (A) a ruptured appendix.
    (B) an ectopic pregnancy.
    (C) cholecystitis.
    (D) kidney stones.

50. Your patient has injured his right arm in a bicycle accident. When assessing the injured extremity, which of the following is most important?
    (A) Check for compartment syndrome.
    (B) Check deep tendon reflexes.
    (C) Do a thorough neurovascular exam.
    (D) Check for position sense (proprioception).

51. When using a bulb syringe device to assist in verification of proper endotracheal tube placement, all of the following are true EXCEPT
    (A) if the bulb syringe easily inflates, the endotracheal tube is correctly placed in the trachea.
    (B) if the bulb syringe does not inflate, the endotracheal tube is placed in the esophagus.
    (C) the cuff on the endotracheal tube must be inflated prior to using a bulb syringe device.
    (D) the cuff on the endotracheal tube should not be inflated prior to using a bulb syringe device.

Questions 52–54 are based on the following scenario:

A 68-year-old woman is complaining of chest pain and shortness of breath. Her blood pressure is 110/64, pulse 60, respirations 32. ECG shows sinus bradycardia with a PR interval of 0.24. Lung sounds reveal crackles in the posterior bases.

52. Management should include
    (A) nitroglycerin gr1/150 mg SL.
    (B) a 200 cc fluid bolus.
    (C) Atropine 0.5 mg to 1.0 mg IVP.
    (D) preparation for immediate transcutaneous pacing.

53. The BP is now 88/50, pulse 50, respirations 40. Lung sounds reveal increased pulmonary congestion. Continued management should include
    (A) Atropine 0.5 mg to 1 mg.
    (B) administering a 200 cc fluid bolus.
    (C) administering Lasix 80 mg IVP.
    (D) immediate transcutaneous pacing.

54. The patient is experiencing severe chest pain, shortness of breath, and becomes unconscious. BP is 72/40 and the ECG now shows the following rhythm.

    Treatment includes
    (A) Atropine 0.5 mg IVP every five minutes to a maximum dose of 0.4 mg/kg.
    (B) Dopamine infusion titrated to a systolic blood pressure >90 mmHg systolic.
    (C) immediate transcutaneous pacing.
    (D) 200 cc fluid bolus and rechecking vital signs.

55. You are providing positive-pressure ventilation to a newborn. Which of the following statements is correct regarding oxygen administration to a newborn?
    (A) An anesthesia bag provides the best ventilation and is easiest to use.
    (B) A large bag-valve is needed to provide adequate tidal volume.
    (C) Never deprive a newborn of oxygen for fear of oxygen toxicity.
    (D) Positive pressure ventilations are often required in newborn resuscitation.

56. An unwanted side effect of Dopamine administration includes
    (A) increased myocardial oxygen demand.
    (B) respiratory depression.
    (C) ventricular dysrhythmias.
    (D) dilation of renal vessels at high doses.

57. The presence of rhonchi in a patient diagnosed with pneumonia indicates
    (A) narrowing of the airways.
    (B) a normal finding in a pneumonia patient.
    (C) the onset of bronchitis.
    (D) mucus in the airways.

58. Which of the following assessment finding would indicate that a pediatric patient is progressing from respiratory distress to respiratory failure?
    (A) Nasal flaring
    (B) Respiratory rate over 32
    (C) Poor muscle tone
    (D) Grunting/head bobbing

59. The recommended dose of lidocaine in the pediatric cardiac arrest patient presenting in ventricular fibrillation is
    (A) 0.001 mg/kg.
    (B) 0.01–0.02 mg/kg.
    (C) 0.1–0.2 mg/kg.
    (D) 1 mg/kg.

Questions 60–62 are based on the following scenario:

You are called to the local elementary school for an unknown medical problem. When you arrive, you are directed to the first-grade teacher Ms. Marsha. The first-grade class is holding a birthday party for Austin, who turned seven today. Austin's mom baked brownies for the party that contained nuts.

60. Ms. Marsha is allergic to nuts. She states that she did not know the brownies contained nuts and ate one five minutes ago. She complains of tightness in her chest that is making it difficult to breathe. She is not able to talk in full sentences. Given this information, you suspect the patient is experiencing
    (A) a simple allergic reaction.
    (B) a severe allergic reaction.
    (C) sensitization.
    (D) delayed hypersensitivity.

61. Ms. Marsha's respiratory distress is becoming worse. Her blood pressure is 74/48, pulse 140, respirations 40. You decide to administer epinephrine. The correct dose and route are
    (A) 0.01–0.03 mg of 1:1,000 solution SQ.
    (B) 0.3–0.5 cc of 1:10,000 solution IV.
    (C) 3–5 ml of 1:10,000 solution IV.
    (D) 0.1–0.3 mg of 1:1,000 solution SQ.

62. There is little change in the patient's condition and on-line medical control orders you to administer 100 mg of diphenhydramine (Benadryl) IV. You would
    (A) administer it slowly since hypotension and sedation may result.
    (B) administer it rapidly to prevent vomiting and headache.
    (C) ask medical control to repeat the dosage because you question 100 mg as being excessive.
    (D) administer it slowly to prevent burning at the injection site.

63. Proper care of the patient with known HIV includes all of the following EXCEPT
    (A) isolation of the patient.
    (B) effective handwashing.
    (C) use of eye protection and gowns where exposure to bodily fluids in large quantities is possible.
    (D) BSI, based on task performed.

64. The elements of a negligence claim include all of the following EXCEPT
    (A) duty to act.
    (B) breach of duty.
    (C) code of conduct.
    (D) proximate cause.

65. The acronym START stands for the "S" in
    (A) suitable.
    (B) simple.
    (C) salvageable.
    (D) sorting.

66. An incomplete or illegible patient care report
    (A) may be acceptable in some areas.
    (B) may cause subsequent caregivers to provide inappropriate treatment based on the report.
    (C) is of no use.
    (D) is useful in the ongoing care and treatment of the patient.

67. Respiratory acidosis is caused by
    (A) an excess of bicarbonate.
    (B) excess carbon dioxide retention.
    (C) a loss of bicarbonate.
    (D) excess carbon dioxide excretion.

68. A healthy female is being transported for preterm labor contractions. Per protocol, she is lying slightly tilted on her left side, is on oxygen via nonrebreather mask, and an IV is established at KVO. You place her on the monitor and notice the following rhythm.

    (A) Sinus rhythm with PACs
    (B) Sinus rhythm with PJCs
    (C) Sinus dysrhythmia
    (D) Sinus rhythm with PVCs

69. The initial dose of adenosine that should be administered is
    (A) 6 mg rapid IV push, repeated in 5 minutes if necessary.
    (B) 6 mg IV push, repeated in 10 minutes.
    (C) 6 mg rapid IV push followed by a 20 cc fluid bolus.
    (D) 12 mg IV push.

70. Cardiac arrest due to ventricular fibrillation requires
    (A) insertion of an ET tube.
    (B) immediate defibrillation.
    (C) administration of lidocaine.
    (D) administration of epinephrine.

71. The Controlled Substance Act of 1970 created five schedules of controlled substances. Schedule 1 drugs are those drugs with
    (A) accepted medical indications, low potential for abuse and dependence.
    (B) accepted medical indications, high potential for abuse or dependence.
    (C) no accepted medical indications, high potential for abuse and dependence.
    (D) accepted medical indications, less abuse potential and low to moderate physical dependence potential.

72. Management of pediatric bradycardia with significant signs and symptoms related to cardiac or respiratory compromise should be treated with
    (A) Atropine.
    (B) lidocaine.
    (C) sodium bicarbonate.
    (D) epinephrine.

73. Signs and symptoms associated with Shaken Baby Syndrome may be difficult to assess in the prehospital setting. Injury resulting from violent shaking might include
    (A) contusions or abrasions visible on the knees of children three to five years old.
    (B) intracranial hemorrhage resulting from torn veins between the brain and skull in children under the age of 24 months.
    (C) a red rash visible on the child's chest and back.
    (D) a spiral fracture of the wrist

74. Identify the anatomical differences in the pediatric airway compared to the adult airway.
    (A) The airway diameter is larger, the larynx is more anterior, the tongue is proportionally smaller.
    (B) The airway diameter is larger, the larynx is more posterior, the tongue is proportionally smaller.
    (C) The airway diameter is smaller, the larynx is more anterior, the tongue is proportionally larger.
    (D) The airway diameter is smaller, the larynx is more posterior, the tongue is proportionally larger.

75. A respiratory pattern characterized by an irregular pattern, rate, and volume with intermittent periods of apnea is
    (A) Cheyne-Stokes.
    (B) Biot's (ataxic).
    (C) central neurogenic hyperventilation.
    (D) agonal.

Questions 76–78 are based on the following scenario:

You are called to attend to a 61-year-old female complaining of headache, vomiting, abdominal pain, and loss of coordination. She has recently been using a gas home-heating device to warm up her bedroom. Her sister lives next door and they always eat every meal together. The patient cannot get out of bed saying she is too tired. She appears to be sleeping now.

76. Upon assessing the patient, you note that she can speak clearly, slowly moves all extremities, and has a blood pressure of 164/86; pulse regular at 104, respiratory rate at 18 with normal effort. She has not eaten since last evening when she ate dinner with her sister. Her sister, however, feels fine. The patient's condition suggests
    (A) food poisoning.
    (B) carbon monoxide poisoning.
    (C) a cardiac disorder.
    (D) transient ischemic attack (TIA).

77. Her pulse oximetry is 99%. This can be misleading because
    (A) pulse oximetry is inaccurate in certain cases of poisoning.
    (B) the hemoglobin is fully saturated with oxygen.
    (C) the carbon dioxide blood level is dangerously low.
    (D) the carbon dioxide level is normal.

78. Which of the following interventions is most important?
    (A) Provide high-flow oxygen.
    (B) Apply a nonrebreather mask.
    (C) Obtain a detailed history from the sister.
    (D) Further assess for acute CVA.

---

79. The normal arterial pH range in the human body is
    (A) 7.0–7.15.
    (B) 7.15–7.35.
    (C) 7.35–7.45.
    (D) 7.45–7.80.

80. Management of cardiogenic shock may include
    (A) administration of morphine.
    (B) administration of IV Dopamine.
    (C) administration of nitroglycerin gr1/150 sublingual.
    (D) establishing an IV 500 cc/hr.

81. _____ seconds are measured in each small square on ECG graph paper.
    (A) 0.01
    (B) 0.4
    (C) 0.04
    (D) 0.20

82. Appropriate professional language on a PCR includes
    (A) medical terminology.
    (B) slang.
    (C) personal opinion.
    (D) personality.

83. Of the following, which is NOT considered an oxygen-deficient environment or confined space?
    (A) A basement
    (B) Storage tanks
    (C) Silos
    (D) Underground vaults

84. You are caring for a 13-year-old tricyclic antidepressant overdose. What cardiac arrhythmia is likely to develop as a result of this type of overdose?
    (A) Tall, peaked t waves
    (B) SVT
    (C) Wide QRS complex and prolonged QT interval
    (D) Narrow QRS complexes with normal PR interval

85. Signs and symptoms of a pregnant patient with preeclampsia include
    (A) elevated BP, increased weight gain, facial edema and seizures.
    (B) elevated BP, abdominal rigidity, and bright red vaginal bleeding.
    (C) elevated BP, normal respirations and normal pulse rate.
    (D) elevated BP, visual disturbance, headache, and edema.

86. You arrive on the scene of a 40-year-old male with a complaint of palpitations and dizziness. Vitals are BP 102/78, pulse 128 slightly irregular, and respirations of 26. A pulse oximeter reading of 86% is obtained. He has no past medical problems. With this information, you suspect
    (A) hyperventilation syndrome.
    (B) hypoxemia.
    (C) congestive heart failure.
    (D) pending respiratory arrest.

87. Which signs/symptoms are NOT considered atypical presentation of myocardial ischemia?
    (A) Neck pain, jaw pain, left arm pain
    (B) Lower extremity pain, shoulder pain, abdominal pain
    (C) Epigastric pain, reproducible pain, sharp or knifelike pain
    (D) Nausea, dizziness, palpitations

88. When performing transcutaneous pacing, the paramedic should increase the _____ delivered until mechanical capture is obtained.
    (A) joules
    (B) milliamps
    (C) rate
    (D) millivolts

89. You are called to a church where a 62-year-old male feels that his pacemaker is not functioning properly. He is conscious and alert but states he feels that he is going to "pass out." You place him on your monitor and observe the following rhythm:

Treatment for this patient should include
(A) oxygen, IV, monitor, and continued observation.
(B) oxygen, IV, monitor, and lidocaine.
(C) oxygen, IV, monitor, nitroglycerin, and aspirin.
(D) oxygen, IV, monitor, cardioversion.

90. Your patient is an ill-appearing four-month-old lying in his mother's arms. The mother tells you that the infant won't take a bottle and cries whenever he moves. Your examination reveals a lethargic infant, warm to touch, with fine pinpoint petechia on the abdomen, chest, and face. The infant's fontanelle appears to be bulging. The information gained on examination should lead you to suspect
(A) bronchiolitis.
(B) meningitis.
(C) croup.
(D) epiglottitis.

91. Advance directives are documents that express the patient's wishes in the event they are unconscious or otherwise unable to express their choice for care. These include living wills, Do Not Resuscitate Orders, and
(A) slow code requests.
(B) durable power of attorney for health care.
(C) artificial care order.
(D) health care denial form.

Questions 92–95 are based on the following scenario:

You respond to a 25-year-old male involved in an industrial accident. Upon arrival, you see that your patient is trapped in a machine. He has suffered a partial amputation of the right leg just above the knee that is bleeding profusely.

92. Your first action is to:
(A) control bleeding.
(B) stabilize the machinery.
(C) do a rapid trauma assessment.
(D) establish two large-bore IVs.

93. The patient remains trapped in the machine. He is awake, alert, and anxious. His blood pressure is 96/44, pulse 142, respirations 26. His skin is pale and moist. He is in what state of shock?
    (A) Decompensated
    (B) Compensated
    (C) Irreversible
    (D) Pneumatic

94. He has been freed from the machinery. Direct pressure and elevation do not stop hemorrhage. The next step would be to apply
    (A) a tourniquet.
    (B) pressure at an arterial point proximal to the injury.
    (C) application of additional trauma dressings.
    (D) a vacuum splint.

95. Despite all efforts to control the bleeding, you are not successful. His pulse is now 52 and very weak. His respirations are 6 and labored. Blood pressure is 78/30. This shock state represents
    (A) decompensated shock.
    (B) compensated shock.
    (C) irreversible shock.
    (D) pneumatic shock.

Questions 96–99 are based on the following scenario:

Your ambulance is assigned to stand by at a building fire. The outside temperature is 103°F and the firefighters are wearing full protective clothing. Approximately 30 minutes into the incident, a firefighter has collapsed and you are assigned to care for him.

96. The patient is a 36-year-old male in good physical condition. He appears anxious and complains of nausea and a headache. He is sweating profusely with cool clammy skin. BP is 116/48, radial pulse is 150 and weak, respirations are 36 and shallow, temperature is 101.2°F. This patient's signs/symptoms indicate:
    (A) heatstroke.
    (B) heat exhaustion.
    (C) heat stress.
    (D) heat fatigue.

97. Treatment for this patient should include all of the following EXCEPT
    (A) removing clothing.
    (B) establishing an IV of normal saline.
    (C) placing the patient in air conditioning.
    (D) administering salt tablets.

98. The patient has developed severe apprehension. Reassessment reveals a BP of 78/0, pulse 154, respirations 36 and shallow. You are unable to take another temperature because he is not cooperating. His skin is extremely hot to touch and he has stopped sweating. On-line medical control has requested that you start rapid active cooling. This can be achieved by
    (A) covering the patient in a sheet that has been soaked in tepid water.
    (B) placing several ice packs under the arms, in the groin, and on the head.
    (C) cold water immersion.
    (D) covering the patient in a sheet that has been soaked in ice water.

99. Which statement is false regarding overcooling of a heatstroke patient?
    (A) It may cause a reflex hypothermia.
    (B) Shivering may result, which can lead to a rise in core temperature.
    (C) Body temperature must be lowered immediately with heatstroke and overcooling is not a concern.
    (D) 102°F should be used as a target temperature to prevent overcooling.

---

100. Which of the following is true regarding frostbite?
    (A) Superficial frostbite involves freezing of the epidermal and subcutaneous tissue.
    (B) Do not thaw frozen flesh if there is any possibility of refreezing.
    (C) Massage the frozen area lightly.
    (D) Do not elevate frozen extremities.

101. Confirmation of endotracheal tube placement should be evaluated
    (A) immediately after insertion.
    (B) each time the patient is moved.
    (C) by at least two methods.
    (D) All of the above.

102. Suctioning (application of negative pressure) should be activated
    (A) upon insertion of the suction catheter.
    (B) upon extraction of the suction catheter.
    (C) both upon insertion and extraction.
    (D) either upon insertion or extraction (it makes no difference).

103. In a pediatric patient, initial defibrillation should be performed at
    (A) 0.5 J/kg.
    (B) 4 J/kg.
    (C) 2 J/kg.
    (D) 100 J.

104. The SA node is located
    (A) high in the right atrium.
    (B) high in the left atrium.
    (C) in the septum.
    (D) high in the left ventricle.

105. You and your partner are overheard in the elevator discussing a patient's injuries from a motor vehicle crash. Your conversation included pertinent personal and medical information about the patient. A call was placed to your supervisor because
    (A) you failed to keep patient confidentiality.
    (B) you failed to discuss the appropriate medical care.
    (C) you failed to speak loudly enough.
    (D) you failed to recall the injuries correctly.

Questions 106 to 110 are based on the following scenario:

A 64-year-old male presents with increased dyspnea. He has a barrel chest, is thin, and pink in color. Clubbing of the fingers is present. Wheezes and rhonchi are present bilaterally in all lobes, and pursed-lip breathing is noted. Vital signs are: blood pressure 162/92, pulse 118 beats per minute, respiratory rate 22.

106. This patient's appearance suggests that he most likely is suffering from
    (A) pneumonia.
    (B) COPD.
    (C) asthma.
    (D) spontaneous pneumothorax.

107. The wheezes auscultated bilaterally indicate
    (A) a narrowing of the airways.
    (B) a partial obstruction by the tongue.
    (C) fluid in the smaller airways.
    (D) a pleural inflammation.

108. The rhonchi auscultated bilaterally indicate
    (A) a partial obstruction by the tongue.
    (B) fluid in the smaller airways.
    (C) excessive mucus in the larger airways.
    (D) a pleural friction rub.

109. The clubbing of the fingers is associated with
    (A) pulsus paradoxus.
    (B) respiratory disease.
    (C) an excess of red blood cells.
    (D) chronic dilation of the bronchioles.

110. The "pink" color of this patient's skin is a result of
    (A) an excess of circulating red blood cells.
    (B) high oxygen blood levels.
    (C) chronic dilation of the bronchioles.
    (D) wheezing.

111. While assessing a patient complaining of abdominal pain, you should first _____ then _____ the abdomen.
    (A) palpate/auscultate
    (B) inspect/percuss
    (C) inspect/ausculate
    (D) palpate/percuss

112. Your crew is dispatched to the home of an obese woman who has fallen. The general rules for lifting and moving this patient include all the following except
    (A) anticipating a lengthy time for backup units to arrive, so move this patient to the best of your ability.
    (B) positioning the load as close to your body as possible.
    (C) bending your knees, letting the large muscles of the legs do the work of lifting.
    (D) taking your time; do not hurry and maintain a wide base of support.

113. You are treating a patient with hyperventilation syndrome due to an anxiety attack. Which acid-base derangement will hyperventilation produce?
    (A) Respiratory acidosis
    (B) Metabolic acidosis
    (C) Respiratory alkalosis
    (D) Metabolic alkalosis

114. While enjoying an "off" day from work, you hear your neighbor screaming. You rush outside to see her pulling her four-year-old child from the swimming pool. The child is limp, blue, and not responsive to any stimulus. What should you do?
    (A) Perform the Heimlich maneuver in an attempt to expel water from the lungs.
    (B) Begin chest compressions.
    (C) Send the mother to call 911; open the airway and initiate rescue breathing.
    (D) Go to your car and get your AED and attach it as soon as possible.

115. You have administered _____ to an eight year old. Drowsiness, decreased mental status, muscle twitching, and seizures are side effects that may result from its administration.
    (A) Atropine
    (B) lidocaine
    (C) calcium chloride
    (D) adenosine

116. The term used to describe normal breath sounds heard over most of the chest wall is
    (A) bronchial.
    (B) adventitious.
    (C) vesicular.
    (D) bronchovesicular.

117. Which of the following medications is not indicated in the treatment of ventricular fibrillation?
    (A) Epinephrine
    (B) Adenosine
    (C) Lidocaine
    (D) Vasopressin

118. Parasympathetic stimulation of the heart causes:
    (A) a decreased heart rate.
    (B) an increased force of contraction.
    (C) dilation of the coronary arteries.
    (D) No effect at all.

119. You are performing rescue breathing. When you initially open the airway, how many initial breaths do you give?
    (A) 1
    (B) 2
    (C) 3
    (D) 4

120. Blind nasotracheal intubation
    (A) should be attempted only on an apneic patient.
    (B) is preferred over oral intubation.
    (C) should be attempted on a patient with spontaneous respirations.
    (D) is contraindicated when facial trauma is present.

121. The lungs are covered by a smooth, moist epithelial layer called the
    (A) visceral pleura.
    (B) parietal pleura.
    (C) visceral peritoneum.
    (D) parietal peritoneum.

122. You are delivering a child in a breech presentation. You have delivered the feet and chest. You note the chest of the child moving and suspect the child is attempting to breathe. You should
    (A) guide the body toward the floor to assist in delivering the head.
    (B) gently pull on the torso to allow the head to be delivered.
    (C) insert two fingers in the vagina to form an airway around the infant's nose and mouth.
    (D) instruct the mother to pant with her next contraction.

123. The compression-ventilation ratio for a newborn in cardiac arrest is
    (A) 5:1.
    (B) 3:1.
    (C) 15:2.
    (D) 5:2.

124. The type of ambulance that is a standard van with forward control integral cab body is a
    (A) Type I ambulance.
    (B) Type II ambulance.
    (C) Type III ambulance.
    (D) medium-duty ambulance.

125. All of the following medications can be administered via endotracheal route EXCEPT
    (A) lidocaine, atropine.
    (B) epinephrine, amiodarone.
    (C) oxygen, epinephrine.
    (D) Narcan, lidocaine.

Questions 126–129 are based on the following scenario:

A 42-year-old male is the victim of a house fire. He has reddened and blistered areas over most of his anterior chest, abdomen, and anterior surfaces of both arms.

126. Using the rule of nines, estimate what percent of BSA he has burned.
  (A) 45%
  (B) 36%
  (C) 22.5%
  (D) 27%

127. Initial treatment for this burn patient would include which of the following?
  (A) Debridement of the blistered skin and antibiotic ointment
  (B) Covering the burn area with gauze and cooling with iced saline
  (C) Administering morphine and then cleaning the burn area with an iodine solution
  (D) Covering the burn area with dry bulky dressings and keeping the patient warm

128. Medical control has asked that you initiate fluid therapy enroute to the hospital. Which of the following statements regarding fluid resuscitation for this burn patient is true?
  (A) The Parkland Formula directs the fluid amount needed for the burn patient. It can be initiated only after a Foley catheter is in place so that accurate intake and output measurements can be monitored.
  (B) Two large-bore catheters are introduced and a bolus of 0.5 ml of normal saline (NS) for every kilogram of the patient's weight multiplied by the percentage of BSA is initiated.
  (C) Two large-bore IVs running NS at a wide open rate for the length of the transport. Do not infuse more than 8,500 mls.
  (D) An IV is not attainable due to the location of the burns.

129. While transporting your burn patient to the burn center, you notice that his voice now sounds hoarse and he is making a "crowing" sound on inspiration. What is the most likely cause?
  (A) Screaming for help while standing inside the burning house
  (B) Fluid overload precipitating pulmonary edema
  (C) Allergic reaction to the by-products of the burning materials
  (D) Anxiety reaction to the traumatic event of being burned

---

130. It is important to compare central and peripheral pulses in the pediatric patient to determine
  (A) the presence of shock.
  (B) skin color.
  (C) mental status.
  (D) airway patency.

131. Cuffed endotracheal tubes are usually not indicated in children under what age?
    (A) Five
    (B) Eight
    (C) Three
    (D) Ten

132. You respond to the home of a 17-year-old male because his father was unable to wake him. The father states that his son was at a party last night and has a history of recreational drug use. He is unconscious and unresponsive. BP is not obtainable, pulse 42 and weak, and respirations of 4. You have orally intubated the patient. Auscultation of lung sounds post intubation reveal breath sounds heard over the right chest and an absence of breath sounds over the left chest. Your next action would be to
    (A) hyperventilate the patient and reassess lung sounds.
    (B) deflate the endotracheal tube cuff, withdraw the tube 2 cm, reinflate the cuff, and reevaluate breath sounds.
    (C) deflate the endotracheal tube cuff, remove the endotracheal tube, and hyperventilate the patient with a bag-valve device.
    (D) observe the patient and monitor his SpO_2 reading for several minutes.

133. The resistance against which the heart must pump is
    (A) afterload.
    (B) blood pressure.
    (C) preload.
    (D) cardiac output.

134. The recommended dose of vasopressin in v fib or pulseless v tach is
    (A) 17 mg/min IV infusion.
    (B) 2–4 mg/min IV infusion.
    (C) 40 units IV repeated once in five minutes.
    (D) 40 units IV in a single dose.

135. A 53-year-old female who is being treated for chronic pain with morphine sulfate continues to complain of pain despite taking her medications as prescribed. The patient is most likely experiencing what response to this medication?
    (A) An allergic reaction
    (B) Tolerance
    (C) Dependence
    (D) Antagonism

136. You are assessing a patient involved in a two-car MVC with severe blunt trauma to the abdomen. You suspect internal hemorrhage. The patient's BP is 100/52 with a pulse rate of 130. You know the elevation in the heart rate is the body's attempt to maintain
    (A) metabolism.
    (B) system integration.
    (C) homeostasis.
    (D) end-organ damage.

137. One reason the respiratory system of a geriatric patient becomes less effective is that
    (A) the muscles of the diaphragm weaken.
    (B) tidal volume increases.
    (C) there is decreased chest wall compliance.
    (D) the lungs become more compliant.

Questions 138–143 are based on the following scenario:

Elly, a 66-year-old female, is unable to get out of bed and her son has called EMS. She responds to verbal stimuli with clear speech, her smile is asymmetrical, she cannot move her left leg, and weakly moves her left arm. Her skin is warm but pale. Vital signs are: Blood pressure 162/88; pulse 110 beats per minute and irregular; respiratory rate is 22 per minute with lung sounds clear bilaterally. A blood glucose reading is 130 mg/dl. The cardiac monitor shows a very irregular, narrow complex tachycardia with no identifiable p waves.

138. Damage to what body system is affecting movement of the left side of her body?
    (A) Cardiovascular system
    (B) Central nervous system
    (C) Pulmonary system
    (D) Endocrine system

139. The patient's asymmetrical smile is most likely a direct result of
    (A) damage to cranial nerve VII.
    (B) injury to the medulla oblongata.
    (C) damage to cranial nerve III.
    (D) cardiac disease.

140. Why was it important to obtain a blood glucose reading on this patient?
    (A) Blood glucose readings can help determine if the patient is an alcoholic.
    (B) Dextrose 50% in water can often reverse the effects of stroke.
    (C) Diabetics are less prone to stroke than healthy individuals.
    (D) Hypoglycemia can mimic stroke.

141. Elly's cardiac rhythm is
    (A) first-degree AV block.
    (B) atrial fibrillation.
    (C) sinus tachycardia.
    (D) second-degree AV block.

142. This cardiac rhythm makes Elly more prone to the development of
    (A) diabetes.
    (B) emboli.
    (C) brain tumors.
    (D) cardiogenic shock.

143. Elly's son states that his mother was fine one hour ago when he talked to her on the telephone. This is important information because:
    (A) there is a six-hour window for treating occlusive strokes with thrombolytics.
    (B) it rules out a problem affecting her cerebral hemispheres.
    (C) it establishes a reference point for the onset of symptoms.
    (D) it clearly proves that Elly has an intracranial hemorrhage.

___

144. You have a patient with a long history of COPD who complains of worsening shortness of breath. He is on continuous 2 LPM of home oxygen. You are concerned that increasing the oxygen flow may eliminate the hypoxic drive to breathe because the hypoxic drive is regulated by
    (A) high PaO_2.
    (B) low PaO_2.
    (C) high oxygen saturation.
    (D) low oxygen saturation.

___

Questions 145 and 146 are based on the following scenario:

You are caring for a patient in ventricular tachycardia. He is lethargic, diaphoretic, pale, and has vomited once. His vital signs are: BP 74/P, pulse 184, respirations 14. You are assigned to manage the airway.

145. Initial management should include
    (A) high-flow oxygen by nonrebreather mask.
    (B) preparation for intubation.
    (C) bag-valve mask ventilations.
    (D) suctioning the airway for vomitus.

146. Your patient becomes unresponsive and apneic. Further airway management should include
    (A) providing ventilations through a nonrebreather mask.
    (B) bag-valve mask ventilation at 12 times per minute.
    (C) endotracheal intubation.
    (D) oral airway insertion and supplemental oxygen by nonrebreather mask.

___

147. Establishing the care and transport priorities for the pediatric patient can be determined by utilizing the "CUPS" assessment. "CUPS" stands for
    (A) critical, unstable, perfect, stable.
    (B) coma, unresponsive, potentially unstable, stable.
    (C) coma, unresponsive, potentially unstable, seizures.
    (D) critical, unstable, potentially unstable, stable.

148. Mixing 2 grams of lidocaine in 500 cc of solution will provide a mixture of
    (A) 1 mg/ml.
    (B) 2 mg/ml.
    (C) 3 mg/ml.
    (D) 4 mg/ml.

149. You encounter a patient with a P-R interval of 0.16, a QRS duration of 0.08, and a regular R-R Interval. This patient is in
    (A) atrial fibrillation.
    (B) sinus rhythm with first-degree heart block.
    (C) sinus rhythm.
    (D) supraventricular tachycardia.

150. You just administered Atropine 0.5 mg to a patient with a symptomatic bradycardia and multifocal PVCs. Suddenly your patient becomes unconscious and goes into ventricular fibrillation. Your next action is to
    (A) administer lidocaine 1.5 mg/kg.
    (B) administer another 0.5 mg of Atropine IVP.
    (C) cardiovert at 100 joules.
    (D) defibrillate at 200 joules.

151. If the amniotic sac has not ruptured and the baby's head emerges, you should
    (A) use a sterile scalpel to carefully open the sac and provide suction before the baby takes a breath.
    (B) delay further delivery and transport immediately for an emergency cesarean section.
    (C) use your fingers to pinch and puncture the sac, then push the sac away from the nose and mouth.
    (D) continue with the delivery, the sac will break on its own once the baby's head is delivered.

Questions 152–155 are based on the following scenario:

You are called to the scene of a 26-year-old female patient who is 27 weeks pregnant and in active labor. The patient states, "The baby is coming." You perform a visual examination of the perineum and notice a prolapsed cord.

152. You would immediately place the patient in which position?
    (A) Hips elevated as much as possible
    (B) Knee-chest position
    (C) Left lateral recumbent position
    (D) Both A and B are correct.

153. You would instruct the patient to
    (A) push with each contraction.
    (B) pant with each contraction.
    (C) bear down.
    (D) hold her breath.

154. Additional treatment would include
    (A) providing oxygen and preparing to assist the mother for a normal delivery.
    (B) with a gloved hand, attempting to push the cord back into the vagina, and transporting with lights and siren.
    (C) with a gloved hand, placing two fingers into the vagina to raise the fetus off the cord, providing oxygen, and transporting.
    (D) attempting to reposition the cord laterally by gently pulling on it.

155. Care for the prolapsed cord would include:
    (A) application of a sterile dressing.
    (B) attempting to reposition the cord.
    (C) doing nothing.
    (D) packing in ice to prevent it from drying.

156. You arrive on scene of a patient who has had steadily worsening chest pain for four hours. He has taken 12 nitroglycerin with no relief. The best description of this type of chest pain is
    (A) stable angina.
    (B) unstable angina.
    (C) Prinzmetal's angina.
    (D) vasospastic angina.

157. A 78-year-old male is alert and oriented to person, place, and time and complains of chest pain and difficulty breathing. You attach him to the ECG and notice a rhythm of 42 with corresponding pulse, a P-R interval of 0.20, and normal R-R intervals. Vitals are BP 76/42, respirations 42. The patient also states that he feels nauseated and dizzy. Treatment for this patient should include
    (A) Atropine 0.5 mg.
    (B) oxygen 3 LPM nasal cannula.
    (C) immediate transvenous pacing.
    (D) Isuprel 2–10 mcg/min.

Questions 158 and 159 are based on the following scenario:

A 5-year-old boy fell 10 feet from a jungle gym at school. Bystanders state that the child lost his balance and fell, striking his left leg on the bars and hitting his head on the ground. Your initial evaluation reveals a child who is lethargic and does not respond appropriately to commands. His respirations are shallow at a rate of 40 with a rapid and weak radial pulse.

158. What is your first priority?
    (A) Splinting the deformed left leg
    (B) Waiting for consent from the mother before giving definitive treatment
    (C) Application of c-collar and securing to backboard for immediate transport
    (D) Rapid c-spine control and airway assistance with BVM and high-flow O_2

159. Which of the following is one of the most important indicators of potential CNS injury?
    (A) Ipsilateral pupil dilatation
    (B) A history of loss of consciousness
    (C) Lethargy
    (D) An elevated heart rate

Questions 160 and 161 are based on the following scenario:

You arrive on scene of a 36-year-old male patient who has ingested 30 levothyroxine that belonged to his mother. You recognize this medication as a thyroid replacement hormone. The ingestion occurred 60 minutes ago.

160. The patient is delirious and sweating profusely. His skin temperature is extremely hot. You suspect
    (A) Grave's syndrome.
    (B) myxedema crises.
    (C) thyroid storm.
    (D) Addison's sign.

161. You attach the ECG monitor and observe a sinus tachycardia of 140 with a corresponding pulse rate. Treatment would include
    (A) expedited transport for definitive care.
    (B) adenocard 6 mg rapid IVP.
    (C) adenocard 12 mg rapid IVP.
    (D) verapamil 2.5 mg slow IVP.

---

162. You respond to a 20-year-old female complaining of dizziness and weakness. She is slow to respond to your questions but admits to taking several diet pills a day in an effort to quickly lose weight. Vitals are blood pressure 98/54, pulse 184, respirations 32, skin is pale and moist. ECG shows the following rhythm.

    Immediate treatment should include
    (A) reassuring the patient that when the medication wears off the symptoms will go away.
    (B) IV, oxygen, continuing to monitor the patient, and transport.
    (C) IV, oxygen, adenocard 6 mg rapid IV push.
    (D) immediate cardioversion with 100 joules.

163. You have been called to the home of a three-year-old child. You are told by the mother he is not eating well, "acting funny," and is not playful. You find a frail-looking small child who is lethargic on examination. Vital signs reveal a respiratory rate of 46 per minute; heart rate is 190 per minute; BP is not obtainable. The patient is given oxygen by nonrebreather mask at 15 LPM and you determine that an IV line is necessary. After three attempts at a peripheral line, you are not able to establish venous access. Of the choices below, select the most appropriate intervention.
    (A) Initiate an IO in the proximal femur and infuse a 20 cc/kg bolus of 5% D5W.
    (B) Initiate an IO in the distal humerus and infuse fluid at a KVO rate.
    (C) Initiate an IO in the proximal tibia and give a 20 cc/kg bolus of normal saline.
    (D) Initiate an IO in the distal radius and infuse fluid wide open to maintain blood pressure.

164. During transport of a child with epiglottitis, he becomes unresponsive and apneic. You are still able to palpate a weak pulse at a rate of 64 per minute. Your immediate action should be to
    (A) apply a nonrebreather mask with 10–15 liters per minute of oxygen.
    (B) insert an OPA and administer bag-valve mask ventilations.
    (C) position the child's head and provide bag-valve mask ventilation with 100% oxygen.
    (D) immediately intubate the child.

165. You respond to a shopping mall for a possible cardiac arrest. When you arrive, you find a male patient in his seventies in cardiac arrest. The mall security officers have an AED attached. The AED is in the process of delivering a shock. Your first response should be to
    (A) establish unresponsiveness.
    (B) open the airway and provide ventilations.
    (C) remove the AED and apply your own monitor.
    (D) allow the AED to deliver the initial shock.

Questions 166 and 167 are based on the following scenario:

You are called to the scene of a patient who was involved in an altercation at the local pool hall. You find one victim in the back alley anxious and screaming for your assistance. You notice immediately that he has clammy skin and a dusky appearance. He has a respiratory rate of 40 and shallow. He tells you that he has been hit multiple times in the chest, abdomen, and back with a pool stick by "two big guys." While assessing his chest you notice multiple contusions to the right side with diminished respirations on the right.

166. What would you suspect?
    (A) Cardiac tamponade
    (B) Hemothorax
    (C) Ruptured diaphragm
    (D) Pneumothorax

167. While enroute to the local trauma center with this patient, you notice that his level of consciousness has decreased and his color has not improved despite 100% O_2 by nonrebreather mask. He is becoming hypotensive and his pulse rate is 140. Respiratory rate remains at 40 and shallow. Ongoing assessment reveals distended neck veins and hyperresonant percussion on the right chest. Your next course of action would be
    (A) oropharyngeal intubation with RSI.
    (B) positive pressure ventilation with BVM.
    (C) needle decompression between the second and third intercostal space anterior chest.
    (D) to stabilize flail segment with a bulky dressing.

Questions 168 and 169 are based on the following scenario:

You are assessing a patient with acute right lower quadrant pain. You suspect acute appendicitis.

168. A common site of pain from appendicitis located one to two inches above the anterior iliac crest in a direct line with the umbilicus is known as
    (A) the volvulus point.
    (B) McBurney's point.
    (C) Murphy's sign.
    (D) Grey-Turner's sign.

169. The presence of rebound tenderness in this patient represents
    (A) peritoneal irritation.
    (B) guarding.
    (C) rupture.
    (D) strangulation.

Questions 170 and 171 are based on the following scenario:

You respond to a patient with shortness of breath. The patient said he was awakened from his sleep with shortness of breath. Assessment reveals vitals: BP 188/94, pulse 116, respiration 36, and a pulse oximeter reading of 88%. Lung sound assessment reveals crackles in the posterior bases.

170. You suspect this patient to be suffering from
    (A) a myocardial infarction.
    (B) angina.
    (C) congestive heart failure.
    (D) a respiratory disorder.

171. As you continue your assessment of this patient, he becomes lethargic. BP is now 198/102, pulse 136, respirations 48, with increased pulmonary congestion. Treatment should include
    (A) preparation for intubation.
    (B) preparation for immediate transcutaneous pacing.
    (C) adenocard 6 mg rapid IVP.
    (D) lidocaine 1.0 mg/kg IVP.

172. You have been called to treat a five-year-old child previously diagnosed with an upper respiratory infection. She now presents with increased work of breathing, fever, and increased cough. The child appears pale, is lying on the couch, and slow to respond. She has obvious nasal flaring with a respiratory rate of 8 per minute. Further history given by the mother reveals that the child has been drinking very little and not eating. In addition, the child has complained of her "tummy" hurting. From the information in the scenario, this child is most likely in
    (A) respiratory distress with impending respiratory failure.
    (B) no acute distress.
    (C) respiratory insufficiency easily corrected with oxygen.
    (D) cardiogenic shock.

Questions 173 to 175 are based on the following scenario:

Your patient rolled a farm tractor over a hill. He has a large puncture wound to his right neck, above the clavicle. It appears that the wound is from a tree branch. Moderate bleeding is present.

173. Care for the puncture wound would include
    (A) application of direct pressure with a bulky trauma dressing.
    (B) application of an occlusive dressing.
    (C) application of a sterile dressing.
    (D) needle decompression.

174. Which transport position would be appropriate for this patient?
    (A) Trendelenburg position
    (B) Left lateral recumbent
    (C) Right lateral recumbent
    (D) Prone

175. A major concern with this type of injury is
    (A) a rib fracture.
    (B) a clavicle fracture.
    (C) a flail chest.
    (D) edema.

Questions 176 and 177 are based on the following scenario:

EMS is called to the scene of a 72-year-old male with a history of cardiac disease. He is unconscious and unresponsive. BP is not obtainable, pulse 140 and weak, respirations 6. After placing him on the monitor, you note the following rhythm.

176. You interpret the rhythm as
    (A) supraventricular tachycardia.
    (B) ventricular tachycardia.
    (C) atrial fibrillation with a rapid ventricular response.
    (D) ventricular fibrillation.

177. Initial treatment of the patient should include:
    (A) synchronized cardioversion.
    (B) defibrillation.
    (C) transcutaneous pacing.
    (D) adenocard 6 mg IVP.

Questions 178–180 are based on the following scenario:

A 22-year-old male is found in an alley with multiple stab wounds to the extremities, abdomen, and chest. BP is 82/40, pulse 142 weak, respirations 10.

178. Your examination reveals distended neck veins, equal breath sounds, and a radial pulse that disappears during inspiration. You suspect:
    (A) a hemothorax.
    (B) a tension pneumothorax.
    (C) a sucking chest wound.
    (D) cardiac tamponade.

179. As you logroll the patient to place him on the long spine board, you inspect his back and discover another stab wound just below the right scapula. You observe blood bubbling out of the wound with each breath. You suspect
    (A) a massive hemothorax.
    (B) a tension pneumothorax.
    (C) an open pneumothorax.
    (D) a hematoma formation.

180. Priority care for this patient would include
    (A) IV fluids to stabilize vital signs.
    (B) closure of the chest wall with an occlusive dressing taped on three sides.
    (C) immediate chest decompression of the right chest.
    (D) rapid transport to a trauma center.

Answer Key

1. A	46. C	91. B	136. C
2. D	47. B	92. B	137. C
3. D	48. B	93. B	138. B
4. B	49. B	94. B	139. A
5. D	50. C	95. A	140. D
6. C	51. C	96. B	141. B
7. C	52. A	97. D	142. B
8. A	53. A	98. A	143. C
9. A	54. C	99. C	144. B
10. B	55. C	100. B	145. D
11. A	56. A	101. D	146. C
12. B	57. D	102. B	147. D
13. B	58. C	103. C	148. D
14. B	59. D	104. A	149. C
15. D	60. B	105. A	150. D
16. D	61. C	106. B	151. C
17. B	62. C	107. A	152. D
18. B	63. A	108. C	153. B
19. B	64. C	109. B	154. C
20. C	65. B	110. A	155. A
21. D	66. B	111. C	156. B
22. B	67. B	112. A	157. A
23. D	68. A	113. C	158. D
24. D	69. C	114. C	159. B
25. A	70. B	115. B	160. C
26. C	71. C	116. C	161. A
27. B	72. D	117. B	162. C
28. C	73. B	118. A	163. C
29. D	74. C	119. B	164. C
30. B	75. B	120. C	165. D
31. A	76. B	121. A	166. D
32. B	77. A	122. C	167. C
33. A	78. A	123. A	168. B
34. D	79. C	124. B	169. A
35. C	80. B	125. B	170. C
36. C	81. C	126. D	171. A
37. D	82. A	127. D	172. A
38. A	83. A	128. B	173. B
39. D	84. C	129. A	174. A
40. D	85. D	130. A	175. D
41. B	86. B	131. B	176. B
42. C	87. A	132. B	177. A
43. A	88. B	133. A	178. D
44. B	89. A	134. D	179. C
45. D	90. B	135. B	180. B

Answer Explanations

1. **(A)** Proper terminology helps to make communication clear, concise, and unambiguous.

2. **(D)** This patient can be treated and transported against his will under involuntary consent. Law enforcement personnel can direct transport and treatment of a patient who is a threat to himself or to others.

3. **(D)** The medical practice act is legislation that governs the practice of medicine to include rules governing the physician's ability to delegate authority to perform medical acts by the paramedic. This legislation varies from one state to another.

4. **(B)** Gastric distension usually occurs with bag-valve mask ventilations prior to intubation. A correctly placed endotracheal tube should not contribute to gastric distension.

5. **(D)** Clear lung sounds do not indicate the presence of a tension pneumothorax.

6. **(C)** The ratio is 15 compressions to 2 ventilations.

7. **(C)** Stimulation of the vagus nerve can occur in many ways. When stimulated, a decrease in heart rate may be observed.

8. **(A)** The PR interval is the time elapsing between the beginning of the p wave and the beginning of the QRS complex. The normal duration of the PR interval is 0.12 to 0.20 seconds. The PR interval represents the time it takes for an electrical impulse to be transmitted from the atria to the ventricles.

9. **(A)** Ecchymosis in the periumbilical area is known as Cullen's sign. Grey-Turner's sign **(B)** is ecchymosis in the flank area. Both may indicate intraabdominal hemorrhage. Mallory-Weiss sign **(D)** is associated with an esophageal tear or laceration that results from excessive vomiting. Peritonitis, **(C)**, is an inflammation of the peritoneum.

10. **(B)** The presence of Cullen's sign may indicate intraabdominal hemorrhage.

11. **(A)** Neurogenic or distributive shock is recognized by hypotension, bradycardia, and a normal initial appearance. **(C)** is something to consider but should not be part of your initial impression. **(B)** is absolutely incorrect. **(D)** is incorrect because this is distributive shock NOT mechanical shock.

12. **(B)** You would suspect injury at the thoracic level between T4 and T10. Memorization of all of the dermatomes is difficult and really not necessary. However, you should have a general knowledge of associated injuries to the spinal nerve plexuses.

13. **(B)** The objective of prehospital fluid resuscitation is to stabilize vital signs until the patient arrives at the hospital. This patient requires close observation since neurogenic shock does not allow the body's normal compensatory mechanisms to work.

14. **(B)** IO infusions will generally improve the patient's condition or improve his or her vascular volume thereby increasing the BP and cardiac output. Osteomyelitis **(A)** can occur if the needle is left in place for longer than 24 hours; fractures **(C)** can occur when the extremity is not well stabilized or an attempt was made at an improper site where the bone is weaker; compartment syndrome **(D)** occurs when extravasation is not detected.

15. **(D)** A 25% dextrose solution is recommended for pediatric patients because it is less viscous than 50% dextrose. This will allow easier administration through a smaller-diameter IV catheter and reduce the occurrence of sclerosis to small peripheral veins.

16. **(D)** A nonrebreather mask can deliver an oxygen concentration of 90–100% at a flow rate of 15 LPM.

17. **(B)** Pulsus paradoxus is defined as a drop in systolic blood pressure of 10 mmHg or more, or the absence of a radial pulse during inspiration.

18. **(B)** Knee deep. Walking in fast-moving water places the person at risk of having an extremity pinned and then being pulled under by the current.

19. **(B)** A side effect of amiodarone administration is vasodilation and hypotension. This is mainly the reason amiodarone is to be administered slow IV. Rapid IV administration of amiodarone may produce profound hypotension.

20. **(C)** This is a basic life support question. If you missed this question, do yourself a favor and review infant, child, and adult CPR prior to taking your certification test.

21. **(D)** Meningitis signs and symptoms include a severe headache, vomiting, fever, and chills of sudden onset. The patient may have a petechial rash and usually has muscle rigidity.

22. **(B)** Lasix is indicated for the treatment of acute pulmonary edema. **(A)** and **(C)** are incorrect because the dose is wrong. **(D)** is not included.

23. **(D)** SIDS is the leading cause of death in American infants under one year of age. The technical definition is: the sudden death of an apparently healthy infant that remains unexplained by history and through autopsy.

24. **(D)** Black. The designation of this patient would be black due to the absence of signs of life and injuries that were possibly incompatible with life. The morgue area should be a triage area away from other treatment areas.

25. **(A)** Green. This patient can be triaged to the green treatment area. The green treatment area is the area where patients require little or no care in preparation for transport.

26. **(C)** Red. This patient has critical injuries that require immediate attention. The red treatment area has the equipment and skilled providers to best care for, stabilize, and transport this patient.

27. **(B)** His history of alcoholism and presentation should lead you to suspect severe pancreatitis. Eighty percent of all cases of pancreatitis are associated with alcoholism.

28. **(C)** His BP of 86/42 and pulse of 138 lead you to believe a shock state is present. His temperature of 104.2°F may indicate sepsis. Severe pancreatitis is associated with septic shock, and when present it has a high mortality rate. **(A)** is incorrect because this scenario did not give you enough information to conclude that excessive vomiting caused hypovolemia. **(B)** is incorrect because the vital signs indicate shock, NOT a normal response to infection.

29. **(D)** Fundamentals of ECG interpretation tell us that the normal duration of a QRS complex is 0.08 to 0.12 seconds.

30. **(B)** The intrinsic firing rate of the AV node is 40–60 beats per minute. The normal pacemaker of the heart is the sinoatrial node with a normal firing rate of 60–100 beats per minute. The third pacemaker of the heart is the Purkinje fibers in the ventricles with a firing rate of 20–40 beats per minute. The internodal pathways do not have pacemaker capabilities.

31. **(A)** The backboard must be tilted on its left side 10–15 degrees to prevent supine hypotension syndrome. Tilting the board will allow the uterus to displace to the left and prevent compression of the inferior vena cava.

32. **(B)** Pediatric administration of lorazepam is 0.05–0.1 mg/kg with repeated doses of 0.05–0.1 mg/kg for persistent seizures.

33. **(A)** CO_2 is a very potent vasodilator. When a patient is hyperventilated, CO_2 is removed and the vessels will become constricted. This vasoconstriction leads to decreased cerebral pressure by decreasing cerebral blood flow.

34. **(D)** A perfect GCS score is 15. A score between 9 and 12 indicates moderate injury while a score of 8 or below represents severe head injury.

35. **(C)** This patient may have ingested 50,000 mg of acetaminophen. A dose of 150 mg/kg of acetaminophen is considered toxic. Unless this patient weighed approximately 334 kg (734 pounds) this is likely to be a toxic dose. Severe acetaminophen toxicity will often result in death within three to six days due to acute liver failure.

36. **(C)** Side effects of Valium or benzodiazepine ingestion include hypotension, respiratory depression, drowsiness, headache, blurred vision, nausea, and vomiting. Tachycardia is a compensatory mechanism of the body in response to the hypotension.

37. **(D)** Narcan is primarily used for complete or partial reversal of opiates. Valium is a benzodiazepine; therefore, Narcan will not reverse its effects. Romazicon is used to reverse effects of benzodiazepines. The administration of Narcan to this patient would not be unreasonable since it is unclear if the patient ingested opiates. A normal dose range of Narcan is 1–2 mg.

38. **(A)** All incident times are to be recorded accurately for legal purposes including; time of call, time of dispatch, time of arrival, time of medication administration, etc.

39. **(D)** An advantage of cellular telephones include promoting a less formal, shorter discussion of EMS events. Disadvantages include lost or broken signals due to geographical area or cell sites.

40. **(D)** Bacteria, viruses, and fungi are all examples of infectious agents that have the potential of causing an infection.

41. **(B)** A nasal cannula will deliver 40% of oxygen at a flow rate of 6 LPM in optimal conditions.

42. **(C)** Look, listen, and feel airflow through the victim's nose or mouth.

43. **(A)** Respiration is defined as the exchange of gases between a living organism and its environment.

44. **(B)** Management of the airway and c-spine are always a priority before other treatments.

45. **(D)** As part of the normal physiologic changes with aging, a decrease occurs in brain weight and size. By the age of 80, the brain loses approximately 3.5 ounces in weight.

46. **(C)** Fluid resuscitation needs to be carefully administered due to the decreased response of the cardiovascular system with age. Reduced circulation, loss of circulatory defense responses, coupled with increased presence of ventricular dysfunction, produce a significant challenge in managing shock in the elderly.

47. **(B)** Positive pressure ventilation of the patient with a flail chest reverses the mechanism that causes the paradoxical chest wall movement, restores tidal volume, and reduces pain of chest wall movement.

48. **(B)** Osteoporosis is common in the geriatric population. This disease process makes bones much more susceptible to hip and other fractures. In severe cases, a simple action such as sneezing may result in a fracture.

49. **(B)** An ectopic pregnancy should be suspected when abdominal pain is present in women of childbearing age who are sexually active. An ectopic pregnancy can be difficult to distinguish from other conditions. The classic triad of symptoms includes abdominal pain, vaginal bleeding, and amenorrhea. Other symptoms include referred pain to the shoulder, nausea, vomiting, or syncope. Signs of shock may be present if the ectopic ruptures.

50. **(C)** It is important to check for pulses, motor, and sensory functions distal to any injury in an extremity. Assessment and documentation of the neurovascular status are required before and after splinting.

51. **(C)** If the endotracheal tube has been placed in the esophagus, inflating the cuff on the endotracheal tube will hold the esophagus open and allow the bulb syringe to inflate. It is important to *not* inflate the endotracheal tube cuff prior to using any bulb syringe device.

52. **(A)** Of the choices listed, nitroglycerin is the best answer since it is indicated for the treatment of chest pain. A fluid bolus **(B)** is not indicated since the patient is not hypotensive and already has evidence of pulmonary congestion (crackles). Atropine **(C)** may be needed if the patient develops unstable signs/symptoms.

53. **(A)** Atropine is indicated for this patient since it appears she is deteriorating (the BP has dropped and there is increased pulmonary congestion). At this point, the application of pacing pads to the patient would not be unreasonable in preparation for the possibility of future deterioration of the patient.

54. **(C)** Immediate transcutaneous pacing is required for a hemodynamically unstable (altered LOC, chest pain, dyspnea, hypotension) bradycardic rhythm.

55. **(C)** If central cyanosis is present, or you are unsure about the adequacy of ventilation, the administration of supplemental oxygen is necessary. Never deprive a newborn of oxygen for fear of oxygen toxicity.

56. **(A)** Dopamine is a vasopressor primarily used by EMS to improve cardiac output in cardiogenic shock. A side effect of Dopamine administration is an increased oxygen demand and workload on the heart. Therefore, Dopamine must be used with caution when cardiac ischemia is suspected.

57. **(D)** Rhonchi are abnormal lung sounds heard on auscultation of airway that is obstructed by thick secretions.

58. **(C)** Nasal flaring, elevated respiratory rate, grunting, and head bobbing all indicate respiratory distress. The development of poor muscle tone indicates the patient is tiring and is an ominous sign of respiratory failure.

59. **(D)** The pediatric dose of lidocaine is 1 mg/kg bolus given IV/IO in cardiac arrest with a presenting rhythm of ventricular fibrillation or pulseless ventricular tachycardia.

60. **(B)** Ms. Marsha is experiencing a severe allergic (anaphylactic) reaction as evidenced by chest tightness, dyspnea, and inability to talk in complete sentences within five minutes of exposure.

61. **(C)** Because this patient is demonstrating pending cardiovascular and respiratory collapse, the administration of intravenous epinephrine is indicated. The correct dose range is 3 to 5 ml of 1:10,000 solution IV.

62. **(C)** The normal dose range of Benadryl is 25 to 50 mg. While there is no doubt this patient is in critical condition, the on-line medical control order to administer such a large dose of Benadryl should be questioned.

63. **(A)** Isolation of the HIV patient is an inappropriate action. Care includes being supportive, using appropriate BSI based on the task being performed, effective handwashing, disinfection of equipment, and care in use of equipment, especially sharps.

64. **(C)** Code of conduct. The four elements of a negligence claim include: the duty to act, breach of duty, actual damages, and proximate cause.

65. **(B)** "Simple." START stands for simple triage and rapid transport. This system focuses on four easily identifiable findings: 1) ability to walk, 2) respiratory effort, 3) pulses/perfusion, 4) neurological status.

66. **(B)** The accuracy and completeness of the patient care report may have a significant impact on ongoing care and treatment of the patient.

67. **(B)** Respiratory acidosis is caused by excess carbon dioxide retention.

68. **(A)** This ECG demonstrates a sinus rhythm with PACs.

69. **(C)** The initial dose of adenosine is 6 mg. Because the half-life of adenosine is so short, all doses should be administered rapid IV push, immediately followed by a 20 cc bolus of fluid.

70. **(B)** Immediate defibrillation is required upon the diagnosis of ventricular fibrillation. Management of the airway is important, but the airway should be maintained by basic methods until defibrillation is performed. Endotracheal intubation may be attempted after defibrillation. Administration of medications is secondary treatment to defibrillation.

71. **(C)** Schedule 1 drugs include heroin, LSD, and mescaline. Schedule 1 drugs pose a high abuse potential and may lead to severe dependence.

72. **(D)** Epinephrine is the drug of choice for symptomatic bradycardia in the pediatric patient. Atropine is effective in the *adult* bradycardic patient since bradycardia is often a result of parasympathetic stimulation; lidocaine is contraindicated in bradycardia.

73. **(B)** The result of violent shaking in a baby less than 24 months old may include damage to nerve tissues deep within the brain and torn veins between the brain and the skull, which can cause severe bleeding.

74. **(C)** The airway diameter in children is smaller than an adult airway; the larynx is more anterior making visualization difficult; the tongue is proportionally larger to the jaw.

75. **(B)** Biot's respiratory pattern is characterized by an irregular pattern, rate, and volume with intermittent periods of apnea. This pattern is seen in patients with increased intracranial pressure.

76. **(B)** The home-heating device in the bedroom, her signs and symptoms, and the fact that her sister is not sick should lead you to suspect carbon monoxide poisoning.

77. **(A)** Because carbon monoxide binds readily with the hemoglobin molecule, the pulse oximetry reading can read normal even though the patient may be hypoxic.

78. **(A)** Providing supplemental oxygen to a patient suffering from carbon monoxide poisoning is essential.

79. **(C)** The normal arterial pH range in the human body is: 7.35–7.45.

80. **(B)** Management of cardiogenic shock may include the administration of IV Dopamine. Dopamine is a vasopressor that increases cardiac output. You would not want to administer morphine or nitroglycerin as they will further lower the blood pressure. An IV at 500 cc/hr is not warranted because administering additional IV fluid to the patient will worsen the condition.

81. **(C)** 0.04 seconds are measured in each small square on the ECG graph paper. Each large block is 0.20 seconds.

82. **(A)** Medical terminology is an integral part of good documentation on a PCR.

83. **(A)** A basement is not an oxygen-deficient environment. Oxygen-deficient/confined spaces include: storage tanks, grain bins or silos, wells, manholes, and underground vaults.

84. **(C)** TCA overdose produces a prolonged QT interval along with widening of the QRS complex. Tall, peaked t waves are most commonly associated with hyperkalemia.

85. **(D)** Common signs and symptoms of preeclampsia include headache, dizziness, confusion, blurred vision, nausea, vomiting, proteinuria, hypertension, and edema.

86. **(B)** A patient with a pulse oximeter reading of 86% with no significant past medical history of pulmonary disorders is considered hypoxic.

87. **(A)** Neck pain, jaw pain, and left arm pain are considered a classic presentation of myocardial ischemia and *not* atypical.

88. **(B)** Milliamps should be increased until mechanical capture is obtained.

89. **(A)** This rhythm indicates a paced rhythm with 1:1 capture. The patient should receive oxygen, IV, monitor, and continued observation. Neither lidocaine nor cardioversion are indicated for this rhythm and nitroglycerin and aspirin are not indicated for the present complaints.

90. **(B)** Recognize the syndrome of fever and petechia as a medical emergency. Inflammation of the meninges will cause the fontanelle to bulge and appear full. Meningitis should be suspected in this patient.

91. **(B)** Durable power of attorney for health care or health care proxy, once signed and witnessed, are effective until the patient revokes them.

92. **(B)** Stabilizing the machinery serves two purposes. First, it assures your safety, and second it will prevent additional injury to the patient. If you choose "control bleeding" **(A)** for your answer, this is important but it does not supersede *your* safety.

93. **(B)** This patient is in compensated shock. His elevated pulse rate (142) and evidence of vasoconstriction (pale moist skin) is able to maintain his blood pressure despite continued blood loss.

94. **(B)** If bleeding still persists after direct pressure and elevation, the next step is to find an arterial pulse point proximal to the wound and apply firm pressure.

95. **(A)** Decompensated shock is when the body can no longer respond to the continued blood loss. This is evident in the scenario by a decreased pulse rate, respirations, and blood pressure.

96. **(B)** Profuse sweating with cool and clammy skin, tachycardia, rapid shallow respiration, and a body temperature over 100°F indicates heat exhaustion.

97. **(D)** Treatment for heat exhaustion includes removal of clothing, removal of the patient from the hot environment, establishing an IV of normal saline, and oral hydration if the patient is able to take fluids. The administration of salt tablets is *not* indicated because they are not readily absorbed through the stomach and can lead to hypernatremia.

98. **(A)** This patient has progressed from heat exhaustion to heatstroke as indicated by severe apprehension, hypotension, hot skin, and the cessation of sweating. Treatment for heatstroke includes removal of clothing, removal of the patient from the hot environment, establishing large-bore IVs of normal saline to run wide open, and rapid active cooling. One method of rapid active cooling is to cover the patient in a sheet that has been soaked in tepid water. Using ice or cold water may cause a reflex hypothermia and cause the patient to shiver, which will raise the body temperature again.

99. **(C)** This choice is false because overcooling of a heatstroke patient will produce a reflex hypothermia and cause the patient to shiver, which will raise the body temperature again. All of the other statements are true regarding overcooling of a heatstroke patient.

100. **(B)** A golden rule for the treatment of frozen flesh is to *never* thaw it, if there is any possibility of refreezing. **(A)** is incorrect because deep frostbite involves freezing of the epidermal and subcutaneous tissue. **(C)** is incorrect because massaging frozen flesh may further damage the tissue, **(D)** is incorrect because you would elevate a frozen extremity.

101. **(D)** Current recommendations for confirmation of endotracheal tube placement should be evaluated immediately after insertion, each time the patient is moved, and by at least two methods.

102. **(B)** Prolonged suctioning has been found to cause hypoxia; therefore, suctioning should be limited to extraction only.

103. **(C)** 2 joules/kg is the recommended energy setting when defibrillation is necessary. Repeat defibrillation is recommended at 4 joules/kg.

104. **(A)** The SA node is located high in the right atrium.

105. **(A)** This was a breach of confidentiality. Any medical or personal information about a patient should not be discussed in public or released without the patient's consent.

106. **(B)** A barrel chest, clubbing of the fingers, and dyspnea are all classic signs of COPD.

107. **(A)** Wheezes indicate narrowing of the airways. Edema and bronchoconstriction are examples of problems that can narrow the airway.

108. **(C)** Rhonchi are rattling sounds with a low pitch and "snoring quality" that is usually associated with excessive mucus or other material in the larger airways.

109. **(B)** Clubbing is a deformity produced by the growth of soft tissue about the fingers or toes. It is associated with chronic cardiac or respiratory disease.

110. **(A)** As part of the body's own compensatory mechanism, a chronic state of low blood oxygen levels will cause an increased production of red blood cells (polycythemia) that give the patient's skin a pink color.

111. **(C)** Inspection is the visual assessment of the patient. Inspection can reveal many important aspects of the patient. Auscultation of abdominal sounds should precede palpation and percussion.

112. **(A)** Proper lifting techniques should be utilized during all patient encounters. Ask for assistance if needed; do not jeopardize the rescuer's or patient's safety.

113. **(C)** Respiratory alkalosis results from an increase in respirations and an excessive elimination of CO_2.

114. **(C)** The lone rescuer should initially provide rescue breathing to the *child* while someone is sent to call 911. AEDs are not currently recommended for infants and children under 25 kg or less than 8 years old. This is basic life support material you must be familiar with before taking your certification exam.

115. **(B)** Lidocaine has central nervous system properties that cause drowsiness, decreased mental status, muscle twitching, and possibility of seizures.

116. **(C)** Vesicular breath sounds are defined as normal sounds heard over most of the chest wall.

117. **(B)** Adenosine is not indicated in the treatment of ventricular fibrillation. Adenosine is useful in the treatment of narrow complex tachycardias. Epinephrine, lidocaine, and vasopressin all have indications in the treatment of ventricular fibrillation.

118. **(A)** The parasympathetic nervous system is a division of the autonomic nervous system that is responsible for controlling vegetative functions. When stimulated, a decreased heart rate is one possible response of the body.

119. **(B)** Two breaths are given.

120. **(C)** Blind nasotracheal intubation requires the patient to have spontaneous respirations because the endotracheal tube is inserted as the patient inhales.

121. **(A)** The lungs are covered by a smooth, moist epithelial layer called the visceral pleura.

122. **(C)** If the infant starts to breathe with its face pressed against the vaginal wall, it is necessary to insert two fingers in the vagina to form an airway around the infant's nose and mouth.

123. **(A)** The ratio is five compressions to one ventilation. This is basic life support material you must be familiar with before taking your certification exam.

124. **(B)** Type II is a standard van-type ambulance. Type I ambulance **(A)** is the design of a conventional truck cab chassis with a modular ambulance body. Type III **(C)** is a specialty van with the larger cab body ambulance. Medium-duty ambulance **(D)** is a larger vehicle designed to handle heavier loads.

125. **(B)** Amiodarone has *not* been approved to be administered via the endotracheal route.

126. **(D)** 27%—chest = 9%, abdomen = 9%, anterior surface of both arms = 9%.

127. **(D)** Manage the burns by covering them with a dry bulky dressing. A dressing reduces air movement past sensitive partial thickness burns, thus reducing pain. Damaged skin loses temperature regulation capacity so it is important to keep the patient covered, even if the environment is not cold. **(B)** is incorrect because the use of ice in any form can worsen the injury because it causes vasoconstriction and reduces blood flow to the already damaged area. **(A)** and **(C)** are incorrect because debridement or cleaning a burn with iodine is not indicated.

128. **(B)** Current fluid resuscitation recommends that two large bore catheters be introduced. When EMS transport time is less than one hour, a bolus of 0.5 ml of normal saline (NS) for every kilogram of the patient's weight multiplied by the percentage of BSA should be initiated.

129. **(A)** Risk factors for inhalation injuries associated with burns include standing in the burn environment (hot gases rise), screaming or yelling in the hot environment (the open glottis allows toxic gases to enter the lower airway), and being trapped in a closed burn environment.

130. **(A)** The presence or absence of shock may be indicated by a difference between the central and peripheral pulses. Pulse differences or deficit may be a sign of poor peripheral perfusion.

131. **(B)** Cuffed endotracheal tubes are not indicated for children under the age of eight. In a child less than eight, the normal anatomic narrowing at the level of the cricoid cartilage provides a "functional cuff," and eliminates the need for a cuffed tracheal tube under most circumstances.

132. **(B)** This patient was most likely intubated in the right mainstem bronchus. Deflating the endotracheal tube cuff, withdrawing the tube slightly, reinflating the cuff, and reevaluating breath sounds is the proper procedure when a right mainstem bronchus intubation is suspected.

133. **(A)** Afterload is defined as the resistance against which the heart must pump. Blood pressure **(B)** is defined as pressure that is exerted on the walls of arteries. Preload **(C)** is defined as the pressure within the ventricles at the end of diastole. Cardiac output **(D)** is defined as the volume of blood ejected from the left ventricle into the arterial system each minute.

134. **(D)** A single dose of 40 units IV is the recommended dose of vasopressin.

135. **(B)** Tolerance is a decreased response to the same amount of a drug after taking the drug over a period of time.

136. **(C)** Homeostasis is the natural tendency of the body to maintain a steady state of equilibrium within the body's internal environment.

137. **(C)** There is no escaping the fact that the body becomes less efficient with age. Decreased chest wall compliance, loss of lung elasticity, air trapping, decreased diffusion of gases, and hypertrophy of the respiratory muscles can all contribute to a less effective respiratory system in a geriatric patient.

138. **(B)** An asymmetrical smile in conjunction with the inability to move her left leg and weakness of the left arm indicate injury to her central nervous system (CNS).

139. **(A)** A patient's ability to smile, frown, lift eyebrows, and wrinkle the forehead is controlled by cranial nerve VII.

140. **(D)** Patients who are hypoglycemic can exhibit signs and symptoms similar to those of a stroke.

141. **(B)** Atrial fibrillation is an irregular, narrow complex rhythm with nondiscernible p waves.

142. **(B)** As the atria fibrillate, they also dilate. This allows for blood to stagnate in the atria and can lead to clot formation.

143. **(C)** Studies suggest that there is a three-hour window between the time of onset of symptoms and time of thrombolytic intervention for treatment to be effective. Establishing a reference point for the onset of symptoms is critical.

144. **(B)** Hypoxic drive to breathe is common in patients with COPD or other degenerative respiratory disorders. Hypoxic drive is regulated by a low PaO_2 (partial pressure of oxygen). Delivering an increased concentration of oxygen may increase the PaO_2 and therefore eliminate the drive to breathe. Note: Do not withhold oxygen from a patient who needs it. If you are concerned about eliminating a patient's hypoxic drive, be prepared to manage the airway.

145. **(D)** Remember the basics! You must first open the airway and suction it before any other airway management.

146. **(C)** Endotracheal intubation is the only choice that is correct. **(A)** is incorrect because you do not ventilate through a nonrebreather mask. **(B)** is incorrect because the ventilation rate is too slow. **(D)** is incorrect because a patient must be breathing to receive oxygen through a nonrebreather mask.

147. **(D)** After completing the initial assessment and providing appropriate treatment for life-threatening emergencies, the "CUPS" assessment can help determine the severity of the patient's condition: "CUPS" stands for: Critical, Unstable, Potentially unstable, Stable.

148. **(D)** This is a simple math for medication administration question. If you missed this question, a review of math is strongly recommended prior to taking your examination.

149. **(C)** Don't overlook the obvious. This question displays the normal values of sinus rhythm.

150. **(D)** Immediate defibrillation is indicated for the treatment of ventricular fibrillation.

151. **(C)** If the amniotic sac is present around the baby's head, use your fingers to pinch the sac and then push it away from the nose and mouth. Using a scalpel or scissors is not recommended.

152. **(D)** Position the mother with the hips elevated as much as possible or in the knee-chest position in an attempt to relieve pressure on the cord.

153. **(B)** You would instruct the patient to pant with each contraction to prevent bearing down and applying pressure on the cord.

154. **(C)** With a gloved hand, place two fingers into the vagina to elevate the presenting part to relieve pressure on the cord. Provide oxygen and rapid transport to a hospital that can perform a cesarean delivery.

155. **(A)** Applying a sterile dressing to the exposed cord will minimize temperature change. If the cord is exposed to room temperature, the temperature of blood flowing to the infant will decrease. This can cause hypothermia. Additionally, a temperature change of the blood may cause the umbilical vessels to spasm resulting in decreased blood flow to the infant.

156. **(B)** Four hours of chest pain with no relief after 12 nitroglycerin is best classified as unstable angina. Stable angina **(A)** is somewhat predictable in onset, severity, character, and response to therapy. Prinzmetal's (or vasospastic angina) **(C and D)** is angina caused by decreased blood flow due to spasm of a vessel.

157. **(A)** The only correct choice is Atropine. Atropine is indicated since the patient presents with chest pain, difficulty breathing, heart rate 42, and BP 76/42. These are considered serious signs and symptoms. A transvenous pacemaker **(C)** is not utilized in EMS. Having a transcutaneous pacemaker available may be useful if the medication is ineffective, an altered LOC is observed, or the patient deteriorates. **(B)** is incorrect because the patient needs high-flow oxygen. **(D)** is incorrect because the dose is incorrect.

158. **(D)** Injured children can rapidly transition from a state of rapid and labored breathing to a state of total exhaustion resulting in respiratory arrest. Airway management is essential.

159. **(B)** A history of loss of consciousness is one of the most important prognostic indicators of potential CNS injury.

160. **(C)** Based on the history of ingestion of 30 thyroid replacement hormone pills and his presentation of an extreme metabolic state, you should suspect thyroid storm.

161. **(A)** Thyroid storm is a true medical emergency that requires expedited transport to definitive care. Drug therapy that will block the effects of the toxic level of thyroid hormone is required. If you chose adenocard or verapamil for your answer, this is incorrect because these medications are not indicated for sinus tachycardia and you simply do not have enough information in this scenario to warrant its use.

162. **(C)** IV, oxygen, and adenocard 6 mg rapid IV push are indicated for this patient. Cardioversion may be needed if the medication fails to convert the rhythm but is not immediately indicated since the patient lacks serious signs/symptoms of chest pain, dyspnea, or hypotension.

163. **(C)** Initiation of an IO line is appropriate after three unsuccessful attempts at a standard peripheral IV line. The best site for placement of the IO line is in proximal tibia. Because of the clinical presentation of the child in this scenario, a 20 cc/kg bolus of normal saline is appropriate.

164. **(C)** Any external manipulation of the epiglottis (i.e., intubation or OPA insertion) can cause complete airway obstruction in the child with epiglottitis. Carefully position the child's head and provide positive pressure ventilation with 100% oxygen.

165. **(D)** The best treatment for a shockable rhythm is defibrillation. If an AED is in the process of delivering a shock, allow it to do so. Removing the AED to apply your own equipment will likely cause a delay in this essential treatment.

166. **(D)** With a history of chest trauma, diminished breath sounds, agitation, increased respiratory rate, along with dusky color, you should suspect pneumothorax.

167. **(C)** The above symptoms are classic for tension pneumothorax, which is a serious and immediate life threat that requires immediate chest decompression.

168. **(B)** McBurney's point is a common site of pain from appendicitis and is located one to two inches above the anterior iliac crest in a direct line with the umbilicus.

169. **(A)** Rebound tenderness is pain on release of the examiner's hand, allowing the patient's abdominal wall to return to its normal position and is usually associated with peritoneal irritation. This assessment finding can be present in other abdominal conditions and is not specific to appendicitis.

170. **(C)** The classic sign/symptoms in this scenario that should lead you to suspect congestive heart failure in this patient is, "They were awakened from their sleep with shortness of breath" and they have signs of pulmonary congestion (crackles) present.

171. **(A)** Of the choices listed, preparation for intubation is the only correct answer.

172. **(A)** Respiratory distress is defined as the inability to maintain gaseous exchange sufficient to meet the needs of the body. Evidence of abnormal respirations (tachypnea or bradypnea) or increased work of breathing, use of accessory muscles, nasal flaring, grunting, and decreased mentation can also signal respiratory distress in the pediatric patient.

173. **(B)** Application of an occlusive dressing is necessary because this is a highly vascular area. An occlusive dressing will prevent air from entering an injured vessel and the development of an air embolism.

174. **(A)** The Trendelenburg position would be appropriate to decrease the potential for air aspiration into an injured vessel. **(B)**, **(C)**, and **(D)** are incorrect because there is a greater potential for air aspiration when in this position.

175. **(D)** Edema is a serious concern because injury to this highly vascular area of the neck can lead to a rapidly expanding hematoma. This hematoma can put pressure on other blood vessels resulting in decreased blood flow to the brain or put pressure on nearby airway structures resulting in an airway management nightmare!

176. **(B)** This ECG demonstrates ventricular tachycardia

177. **(A)** Treatment of this unstable patient is synchronous cardioversion. Defibrillation **(B)** is not indicated since the patient has a pulse. If this patient were pulseless, the treatment would include defibrillation.

178. **(D)** The diagnosis of cardiac tamponade often relies upon symptoms. Hypotension, distended neck veins, and muffled heart sounds are classic symptoms of cardiac tamponade and are known as Beck's triad. If the patient loses his peripheral pulse during inspiration, it is suggestive of pulsus paradoxus and the presence of cardiac tamponade.

179. **(C)** An open pneumothorax (sucking chest wound) includes a sucking or bubbling sound as air moves in and out of the chest wall. Bleeding is usually present and frothing of the blood may occur as the air and blood combine.

180. **(B)** Treatment of an open pneumothorax includes closing the chest wall by application of an occlusive dressing that is taped on three sides. **(A)** may be necessary, but it is not a more important priority than sealing the chest. **(D)** is necessary for this patient but sealing the chest should be performed on-scene, prior to rapid transport to a trauma center. **(C)** is incorrect because this patient does not have a tension pneumothorax although he will need to be monitored closely because an open pneumothorax can rapidly transition into a tension pneumothorax.

NOTES

NOTES

CHAPTER 10

Practice Test 3

Practice Test 3 follows the same format as the others and consists of questions from each chapter in the following breakdown:

• Airway and Breathing	26–34 questions
• Cardiology	29–37 questions
• Trauma	26–34 questions
• Medical Emergencies	26–34 questions
• Obstetrics/Pediatrics	24–32 questions
• Operations	25–33 questions
Total	**180 questions**

Allow yourself 180 minutes to take the test and again hold yourself to a high standard for this practice test by scoring 85% or better. This is achievable by answering 153 questions correctly.

All ECG rhythm strips used in this test are six-second strips.

CHAPTER 10—PRACTICE TEST 3

Answer Sheet

1. Ⓐ Ⓑ Ⓒ Ⓓ	31. Ⓐ Ⓑ Ⓒ Ⓓ	61. Ⓐ Ⓑ Ⓒ Ⓓ	91. Ⓐ Ⓑ Ⓒ Ⓓ	121. Ⓐ Ⓑ Ⓒ Ⓓ	151. Ⓐ Ⓑ Ⓒ Ⓓ
2. Ⓐ Ⓑ Ⓒ Ⓓ	32. Ⓐ Ⓑ Ⓒ Ⓓ	62. Ⓐ Ⓑ Ⓒ Ⓓ	92. Ⓐ Ⓑ Ⓒ Ⓓ	122. Ⓐ Ⓑ Ⓒ Ⓓ	152. Ⓐ Ⓑ Ⓒ Ⓓ
3. Ⓐ Ⓑ Ⓒ Ⓓ	33. Ⓐ Ⓑ Ⓒ Ⓓ	63. Ⓐ Ⓑ Ⓒ Ⓓ	93. Ⓐ Ⓑ Ⓒ Ⓓ	123. Ⓐ Ⓑ Ⓒ Ⓓ	153. Ⓐ Ⓑ Ⓒ Ⓓ
4. Ⓐ Ⓑ Ⓒ Ⓓ	34. Ⓐ Ⓑ Ⓒ Ⓓ	64. Ⓐ Ⓑ Ⓒ Ⓓ	94. Ⓐ Ⓑ Ⓒ Ⓓ	124. Ⓐ Ⓑ Ⓒ Ⓓ	154. Ⓐ Ⓑ Ⓒ Ⓓ
5. Ⓐ Ⓑ Ⓒ Ⓓ	35. Ⓐ Ⓑ Ⓒ Ⓓ	65. Ⓐ Ⓑ Ⓒ Ⓓ	95. Ⓐ Ⓑ Ⓒ Ⓓ	125. Ⓐ Ⓑ Ⓒ Ⓓ	155. Ⓐ Ⓑ Ⓒ Ⓓ
6. Ⓐ Ⓑ Ⓒ Ⓓ	36. Ⓐ Ⓑ Ⓒ Ⓓ	66. Ⓐ Ⓑ Ⓒ Ⓓ	96. Ⓐ Ⓑ Ⓒ Ⓓ	126. Ⓐ Ⓑ Ⓒ Ⓓ	156. Ⓐ Ⓑ Ⓒ Ⓓ
7. Ⓐ Ⓑ Ⓒ Ⓓ	37. Ⓐ Ⓑ Ⓒ Ⓓ	67. Ⓐ Ⓑ Ⓒ Ⓓ	97. Ⓐ Ⓑ Ⓒ Ⓓ	127. Ⓐ Ⓑ Ⓒ Ⓓ	157. Ⓐ Ⓑ Ⓒ Ⓓ
8. Ⓐ Ⓑ Ⓒ Ⓓ	38. Ⓐ Ⓑ Ⓒ Ⓓ	68. Ⓐ Ⓑ Ⓒ Ⓓ	98. Ⓐ Ⓑ Ⓒ Ⓓ	128. Ⓐ Ⓑ Ⓒ Ⓓ	158. Ⓐ Ⓑ Ⓒ Ⓓ
9. Ⓐ Ⓑ Ⓒ Ⓓ	39. Ⓐ Ⓑ Ⓒ Ⓓ	69. Ⓐ Ⓑ Ⓒ Ⓓ	99. Ⓐ Ⓑ Ⓒ Ⓓ	129. Ⓐ Ⓑ Ⓒ Ⓓ	159. Ⓐ Ⓑ Ⓒ Ⓓ
10. Ⓐ Ⓑ Ⓒ Ⓓ	40. Ⓐ Ⓑ Ⓒ Ⓓ	70. Ⓐ Ⓑ Ⓒ Ⓓ	100. Ⓐ Ⓑ Ⓒ Ⓓ	130. Ⓐ Ⓑ Ⓒ Ⓓ	160. Ⓐ Ⓑ Ⓒ Ⓓ
11. Ⓐ Ⓑ Ⓒ Ⓓ	41. Ⓐ Ⓑ Ⓒ Ⓓ	71. Ⓐ Ⓑ Ⓒ Ⓓ	101. Ⓐ Ⓑ Ⓒ Ⓓ	131. Ⓐ Ⓑ Ⓒ Ⓓ	161. Ⓐ Ⓑ Ⓒ Ⓓ
12. Ⓐ Ⓑ Ⓒ Ⓓ	42. Ⓐ Ⓑ Ⓒ Ⓓ	72. Ⓐ Ⓑ Ⓒ Ⓓ	102. Ⓐ Ⓑ Ⓒ Ⓓ	132. Ⓐ Ⓑ Ⓒ Ⓓ	162. Ⓐ Ⓑ Ⓒ Ⓓ
13. Ⓐ Ⓑ Ⓒ Ⓓ	43. Ⓐ Ⓑ Ⓒ Ⓓ	73. Ⓐ Ⓑ Ⓒ Ⓓ	103. Ⓐ Ⓑ Ⓒ Ⓓ	133. Ⓐ Ⓑ Ⓒ Ⓓ	163. Ⓐ Ⓑ Ⓒ Ⓓ
14. Ⓐ Ⓑ Ⓒ Ⓓ	44. Ⓐ Ⓑ Ⓒ Ⓓ	74. Ⓐ Ⓑ Ⓒ Ⓓ	104. Ⓐ Ⓑ Ⓒ Ⓓ	134. Ⓐ Ⓑ Ⓒ Ⓓ	164. Ⓐ Ⓑ Ⓒ Ⓓ
15. Ⓐ Ⓑ Ⓒ Ⓓ	45. Ⓐ Ⓑ Ⓒ Ⓓ	75. Ⓐ Ⓑ Ⓒ Ⓓ	105. Ⓐ Ⓑ Ⓒ Ⓓ	135. Ⓐ Ⓑ Ⓒ Ⓓ	165. Ⓐ Ⓑ Ⓒ Ⓓ
16. Ⓐ Ⓑ Ⓒ Ⓓ	46. Ⓐ Ⓑ Ⓒ Ⓓ	76. Ⓐ Ⓑ Ⓒ Ⓓ	106. Ⓐ Ⓑ Ⓒ Ⓓ	136. Ⓐ Ⓑ Ⓒ Ⓓ	166. Ⓐ Ⓑ Ⓒ Ⓓ
17. Ⓐ Ⓑ Ⓒ Ⓓ	47. Ⓐ Ⓑ Ⓒ Ⓓ	77. Ⓐ Ⓑ Ⓒ Ⓓ	107. Ⓐ Ⓑ Ⓒ Ⓓ	137. Ⓐ Ⓑ Ⓒ Ⓓ	167. Ⓐ Ⓑ Ⓒ Ⓓ
18. Ⓐ Ⓑ Ⓒ Ⓓ	48. Ⓐ Ⓑ Ⓒ Ⓓ	78. Ⓐ Ⓑ Ⓒ Ⓓ	108. Ⓐ Ⓑ Ⓒ Ⓓ	138. Ⓐ Ⓑ Ⓒ Ⓓ	168. Ⓐ Ⓑ Ⓒ Ⓓ
19. Ⓐ Ⓑ Ⓒ Ⓓ	49. Ⓐ Ⓑ Ⓒ Ⓓ	79. Ⓐ Ⓑ Ⓒ Ⓓ	109. Ⓐ Ⓑ Ⓒ Ⓓ	139. Ⓐ Ⓑ Ⓒ Ⓓ	169. Ⓐ Ⓑ Ⓒ Ⓓ
20. Ⓐ Ⓑ Ⓒ Ⓓ	50. Ⓐ Ⓑ Ⓒ Ⓓ	80. Ⓐ Ⓑ Ⓒ Ⓓ	110. Ⓐ Ⓑ Ⓒ Ⓓ	140. Ⓐ Ⓑ Ⓒ Ⓓ	170. Ⓐ Ⓑ Ⓒ Ⓓ
21. Ⓐ Ⓑ Ⓒ Ⓓ	51. Ⓐ Ⓑ Ⓒ Ⓓ	81. Ⓐ Ⓑ Ⓒ Ⓓ	111. Ⓐ Ⓑ Ⓒ Ⓓ	141. Ⓐ Ⓑ Ⓒ Ⓓ	171. Ⓐ Ⓑ Ⓒ Ⓓ
22. Ⓐ Ⓑ Ⓒ Ⓓ	52. Ⓐ Ⓑ Ⓒ Ⓓ	82. Ⓐ Ⓑ Ⓒ Ⓓ	112. Ⓐ Ⓑ Ⓒ Ⓓ	142. Ⓐ Ⓑ Ⓒ Ⓓ	172. Ⓐ Ⓑ Ⓒ Ⓓ
23. Ⓐ Ⓑ Ⓒ Ⓓ	53. Ⓐ Ⓑ Ⓒ Ⓓ	83. Ⓐ Ⓑ Ⓒ Ⓓ	113. Ⓐ Ⓑ Ⓒ Ⓓ	143. Ⓐ Ⓑ Ⓒ Ⓓ	173. Ⓐ Ⓑ Ⓒ Ⓓ
24. Ⓐ Ⓑ Ⓒ Ⓓ	54. Ⓐ Ⓑ Ⓒ Ⓓ	84. Ⓐ Ⓑ Ⓒ Ⓓ	114. Ⓐ Ⓑ Ⓒ Ⓓ	144. Ⓐ Ⓑ Ⓒ Ⓓ	174. Ⓐ Ⓑ Ⓒ Ⓓ
25. Ⓐ Ⓑ Ⓒ Ⓓ	55. Ⓐ Ⓑ Ⓒ Ⓓ	85. Ⓐ Ⓑ Ⓒ Ⓓ	115. Ⓐ Ⓑ Ⓒ Ⓓ	145. Ⓐ Ⓑ Ⓒ Ⓓ	175. Ⓐ Ⓑ Ⓒ Ⓓ
26. Ⓐ Ⓑ Ⓒ Ⓓ	56. Ⓐ Ⓑ Ⓒ Ⓓ	86. Ⓐ Ⓑ Ⓒ Ⓓ	116. Ⓐ Ⓑ Ⓒ Ⓓ	146. Ⓐ Ⓑ Ⓒ Ⓓ	176. Ⓐ Ⓑ Ⓒ Ⓓ
27. Ⓐ Ⓑ Ⓒ Ⓓ	57. Ⓐ Ⓑ Ⓒ Ⓓ	87. Ⓐ Ⓑ Ⓒ Ⓓ	117. Ⓐ Ⓑ Ⓒ Ⓓ	147. Ⓐ Ⓑ Ⓒ Ⓓ	177. Ⓐ Ⓑ Ⓒ Ⓓ
28. Ⓐ Ⓑ Ⓒ Ⓓ	58. Ⓐ Ⓑ Ⓒ Ⓓ	88. Ⓐ Ⓑ Ⓒ Ⓓ	118. Ⓐ Ⓑ Ⓒ Ⓓ	148. Ⓐ Ⓑ Ⓒ Ⓓ	178. Ⓐ Ⓑ Ⓒ Ⓓ
29. Ⓐ Ⓑ Ⓒ Ⓓ	59. Ⓐ Ⓑ Ⓒ Ⓓ	89. Ⓐ Ⓑ Ⓒ Ⓓ	119. Ⓐ Ⓑ Ⓒ Ⓓ	149. Ⓐ Ⓑ Ⓒ Ⓓ	179. Ⓐ Ⓑ Ⓒ Ⓓ
30. Ⓐ Ⓑ Ⓒ Ⓓ	60. Ⓐ Ⓑ Ⓒ Ⓓ	90. Ⓐ Ⓑ Ⓒ Ⓓ	120. Ⓐ Ⓑ Ⓒ Ⓓ	150. Ⓐ Ⓑ Ⓒ Ⓓ	180. Ⓐ Ⓑ Ⓒ Ⓓ

1. Unlawful touching of an individual without his or her consent could leave the paramedic open for allegations of
   (A) assault.
   (B) battery.
   (C) abandonment.
   (D) false imprisonment.

2. The body's first line of defense against infection is
   (A) the skin.
   (B) the respiratory system.
   (C) the G.I. system.
   (D) humoral response.

3. You and your partner are treating a 16-year-old female with lower abdominal pain. The patient's husband arrives and informs you his wife may be pregnant. You can treat this patient without parental consent based on:
   (A) the nonurgent doctrine.
   (B) that emancipated minors are considered adults.
   (C) that she is mentally competent.
   (D) that the consent is involuntary.

4. The phrenic nerve originates from which spinal nerves?
   (A) C1–C2–C3
   (B) C3–C4–C5
   (C) C5–C6–C7
   (D) C6–C7–T1

5. Nasotracheal intubation is contraindicated in a patient with
   (A) clenched teeth.
   (B) a history of recent sinus infections.
   (C) a suspected basilar skull fracture.
   (D) facial trauma.

Questions 6–8 are based on the following scenario:

You arrive on-scene of a patient who presented in ventricular fibrillation. After immediately defibrillating the patient at 200, 300, and 360 joules, no vital signs are obtainable and you note the following rhythm on the monitor:

6. Initial treatment should include
   (A) immediate transcutaneous pacing.
   (B) Atropine 1 mg IVP.
   (C) epinephrine 1 mg IVP.
   (D) vasopressin 40 units IVP.

7. There is no change in the patient's condition. Continued treatment should include
   (A) immediate transcutaneous pacing.
   (B) Atropine 1 mg IVP.
   (C) epinephrine 1 mg IVP.
   (D) vasopressin 40 units IVP.

8. Treatable causes of PEA include all of the following EXCEPT
   (A) hypoxia.
   (B) hypervolemia.
   (C) acidosis.
   (D) a tension pneumothorax.

---

9. A child has suffered multisystem trauma and IV access cannot be obtained. You determine the best course of action would be to establish an IO. A contraindication for IO insertion is
   (A) that the child is under one year old.
   (B) that the child is apneic and pulseless.
   (C) a fracture of the lower extremity.
   (D) a previous attempt in the opposite leg.

10. A stab wound to the stomach or small intestine would cause gastric contents to enter the peritoneal cavity. Presentation would include
   (A) a rapid onset of cramping pain.
   (B) referred pain to the left shoulder.
   (C) a gradual onset of pain throughout the abdomen.
   (D) a rapid onset of sharp pain, diffuse throughout the abdomen.

11. Which of the following would you expect to cause the greatest cavitation?
    (A) a hunting knife
    (B) a bullet from a handgun
    (C) a bullet from a rifle
    (D) an arrow

12. A syndrome that develops as a complication of an illness such as multisystem trauma, severe sepsis, or toxic inhalation is termed
    (A) adult respiratory syndrome (ARDS).
    (B) pneumonia syndrome (PS).
    (C) chronic obstructive pulmonary disease (COPD).
    (D) congestive heart failure (CHF).

13. A respiratory pattern characterized by a gradually increasing rate and tidal volume followed by a gradual decrease with intermittent periods of apnea is
    (A) Cheyne-Stokes.
    (B) Biot's (ataxic).
    (C) central neurogenic hyperventilation.
    (D) agonal.

14. Functions of an EMS dispatcher include all of the following EXCEPT
    (A) call taking.
    (B) proper diagnosis of the caller's illness.
    (C) alerting and directing the EMS response.
    (D) giving prearrival instructions to the caller.

15. A priority in evaluating a two-year-old with diarrhea and vomiting includes determining:
    (A) a temperature elevation.
    (B) a viral infection.
    (C) a respiratory infection.
    (D) adequate hydration.

16. The proper size oropharyngeal airway is determined by measuring
    (A) from the tip of the nose to the center of the chin.
    (B) from the corner of the mouth to the tip of the chin.
    (C) from the corner of the mouth to the tip of the ear lobe at the angle of the jaw.
    (D) from the center of the mouth to the tip of the ear lobe at the angle of the jaw.

17. Where should you place your hands on the chest of an adult victim when you are performing chest compressions?
    (A) On the top of the sternum
    (B) On the lower one third of the sternum
    (C) On the lower half of the sternum, at the nipple line
    (D) Over the very bottom of the sternum

18. Ecchymosis in the flank area associated with intraabdominal hemorrhage is known as
    (A) peritonitis.
    (B) Cullen's sign.
    (C) Mallory-Weiss sign.
    (D) Grey-Turner's sign.

19. On an ECG tracing, the t wave indicates
    (A) depolarization of the atria.
    (B) repolarization of the atria.
    (C) depolarization of the ventricles.
    (D) repolarization of the ventricles.

20. The effect of Dopamine administration at an infusion rate greater than 20 mcg/kg/minute includes
    (A) arterial vasoconstriction only.
    (B) venous vasoconstriction only.
    (C) both arterial and venous peripheral vasoconstriction.
    (D) improved renal blood flow.

21. Cardiogenic shock can result in all of the following EXCEPT
    (A) dysrhythmias.
    (B) hypertension.
    (C) respiratory failure.
    (D) elevated heart rate.

22. The period of the cardiac cycle when stimulation may produce depolarization is
    (A) the refractory period.
    (B) the decompensation period.
    (C) the absolute refractory period.
    (D) the relative refractory period.

23. At the scene of an MVC, your ambulance should be parked at least 100 feet from the accident, uphill and upwind to ensure
    (A) the safety of the vehicle.
    (B) the safety of your crew.
    (C) that the crime scene is not violated.
    (D) clear distance for secondary units to arrive.

Questions 24 and 25 are based on the following scenario:

You are called to attend to a 51-year-old male who fell in his living room. His wife states that he has been very depressed and has not eaten or drunk anything for the past 24 hours. You notice that the patient has a stonelike face, muscular rigidity, and is exhibiting "pill-rolling" movements.

24. These are all signs of
    (A) multiple sclerosis.
    (B) Bell's palsy.
    (C) Parkinson's disease.
    (D) vertebral disc disease.

25. In managing this patient, it is important to
    (A) start an intravenous line.
    (B) determine a blood glucose level.
    (C) apply a cardiac monitor.
    (D) All of the above are correct.

26. Which device listed below would be most effective in determining if an endotracheal tube is placed in the stomach?
    (A) Pulse oximeter
    (B) CPAP device
    (C) Peak flow meter
    (D) End-tidal CO_2 detector

27. Which of the following best describes the effects of pericardial tamponade?
    (A) Cardiac output increases, and central venous pressure falls.
    (B) Cardiac output is reduced, and central venous pressure rises.
    (C) Cardiac output increases, and venous pressure is not affected.
    (D) Cardiac output is not affected, and central venous pressure falls.

28. Which of the following vital signs is most likely present in a 13-year-old with spinal shock?
    (A) B/P 64/30; pulse 56 per minute
    (B) B/P 64/30; pulse 150 per minute
    (C) B/P 160/100; pulse 56 per minute
    (D) B/P 160/100; pulse 150 per minute

29. In caring for an infant burn patient, the rule of nines assigns _____ percent of the body surface area to the head.
    A) 9%
    B) 4½%
    C) 18%
    D) 36%

30. You have intubated a six-week-old infant found in respiratory arrest. While performing ventilations, the child becomes blue and the pulse rate drops into the lower 50s. Your next step should be to
    (A) check the pulse oximeter reading.
    (B) administer epinephrine down the endotracheal tube to correct the bradycardia.
    (C) auscultate the chest.
    (D) administer Atropine.

31. Commonly mandated injuries that are reportable to local authorities include all of the following EXCEPT
    (A) falls greater than 10 feet.
    (B) child abuse or neglect.
    (C) animal bites.
    (D) gunshot/stab wounds.

Questions 32 and 33 are based on the following scenario:

You are called to the scene of a stabbing. You find one victim lying supine on the ground in a large pool of blood with multiple lacerations to the abdomen. The scene is secure. Your initial assessment finds a patient responding only to pain with no peripheral pulse and a respiratory rate of 8.

32. Priority care of this patient would be
    (A) MAST trousers and IV wide open.
    (B) BVM ventilations and moist saline dressings to the abdomen.
    (C) intubation and fluid resuscitation.
    (D) peritoneal lavage.

33. While transporting this patient to the hospital, a large section of bowel protrudes through one of the lacerations. Your management would be to
    (A) increase pressure in the abdominal compartment of MAST trousers.
    (B) replace the protruding bowel and apply a pressure dressing.
    (C) make a note, no treatment necessary except to notify medical control.
    (D) gently cover with moistened gauze and nonadherent material as a dressing.

---

34. You need to administer epinephrine to a 26-year-old male who is short of breath after receiving radiologic contrast material. The standard subcutaneous dose is
    (A) 0.1–0.3 mg 1:1,000 solution.
    (B) 0.1–0.3 mg 1:10,000 solution.
    (C) 0.5–1.0 mg 1:1,000.
    (D) 0.3–0.5 mg 1:1,000 solution.

35. Of the following hepatitis groups, which is not transmitted via blood?
    (A) Hepatitis A
    (B) Hepatitis B
    (C) Hepatitis C
    (D) Hepatitis D

36. Which of the following is most likely to cause shock in a child?
    (A) Laceration to the face
    (B) Fractured radius
    (C) Cerebral edema
    (D) Splenic injury

37. After bag-valve mask ventilation is performed on a two-year-old patient with impending respiratory failure, the child fails to improve. You determine that the best course of action would be to intubate. However, the patient is awake with an intact gag reflex. Rapid sequence Intubation is preferred in this setting. Using Atropine, midazolam, and succinylcholine as the medications of choice for RSI, the correct dosage of succinylcholine for this two-year-old would be
    (A) 0.01 mg/kg.
    (B) 0.1 mg/kg.
    (C) 1.0 mg/kg.
    (D) None of the above are the correct dosage.

38. You arrive at the scene of a car that struck a telephone pole. You find a 17-year-old female ejected from her vehicle, lying 25 feet from the point of impact. Which of the following is an acceptable method of opening her airway?
    (A) Modified jaw thrust
    (B) Neck extension
    (C) Neck flexion
    (D) Sellick's maneuver

39. An infant should not be suctioned for more than
    (A) 15 seconds.
    (B) 5 seconds.
    (C) 10 seconds.
    (D) 20 seconds.

40. Which of the following facial injuries involves a fracture of both the maxillary and nasal bone?
    (A) Mandibular fracture
    (B) LeFort I
    (C) LeFort II
    (D) LeFort III

41. A burn victim with suspected thermal or chemical airway burns needs close monitoring for signs of respiratory compromise. Appropriate management would include
    (A) immediate intubation using RSI upon all inhalation injuries.
    (B) using cool nebulized oxygen in a blow-by manner with a simple pocket mask to prevent further mucosal tissue damage.
    (C) providing high-flow oxygen by nonrebreather mask at 15 liters per minute once the airway has been secured.
    (D) suspecting cyanide toxicity and administering the sulfur-containing antidote.

42. Documentation of a patient's refusal for care or transport should include all of the following EXCEPT
    (A) the patient's insurance information.
    (B) the paramedic's advice to the patient.
    (C) on-line medical control's advice.
    (D) a complete narrative of the event.

43. You are treating a patient with diabetic ketoacidosis. The patient is tachycardic and has deep, rapid respirations. The most likely cause for the deep, rapid respirations is that
    (A) the body is compensating for a low pH by increasing respirations.
    (B) the body is compensating for a high pH by increasing respirations.
    (C) the body is compensating for an excess of HCO_3 by increasing respirations.
    (D) the body is compensating for a decrease in H+ ions by increasing respirations.

44. A patient is involved in a motor vehicle crash and is semiconscious. Vitals BP 92/54, pulse 110, respirations 24. ECG shows the following rhythm:

Which treatment is appropriate?
(A) Immediate cardioversion
(B) Immediate defibrillation
(C) Lidocaine 1 mg/kg
(D) Continued observation

45. On an ECG tracing, the QRS complex indicates
(A) depolarization of the atria.
(B) repolarization of the atria.
(C) depolarization of the ventricles.
(D) repolarization of the ventricles.

46. Which term best describes the following definition: Disease of arterial vessels marked by thickening, hardening, and loss of elasticity in the arterial walls?
(A) Atherosclerosis
(B) Arterionecrosis
(C) Arteriosclerosis
(D) Angina

47. The minimum-size bag-valve mask device used for neonates, infants, and children should be
(A) 250 ml.
(B) 450 ml.
(C) 750 ml.
(D) 1,000 ml.

48. Your EMS unit is called to attend to a 79-year-old female who experienced an abrupt onset of facial drooping, dysphasia, and marked hemiparesis. Upon examination, she is now alert and oriented, speech clear, and moves all extremities well. Vital signs are normal. Your assessment findings lead you to suspect
(A) a stroke.
(B) a transient ischemic attack.
(C) Alzheimer's disease.
(D) amyotrophic lateral sclerosis.

49. A patient experiencing Addisonian crisis may display which of the following signs/symptoms?
    (A) Increased appetite, hypoglycemia, hyperthermia
    (B) Extreme hypertension, elevated temperature, vomiting
    (C) Cardiovascular collapse, hypotension, hypoglycemia
    (D) Coma secondary to hypothyroidism

50. Findings that require no medical intervention, but require documentation as evidence of a thorough history and exam are termed
    (A) negative responses.
    (B) positive therapeutics.
    (C) noteworthy responses.
    (D) pertinent negatives.

51. You have successfully resuscitated a patient who suffered a cardiac arrest. You are enroute to the hospital when the patient wakes up and is not tolerating the endotracheal tube. The medical director at the receiving hospital has ordered you to extubate the patient. All of the following should be done except to
    (A) remove the endotracheal tube on a cough or expiration.
    (B) deflate the endotracheal tube cuff completely.
    (C) remove the endotracheal tube slowly.
    (D) provide supplemental oxygen once the tube is removed.

Questions 52–55 are based on the following scenario:

You are on duty at your EMS service when you are called to respond to a car that struck a light pole. As you arrive on scene you notice that power lines are down on top of the car. The driver is hanging halfway out of the driver's side window, unconscious, with slow, snoring-type respirations.

52. What is your first priority?
    (A) In-line stabilization of the c-spine and modified jaw thrust
    (B) Removal of the wire from the top of the car and proceeding with caution
    (C) C-spine stabilization and oral pharyngeal airway with BVM ventilations
    (D) Calling the power company for assistance prior to starting patient care

53. After the patient is removed from the car, a rapid trauma survey shows a GCS of 9, B/P 178/100, pulse 56, and respirations 34 and irregular. What is your differential diagnosis from this assessment?
    (A) Hypoglycemia
    (B) Hyperglycemia
    (C) Cushing's syndrome
    (D) CVA

54. To manage the airway of this patient appropriately you would
    (A) administer 100% O_2 with BVM at 30 breaths per minute.
    (B) administer 100% nonrebreather mask on 10 liters of O_2.
    (C) apply a nasal cannula with 10 liters.
    (D) intubate and hyperoxygenate with BVM at a rate of 24 breaths per minute.

55. You have established two large-bore IVs of normal saline. Choose the appropriate rate.
    (A) Enough fluid to maintain stable vital signs
    (B) Both lines wide open
    (C) TKO
    (D) 500 cc bolus

Questions 56–58 are based on the following scenario:

You are dispatched to a local department store when a concerned customer notices an infant left unattended in a car. It is bitterly cold outside. Once you gain entry into the car, you find the infant to be dusky in color with no activity or movement. The respiratory rate is 12 per minute and irregular with grunting and short sighs. The heart rate is 64 per minute with weak central pulses. The infant's hands and feet are cold to touch. Capillary refill is five seconds.

56. Your immediate action would be to
    (A) start CPR.
    (B) ventilate with a bag-valve mask device and 100% oxygen.
    (C) give oxygen by blow-by.
    (D) intubate the infant.

57. After the above treatment is given, the infant does not improve. The ECG shows narrow complexes with p waves. The rate is 64 per minute. Your next action would be to
    (A) obtain IV/IO access and give Atropine for the bradycardia.
    (B) obtain IV/IO access and give Atropine 0.01–0.02 mg/kg.
    (C) obtain IV/IO access and give 0.01 mg/kg of 1:1,000 epinephrine.
    (D) obtain IV/IO access and give 0.01 mg/kg of 1:10,000 epinephrine.

58. After obtaining venous access and delivering the pharmacological intervention, the patient's heart rate increases to 130 per minute with strong central pulses but no peripheral pulses. To further stabilize the infant, the next course of action should be to
    (A) repeat the Atropine dose.
    (B) repeat the epinephrine dose.
    (C) continue CPR.
    (D) begin rewarming the patient.

---

59. A telephone is an example of a _____ communication system.
    (A) simplex
    (B) duplex
    (C) multiplex
    (D) trunked

60. You are the triage officer at a car verses bus collision. Your first victim is approximately 30 years old, awake, alert, and oriented. He is the driver of the car that collided with the bus head on. He complains of lower abdominal pain and has obvious deformity to both femurs. Respirations 24, pulse 140, BP 80/p, capillary refill >2 sec. How would you triage the following patient?
    (A) Green
    (B) Yellow
    (C) Red
    (D) Black

61. You respond to a 72-year-old man with syncope. He is sitting in the kitchen when you arrive. He is alert and oriented to person, place, and time. He complains of dizziness. Current vitals are BP 108/60; pulse 96 slightly irregular, and respirations of 28. Pulse oximeter reading is 97%. ECG shows a sinus rhythm with occasional PVCs. This patient should receive oxygen
    (A) by nasal cannula at 3 LPM.
    (B) by nonrebreather mask.
    (C) Oxygen application is not required.
    (D) by nasal cannula at 6 LPM.

62. All of the following are reasons for a pulse oximeter to read "Error" EXCEPT
    (A) low capillary blood flow.
    (B) peripheral vasoconstriction.
    (C) extremity movement.
    (D) hyperthermia.

63. When confirming endotracheal tube placement, it is imperative to auscultate:
    (A) at the midaxillary line.
    (B) over the trachea.
    (C) over the epigastrium.
    (D) All of the above.

64. To prevent over- or undertransfusion of blood from the umbilical cord to the newborn, correct positioning of the newborn until the umbilical cord is clamped should be
    (A) at the level of the vagina.
    (B) at a higher level than the placenta.
    (C) at a level lower than the vagina.
    (D) placed in the left lateral recumbent position.

65. Of the statements below, identify that which is true concerning pediatric airway management.
    (A) the Sellick maneuver is not appropriate for use in the child.
    (B) Nasotracheal intubation is the preferred method of intubation.
    (C) Cuffed endotracheal tubes can be used in children.
    (D) Bradycardia can result from suctioning a child.

66. You have a patient with a history of metastatic brain cancer. He opens his eyes to pain, and answers questions with incomprehensible sounds. When you start an IV in his left arm, he withdraws from the IV needle piercing the skin. You would calculate his Glasgow Coma Scale to be
    (A) 9.
    (B) 11.
    (C) 7.
    (D) 4.

67. Acute coronary syndrome is defined as
    (A) a sudden ischemic disorder of the heart.
    (B) a myocardial infarction.
    (C) congestive heart failure.
    (D) triple vessel disease.

68. The following statements regarding scene safety with regard to helicopter and air medical transport are all true EXCEPT that
    (A) generally a helicopter requires a landing zone of approximately 100 feet by 100 feet.
    (B) you should approach a helicopter from the rear, nearest the tail rotor for safe loading and unloading.
    (C) you should ensure the landing zone is clear of wires, loose debris, towers, or vehicles.
    (D) you should mark the landing zone with a single flare and do not shine lights directly into pilot's eyes.

69. You are treating a six-month-old infant who presents as "fussy." The infant is crying and has a respiratory rate of 40 per minute. She has pink skin with a capillary refill of two seconds. The cardiac monitor shows a narrow complex tachycardia of 260 beats per minute. Based on this assessment, the correct pharmacological intervention to control the rate would be
    (A) adenosine 0.1 mg/kg IV.
    (B) amiodarone 5 mg/kg IV over 20 minutes.
    (C) procainamide 15 mg/kg IV over 30 minutes.
    (D) lidocaine 1 mg/kg IV bolus.

70. Anatomical dead space is
    (A) the volume of air in the trachea, bronchi, and air passages that does not reach the alveoli during respiration.
    (B) the volume of air in the trachea, bronchi, and air passages that is available for gas exchange during respiration.
    (C) the volume of air in the alveoli that does not contribute to oxygen-carbon dioxide exchange.
    (D) the volume of air in the alveoli that contributes to oxygen-carbon dioxide exchange during respiration.

Questions 71–73 are based on the following scenario:

It is 11:30 A.M. and you respond to a 21-year-old male with a complaint of vomiting. His friends tell you that he was celebrating his twenty-first birthday last night and had an excessive amount of alcohol to drink. EMS was called because he has been vomiting for the past 45 minutes. Your patient is in the bathroom. He is conscious, alert, oriented, and experiencing excessive dry heaves at this time. He states that he drank beer most of the night and then started drinking shots of whiskey with his friends. His last drink was approximately six hours ago.

71. You note the presence of specks of blood on the toilet. He has no history of GI problems and takes no medications. You suspect the bleeding is
    (A) caused by acute gastritis.
    (B) the result of a Mallory-Weiss tear.
    (C) caused by acute peptic ulcer disease.
    (D) caused by acute duodenitis.

72. As you assess the patient, you note that the scleras of his eyes are dramatically blood red. This is most likely the result of
    (A) hyphema.
    (B) subconjunctival hemorrhage.
    (C) conjunctivitis.
    (D) the result of blunt trauma.

73. You are ordered by medical control to administer Phenergan (promethazine) to this patient. The proper dose range and route should be
    (A) 12.5 to 25 mg IV or deep IM.
    (B) 12.5 to 25 mg SQ, IV or deep IM.
    (C) 25 to 50 mg IV or deep IM.
    (D) 25 mg IV only. IM injection of this medication is not recommended.

---

74. Patients with chronic obstructive pulmonary disease (COPD) often breathe through pursed lips to increase pressure in the lungs. This method of breathing helps in
    (A) decreasing the blood carbon dioxide levels.
    (B) preventing alveolar collapse.
    (C) preventing the loss of elasticity in the lungs.
    (D) reversing peripheral vasoconstriction.

75. Suctioning of the infant's mouth and nose should be performed after
    (A) the cord is clamped and cut.
    (B) the infant begins to cry.
    (C) the chest has been delivered.
    (D) the head has been delivered.

76. When caring for a pediatric patient, the standard dose of epinephrine for pulseless arrest or symptomatic bradycardia is
    (A) 0.1 mg/kg IV/IO of 1:1,000.
    (B) 0.01 mg/kg IV/IO of 1:10,000.
    (C) 0.01 mg/kg IV/IO of 1:1,000.
    (D) 0.1 mg/kg IV/IO of 1:10,000.

77. A respiratory pattern characterized by slow, shallow, irregular respirations is
    (A) Cheyne-Stokes.
    (B) Biot's (ataxic).
    (C) central neurogenic hyperventilation.
    (D) bradypnea.

78. Exercising the degree of care, skill, and judgment that would be expected under like
    or similar circumstances by a similarly trained, reasonable paramedic in a similar
    community or location is the definition of
    (A) duty to act.
    (B) standard of care.
    (C) malfeasance.
    (D) proximate cause.

79. Which of the following definitions best describes a disaster?
    (A) A motor vehicle collision with two to three patients
    (B) An everyday incident that generates three or more patients
    (C) A bus or train collision with 25–30 injured
    (D) An incident that overwhelms resources and may damage the infrastructure
        of a region

80. How often should you provide rescue breaths for a child who is apneic?
    (A) 20 breaths per minute
    (B) 12–20 breaths per minute
    (C) once every 5 seconds
    (D) once every 10 seconds

81. The recommended dose of vasopressin in ventricular fibrillation is
    (A) 40 mg IV repeated once in 10 minutes.
    (B) 20 mg IV one time only.
    (C) 40 mg IV one time only.
    (D) 40 units IV one time only.

82. All of the following are appropriate end points for procainamide administration
    EXCEPT
    (A) 17 mcg/kg administered.
    (B) hypotension.
    (C) widening of the QRS complex greater than 50%.
    (D) that the dysrhythmia is suppressed.

83. Calcium chloride is indicated for a dialysis patient in
    (A) cardiac arrest with refractory v fib.
    (B) symptomatic bradycardia.
    (C) cardiac arrest with known or suspected hyperkalemia.
    (D) cardiac arrest with pulseless electrical activity.

84. Advantages of the Esophageal Tracheal CombiTube include all of the following
    except that
    (A) insertion is rapid and easy.
    (B) it can be used on trauma patients.
    (C) it can provide ventilation if placed in the esophagus.
    (D) it can be used with pediatric patients.

85. The normal value for PCO_2 is
    (A) 7.35 to 7.45.
    (B) 22 to 26 mEq/liter.
    (C) 35 to 45 mmHg.
    (D) 80 to 100 mmHg.

86. During what month of gestation does the uterus rise out of the pelvic cavity and become more susceptible to blunt trauma?
    (A) Third month
    (B) Seventh month
    (C) Fifth month
    (D) Second month

87. On the first day of summer vacation, you are called to a rooftop for a 17-year-old female who was sun bathing. She is alert and oriented and states that she was using lotion without any SPF protection to "speed up her tan." She was in the sun from 9:00 A.M. to 2:00 P.M. She is in significant pain and requests that you help her off the rooftop. She has blisters covering the entire front of her body. You should consider this patient to have
    (A) first-degree burns.
    (B) minor burns.
    (C) nothing to worry about.
    (D) critical burns.

88. Disadvantages of a simplex system may include that
    (A) the process is slower and more formal.
    (B) either party can interrupt the other party as necessary.
    (C) voice transmission may interfere with data transmission.
    (D) the simplex system facilitates discussion.

Questions 89 and 90 are based on the following scenario:

You are called to assist a 25-year-old known Type I diabetic patient who is complaining of abdominal pain, vomiting, and lethargy. His glucometer reading is 510. Vitals include B/P 122/70, pulse 118, respirations 34.

89. The highest treatment priority for this patient is to:
    (A) reverse alkalosis by hyperventilation.
    (B) administer the patient's next scheduled dose of insulin intravenously.
    (C) correct fluid volume deficit.
    (D) administer morphine to provide for pain management.

90. One week later you are called to the same home. His glucometer now reads 66. You may encounter all of the following symptoms of hypoglycemia EXCEPT
    (A) altered mental status.
    (B) hot, dry skin.
    (C) bizarre behavior.
    (D) hunger.

Questions 91 and 92 are based on the following scenario:

You respond to the local college campus soccer field for a 20-year-old female patient with a complaint of severe muscle cramps. The temperature is 88 degrees with high humidity. The patient just finished a strenuous workout when the cramps began. Her skin is hot to touch and she is sweating profusely.

91. You suspect this patient is suffering
    (A) heatstroke.
    (B) heat exhaustion.
    (C) heat cramps.
    (D) exercise-induced fatigue.

92. Treatment should include
    (A) oral hydration if the patient is able to take fluids.
    (B) two large-bore IVs of normal saline wide open.
    (C) initiating rapid active cooling.
    (D) Both A and C are correct.

Questions 93 and 94 are based on the following scenario:

You are called to a local homeless shelter for a gentleman with complaint of cough for two to three weeks, night sweats, and weight loss.

93. You suspect
    (A) hepatitis A.
    (B) HIV.
    (C) TB–tuberculosis.
    (D) meningitis.

94. You diagnose the above illness appropriately and know the disease is spread through
    (A) exposure to blood.
    (B) exposure through airborne droplets.
    (C) exposure to body fluids.
    (D) direct physical contact.

---

95. The major concern with a prolapsed cord is that it
    (A) will dry, become contaminated, and infection may result.
    (B) will delay delivery.
    (C) will be compressed and reduce blood flow to the infant resulting in hypoxia.
    (D) when exposed to room temperature, will lower the temperature of the blood going to the infant.

96. You need to administer diazepam for a three-year-old in status epilepticus. He weighs 15 kg. An acceptable dose range is:
    (A) 1.5–4.5 mg
    (B) 1.0–3.5 mg
    (C) 2.0–5 mg
    (D) 0.01 mg/kg

97. When blood levels of carbon dioxide or hydrogen ions increase above normal, the respiratory center of the brain responds by
    (A) decreasing the rate and increasing the depth of respiration.
    (B) increasing the rate and depth of respiration.
    (C) increasing the rate and decreasing the depth of respiration.
    (D) decreasing the rate and decreasing the depth of respiration.

98. A second dose of amiodarone is necessary for a patient in v fib. The dose to be administered is
    (A) 300 mg IV.
    (B) 150 mg IV.
    (C) 100 mg IV.
    (D) 40 units IV.

99. What is the proper ratio of chest compressions to ventilations while performing two-person CPR on an adult?
    (A) 15 compressions to 2 ventilations
    (B) 5 compressions to 1 ventilation
    (C) 15 compressions to 1 ventilation
    (D) 5 compressions to 2 ventilations

100. All of the following are treatable causes of pulseless electrical activity EXCEPT
    (A) hypothermia, hypovolemia, cardiac tamponade, acidosis.
    (B) hypovolemia, tension pneumothorax, hyperthermia, hyperkalemia.
    (C) acidosis, coronary thrombosis, pulmonary embolism.
    (D) tension pneumothorax, hyperkalemia, coronary thrombosis.

101. The pathophysiology of Type II diabetes mellitus includes polydipsia, polyuria, and _____ .
    (A) polyphagia.
    (B) polycythemia.
    (C) alkalosis.
    (D) glycosuria.

102. Signs and symptoms of _____ include: agitation, emotional changes, insomnia, heat intolerance, weight loss, and exophthalmos.
    (A) myxedema
    (B) malaise
    (C) Grave's disease
    (D) hypothyroidism

103. You are delivering a child when you observe the umbilical cord wrapped around the neck. Your first action should be
    (A) to stop delivery and delay as long as possible.
    (B) to gently remove the cord from around the neck.
    (C) to immediately cut the cord and remove it from around the neck.
    (D) rapid transportation to the delivery room.

104. The standards known as _____ are a major influence on safety
     standards, standardizing the look and manufacturing designs of ambulances.
     (A) medical equipment standards
     (B) essential equipment standards
     (C) DOT KKK 1822 D specs
     (D) gold standard

105. Parenteral routes of drug administration include all of the following EXCEPT
     (A) sublingual.
     (B) intravenous.
     (C) intramuscular.
     (D) topical.

106. _____ are the primary solutions used for intravenous therapy in
     the prehospital setting:
     (A) Colloids
     (B) Blood products
     (C) Hypotonic solutions
     (D) Crystalloids

107. A 49-year-old with COPD is tired, confused, and in severe respiratory distress.
     His altered mental status is most likely caused by
     (A) carbon dioxide excretion.
     (B) hypoxia.
     (C) tachypnea.
     (D) Both A and B are correct.

108. The area where the trachea divides into the right and left mainstem bronchi is
     known as the
     (A) pleura.
     (B) xiphoid process.
     (C) carina.
     (D) sternal angle.

Questions 109 and 110 are based on the following scenario:

You arrive on the scene of a trench collapse. There are three trapped victims who are
buried to the midchest. The rescue will take several hours because they will need to be
dug out by hand.

109. Crushing syndrome is a significant concern because crush injuries release toxins
     into the central circulation that can cause:
     (A) alkalosis.
     (B) increased renal function.
     (C) cardiac dysrhythmias.
     (D) dyspnea.

110. The following medications would be given to this patient to combat the effects of Crushing syndrome:
    (A) Narcan.
    (B) oxygen.
    (C) Atropine.
    (D) sodium bicarbonate.

---

111. To administer 2 mg/min of lidocaine using the mixture of 2 grams in 500 cc and 60 gtt/ml tubing, you will administer how many drops a minute?
    (A) 15
    (B) 30
    (C) 45
    (D) 60

Questions 112 and 113 are based on the following scenario:

You are sent to a private residence for a 13-month-old child with a barky cough. On arrival, you find the child being held in his mother's arms. He is awake, slow to respond, and visibly uncomfortable. Initial vital signs reveal a pulse of 170, respiratory rate of 46, and a blood pressure of 90/52. The barky cough is audible without a stethoscope but lung sounds reveal inspiratory stridor at rest. There is use of accessory muscles and you note nasal flaring.

112. From the information given in the scenario, you would suspect the child to be suffering from
    (A) epiglottitis.
    (B) croup.
    (C) bronchiolitis.
    (D) common cold.

113. This child can be categorized as a child who is experiencing
    (A) respiratory arrest.
    (B) respiratory insufficiency.
    (C) prerespiratory arrest.
    (D) respiratory failure.

---

114. Breath sounds, such as crackles and rhonchi that are not normally heard are defined as _____ breath sounds.
    (A) bronchial
    (B) adventitious
    (C) vesicular
    (D) bronchovesicular

115. The body responds to cold water by rapidly losing heat. Protective measures exist within the body, which stimulates a parasympathetic response, decreasing heart rate, causing peripheral vasoconstriction and shunting blood to the core. This cold protective response is known as the:
    (A) mammalian dive reflex.
    (B) core shunt mechanism.
    (C) cold survival mechanism.
    (D) physiologic shunt response.

116. Your patient in ventricular tachycardia is lethargic, diaphoretic, and pale and has vomited once. His vital signs are: BP 54/P, pulse 184, respirations 14. Describe your management of this patient.
    (A) 200 cc fluid bolus, nitroglycerin gr1/150 sublingual, Lidocaine
    (B) ABCs, high-flow oxygen, cardioversion
    (C) ABCs, high-flow oxygen, IV, adenocard 6 mg IV
    (D) intubation, IV, Dopamine infusion

117. What is the initial and repeat dosing schedule for sodium bicarbonate administration?
    (A) 1 amp; the repeat dose is ½ amp every 10 minutes
    (B) 1 mEq/kg; the repeat dose is ½ the initial dose in 10 minutes
    (C) 1 mg/kg; the repeat dose is ½ the initial dose in 10 minutes
    (D) 1 mEq/kg; the repeat dose is 1 mEq/kg in 10 minutes

118. You are assessing a newborn infant who presents with respiratory distress. Physical findings reveal that the patient has a low birth weight, small head, and small eye openings. Besides the obvious respiratory distress initially described, you might suspect the infant to be suffering from
    (A) heroin overdose.
    (B) crack cocaine ingestion.
    (C) fetal alcohol syndrome.
    (D) apnea of infancy.

Questions 119–122 are based on the following scenario:

You are called to the residence of a 58-year-old male. He is vomiting over the side of the front porch when you arrive. You observe many empty bottles of whiskey and beer on the porch. You have been at this residence in the past and recall that this patient has a history of alcoholism and liver cirrhosis.

119. The patient is conscious but slow to respond and appears highly intoxicated. He asks for your help and falls to the floor. His appearance is pale and diaphoretic with a blood pressure of 90/64, pulse 144, respirations 36. You note that the porch is covered in coffee-ground emesis. This patient is most likely suffering
    (A) a Mallory-Weiss tear.
    (B) a ruptured esophageal varices.
    (C) acute portal hypertension.
    (D) an acute abdominal aortic aneurysm rupture.

120. His appearance and vital signs indicate
    (A) acute withdrawal from alcohol.
    (B) compensated shock.
    (C) acute alcohol intoxication.
    (D) alcohol psychosis.

121. Treatment for this patient should include
    (A) close monitoring of airway patency to prevent aspiration, administration of Phenergan to control emesis.
    (B) close monitoring of airway patency, administration of supplemental oxygen, establishing intravenous access, and treatment for shock.
    (C) administering supplemental oxygen, administration of Phenergan to control emesis, and treatment for shock.
    (D) monitoring airway, administering oxygen 3 to 6 liters nasal cannula, transporting for alcohol detoxification.

122. During transport to the hospital, your patient has several additional episodes of vomiting. It starts as coffee-ground emesis that quickly changes to bright red blood. He is less responsive with intermediate periods of syncope. Blood pressure is 82/64 pulse 148, respirations 40. You know that
    (A) his change in mental status is secondary to the effects of the alcohol.
    (B) his vital signs and change in mental status indicate decompensated shock.
    (C) his condition is serious and rapid transport is necessary.
    (D) Both B and C are correct.

___

123. You are one of many local EMS workers who just completed working the scene of a devastating plane crash that left several hundred people dead or injured. You and your crew are called in for CISD (Critical Incident Stress Debriefing). You understand this to be
    (A) a technique for reducing stress on scene that includes fluid replacement, food services, and change of assignments.
    (B) a formal, structured, planned intervention done by a trained team within 24–72 hours after a traumatic event. The team includes mental health workers and peers.
    (C) a spontaneous post-call discussion of the events.
    (D) a short informal meeting that gives the crew a chance to vent and verbalize their feelings about this incident.

124. You are transporting a patient who has been exposed to a hazardous material. You have come into contact with this patient with level D hazmat protection equipment on. You have most likely experienced:
    (A) a secondary exposure.
    (B) a primary contamination.
    (C) a tertiary contamination.
    (D) no contamination; this level of hazmat protection is sufficient.

125. A normal PR interval is _____ to _____ seconds.
    (A) 0.12–0.20
    (B) 0.10–0.20
    (C) 0.04–0.10
    (D) 0.08–0.10

126. Management of left ventricular failure in the prehospital setting may include
    (A) placing the patient supine on the cot.
    (B) increasing venous return to the heart.
    (C) administering IV furosemide and morphine.
    (D) administering 3 liters oxygen by nasal cannula.

127. Your patient is complaining of back and flank pain described as a tearing sensation. Inspection of the abdomen reveals a pulsatile mass. Treatment includes
    (A) palpation of the mass.
    (B) gentle handling and rapid transport.
    (C) administration of Lasix 40 mg IV.
    (D) administering lidocaine 100 mg IV.

128. Which of the following correctly describes the flow of air from outside the body into the trachea?
    (A) Nose, nasopharynx, laryngopharynx, oropharynx, larynx, trachea
    (B) Nose, nasopharynx, larynx, laryngopharynx, oropharynx, trachea
    (C) Nose, nasal cavities, nasopharynx, oropharynx, laryngopharynx, larynx, trachea
    (D) Nose, nasal cavities, laryngopharynx, nasopharynx, oropharynx, larynx, trachea

---

Questions 129 and 130 are based on the following scenario:

You arrive on the scene of a 25-year-old female who states she is 9 months pregnant and is in apparent labor. The patient states she is gravida 3, para 2. She states her "water broke" about 15 minutes ago and the baby is coming. Vital signs are: BP 152/86, pulse 96, respirations 24.

129. The term "gravida" means
    (A) number of live children.
    (B) number of pregnancies.
    (C) number of miscarriages.
    (D) time period for intrauterine fetal development.

130. Upon visual examination, you notice that crowning is present. You should
    (A) place the patient in the right lateral recumbent position and transport.
    (B) prepare for delivery because birth of the baby is imminent.
    (C) place the patient in the knee to chest position and transport with lights and siren.
    (D) place patient on her left side because birth of the baby will be delayed.

---

131. A 33-year-old man has just finished playing basketball. He is complaining of chest discomfort. Physical examination shows a rapid pulse, BP 128/64, respirations 30. ECG monitor shows the following rhythm:

Treatment includes
    (A) adenocard 6 mg IV.
    (B) cardioversion 100 joules.
    (C) continuing to assess and monitor the patient.
    (D) defibrillation.

Questions 132–134 are based on the following scenario:

You are caring for a 77-year-old male patient who is short of breath. He has a history of COPD and is on home oxygen at 3 LPM by nasal cannula. He is alert and oriented to person, place, and time but only able to speak in two- to three-word sentences. BP 148/92, pulse 124, respirations of 28.

132. What does the patient's ability to speak in two- to three-word sentences indicate?
    (A) Respiratory alkalosis is present.
    (B) There is inadequate tidal volume.
    (C) His condition is improving.
    (D) Respiratory acidosis is present.

133. You observe this patient utilizing pursed-lip breathing technique. Which statement is correct regarding pursed-lip breathing?
    (A) It is not usually used by COPD patients.
    (B) It may eliminate the hypoxic drive to breathe.
    (C) It helps improve tidal volume.
    (D) It helps maintain pressure within the airways.

134. The development of which sign/symptom in this patient would lead you to believe he is significantly decompensating?
    (A) Decreased level of consciousness
    (B) JVD
    (C) Cyanosis
    (D) A rise in blood pressure

---

135. Personal protective equipment used to operate safely in the rescue environment includes all of the following EXCEPT
    (A) head protection.
    (B) eye protection.
    (C) hand protection.
    (D) throat and neck protection.

136. You are treating a 50-kg child who was found to be unconscious. The cardiac monitor attached to the patient shows a heart rate of 200 beats per minute with narrow QRS complexes. You palpate a weak pulse; blood pressure is 60/32. Oxygen is being delivered and an IV line has been established. Initial management of this patient would include
    (A) giving adenocard 6 mg IVP.
    (B) synchronizing cardioversion at 25 joules.
    (C) synchronizing cardioversion at 100 joules.
    (D) transporting with continued assessment.

137. You are called for an unresponsive 29-year-old man. Bystanders report that he has been drinking heavily all day. Assessment reveals the patient to be responsive only to painful stimuli. He is breathing at a rate of four to six times per minute and shallow. How would you manage this patient's airway?
    (A) Nasal cannula at 2–4 LPM
    (B) Simple face mask at 4–6 LPM
    (C) Nonrebreather mask at 10–15 LPM
    (D) Bag-valve device with a reservoir at 10–15 LPM

138. Which head injury will likely result in immediate neurological signs/symptoms with rapid deterioration?
    (A) Concussion
    (B) Contusion
    (C) Subdural hematoma
    (D) Epidural hematoma

Questions 139–144 are based on the following scenario:

Your EMS team is called to attend to an 18-year-old male named Todd who is having a severe asthma attack in the lunchroom at his high school. He is leaning forward and bracing himself on his desk. He has accessory muscle use, is pale, and diaphoretic. He is awake and alert but appears very tired. His vital signs are as follows: blood pressure 158/90, pulse 132, respiratory rate 32 and extremely labored.

139. Upon auscultation of Todd's chest you note breath sounds heard only in the upper lobes with very little wheezing bilaterally. This is significant because it shows
    (A) bronchoconstriction with air trapping.
    (B) that the lack of prominent wheezes rules out an asthma attack.
    (C) bronchodilation with adequate tidal volume.
    (D) that the patient is not hypoxic.

140. Todd's fatigue is significant in that it tells you
    (A) he is not in any danger of respiratory failure.
    (B) he is exchanging gases well in his lungs.
    (C) he is in danger of respiratory failure.
    (D) his condition is going to improve soon.

141. Todd is tachycardic at a rate of 132 beats per minute and has pale and diaphoretic skin. What is causing these signs?
    (A) Hypoxia.
    (B) Suppression of the sympathetic nervous system.
    (C) Release of epinephrine and norepinephrine.
    (D) Both A and C are correct.

142. Why is Todd able to talk only in short, broken phrases?
    (A) His tachycardia is impairing perfusion.
    (B) He is in left ventricular failure.
    (C) His tidal volume is inadequate for him to speak in full sentences.
    (D) He is hypoxic.

143. Which intervention will assist in dilating Todd's airways?
     (A) Supplemental oxygen via nonrebreather mask at 15 LPM
     (B) Administration of a nebulized beta-2 agonist
     (C) Allowing Todd to continue to sit upright
     (D) Starting an intravenous solution

144. What medication can be administered into the subcutaneous tissues to help allevi-
     ate Todd's respiratory distress?
     (A) Benadryl 25 mg
     (B) Epinephrine 1:10,000, 1 mg
     (C) Benadryl 5 mg
     (D) Epinephrine 1:1,000, 0.3 mg

---

145. You respond to a possible drowning call. On arrival, you find bystander CPR in
     progress on a male patient in his thirties. Your first action should be
     (A) to take over CPR from the bystanders.
     (B) immediate defibrillation.
     (C) to stop bystander CPR to assess ABCs.
     (D) to open the airway and suction if necessary.

146. The recommended dose of aspirin for a patient experiencing chest pain is:
     (A) 325 mg.
     (B) 162–325 mg.
     (C) 81 mg.
     (D) 650 mg.

147. You just delivered three stacked shocks to a patient in ventricular fibrillation. The
     monitor now shows asystole. You confirm in two leads. Your next action is to
     (A) administer Atropine 1 mgIVP.
     (B) consider immediate transcutaneous pacing.
     (C) administer fluid bolus 200 cc.
     (D) defibrillate at 360 joules.

148. You are called to the scene of a mass casualty incident where you are responsible
     for the triage transportation decisions. Which of the following patients would be
     the first to be transported to the local trauma center?
     (A) a 50-year-old man complaining of knee and ankle pain.
     (B) an 18-year-old female with a five-minute lapse of consciousness after being
         struck in the head
     (C) a 25-year-old female, eight months pregnant with partial thickness burns on her
         arms and legs covering 5% of her BSA
     (D) a 32-year-old male with a large piece of metal impaled in his left foot

149. You have been summoned to a local residence for a child who fell. On arrival, you find a seven-year-old boy supporting his left arm with his right hand. You note that the boy also has what appears to be some swelling around his right eye. You also note bruises in various stages of healing on his chest and lower back. His parents are upstairs, providing no comfort or support to the boy. Given this information, you suspect
    (A) "coining."
    (B) "rubbing."
    (C) child abuse.
    (D) shaken baby syndrome.

150. Normal intrathoracic pressure
    (A) exceeds atmospheric pressure.
    (B) is equal to atmospheric pressure.
    (C) is less than atmospheric pressure.
    (D) None of the above

151. The presence of pulmonary congestion indicated by abnormal lung sounds such as crackles (rales) in a patient complaining of chest pain may indicate
    (A) hypotension.
    (B) increased vagal tone.
    (C) increased stroke volume.
    (D) left ventricular failure.

152. When the body is not able to use glucose as a primary source of energy, what occurs?
    (A) Adipose cells begin breaking down resulting in hyperglycemia.
    (B) Adipose cells begin breaking down resulting in hypoglycemia.
    (C) Adipose cells begin breaking down resulting in hyperinsulinism.
    (D) Adipose cells begin breaking down resulting in ketoacidosis.

Questions 153 and 154 are based on the following scenario:

A patient weighing 220 pounds presents in this rhythm:

153. Management should include
    (A) amiodarone 300 mg IV.
    (B) lidocaine 180 mg IV.
    (C) procainamide 4 mg/min IV.
    (D) magnesium 1 mg IV.

154. Further management for the rhythm includes
    (A) amiodarone 150 mg IV.
    (B) vasopressin 20 mg IV.
    (C) procainamide 4 mg/min up to a total of 17 mg/kg IV.
    (D) magnesium 1 gram IV.

155. You are caring for a 24-year-old male who wrecked his four-wheeler. He states that his handlebar struck him in the stomach. He has bruising and tenderness in the abdomen and you suspect bowel rupture. This condition can lead to _____ and the development of serious complications.
    (A) peritonitis
    (B) diaphragm dysfunction
    (C) gastric distention
    (D) herniated bowel

156. You are called for a 54-year-old woman who is unconscious. Your assessment reveals the patient to be apneic and pulseless. Initial management of this patient's airway should include
    (A) assisted ventilation with a bag-valve device at 6–10 LPM.
    (B) assisted ventilation with a nonrebreather mask at 10–15 LPM.
    (C) immediate nasotracheal intubation and ventilation with a bag-valve device.
    (D) insertion of an oropharyngeal airway and ventilation with a bag-valve device.

Questions 157–159 are based on the following scenario:

You have a female patient at 39 weeks gestation. She has regular contractions lasting 45–60 seconds at one- to two-minute intervals and is crowning.

157. Contraction intervals are correctly measured
    (A) from the beginning of one contraction to the end.
    (B) from the end of one contraction to the end of the next.
    (C) from the beginning of one contraction to the beginning of the next.
    (D) from the end of one contraction to the beginning of the next.

158. Contraction length is correctly measured
    (A) from the beginning of one contraction to the end.
    (B) from the end of one contraction to the end of the next.
    (C) from the beginning of one contraction to the beginning of the next.
    (D) from the end of one contraction to the beginning of the next.

159. Treatment for this patient should include
    (A) transport since delivery will not occur immediately.
    (B) preparation for delivery.
    (C) starting immediate transportation to the hospital.
    (D) placing her on her left side and administering oxygen.

160. You are called to the scene of a single-car MVC involving a 25-year-old female who is 30 weeks pregnant. What normal physiological alterations take place during pregnancy that may affect your assessment of this patient?
    (A) Increased blood pressure and increased pulse
    (B) Increased blood pressure and decreased pulse
    (C) Decreased blood pressure and decreased pulse
    (D) Decreased blood pressure and increased pulse

Questions 161–163 are based on the following scenario:

You are called to a scene of a motor vehicle collision (MVC). During your initial assessment, you find an unresponsive 32-year-old male with multiple contusions to his face and head. He has snoring respirations and a weak, thready peripheral pulse.

161. Your first action would be
    (A) to control any major bleeding.
    (B) rapid extrication.
    (C) to open the airway with a modified jaw thrust and immobilize the cervical spine.
    (D) endotracheal intubation and starting two large-bore intravenous lines with normal saline and run at "wide open" rate.

162. Your partner performs a rapid trauma survey and finds him lethargic, very pale, with cool and clammy skin. He has contusions, crepitus and diminished breath sounds on the right side of the chest. BP 74/50, pulse of 140 centrally, no peripheral pulse found at this time, and respirations 32 and shallow. What is the most likely cause of these findings?
    (A) Beck's triad
    (B) A hemopneumothorax
    (C) Cushing's syndrome
    (D) A ruptured liver

163. These critical findings should have been found in what length of time?
    (A) Five minutes
    (B) Ten minutes
    (C) Less than two minutes
    (D) Three to six minutes

---

164. A 16-month-old child presents with seizures. Airway assessment reveals copious secretions. Breath sounds are present and coarse bilaterally. Heart rate is regular with weak pulses. After suctioning the airway and assisting ventilations, you are able to establish IV access. Identify those that can cause seizures in this age group:
    (A) Bronchiolitis, croup, fever
    (B) Drug overdose, hyperglycemia, pneumonia
    (C) Hypoglycemia, fever, drug overdose
    (D) Hyperglycemia, pneumonia, fever

165. The time elapsing between the beginning of the p wave and the beginning of the QRS complex on the electrocardiogram is
(A) the QRS complex.
(B) first-degree heart block.
(C) QT interval.
(D) PR interval.

166. Vasopressin is useful in the management of
(A) complete heart block.
(B) PSVT.
(C) ventricular fibrillation.
(D) torsades de pointes.

Questions 167 and 168 are based on the following scenario:

A 42-year-old male presents with severe pain in the left flank area with no history or signs of trauma. The patient has excruciating colicky pain with intermittent vomiting.

167. What problem would you suspect as the cause of the patient's discomfort?
(A) An abdominal aortic aneurysm
(B) Appendicitis
(C) A gallbladder attack
(D) Renal calculi

168. Treatment for this patient would include
(A) IV fluids and morphine.
(B) nasogastric tube to decompress the stomach.
(C) NTG and aspirin.
(D) PASG and two large-bore IVs wide open.

169. You have performed a Rapid Trauma Survey on a child and are prepared to transport. In which situation is it appropriate to perform the detailed exam enroute to the hospital?
(A) A fracture of the humerus
(B) An amputated thumb
(C) Mottled skin with tachycardia
(D) A fractured tibia with numbness in the foot

170. You respond to a bee sting call and find a six-year-old with a full body rash. He has no respiratory difficulty at this time. You are going to administer Benadryl. The correct dose is
(A) 25 mg.
(B) 50 mg.
(C) 1 mg/kg.
(D) 0.5 mg/kg.

171. During transport of a seven-year-old male who has sustained multisystem trauma, you determine the need for fluid resuscitation. Appropriate administration of fluid would be to
    (A) rapidly infuse 250–300 cc of dextrose 5% in water.
    (B) rapidly infuse 350 cc of dextrose 5% in water.
    (C) determine the child's weight in kilograms and administer a 20 cc/kg bolus of an isotonic crystalloid.
    (D) give an immediate rapid infusion of normal saline, reassess, and then give additional boluses as needed.

172. You are evaluating a male patient with complaints of a "tearing sensation" epigastric pain. He tells you that the pain began two hours ago after eating lunch. He says he has never experienced any pain like this. He rates the pain as a 10, and states that it is radiating into his back and shoulder. Based on the information provided, you suspect the pain may be the result of
    (A) a myocardial infarction.
    (B) a hiatal hernia.
    (C) an aortic aneurysm.
    (D) gastric esophageal reflux disease.

173. A 68-year-old male suffered a syncopal episode while golfing. The cardiac monitor shows a sinus tachycardia at 142 beats/minute without ectopy. His blood pressure is presently 78/42. Despite a 200 cc fluid bolus the patient remains hypotensive. The patient has an altered mental status with cool and diaphoretic skin. Of the following, which is not likely to be considered for administration to this patient?
    (A) Dopamine
    (B) Nitroglycerin
    (C) A second fluid bolus
    (D) High-flow oxygen

Questions 174–177 are based on the following scenario:

You respond to an explosion at a local fireworks production factory. The explosion rocked the ground several blocks away. There are multiple patients.

174. The mechanism of injury from a blast or explosion can be from three factors: primary, secondary, and tertiary. The mechanism of injury of a patient who suffers injuries from being struck by material propelled by the blast force is considered
    (A) a primary mechanism of injury.
    (B) a secondary mechanism of injury.
    (C) a tertiary mechanism of injury.
    (D) All of the above

175. The mechanism of injury of a patient being thrown and impacting the ground or other object is considered
    (A) a primary mechanism of injury.
    (B) a secondary mechanism of injury.
    (C) a tertiary mechanism of injury.
    (D) All of the above

176. Your first patient is a 43-year-old male with burns over the front of his right arm, upper chest, and the front of his right leg. Using the rule of nines, what percent of burns does this patient have?
    (A) 27%
    (B) 22.5%
    (C) 18%
    (D) 35%

177. This patient is hoarse, has singed nasal hair, is coughing up charcoal-colored sputum, and has developed inspiratory stridor. Treatment should include
    (A) high-flow oxygen via simple mask.
    (B) immediate endotracheal intubation.
    (C) continuing to monitor for complications.
    (D) humidified oxygen via nasal cannula.

Question 178 and 179 are based on the following scenario:

A 62-year-old male fainted while working in the yard. His current vitals are BP 108/64, pulse 102 and irregular, and respirations 24. ECG shows the following rhythm:

178. You interpret his ECG rhythm as
    (A) second-degree heart block.
    (B) sinus rhythm.
    (C) atrial fibrillation.
    (D) sinus bradycardia.

179. The patient complains of feeling that he is going to black out again. Vitals are unchanged. Treatment for the patient should include
    (A) oxygen, monitoring, IV, observation, and transport.
    (B) oxygen, monitoring, IV, Atropine.
    (C) oxygen, monitoring, IV, adenocard.
    (D) oxygen, monitoring, IV, synchronized cardioversion.

---

180. You respond to the local high school football practice field for a sports injury. The coach tells you that the patient made a tackle and after the play did not get up. Your patient is supine on the ground with all of his equipment on. He is awake but slow to answer questions. You should remove the football helmet if
    (A) a c-spine injury is suspected.
    (B) you do not have easy access to the airway.
    (C) you suspect the patient had a loss of consciousness.
    (D) the patient has numbness in his hands.

Answer Key

1. B	46. C	91. C	136. B
2. A	47. B	92. A	137. D
3. B	48. B	93. C	138. D
4. B	49. C	94. B	139. A
5. C	50. D	95. C	140. C
6. C	51. C	96. A	141. D
7. B	52. D	97. B	142. C
8. B	53. C	98. B	143. B
9. C	54. D	99. A	144. D
10. D	55. A	100. B	145. C
11. C	56. B	101. A	146. B
12. A	57. D	102. C	147. B
13. A	58. D	103. B	148. B
14. B	59. B	104. C	149. C
15. D	60. C	105. A	150. C
16. C	61. B	106. D	151. D
17. C	62. D	107. B	152. D
18. D	63. D	108. C	153. A
19. D	64. A	109. C	154. A
20. C	65. D	110. D	155. A
21. B	66. A	111. B	156. D
22. D	67. A	112. B	157. C
23. B	68. B	113. D	158. A
24. C	69. A	114. B	159. B
25. D	70. A	115. A	160. D
26. D	71. B	116. B	161. C
27. B	72. B	117. B	162. B
28. A	73. A	118. C	163. C
29. C	74. B	119. B	164. C
30. C	75. D	120. B	165. D
31. A	76. B	121. B	166. C
32. C	77. D	122. D	167. D
33. D	78. B	123. B	168. A
34. D	79. D	124. A	169. C
35. A	80. A	125. A	170. C
36. D	81. D	126. C	171. C
37. C	82. A	127. B	172. C
38. A	83. D	128. C	173. B
39. B	84. D	129. B	174. B
40. C	85. C	130. B	175. C
41. C	86. C	131. A	176. B
42. A	87. D	132. B	177. B
43. A	88. A	133. D	178. C
44. C	89. C	134. C	179. A
45. C	90. B	135. D	180. B

Answer Explanations

1. **(B)** Battery is the unlawful touching of someone without his or her consent.

2. **(A)** The skin is the body's first line of defense against infectious agents.

3. **(B)** Care for this patient would not require parental consent because the patient is married and therefore an emancipated minor.

4. **(B)** The phrenic nerve originates from spinal nerves C3–C4–C5.

5. **(C)** A suspected basilar skull fracture is a contraindication for nasotracheal intubation because the distal tip of the endotracheal tube could enter the cranial cavity through the fracture site.

6. **(C)** Epinephrine is the first medication to be administered in the pulseless electrical activity algorithm.

7. **(B)** Atropine 1 mg follows the administration of epinephrine in pulseless electrical activity algorithm.

8. **(B)** Hypervolemia is NOT considered a treatable cause of PEA.

9. **(C)** A fracture of the lower extremity is a contraindication to an IO insertion.

10. **(D)** Injury to the stomach or small bowel that allows digestive enzymes to enter the peritoneal cavity can cause a rapid development of sharp pain throughout the abdomen. This is a serious concern because peritonitis can develop and lead to complications.

11. **(C)** Ballistics is the study of projectiles in motion. Studies suggest that wounds from rifle bullets are two to four times more lethal than handgun bullets due to mass energy and velocity.

12. **(A)** ARDS is a form of pulmonary edema that occurs as a response to a wide variety of lung injury insults.

13. **(A)** Cheyne-Stokes respiratory pattern is characterized by a gradually increasing rate and tidal volume followed by a gradual decrease with intermittent periods of apnea. This breathing pattern is usually seen in patients with brain injury or elderly patients with terminal illness.

14. **(B)** It is not the role of the EMS dispatcher to diagnose the nature of the illness. EMS dispatchers serve by receiving the call, taking information regarding the nature of the event, and providing prearrival instructions to assist prior to the EMS units arrival.

15. **(D)** Of the choices listed, evaluating the patient for adequate hydration is the top priority. Evaluating the patient's temperature and the presence of infection are necessary but secondary to determining adequate hydration.

16. **(C)** The proper size oropharyngeal airway (OPA) is determined by measuring from the corner of the mouth to the tip of the earlobe at the angle of the jaw. It is essential the OPA be sized appropriately because improper sizing can lead to airway obstruction.

17. **(C)** You should place your hands on the lower half of the sternum, at the nipple line

18. **(D)** Ecchymosis in the flank area associated with intraabdominal hemorrhage is known as Grey-Turner sign. Ecchymosis in the periumbilical area is known as Cullen's sign **(B)**. Mallory-Weiss sign **(C)** is associated with an esophageal tear or laceration that results from excessive vomiting. Peritonitis, **(A)**, is inflammation of the peritoneum.

19. **(D)** The t-wave reflects repolarization of the ventricles.

20. **(C)** Dopamine at 1–2 mcg/kg/min administration causes renal artery dilation to occur. At 2–10 mcg/kg/min, it primarily affects beta receptors. At 10–15 mcg/kg/min, it primarily affects both alpha and beta receptors. At 15–20 mcg/kg/min it primarily affects alpha receptors.

21. **(B)** Cardiogenic shock is the most severe form of pump failure that often results in dysrhythmias, hypotension, respiratory failure, and possibly organ failure. The heart rate is initially elevated as the body attempts to compensate for the shock. Hypertension will not be present in cardiogenic shock.

22. **(D)** The period of the cardiac cycle when a significantly strong stimulus may produce depolarization is the relative refractory period. The period of the cardiac cycle when stimulation will not produce depolarization is the absolute refractory period **(C)**. The refractory period **(A)** is a period of time when myocardial cells have not yet completely repolarized and cannot be stimulated again. **(B)** is not a term used in cardiology.

23. **(B)** The number one priority of every EMS call is assurance of the crew's personal safety.

24. **(C)** Parkinson's disease is characterized by tremor, rigidity of muscles, bradykinesia, and impaired balance. It affects 500,000 Americans.

25. **(D)** Starting an intravenous line will allow access for medications if necessary, determining the blood glucose level will show if the altered mental status is due to hypoglycemia, and applying a cardiac monitor will determine if there is a rhythm disturbance.

26. **(D)** This instrument measures the presence or absence of carbon dioxide in the sampled gas at the tip of the endotracheal tube. It can be used as an assessment tool to help determine proper endotracheal tube placement.

27. **(B)** In pericardial tamponade, the pericardial sac fills with fluid and compresses the heart. This impairs ventricular filling. The result is a decrease in cardiac output (the left ventricle cannot effectively fill and pump) and an increase in central venous pressure (venous blood returning to the heart is impaired and the right ventricle cannot fill or pump effectively).

28. **(A)** Spinal shock (neurogenic) is a distributive shock producing hypotension relative to an increase in the vascular space in the absence of a loss of body fluids. A spinal cord injury results in a "lack of communication" between the brain and the body so there is no response to catecholamine release resulting in bradycardia and hypotension.

29. **(C)** Using the rule of nines, the head of an infant is assigned 18% body surface area.

30. **(C)** Auscultation of the chest for proper endotracheal tube placement is necessary. If lung sounds are diminished or absent, it may be necessary to extubate, ventilate, reassess, and then reintubate.

31. **(A)** Falls of greater than 10 feet are not reportable injuries. Injuries reportable to local authorities include spouse abuse, child abuse or neglect, elder abuse, sexual assault, gunshot/stab wounds, animal bites, and communicable diseases.

32. **(C)** Priority for this patient who presents with respiratory compromise and hypovolemia is airway support and fluid resuscitation.

33. **(D)** Intestines should never be pushed back into the abdominal compartment. A moist nonadherent dressing should be gently placed over the bowel to prevent it from "drying out" because of the risk of irreversible damage.

34. **(D)** The standard adult dose of subcutaneous epinephrine in the treatment of allergic reaction is 0.3–0.5 mg of 1:1,000 solution.

35. **(A)** Hepatitis A is transmitted via the oral/fecal route.

36. **(D)** The spleen is a blood-filled organ located in the left upper quadrant. Blunt trauma can cause injury to the spleen resulting in blood loss and shock. The spleen is the most injured organ resulting in *shock*, while the liver is the most injured organ resulting in *death* of a pediatric patient.

37. **(C)** 1.0 mg/kg of succinylcholine is the recommended dose for this patient. There are no contraindications to its use in this scenario.

38. **(A)** This is a trauma victim and should be managed utilizing c-spine precautions. **(A)** is the only correct answer. Using any other option would potentiate a cervical spine injury.

39. **(B)** Suctioning should not exceed 5 seconds in a pediatric patient and 15 seconds in an adult patient.

40. **(C)** This is a difficult question. If you knew this answer, pat yourself on the back. A LeFort II fracture involves both the maxillary and nasal bones.

41. **(C)** Of the choices listed, provide high-flow oxygen by nonrebreather mask at 15 liters per minute once the airway has been assured is correct. **(A)** is incorrect because it states "ALL" inhalation injury. **(B)** is incorrect because the patient requires high-flow oxygen. **(D)** is incorrect because the scenario does not give enough information to conclude cyanide toxicity.

42. **(A)** The patient's insurance information is not a necessary part of documentation included in a patient care refusal.

43. **(A)** The brain recognizes a decrease in pH or excess of H+ ions and attempts to compensate by increasing the respiratory effort.

44. **(C)** Lidocaine 1 mg/kg is indicated for the treatment of bigeminal PVCs.

45. **(C)** The QRS complex reflects ventricular depolarization. The Q-wave is the first negative deflection after the p wave; the r wave is the first positive deflection after the p wave; and the s wave is the first negative deflection after the r wave. All three waves are not always present.

46. **(C)** Arteriosclerosis is a disease of the arterial vessel marked by thickening, hardening, and loss of elasticity in the arterial walls. Atherosclerosis **(A)** is the most common form of arteriosclerosis usually involving medium-sized and large arteries. Arteriolonecrosis, **(B)**, is destruction (necrosis) of the arteriole. Angina, **(D)**, is chest discomfort associated with a deficiency of oxygen supply to the heart muscle.

47. **(B)** The minimum-size bag-valve mask device used for neonates, infants, and children should be 450 ml: Although it is likely that the bag-valve mask will not deliver 450 ml of volume, it is important to have a device capable of delivering excessive volumes because, as the bag is compressed, there is dead space, from which air cannot be fully expelled.

48. **(B)** Since her signs and symptoms disappeared rapidly, and she has no neurological deficits, she most likely suffered a transient ischemic attack. TIA is considered a significant warning sign for the development of a stroke.

49. **(C)** Presentation of adrenal insufficiency (Addisonian crisis) may include cardiovascular collapse, hypotension, and hypoglycemia. These serious signs/symptoms are attributed to major disturbances in the water and electrolyte balance within the body.

50. **(D)** Pertinent negatives are findings that require no medical treatment but help to show the completeness of the paramedics' history and exam on the PCR.

51. **(C)** The ET tube must be removed swiftly on a cough or expiration.

52. **(D)** Your safety is the first priority. Do not approach the car until you are notified by the proper officials that the power has been turned off.

53. **(C)** Cushing's or herniation syndrome is manifested by hypertension, bradycardia, and erratic respirations. This patient has a GCS score of 9, hypertension (178/100), bradycardia (56), and irregular respirations, which indicate head injury with Cushing's syndrome.

54. **(D)** Intubation and supplemental oxygen are essential. You would hyperventilate this patient because he or she exhibits signs/symptoms of increased intracranial pressure (Cushing's syndrome).

55. **(A)** The objective of prehospital fluid resuscitation is to stabilize vital signs until the patient arrives at the hospital.

56. **(B)** Recognize that the infant has inadequate oxygenation (dusky color) and immediately begin bag-valve mask ventilation with 100% oxygen.

57. **(D)** Epinephrine 1:10,000 solution should be given at 0.01 mg/kg IV/IO for persistent bradycardia unresponsive to ventilation.

58. **(D)** Considering the ambient temperature to be very cold in this scenario, hypothermia is a significant cause of the patient's presentation. Begin rewarming the patient.

59. **(B)** A duplex communication system allows the user to both listen and speak at the same time. A simplex system **(A)** allows you to listen or speak at one time. A multiplex system **(C)** allows a person to listen and speak, as well as transmit data. A trunked system, **(D)**, pools all frequencies and routes transmissions to the next available frequency.

60. **(C)** This patient should be tagged Red with immediate life threats including the possibility of bilateral femur fractures and intraabdominal bleeding.

61. **(B)** This patient needs oxygen by nonrebreather mask. He has an increased respiratory rate and PVCs on the monitor that may indicate hypoxia. A normal pulse oximeter of 97% is a welcome finding but oxygen should not be withheld based on this reading. Always remember to treat your patient and not the pulse oximeter.

62. **(D)** Hyperthermia will not cause the pulse oximeter error.

63. **(D)** All of the above are correct. Auscultating individual lung fields is of great benefit because they help to confirm tube placement. Auscultation of the epigastrium is beneficial because it will help to verify improper tube placement or problems with the cuff seal of the tube.

64. **(A)** Keep the newborn at the same level of the vagina with the head slightly lower than the rest of the body. This will prevent over- or undertransfusion of blood from the umbilical cord to the newborn and facilitate drainage of secretions from the nose and mouth to help prevent aspiration.

65. **(D)** Suctioning may result in bradycardia from stimulation of the vagus nerve, particularly in children less than six months old. Do not use *prolonged* suction attempts.

66. **(A)** You should always have a Glasgow Coma Scale chart available to reference in your EMS practice. Unfortunately, you may not have a chart to reference on a certification exam. Therefore, you must be familiar with its contents. This patient has a GCS score of 9—eye opening = 2, verbal response = 3, motor response = 4.

67. **(A)** Acute coronary syndrome is defined as a sudden ischemic disorder of the heart. If you are not familiar with this terminology, it is strongly recommended that you review Chapter Six of the American Heart Association ACLS Providers manual.

68. **(B)** The helicopter should be approached cautiously in a crouched position away from the tail rotor. Approach a helicopter that is on a slight incline from the downhill side.

69. **(A)** In a pediatric patient, adenosine given at 0.1 mg/kg IV is indicated to correct a stable tachycardia.

70. **(A)** Anatomical dead space is defined as the volume of air in the trachea, bronchi, and air passages containing air that does not reach the alveoli during respiration.

71. **(B)** An esophageal tear or laceration that results from excessive vomiting is known as a Mallory-Weiss tear. While you may suspect this type of injury, it is difficult to be 100% certain. Do not rule out more serious causes of upper GI bleeding.

72. **(B)** A subconjunctival hemorrhage involves rupture of small blood vessels in the subconjunctival space resulting in the "white" of the eye becoming blood red. This may occur after a strong sneeze or excessive vomiting. While it looks dramatic, this type of hemorrhage usually clears without intervention and rarely causes any residual problems.

73. **(A)** The usual dose range of Phenergan is 12.5 to 25 mg. It can be administered slow IVP or by deep IM injection. SQ administration is not indicated.

74. **(B)** Pursed-lip breathing technique helps maintain pressure within the airways (even during exhalation) to support bronchial walls that have been damaged as a result of disease.

75. **(D)** This is one of the most basic OB questions you can be asked. If you missed this question, you need to review childbirth.

76. **(B)** 0.01 mg/kg IV/IO of 1:10,000 solution is the recommended dose of epinephrine for pediatric cardiac arrest and/or symptoms of bradycardia.

77. **(D)** Bradypnea respiratory pattern is characterized by slow, shallow, irregular respirations. This breathing pattern can be associated with stroke or several other nervous system diseases.

78. **(B)** Standard of care can be established by court testimony, reference to published codes, standard criteria, and standards appropriate for the situation.

79. **(D)** A disaster is an incident that may generate hundreds of patients, may overwhelm the existing resources, and may damage the infrastructure of the region shutting down railroads, hospitals, and other normal operations.

80. **(A)** This is a basic life support question to which you must know the correct answer. If you missed this question, do yourself a favor and review infant, child, and adult CPR prior to taking your certification exam.

81. **(D)** Vasopressin is indicated in ventricular fibrillation at a dose of 40 *units* IV to be administered as a *one-time* dose.

82. **(A)** 17 mcg/kg is incorrect because procainamide is delivered in mg/kg.

83. **(D)** Calcium chloride may by useful in a dialysis patient in cardiac arrest with PEA. Dialysis patients often suffer from hyperkalemia as a result of their disease process.

84. **(D)** The Esophageal Tracheal CombiTube is not indicated for pediatric patients due to its large diameter and the risk of perforation of the esophagus.

85. **(C)** The normal value for PCO_2 is 35 to 45 mmHg. A high PCO_2 is considered respiratory acidosis. A low PCO_2 is considered respiratory alkalosis.

86. **(C)** After the third month of gestation the fetus and uterus grow rapidly. After the fifth month of pregnancy, the uterus rises out of the pelvis and is more prone to injury.

87. **(D)** This should be classified as a critical burn with over 50% body surface area containing second-degree burns.

88. **(A)** In a simplex system the user is able to only listen or speak. The major disadvantages include the process being slower, more formal, and not facilitating discussion.

89. **(C)** This patient has diabetic ketoacidosis and is likely to be profoundly dehydrated because excess glucose acts as an osmotic diuretic. Fluid replacement with normal saline should be started immediately.

90. **(B)** The signs and symptoms of hypoglycemia are many and varied. Altered mental status including irritability, bizarre behavior, or agitation is often the most important and early indicator of a problem. Other signs/symptoms may include diaphoresis, tachycardia, weakness, and headache. Coma may be present in severe cases.

91. **(C)** Heat cramps are acute painful spasms of the voluntary muscles following strenuous activities in a hot environment.

92. **(A)** Treatment for heat cramps include removing the patient from the hot environment and administration of oral saline solution or sport drinks for hydration. If oral fluids cannot be administered because of nausea, an IV line of normal saline may be needed. **(C)** and **(B)** are incorrect because rapid cooling is indicated for heatstroke NOT heat cramps and two large-bore IVs wide open are NOT indicated for heat cramps.

93. **(C)** Tuberculosis presents with a chronic cough persistent for two to three weeks, low-grade fever, and night sweats. Certain populations are at a higher risk of developing TB including children <3 years old and geriatric patients.

94. **(B)** Tuberculosis is transmitted through exposure to airborne droplets, and prolonged close exposure to a person with active TB.

95. **(C)** The major concern with a prolapsed cord is compression of the cord by the head of the infant. This can result in a reduced blood flow to the infant and lead to fetal hypoxia.

96. **(A)** The dose range for diazepam is 0.1–0.3 mg/kg. A 15 kg patient would receive 1.5 to 4.5 mg of medication.

97. **(B)** Rate and depth of respiration are increased to eliminate excess CO_2 and therefore decreasing hydrogen ion concentrations. This is a normal compensatory mechanism of the body.

98. **(B)** The correct second dose of amiodarone for a patient in v fib is 150 mg IVP.

99. **(A)** This a basic life support question to which you must know the correct answer. If you missed this question, do yourself a favor and review infant, child, and adult CPR prior to taking your certification test.

100. **(B)** Hyperthermia is not considered a treatable cause of pulseless electrical activity. All of the following are considered treatable causes of PEA: hypovolemia, hypoxia, acidosis, hyper/hypokalemia, hypothermia, drug overdose, cardiac tamponade, tension pneumothorax, coronary thrombosis, and pulmonary embolism.

101. **(A)** Polydipsia (excessive thirst), polyuria (excessive urination), and polyphagia (excessive hunger) are just a few symptoms of untreated diabetes mellitus.

102. **(C)** You must be familiar with signs and symptoms of the most common endocrine disorders. Agitation, emotional changes, insomnia, heat intolerance, weight loss, and exophthalmos are all common in Graves' disease. Graves' disease is the result of thyrotoxicosis (excessive thyroid hormones).

103. **(B)** Initial care for nuchal cord (cord around the neck) is to first try to gently remove the cord from around the neck. If this is not successful and the cord is so tight that it is inhibiting labor, it will be necessary to clamp the cord in two places and cut between the clamps.

104. **(C)** The DOT KKK 1822 D specs outline the design and manufacturing specifications produced by the Federal General Services Administrative Automotive Commodity Center.

105. **(A)** Parenteral routes for delivery of medication include all those areas outside the gastrointestinal tract. Parenteral routes include intravenous, endotracheal, intramuscular, subcutaneous, topical and inhalation. The sublingual route administers the drug through the enteral route, or through the gastrointestinal tract.

106. **(D)** Crystalloids are the primary solutions used for intravenous fluid therapies in the prehospital setting.

107. **(B)** Hypoxia can affect the brain at the cellular level resulting in a decreased mental status.

108. **(C)** This is a basic anatomy and physiology question. The area where the trachea divides into the right and left mainstem bronchi is known as the carina.

109. **(C)** Crushing syndrome is a complex process. Part of this process causes toxin production including an increased potassium level. One of the major concerns with releasing a body part that has been crushed for several hours is the release of toxins into the circulating blood volume, which can lead to cardiac arrhythmia and immediate death.

110. **(D)** Crushing syndrome creates lactic acid due to anaerobic metabolism that takes place within the crushed body part. One of the major concerns with releasing a body part that has been crushed for several hours is the release of the lactic acid and other toxins into the circulating blood volume that can lead to profound metabolic acidosis. Sodium bicarbonate is indicated in the treatment of Crushing syndrome.

111. **(B)** Two grams of lidocaine in 500 cc of solution will provide a mixture of 4 mg/ml. To deliver 2 mg/min using 60 gtt/ml tubing, you need to administer 30 drops per minute.

112. **(B)** Croup is a viral infection of the upper airway that causes inflammation of the subglottic region that can lead to airway obstruction. Inspiratory stridor is often present. Other assessment findings include nasal flaring, tracheal tugging, or retractions. The vital signs of this patient are compensatory to the airway obstruction.

113. **(D)** Respiratory failure is evident for the following reasons: tachypnea, tachycardia, nasal flaring, retractions, audible airway noises (stridor/barky) cough, and slowness to respond, which indicates a decreased level of consciousness.

114. **(B)** Adventitious breath sounds are considered abnormal sounds such as crackles and rhonchi.

115. **(A)** The mammalian dive reflex is a protective physiologic response, which increases survivability by shunting blood to the core, decreasing heart rate and dropping blood pressure. These factors are affected by the person's age, water temperature, and health status.

116. **(B)** ABCs and high-flow oxygen are indicated for this patient and cardioversion needs to be performed because the patient is in ventricular tachycardia *with a pulse*.

117. **(B)** Sodium bicarbonate has been in use for a long time. Current dosing instructions include 1 mEq/kg for the initial dose and half the initial dose or 0.5 mEq/kg for the second dose. It is suggested the repeat dose be given 10 minutes after the first.

118. **(C)** Characteristics of a newborn with fetal alcohol syndrome include low birth weight, small head, and small eye openings.

119. **(B)** The patient's past medical history and presentation should lead you to the conclusion of ruptured esophageal varices. **(A)** is incorrect because a Mallory-Weiss tear is usually not associated with significant blood loss. **(C)** and **(D)** are incorrect because the scenario does not give enough information to conclude this.

120. **(B)** This patient is experiencing compensated shock as evidence by his elevated pulse rate (144), evidence of vasoconstriction (pale moist skin), and his ability to maintain his blood pressure.

121. **(B)** As always, the airway is your priority. You must protect the airway and prevent aspiration of emesis. Supplemental oxygen, establishing intravenous access, and treating this patient for shock are required. **(A)** and **(C)** are incorrect because Phenergan potentiates the effects of alcohol. **(D)** is incorrect because the patient requires supplemental oxygen and transport to an acute care hospital.

122. **(D)** Both **(B)** and **(C)** are correct. His vital signs indicate decompensated shock and rapid transport is necessary. While it is true alcohol is a CNS depressant and can alter mental status, you cannot assume this is the cause of his change in mental status since decompensated shock is present; therefore, **(A)** is incorrect.

123. **(B)** CISD is a formal, structured, planned intervention performed by a CISM (critical incident stress management) team, which includes mental health workers and peers. The intervention should take place within 24–72 hours after a traumatic event.

124. **(A)** A secondary contamination; Level D hazmat protection equipment is the lowest level of protection. Level D equipment consists of structural firefighting, or turn-out gear. Secondary contamination occurs when an uncontaminated person comes in contact with a contaminated person.

125. **(A)** Fundamentals of ECG interpretation tell us that a normal PR interval is 0.12 to 0.20 seconds.

126. **(C)** Administration of IV furosemide and morphine are appropriate in the prehospital management of left ventricular failure. You want to place the patient in a sitting position to facilitate breathing, NOT supine. Increasing venous return to the heart will worsen the condition. Administration of oxygen should be at a high-flow rate.

127. **(B)** Back and flank pain described as a tearing sensation and a pulsating abdominal mass are classic signs of an abdominal aortic aneurysm. Gentle handling and rapid transport to the hospital are essential once the diagnosis is made. Palpating the mass **(A)** is contraindicated and may worsen the condition. **(C)** and **(D)** are not indicated for this patient.

128. **(C)** This is a simple anatomy and physiology question. The nose, nasal cavities, nasopharynx, oropharynx, laryngopharynx, larynx, and trachea correctly describe the flow of air.

129. **(B)** Gravida or gravidity refers to the number of times a women has been pregnant. If you did not know this common terminology, you must review obstetric medical terminology.

130. **(B)** Preparation for delivery is necessary. The information presented in this scenario should lead you to believe that delivery of the baby is imminent.

131. **(A)** Treatment for this patient includes adenocard 6 mg IVP since chest pain is present. This scenario does not present an unstable patient and therefore cardioversion **(B)** is not indicated. Assessment and monitoring the patient will be done but this is not the best choice since adenocard is indicated. **(D)** is not indicated.

132. **(B)** A patient who is not able to speak in full sentences due to breathing difficulty does not have an adequate tidal volume. This assessment finding can be a significant warning sign of pending respiratory failure.

133. **(D)** Pursed-lip breathing technique helps maintain pressure within the airways (even during exhalation) to support bronchial walls that have been damaged as a result of disease.

134. **(C)** Cyanosis is correct because the question asks about *significant* decompensation. Decreased level of consciousness **(A)** is an *early* indicator of decompensation. Proper care should be instituted to hopefully prevent the development of significant decompensation. This is an example of how test-taking skills come in handy. You must understand what the question is asking to choose the correct answer. **(B)** and **(D)** may or may not be present depending on the cause of the respiratory difficulty.

135. **(D)** No specific equipment is designed for throat and neck protection. PPE used to safely operate in rescue operations includes eye protection, head protection, hand protection, personal flotation devices, thermal protection, high-visibility clothing, and specialized footwear.

136. **(B)** The child is unstable (decreased LOC, rapid heart rate, and hypotension). Synchronized cardioversion should be provided at 0.5–1.0 joules per kilogram.

137. **(D)** Breathing must be supported with a bag-valve device with supplemental high-flow oxygen. This patient's breathing is too slow and too shallow for the patient to receive enough oxygen for proper gas exchange to take place.

138. **(D)** An epidural hematoma involves arterial vessels. Because the bleeding is arterial, intracranial pressure builds rapidly, compressing the cerebrum and increasing pressure within the skull. As the pressure rapidly builds, the patient will immediately display neurological signs/symptoms.

139. **(A)** This assessment finding indicates that there is bronchoconstriction and air trapping. This serious condition results in decreased air exchange in the lungs and can lead to profound hypoxia.

140. **(C)** Fatigue in this situation indicates that the patient is becoming tired. This is an ominous sign of pending respiratory failure and the development of respiratory arrest.

141. **(D)** Both hypoxia and anxiety cause activation of the sympathetic nervous system and the release of epinephrine and norepinephrine, which causes diaphoresis, elevation of the heart rate (tachycardia), and peripheral vasoconstriction (pale skin).

142. **(C)** Because of the air trapping, the patient does not have enough air (tidal volume) available to speak.

143. **(B)** A nebulized beta 2 agonist (such as albuterol) delivered by mask or hand-held device using 5–10 LPM of oxygen can assist in bronchodilation.

144. **(D)** Subcutaneous epinephrine is an option to treat cases of severe asthma because of its beta 2 agonist properties.

145. **(C)** Bystander CPR is a courageous effort to save a life and is important in the chain of survival, but there are times when bystanders perform CPR inappropriately. As an EMS provider, you must stop bystander CPR and verify a patent airway, the absence of breathing, and pulselessness when you arrive on scene.

146. **(B)** 162–325 mg is the current recommended dose of aspirin for a patient experiencing chest pain/acute coronary syndrome.

147. **(B)** According to the ACLS algorithm, immediate transcutaneous pacing should be considered early in asystole when the patient is witnessed going into asystole.

148. **(B)** Of the choices listed, the patient with a possible head injury should be transported first. **(A)**, **(C)**, and **(D)** are all isolated injuries that do not pose an immediate life threat that a head injury is capable of.

149. **(C)** Child abuse is prevalent in all socioeconomic groups. With the parents at home, yet away from the child, offering no consolation is a standard "red flag" signal to child abuse. The swelling around the right eye and the evidence of unexplained bruises might also indicate child abuse. Since the child is seven years old, shaken baby syndrome **(D)** is not correct. "Rubbing" and "coining" (**A** and **B**) are characteristic cultural differences that must be recognized and documented but not suspected child abuse.

150. **(C)** Normal intrathoracic pressure is less than atmospheric pressure. At rest (when not inhaling or exhaling), intrathoracic and atmospheric pressures are equal. On inhalation, the thoracic cavity enlarges, the pressure inside the lungs drop, and air is drawn into the lungs (thorax). The thoracic cavity is a negative pressure system.

151. **(D)** Left ventricular failure occurs when the heart fails as an effective forward pump, which causes backpressure of blood into pulmonary circulation. When the backpressure becomes high enough, it forces the blood into the capillaries of the alveoli resulting in pulmonary congestion. Adventitious lung sounds such as crackles (rales) are commonly present in left ventricular failure.

152. **(D)** When the body is not able to use glucose as a primary source of energy, the body starts to break down adipose (fat) tissue as a source of energy. This fat-based metabolism results in a rise of blood ketones, which can lead to ketoacidosis.

153. **(A)** This rhythm is ventricular fibrillation. Of the choices listed, amiodarone 300 mg is indicated. The dose of lidocaine and procainamide are incorrect (**B** and **C**). Magnesium (**D**) is not indicated.

154. **(A)** If a second dose of amiodarone is needed in the treatment of ventricular fibrillation, the correct dose is 150 mg.

155. **(A)** Rupture of the stomach or small bowel that allows digestive enzymes to enter the peritoneal cavity can cause peritonitis, which can lead to infection and serious complications.

156. **(D)** Of the choices listed, insertion of an oropharyngeal airway and ventilating with a bag-valve device is the best answer. (**A**) is incorrect because the oxygen flow setting is too low; it should be at least 15 LPM. (**B**) is incorrect because it utilizes a nonrebreather mask to assist ventilations. Nonrebreathers are not designed for or capable of assisting ventilations. (**C**) is incorrect because an apneic patient cannot be nasotracheally intubated.

157. **(C)** Contraction intervals are correctly measured from the beginning of one contraction to the beginning of the next. Many healthcare providers incorrectly measure intervals from the end of one contraction to the beginning of the next.

158. **(A)** Contraction length is correctly measured from the beginning of the contraction to the end of that contraction.

159. **(B)** Regular contractions lasting 45–60 seconds at one- to two-minute intervals and crowning indicates delivery is imminent.

160. **(D)** Normal physiological changes to vital signs during the second trimester of pregnancy include a drop in blood pressure 10–15 mmHg due to a reduction in peripheral vascular resistance. The heart rate will increase 10–20 beats per minute due to an increased maternal blood volume. Note: The blood pressure will rise back to baseline in the third trimester. Keep these normal changes in mind when assessing a pregnant trauma patient.

161. **(C)** Open the airway with a modified jaw thrust and immobilize the cervical spine. Always remember the ABCs.

162. **(B)** With the information given: hypotension, absent peripheral pulses, diminished breath sounds on the right with chest trauma on the right, a hemopneumothorax is likely.

163. **(C)** This patient received an initial assessment and rapid trauma survey to identify all life threats. It is recommended that these assessment steps be performed in two minutes or less.

164. **(C)** Hypoglycemia, fever, drug overdoses, or hypoxia are common causes of seizures in an infant.

165. **(D)** The PR interval is the time elapsing between the beginning of the p wave and the beginning of the QRS complex. The normal duration of the PR interval is 0.12 to 0.20 seconds.

166. **(C)** Vasopressin is indicated in the management of ventricular fibrillation and pulseless ventricular tachycardia.

167. **(D)** Sudden onset of flank pain, excruciating colicky pain, and vomiting are considered classic signs and symptoms of renal calculi (kidney stones).

168. **(A)** Prehospital care should be focused on comfort and support. Give nothing by mouth, establish an IV line for medication administration, an antiemetic may be indicated, and pain management is important. Note: While there may be concern about the use of pain medication in "undiagnosed" abdominal pain or that administration of pain medication may mask symptoms and make in-hospital assessment more difficult, the use of morphine is NOT contraindicated in renal calculi.

169. **(C)** A sign of poor perfusion includes mottled skin and tachycardia. This is indicative of shock and a detailed exam should be performed enroute to the hospital. Other indicators of shock include weak peripheral pulses and prolonged capillary refill time.

170. **(C)** The recommended dose of Benadryl for a pediatric patient with an allergic reaction is 1 mg/kg.

171. **(C)** Fluid resuscitation for multisystem trauma in the pediatric patient includes a bolus of an isotonic crystalloid at 20 cc/kg. Reassess and repeat as needed.

172. **(C)** A severe "tearing sensation" epigastric pain that radiates into the back and shoulders is classic description of pain often associated with an aortic aneurysm.

173. **(B)** Nitroglycerin is not indicated for this patient because of the presence of hypotension.

174. **(B)** Secondary mechanism of injury from a blast or explosion is defined as any injury sustained from being struck by material propelled by the blast force.

175. **(C)** Tertiary mechanism of injury from a blast or explosion is defined as any injury sustained from being thrown and impacting the ground or other objects.

176. **(B)** 22.5%—front of right arm = 4½%, upper chest = 9%, front of right leg = 9%.

177. **(B)** Your concern with this patient is complete airway obstruction secondary to swelling of the airway. Immediate endotracheal intubation is indicated.

178. **(C)** This ECG demonstrates atrial fibrillation

179. **(A)** Treatment for this patient would include oxygen, IV, continued monitoring and observation. Studies have shown that atrial fibrillation can decrease cardiac output as much as 33%. This patient should be transported for evaluation, especially if this rhythm is a new development for the patient.

180. **(B)** Unless special circumstances exist such as respiratory distress or airway compromise, the helmet should not be removed by EMS. This question asks when you *should* remove the helmet. Not having easy access to the airway is the best choice.

NOTES

APPENDIX

Additional Practice Test Answer Sheets

This appendix contains seven additional answer sheets that can be used for the Practice Tests in Chapters Eight, Nine, and Ten.

PRACTICE TEST ANSWER SHEET

Test ____

1. Ⓐ Ⓑ Ⓒ Ⓓ	31. Ⓐ Ⓑ Ⓒ Ⓓ	61. Ⓐ Ⓑ Ⓒ Ⓓ	91. Ⓐ Ⓑ Ⓒ Ⓓ	121. Ⓐ Ⓑ Ⓒ Ⓓ	151. Ⓐ Ⓑ Ⓒ Ⓓ
2. Ⓐ Ⓑ Ⓒ Ⓓ	32. Ⓐ Ⓑ Ⓒ Ⓓ	62. Ⓐ Ⓑ Ⓒ Ⓓ	92. Ⓐ Ⓑ Ⓒ Ⓓ	122. Ⓐ Ⓑ Ⓒ Ⓓ	152. Ⓐ Ⓑ Ⓒ Ⓓ
3. Ⓐ Ⓑ Ⓒ Ⓓ	33. Ⓐ Ⓑ Ⓒ Ⓓ	63. Ⓐ Ⓑ Ⓒ Ⓓ	93. Ⓐ Ⓑ Ⓒ Ⓓ	123. Ⓐ Ⓑ Ⓒ Ⓓ	153. Ⓐ Ⓑ Ⓒ Ⓓ
4. Ⓐ Ⓑ Ⓒ Ⓓ	34. Ⓐ Ⓑ Ⓒ Ⓓ	64. Ⓐ Ⓑ Ⓒ Ⓓ	94. Ⓐ Ⓑ Ⓒ Ⓓ	124. Ⓐ Ⓑ Ⓒ Ⓓ	154. Ⓐ Ⓑ Ⓒ Ⓓ
5. Ⓐ Ⓑ Ⓒ Ⓓ	35. Ⓐ Ⓑ Ⓒ Ⓓ	65. Ⓐ Ⓑ Ⓒ Ⓓ	95. Ⓐ Ⓑ Ⓒ Ⓓ	125. Ⓐ Ⓑ Ⓒ Ⓓ	155. Ⓐ Ⓑ Ⓒ Ⓓ
6. Ⓐ Ⓑ Ⓒ Ⓓ	36. Ⓐ Ⓑ Ⓒ Ⓓ	66. Ⓐ Ⓑ Ⓒ Ⓓ	96. Ⓐ Ⓑ Ⓒ Ⓓ	126. Ⓐ Ⓑ Ⓒ Ⓓ	156. Ⓐ Ⓑ Ⓒ Ⓓ
7. Ⓐ Ⓑ Ⓒ Ⓓ	37. Ⓐ Ⓑ Ⓒ Ⓓ	67. Ⓐ Ⓑ Ⓒ Ⓓ	97. Ⓐ Ⓑ Ⓒ Ⓓ	127. Ⓐ Ⓑ Ⓒ Ⓓ	157. Ⓐ Ⓑ Ⓒ Ⓓ
8. Ⓐ Ⓑ Ⓒ Ⓓ	38. Ⓐ Ⓑ Ⓒ Ⓓ	68. Ⓐ Ⓑ Ⓒ Ⓓ	98. Ⓐ Ⓑ Ⓒ Ⓓ	128. Ⓐ Ⓑ Ⓒ Ⓓ	158. Ⓐ Ⓑ Ⓒ Ⓓ
9. Ⓐ Ⓑ Ⓒ Ⓓ	39. Ⓐ Ⓑ Ⓒ Ⓓ	69. Ⓐ Ⓑ Ⓒ Ⓓ	99. Ⓐ Ⓑ Ⓒ Ⓓ	129. Ⓐ Ⓑ Ⓒ Ⓓ	159. Ⓐ Ⓑ Ⓒ Ⓓ
10. Ⓐ Ⓑ Ⓒ Ⓓ	40. Ⓐ Ⓑ Ⓒ Ⓓ	70. Ⓐ Ⓑ Ⓒ Ⓓ	100. Ⓐ Ⓑ Ⓒ Ⓓ	130. Ⓐ Ⓑ Ⓒ Ⓓ	160. Ⓐ Ⓑ Ⓒ Ⓓ
11. Ⓐ Ⓑ Ⓒ Ⓓ	41. Ⓐ Ⓑ Ⓒ Ⓓ	71. Ⓐ Ⓑ Ⓒ Ⓓ	101. Ⓐ Ⓑ Ⓒ Ⓓ	131. Ⓐ Ⓑ Ⓒ Ⓓ	161. Ⓐ Ⓑ Ⓒ Ⓓ
12. Ⓐ Ⓑ Ⓒ Ⓓ	42. Ⓐ Ⓑ Ⓒ Ⓓ	72. Ⓐ Ⓑ Ⓒ Ⓓ	102. Ⓐ Ⓑ Ⓒ Ⓓ	132. Ⓐ Ⓑ Ⓒ Ⓓ	162. Ⓐ Ⓑ Ⓒ Ⓓ
13. Ⓐ Ⓑ Ⓒ Ⓓ	43. Ⓐ Ⓑ Ⓒ Ⓓ	73. Ⓐ Ⓑ Ⓒ Ⓓ	103. Ⓐ Ⓑ Ⓒ Ⓓ	133. Ⓐ Ⓑ Ⓒ Ⓓ	163. Ⓐ Ⓑ Ⓒ Ⓓ
14. Ⓐ Ⓑ Ⓒ Ⓓ	44. Ⓐ Ⓑ Ⓒ Ⓓ	74. Ⓐ Ⓑ Ⓒ Ⓓ	104. Ⓐ Ⓑ Ⓒ Ⓓ	134. Ⓐ Ⓑ Ⓒ Ⓓ	164. Ⓐ Ⓑ Ⓒ Ⓓ
15. Ⓐ Ⓑ Ⓒ Ⓓ	45. Ⓐ Ⓑ Ⓒ Ⓓ	75. Ⓐ Ⓑ Ⓒ Ⓓ	105. Ⓐ Ⓑ Ⓒ Ⓓ	135. Ⓐ Ⓑ Ⓒ Ⓓ	165. Ⓐ Ⓑ Ⓒ Ⓓ
16. Ⓐ Ⓑ Ⓒ Ⓓ	46. Ⓐ Ⓑ Ⓒ Ⓓ	76. Ⓐ Ⓑ Ⓒ Ⓓ	106. Ⓐ Ⓑ Ⓒ Ⓓ	136. Ⓐ Ⓑ Ⓒ Ⓓ	166. Ⓐ Ⓑ Ⓒ Ⓓ
17. Ⓐ Ⓑ Ⓒ Ⓓ	47. Ⓐ Ⓑ Ⓒ Ⓓ	77. Ⓐ Ⓑ Ⓒ Ⓓ	107. Ⓐ Ⓑ Ⓒ Ⓓ	137. Ⓐ Ⓑ Ⓒ Ⓓ	167. Ⓐ Ⓑ Ⓒ Ⓓ
18. Ⓐ Ⓑ Ⓒ Ⓓ	48. Ⓐ Ⓑ Ⓒ Ⓓ	78. Ⓐ Ⓑ Ⓒ Ⓓ	108. Ⓐ Ⓑ Ⓒ Ⓓ	138. Ⓐ Ⓑ Ⓒ Ⓓ	168. Ⓐ Ⓑ Ⓒ Ⓓ
19. Ⓐ Ⓑ Ⓒ Ⓓ	49. Ⓐ Ⓑ Ⓒ Ⓓ	79. Ⓐ Ⓑ Ⓒ Ⓓ	109. Ⓐ Ⓑ Ⓒ Ⓓ	139. Ⓐ Ⓑ Ⓒ Ⓓ	169. Ⓐ Ⓑ Ⓒ Ⓓ
20. Ⓐ Ⓑ Ⓒ Ⓓ	50. Ⓐ Ⓑ Ⓒ Ⓓ	80. Ⓐ Ⓑ Ⓒ Ⓓ	110. Ⓐ Ⓑ Ⓒ Ⓓ	140. Ⓐ Ⓑ Ⓒ Ⓓ	170. Ⓐ Ⓑ Ⓒ Ⓓ
21. Ⓐ Ⓑ Ⓒ Ⓓ	51. Ⓐ Ⓑ Ⓒ Ⓓ	81. Ⓐ Ⓑ Ⓒ Ⓓ	111. Ⓐ Ⓑ Ⓒ Ⓓ	141. Ⓐ Ⓑ Ⓒ Ⓓ	171. Ⓐ Ⓑ Ⓒ Ⓓ
22. Ⓐ Ⓑ Ⓒ Ⓓ	52. Ⓐ Ⓑ Ⓒ Ⓓ	82. Ⓐ Ⓑ Ⓒ Ⓓ	112. Ⓐ Ⓑ Ⓒ Ⓓ	142. Ⓐ Ⓑ Ⓒ Ⓓ	172. Ⓐ Ⓑ Ⓒ Ⓓ
23. Ⓐ Ⓑ Ⓒ Ⓓ	53. Ⓐ Ⓑ Ⓒ Ⓓ	83. Ⓐ Ⓑ Ⓒ Ⓓ	113. Ⓐ Ⓑ Ⓒ Ⓓ	143. Ⓐ Ⓑ Ⓒ Ⓓ	173. Ⓐ Ⓑ Ⓒ Ⓓ
24. Ⓐ Ⓑ Ⓒ Ⓓ	54. Ⓐ Ⓑ Ⓒ Ⓓ	84. Ⓐ Ⓑ Ⓒ Ⓓ	114. Ⓐ Ⓑ Ⓒ Ⓓ	144. Ⓐ Ⓑ Ⓒ Ⓓ	174. Ⓐ Ⓑ Ⓒ Ⓓ
25. Ⓐ Ⓑ Ⓒ Ⓓ	55. Ⓐ Ⓑ Ⓒ Ⓓ	85. Ⓐ Ⓑ Ⓒ Ⓓ	115. Ⓐ Ⓑ Ⓒ Ⓓ	145. Ⓐ Ⓑ Ⓒ Ⓓ	175. Ⓐ Ⓑ Ⓒ Ⓓ
26. Ⓐ Ⓑ Ⓒ Ⓓ	56. Ⓐ Ⓑ Ⓒ Ⓓ	86. Ⓐ Ⓑ Ⓒ Ⓓ	116. Ⓐ Ⓑ Ⓒ Ⓓ	146. Ⓐ Ⓑ Ⓒ Ⓓ	176. Ⓐ Ⓑ Ⓒ Ⓓ
27. Ⓐ Ⓑ Ⓒ Ⓓ	57. Ⓐ Ⓑ Ⓒ Ⓓ	87. Ⓐ Ⓑ Ⓒ Ⓓ	117. Ⓐ Ⓑ Ⓒ Ⓓ	147. Ⓐ Ⓑ Ⓒ Ⓓ	177. Ⓐ Ⓑ Ⓒ Ⓓ
28. Ⓐ Ⓑ Ⓒ Ⓓ	58. Ⓐ Ⓑ Ⓒ Ⓓ	88. Ⓐ Ⓑ Ⓒ Ⓓ	118. Ⓐ Ⓑ Ⓒ Ⓓ	148. Ⓐ Ⓑ Ⓒ Ⓓ	178. Ⓐ Ⓑ Ⓒ Ⓓ
29. Ⓐ Ⓑ Ⓒ Ⓓ	59. Ⓐ Ⓑ Ⓒ Ⓓ	89. Ⓐ Ⓑ Ⓒ Ⓓ	119. Ⓐ Ⓑ Ⓒ Ⓓ	149. Ⓐ Ⓑ Ⓒ Ⓓ	179. Ⓐ Ⓑ Ⓒ Ⓓ
30. Ⓐ Ⓑ Ⓒ Ⓓ	60. Ⓐ Ⓑ Ⓒ Ⓓ	90. Ⓐ Ⓑ Ⓒ Ⓓ	120. Ⓐ Ⓑ Ⓒ Ⓓ	150. Ⓐ Ⓑ Ⓒ Ⓓ	180. Ⓐ Ⓑ Ⓒ Ⓓ

PRACTICE TEST ANSWER SHEET

Test _____

1. Ⓐ Ⓑ Ⓒ Ⓓ	31. Ⓐ Ⓑ Ⓒ Ⓓ	61. Ⓐ Ⓑ Ⓒ Ⓓ	91. Ⓐ Ⓑ Ⓒ Ⓓ	121. Ⓐ Ⓑ Ⓒ Ⓓ	151. Ⓐ Ⓑ Ⓒ Ⓓ
2. Ⓐ Ⓑ Ⓒ Ⓓ	32. Ⓐ Ⓑ Ⓒ Ⓓ	62. Ⓐ Ⓑ Ⓒ Ⓓ	92. Ⓐ Ⓑ Ⓒ Ⓓ	122. Ⓐ Ⓑ Ⓒ Ⓓ	152. Ⓐ Ⓑ Ⓒ Ⓓ
3. Ⓐ Ⓑ Ⓒ Ⓓ	33. Ⓐ Ⓑ Ⓒ Ⓓ	63. Ⓐ Ⓑ Ⓒ Ⓓ	93. Ⓐ Ⓑ Ⓒ Ⓓ	123. Ⓐ Ⓑ Ⓒ Ⓓ	153. Ⓐ Ⓑ Ⓒ Ⓓ
4. Ⓐ Ⓑ Ⓒ Ⓓ	34. Ⓐ Ⓑ Ⓒ Ⓓ	64. Ⓐ Ⓑ Ⓒ Ⓓ	94. Ⓐ Ⓑ Ⓒ Ⓓ	124. Ⓐ Ⓑ Ⓒ Ⓓ	154. Ⓐ Ⓑ Ⓒ Ⓓ
5. Ⓐ Ⓑ Ⓒ Ⓓ	35. Ⓐ Ⓑ Ⓒ Ⓓ	65. Ⓐ Ⓑ Ⓒ Ⓓ	95. Ⓐ Ⓑ Ⓒ Ⓓ	125. Ⓐ Ⓑ Ⓒ Ⓓ	155. Ⓐ Ⓑ Ⓒ Ⓓ
6. Ⓐ Ⓑ Ⓒ Ⓓ	36. Ⓐ Ⓑ Ⓒ Ⓓ	66. Ⓐ Ⓑ Ⓒ Ⓓ	96. Ⓐ Ⓑ Ⓒ Ⓓ	126. Ⓐ Ⓑ Ⓒ Ⓓ	156. Ⓐ Ⓑ Ⓒ Ⓓ
7. Ⓐ Ⓑ Ⓒ Ⓓ	37. Ⓐ Ⓑ Ⓒ Ⓓ	67. Ⓐ Ⓑ Ⓒ Ⓓ	97. Ⓐ Ⓑ Ⓒ Ⓓ	127. Ⓐ Ⓑ Ⓒ Ⓓ	157. Ⓐ Ⓑ Ⓒ Ⓓ
8. Ⓐ Ⓑ Ⓒ Ⓓ	38. Ⓐ Ⓑ Ⓒ Ⓓ	68. Ⓐ Ⓑ Ⓒ Ⓓ	98. Ⓐ Ⓑ Ⓒ Ⓓ	128. Ⓐ Ⓑ Ⓒ Ⓓ	158. Ⓐ Ⓑ Ⓒ Ⓓ
9. Ⓐ Ⓑ Ⓒ Ⓓ	39. Ⓐ Ⓑ Ⓒ Ⓓ	69. Ⓐ Ⓑ Ⓒ Ⓓ	99. Ⓐ Ⓑ Ⓒ Ⓓ	129. Ⓐ Ⓑ Ⓒ Ⓓ	159. Ⓐ Ⓑ Ⓒ Ⓓ
10. Ⓐ Ⓑ Ⓒ Ⓓ	40. Ⓐ Ⓑ Ⓒ Ⓓ	70. Ⓐ Ⓑ Ⓒ Ⓓ	100. Ⓐ Ⓑ Ⓒ Ⓓ	130. Ⓐ Ⓑ Ⓒ Ⓓ	160. Ⓐ Ⓑ Ⓒ Ⓓ
11. Ⓐ Ⓑ Ⓒ Ⓓ	41. Ⓐ Ⓑ Ⓒ Ⓓ	71. Ⓐ Ⓑ Ⓒ Ⓓ	101. Ⓐ Ⓑ Ⓒ Ⓓ	131. Ⓐ Ⓑ Ⓒ Ⓓ	161. Ⓐ Ⓑ Ⓒ Ⓓ
12. Ⓐ Ⓑ Ⓒ Ⓓ	42. Ⓐ Ⓑ Ⓒ Ⓓ	72. Ⓐ Ⓑ Ⓒ Ⓓ	102. Ⓐ Ⓑ Ⓒ Ⓓ	132. Ⓐ Ⓑ Ⓒ Ⓓ	162. Ⓐ Ⓑ Ⓒ Ⓓ
13. Ⓐ Ⓑ Ⓒ Ⓓ	43. Ⓐ Ⓑ Ⓒ Ⓓ	73. Ⓐ Ⓑ Ⓒ Ⓓ	103. Ⓐ Ⓑ Ⓒ Ⓓ	133. Ⓐ Ⓑ Ⓒ Ⓓ	163. Ⓐ Ⓑ Ⓒ Ⓓ
14. Ⓐ Ⓑ Ⓒ Ⓓ	44. Ⓐ Ⓑ Ⓒ Ⓓ	74. Ⓐ Ⓑ Ⓒ Ⓓ	104. Ⓐ Ⓑ Ⓒ Ⓓ	134. Ⓐ Ⓑ Ⓒ Ⓓ	164. Ⓐ Ⓑ Ⓒ Ⓓ
15. Ⓐ Ⓑ Ⓒ Ⓓ	45. Ⓐ Ⓑ Ⓒ Ⓓ	75. Ⓐ Ⓑ Ⓒ Ⓓ	105. Ⓐ Ⓑ Ⓒ Ⓓ	135. Ⓐ Ⓑ Ⓒ Ⓓ	165. Ⓐ Ⓑ Ⓒ Ⓓ
16. Ⓐ Ⓑ Ⓒ Ⓓ	46. Ⓐ Ⓑ Ⓒ Ⓓ	76. Ⓐ Ⓑ Ⓒ Ⓓ	106. Ⓐ Ⓑ Ⓒ Ⓓ	136. Ⓐ Ⓑ Ⓒ Ⓓ	166. Ⓐ Ⓑ Ⓒ Ⓓ
17. Ⓐ Ⓑ Ⓒ Ⓓ	47. Ⓐ Ⓑ Ⓒ Ⓓ	77. Ⓐ Ⓑ Ⓒ Ⓓ	107. Ⓐ Ⓑ Ⓒ Ⓓ	137. Ⓐ Ⓑ Ⓒ Ⓓ	167. Ⓐ Ⓑ Ⓒ Ⓓ
18. Ⓐ Ⓑ Ⓒ Ⓓ	48. Ⓐ Ⓑ Ⓒ Ⓓ	78. Ⓐ Ⓑ Ⓒ Ⓓ	108. Ⓐ Ⓑ Ⓒ Ⓓ	138. Ⓐ Ⓑ Ⓒ Ⓓ	168. Ⓐ Ⓑ Ⓒ Ⓓ
19. Ⓐ Ⓑ Ⓒ Ⓓ	49. Ⓐ Ⓑ Ⓒ Ⓓ	79. Ⓐ Ⓑ Ⓒ Ⓓ	109. Ⓐ Ⓑ Ⓒ Ⓓ	139. Ⓐ Ⓑ Ⓒ Ⓓ	169. Ⓐ Ⓑ Ⓒ Ⓓ
20. Ⓐ Ⓑ Ⓒ Ⓓ	50. Ⓐ Ⓑ Ⓒ Ⓓ	80. Ⓐ Ⓑ Ⓒ Ⓓ	110. Ⓐ Ⓑ Ⓒ Ⓓ	140. Ⓐ Ⓑ Ⓒ Ⓓ	170. Ⓐ Ⓑ Ⓒ Ⓓ
21. Ⓐ Ⓑ Ⓒ Ⓓ	51. Ⓐ Ⓑ Ⓒ Ⓓ	81. Ⓐ Ⓑ Ⓒ Ⓓ	111. Ⓐ Ⓑ Ⓒ Ⓓ	141. Ⓐ Ⓑ Ⓒ Ⓓ	171. Ⓐ Ⓑ Ⓒ Ⓓ
22. Ⓐ Ⓑ Ⓒ Ⓓ	52. Ⓐ Ⓑ Ⓒ Ⓓ	82. Ⓐ Ⓑ Ⓒ Ⓓ	112. Ⓐ Ⓑ Ⓒ Ⓓ	142. Ⓐ Ⓑ Ⓒ Ⓓ	172. Ⓐ Ⓑ Ⓒ Ⓓ
23. Ⓐ Ⓑ Ⓒ Ⓓ	53. Ⓐ Ⓑ Ⓒ Ⓓ	83. Ⓐ Ⓑ Ⓒ Ⓓ	113. Ⓐ Ⓑ Ⓒ Ⓓ	143. Ⓐ Ⓑ Ⓒ Ⓓ	173. Ⓐ Ⓑ Ⓒ Ⓓ
24. Ⓐ Ⓑ Ⓒ Ⓓ	54. Ⓐ Ⓑ Ⓒ Ⓓ	84. Ⓐ Ⓑ Ⓒ Ⓓ	114. Ⓐ Ⓑ Ⓒ Ⓓ	144. Ⓐ Ⓑ Ⓒ Ⓓ	174. Ⓐ Ⓑ Ⓒ Ⓓ
25. Ⓐ Ⓑ Ⓒ Ⓓ	55. Ⓐ Ⓑ Ⓒ Ⓓ	85. Ⓐ Ⓑ Ⓒ Ⓓ	115. Ⓐ Ⓑ Ⓒ Ⓓ	145. Ⓐ Ⓑ Ⓒ Ⓓ	175. Ⓐ Ⓑ Ⓒ Ⓓ
26. Ⓐ Ⓑ Ⓒ Ⓓ	56. Ⓐ Ⓑ Ⓒ Ⓓ	86. Ⓐ Ⓑ Ⓒ Ⓓ	116. Ⓐ Ⓑ Ⓒ Ⓓ	146. Ⓐ Ⓑ Ⓒ Ⓓ	176. Ⓐ Ⓑ Ⓒ Ⓓ
27. Ⓐ Ⓑ Ⓒ Ⓓ	57. Ⓐ Ⓑ Ⓒ Ⓓ	87. Ⓐ Ⓑ Ⓒ Ⓓ	117. Ⓐ Ⓑ Ⓒ Ⓓ	147. Ⓐ Ⓑ Ⓒ Ⓓ	177. Ⓐ Ⓑ Ⓒ Ⓓ
28. Ⓐ Ⓑ Ⓒ Ⓓ	58. Ⓐ Ⓑ Ⓒ Ⓓ	88. Ⓐ Ⓑ Ⓒ Ⓓ	118. Ⓐ Ⓑ Ⓒ Ⓓ	148. Ⓐ Ⓑ Ⓒ Ⓓ	178. Ⓐ Ⓑ Ⓒ Ⓓ
29. Ⓐ Ⓑ Ⓒ Ⓓ	59. Ⓐ Ⓑ Ⓒ Ⓓ	89. Ⓐ Ⓑ Ⓒ Ⓓ	119. Ⓐ Ⓑ Ⓒ Ⓓ	149. Ⓐ Ⓑ Ⓒ Ⓓ	179. Ⓐ Ⓑ Ⓒ Ⓓ
30. Ⓐ Ⓑ Ⓒ Ⓓ	60. Ⓐ Ⓑ Ⓒ Ⓓ	90. Ⓐ Ⓑ Ⓒ Ⓓ	120. Ⓐ Ⓑ Ⓒ Ⓓ	150. Ⓐ Ⓑ Ⓒ Ⓓ	180. Ⓐ Ⓑ Ⓒ Ⓓ

PRACTICE TEST ANSWER SHEET

Test ____

1. Ⓐ Ⓑ Ⓒ Ⓓ	31. Ⓐ Ⓑ Ⓒ Ⓓ	61. Ⓐ Ⓑ Ⓒ Ⓓ	91. Ⓐ Ⓑ Ⓒ Ⓓ	121. Ⓐ Ⓑ Ⓒ Ⓓ	151. Ⓐ Ⓑ Ⓒ Ⓓ
2. Ⓐ Ⓑ Ⓒ Ⓓ	32. Ⓐ Ⓑ Ⓒ Ⓓ	62. Ⓐ Ⓑ Ⓒ Ⓓ	92. Ⓐ Ⓑ Ⓒ Ⓓ	122. Ⓐ Ⓑ Ⓒ Ⓓ	152. Ⓐ Ⓑ Ⓒ Ⓓ
3. Ⓐ Ⓑ Ⓒ Ⓓ	33. Ⓐ Ⓑ Ⓒ Ⓓ	63. Ⓐ Ⓑ Ⓒ Ⓓ	93. Ⓐ Ⓑ Ⓒ Ⓓ	123. Ⓐ Ⓑ Ⓒ Ⓓ	153. Ⓐ Ⓑ Ⓒ Ⓓ
4. Ⓐ Ⓑ Ⓒ Ⓓ	34. Ⓐ Ⓑ Ⓒ Ⓓ	64. Ⓐ Ⓑ Ⓒ Ⓓ	94. Ⓐ Ⓑ Ⓒ Ⓓ	124. Ⓐ Ⓑ Ⓒ Ⓓ	154. Ⓐ Ⓑ Ⓒ Ⓓ
5. Ⓐ Ⓑ Ⓒ Ⓓ	35. Ⓐ Ⓑ Ⓒ Ⓓ	65. Ⓐ Ⓑ Ⓒ Ⓓ	95. Ⓐ Ⓑ Ⓒ Ⓓ	125. Ⓐ Ⓑ Ⓒ Ⓓ	155. Ⓐ Ⓑ Ⓒ Ⓓ
6. Ⓐ Ⓑ Ⓒ Ⓓ	36. Ⓐ Ⓑ Ⓒ Ⓓ	66. Ⓐ Ⓑ Ⓒ Ⓓ	96. Ⓐ Ⓑ Ⓒ Ⓓ	126. Ⓐ Ⓑ Ⓒ Ⓓ	156. Ⓐ Ⓑ Ⓒ Ⓓ
7. Ⓐ Ⓑ Ⓒ Ⓓ	37. Ⓐ Ⓑ Ⓒ Ⓓ	67. Ⓐ Ⓑ Ⓒ Ⓓ	97. Ⓐ Ⓑ Ⓒ Ⓓ	127. Ⓐ Ⓑ Ⓒ Ⓓ	157. Ⓐ Ⓑ Ⓒ Ⓓ
8. Ⓐ Ⓑ Ⓒ Ⓓ	38. Ⓐ Ⓑ Ⓒ Ⓓ	68. Ⓐ Ⓑ Ⓒ Ⓓ	98. Ⓐ Ⓑ Ⓒ Ⓓ	128. Ⓐ Ⓑ Ⓒ Ⓓ	158. Ⓐ Ⓑ Ⓒ Ⓓ
9. Ⓐ Ⓑ Ⓒ Ⓓ	39. Ⓐ Ⓑ Ⓒ Ⓓ	69. Ⓐ Ⓑ Ⓒ Ⓓ	99. Ⓐ Ⓑ Ⓒ Ⓓ	129. Ⓐ Ⓑ Ⓒ Ⓓ	159. Ⓐ Ⓑ Ⓒ Ⓓ
10. Ⓐ Ⓑ Ⓒ Ⓓ	40. Ⓐ Ⓑ Ⓒ Ⓓ	70. Ⓐ Ⓑ Ⓒ Ⓓ	100. Ⓐ Ⓑ Ⓒ Ⓓ	130. Ⓐ Ⓑ Ⓒ Ⓓ	160. Ⓐ Ⓑ Ⓒ Ⓓ
11. Ⓐ Ⓑ Ⓒ Ⓓ	41. Ⓐ Ⓑ Ⓒ Ⓓ	71. Ⓐ Ⓑ Ⓒ Ⓓ	101. Ⓐ Ⓑ Ⓒ Ⓓ	131. Ⓐ Ⓑ Ⓒ Ⓓ	161. Ⓐ Ⓑ Ⓒ Ⓓ
12. Ⓐ Ⓑ Ⓒ Ⓓ	42. Ⓐ Ⓑ Ⓒ Ⓓ	72. Ⓐ Ⓑ Ⓒ Ⓓ	102. Ⓐ Ⓑ Ⓒ Ⓓ	132. Ⓐ Ⓑ Ⓒ Ⓓ	162. Ⓐ Ⓑ Ⓒ Ⓓ
13. Ⓐ Ⓑ Ⓒ Ⓓ	43. Ⓐ Ⓑ Ⓒ Ⓓ	73. Ⓐ Ⓑ Ⓒ Ⓓ	103. Ⓐ Ⓑ Ⓒ Ⓓ	133. Ⓐ Ⓑ Ⓒ Ⓓ	163. Ⓐ Ⓑ Ⓒ Ⓓ
14. Ⓐ Ⓑ Ⓒ Ⓓ	44. Ⓐ Ⓑ Ⓒ Ⓓ	74. Ⓐ Ⓑ Ⓒ Ⓓ	104. Ⓐ Ⓑ Ⓒ Ⓓ	134. Ⓐ Ⓑ Ⓒ Ⓓ	164. Ⓐ Ⓑ Ⓒ Ⓓ
15. Ⓐ Ⓑ Ⓒ Ⓓ	45. Ⓐ Ⓑ Ⓒ Ⓓ	75. Ⓐ Ⓑ Ⓒ Ⓓ	105. Ⓐ Ⓑ Ⓒ Ⓓ	135. Ⓐ Ⓑ Ⓒ Ⓓ	165. Ⓐ Ⓑ Ⓒ Ⓓ
16. Ⓐ Ⓑ Ⓒ Ⓓ	46. Ⓐ Ⓑ Ⓒ Ⓓ	76. Ⓐ Ⓑ Ⓒ Ⓓ	106. Ⓐ Ⓑ Ⓒ Ⓓ	136. Ⓐ Ⓑ Ⓒ Ⓓ	166. Ⓐ Ⓑ Ⓒ Ⓓ
17. Ⓐ Ⓑ Ⓒ Ⓓ	47. Ⓐ Ⓑ Ⓒ Ⓓ	77. Ⓐ Ⓑ Ⓒ Ⓓ	107. Ⓐ Ⓑ Ⓒ Ⓓ	137. Ⓐ Ⓑ Ⓒ Ⓓ	167. Ⓐ Ⓑ Ⓒ Ⓓ
18. Ⓐ Ⓑ Ⓒ Ⓓ	48. Ⓐ Ⓑ Ⓒ Ⓓ	78. Ⓐ Ⓑ Ⓒ Ⓓ	108. Ⓐ Ⓑ Ⓒ Ⓓ	138. Ⓐ Ⓑ Ⓒ Ⓓ	168. Ⓐ Ⓑ Ⓒ Ⓓ
19. Ⓐ Ⓑ Ⓒ Ⓓ	49. Ⓐ Ⓑ Ⓒ Ⓓ	79. Ⓐ Ⓑ Ⓒ Ⓓ	109. Ⓐ Ⓑ Ⓒ Ⓓ	139. Ⓐ Ⓑ Ⓒ Ⓓ	169. Ⓐ Ⓑ Ⓒ Ⓓ
20. Ⓐ Ⓑ Ⓒ Ⓓ	50. Ⓐ Ⓑ Ⓒ Ⓓ	80. Ⓐ Ⓑ Ⓒ Ⓓ	110. Ⓐ Ⓑ Ⓒ Ⓓ	140. Ⓐ Ⓑ Ⓒ Ⓓ	170. Ⓐ Ⓑ Ⓒ Ⓓ
21. Ⓐ Ⓑ Ⓒ Ⓓ	51. Ⓐ Ⓑ Ⓒ Ⓓ	81. Ⓐ Ⓑ Ⓒ Ⓓ	111. Ⓐ Ⓑ Ⓒ Ⓓ	141. Ⓐ Ⓑ Ⓒ Ⓓ	171. Ⓐ Ⓑ Ⓒ Ⓓ
22. Ⓐ Ⓑ Ⓒ Ⓓ	52. Ⓐ Ⓑ Ⓒ Ⓓ	82. Ⓐ Ⓑ Ⓒ Ⓓ	112. Ⓐ Ⓑ Ⓒ Ⓓ	142. Ⓐ Ⓑ Ⓒ Ⓓ	172. Ⓐ Ⓑ Ⓒ Ⓓ
23. Ⓐ Ⓑ Ⓒ Ⓓ	53. Ⓐ Ⓑ Ⓒ Ⓓ	83. Ⓐ Ⓑ Ⓒ Ⓓ	113. Ⓐ Ⓑ Ⓒ Ⓓ	143. Ⓐ Ⓑ Ⓒ Ⓓ	173. Ⓐ Ⓑ Ⓒ Ⓓ
24. Ⓐ Ⓑ Ⓒ Ⓓ	54. Ⓐ Ⓑ Ⓒ Ⓓ	84. Ⓐ Ⓑ Ⓒ Ⓓ	114. Ⓐ Ⓑ Ⓒ Ⓓ	144. Ⓐ Ⓑ Ⓒ Ⓓ	174. Ⓐ Ⓑ Ⓒ Ⓓ
25. Ⓐ Ⓑ Ⓒ Ⓓ	55. Ⓐ Ⓑ Ⓒ Ⓓ	85. Ⓐ Ⓑ Ⓒ Ⓓ	115. Ⓐ Ⓑ Ⓒ Ⓓ	145. Ⓐ Ⓑ Ⓒ Ⓓ	175. Ⓐ Ⓑ Ⓒ Ⓓ
26. Ⓐ Ⓑ Ⓒ Ⓓ	56. Ⓐ Ⓑ Ⓒ Ⓓ	86. Ⓐ Ⓑ Ⓒ Ⓓ	116. Ⓐ Ⓑ Ⓒ Ⓓ	146. Ⓐ Ⓑ Ⓒ Ⓓ	176. Ⓐ Ⓑ Ⓒ Ⓓ
27. Ⓐ Ⓑ Ⓒ Ⓓ	57. Ⓐ Ⓑ Ⓒ Ⓓ	87. Ⓐ Ⓑ Ⓒ Ⓓ	117. Ⓐ Ⓑ Ⓒ Ⓓ	147. Ⓐ Ⓑ Ⓒ Ⓓ	177. Ⓐ Ⓑ Ⓒ Ⓓ
28. Ⓐ Ⓑ Ⓒ Ⓓ	58. Ⓐ Ⓑ Ⓒ Ⓓ	88. Ⓐ Ⓑ Ⓒ Ⓓ	118. Ⓐ Ⓑ Ⓒ Ⓓ	148. Ⓐ Ⓑ Ⓒ Ⓓ	178. Ⓐ Ⓑ Ⓒ Ⓓ
29. Ⓐ Ⓑ Ⓒ Ⓓ	59. Ⓐ Ⓑ Ⓒ Ⓓ	89. Ⓐ Ⓑ Ⓒ Ⓓ	119. Ⓐ Ⓑ Ⓒ Ⓓ	149. Ⓐ Ⓑ Ⓒ Ⓓ	179. Ⓐ Ⓑ Ⓒ Ⓓ
30. Ⓐ Ⓑ Ⓒ Ⓓ	60. Ⓐ Ⓑ Ⓒ Ⓓ	90. Ⓐ Ⓑ Ⓒ Ⓓ	120. Ⓐ Ⓑ Ⓒ Ⓓ	150. Ⓐ Ⓑ Ⓒ Ⓓ	180. Ⓐ Ⓑ Ⓒ Ⓓ

PRACTICE TEST ANSWER SHEET

Test _____

1. Ⓐ Ⓑ Ⓒ Ⓓ	31. Ⓐ Ⓑ Ⓒ Ⓓ	61. Ⓐ Ⓑ Ⓒ Ⓓ	91. Ⓐ Ⓑ Ⓒ Ⓓ	121. Ⓐ Ⓑ Ⓒ Ⓓ	151. Ⓐ Ⓑ Ⓒ Ⓓ
2. Ⓐ Ⓑ Ⓒ Ⓓ	32. Ⓐ Ⓑ Ⓒ Ⓓ	62. Ⓐ Ⓑ Ⓒ Ⓓ	92. Ⓐ Ⓑ Ⓒ Ⓓ	122. Ⓐ Ⓑ Ⓒ Ⓓ	152. Ⓐ Ⓑ Ⓒ Ⓓ
3. Ⓐ Ⓑ Ⓒ Ⓓ	33. Ⓐ Ⓑ Ⓒ Ⓓ	63. Ⓐ Ⓑ Ⓒ Ⓓ	93. Ⓐ Ⓑ Ⓒ Ⓓ	123. Ⓐ Ⓑ Ⓒ Ⓓ	153. Ⓐ Ⓑ Ⓒ Ⓓ
4. Ⓐ Ⓑ Ⓒ Ⓓ	34. Ⓐ Ⓑ Ⓒ Ⓓ	64. Ⓐ Ⓑ Ⓒ Ⓓ	94. Ⓐ Ⓑ Ⓒ Ⓓ	124. Ⓐ Ⓑ Ⓒ Ⓓ	154. Ⓐ Ⓑ Ⓒ Ⓓ
5. Ⓐ Ⓑ Ⓒ Ⓓ	35. Ⓐ Ⓑ Ⓒ Ⓓ	65. Ⓐ Ⓑ Ⓒ Ⓓ	95. Ⓐ Ⓑ Ⓒ Ⓓ	125. Ⓐ Ⓑ Ⓒ Ⓓ	155. Ⓐ Ⓑ Ⓒ Ⓓ
6. Ⓐ Ⓑ Ⓒ Ⓓ	36. Ⓐ Ⓑ Ⓒ Ⓓ	66. Ⓐ Ⓑ Ⓒ Ⓓ	96. Ⓐ Ⓑ Ⓒ Ⓓ	126. Ⓐ Ⓑ Ⓒ Ⓓ	156. Ⓐ Ⓑ Ⓒ Ⓓ
7. Ⓐ Ⓑ Ⓒ Ⓓ	37. Ⓐ Ⓑ Ⓒ Ⓓ	67. Ⓐ Ⓑ Ⓒ Ⓓ	97. Ⓐ Ⓑ Ⓒ Ⓓ	127. Ⓐ Ⓑ Ⓒ Ⓓ	157. Ⓐ Ⓑ Ⓒ Ⓓ
8. Ⓐ Ⓑ Ⓒ Ⓓ	38. Ⓐ Ⓑ Ⓒ Ⓓ	68. Ⓐ Ⓑ Ⓒ Ⓓ	98. Ⓐ Ⓑ Ⓒ Ⓓ	128. Ⓐ Ⓑ Ⓒ Ⓓ	158. Ⓐ Ⓑ Ⓒ Ⓓ
9. Ⓐ Ⓑ Ⓒ Ⓓ	39. Ⓐ Ⓑ Ⓒ Ⓓ	69. Ⓐ Ⓑ Ⓒ Ⓓ	99. Ⓐ Ⓑ Ⓒ Ⓓ	129. Ⓐ Ⓑ Ⓒ Ⓓ	159. Ⓐ Ⓑ Ⓒ Ⓓ
10. Ⓐ Ⓑ Ⓒ Ⓓ	40. Ⓐ Ⓑ Ⓒ Ⓓ	70. Ⓐ Ⓑ Ⓒ Ⓓ	100. Ⓐ Ⓑ Ⓒ Ⓓ	130. Ⓐ Ⓑ Ⓒ Ⓓ	160. Ⓐ Ⓑ Ⓒ Ⓓ
11. Ⓐ Ⓑ Ⓒ Ⓓ	41. Ⓐ Ⓑ Ⓒ Ⓓ	71. Ⓐ Ⓑ Ⓒ Ⓓ	101. Ⓐ Ⓑ Ⓒ Ⓓ	131. Ⓐ Ⓑ Ⓒ Ⓓ	161. Ⓐ Ⓑ Ⓒ Ⓓ
12. Ⓐ Ⓑ Ⓒ Ⓓ	42. Ⓐ Ⓑ Ⓒ Ⓓ	72. Ⓐ Ⓑ Ⓒ Ⓓ	102. Ⓐ Ⓑ Ⓒ Ⓓ	132. Ⓐ Ⓑ Ⓒ Ⓓ	162. Ⓐ Ⓑ Ⓒ Ⓓ
13. Ⓐ Ⓑ Ⓒ Ⓓ	43. Ⓐ Ⓑ Ⓒ Ⓓ	73. Ⓐ Ⓑ Ⓒ Ⓓ	103. Ⓐ Ⓑ Ⓒ Ⓓ	133. Ⓐ Ⓑ Ⓒ Ⓓ	163. Ⓐ Ⓑ Ⓒ Ⓓ
14. Ⓐ Ⓑ Ⓒ Ⓓ	44. Ⓐ Ⓑ Ⓒ Ⓓ	74. Ⓐ Ⓑ Ⓒ Ⓓ	104. Ⓐ Ⓑ Ⓒ Ⓓ	134. Ⓐ Ⓑ Ⓒ Ⓓ	164. Ⓐ Ⓑ Ⓒ Ⓓ
15. Ⓐ Ⓑ Ⓒ Ⓓ	45. Ⓐ Ⓑ Ⓒ Ⓓ	75. Ⓐ Ⓑ Ⓒ Ⓓ	105. Ⓐ Ⓑ Ⓒ Ⓓ	135. Ⓐ Ⓑ Ⓒ Ⓓ	165. Ⓐ Ⓑ Ⓒ Ⓓ
16. Ⓐ Ⓑ Ⓒ Ⓓ	46. Ⓐ Ⓑ Ⓒ Ⓓ	76. Ⓐ Ⓑ Ⓒ Ⓓ	106. Ⓐ Ⓑ Ⓒ Ⓓ	136. Ⓐ Ⓑ Ⓒ Ⓓ	166. Ⓐ Ⓑ Ⓒ Ⓓ
17. Ⓐ Ⓑ Ⓒ Ⓓ	47. Ⓐ Ⓑ Ⓒ Ⓓ	77. Ⓐ Ⓑ Ⓒ Ⓓ	107. Ⓐ Ⓑ Ⓒ Ⓓ	137. Ⓐ Ⓑ Ⓒ Ⓓ	167. Ⓐ Ⓑ Ⓒ Ⓓ
18. Ⓐ Ⓑ Ⓒ Ⓓ	48. Ⓐ Ⓑ Ⓒ Ⓓ	78. Ⓐ Ⓑ Ⓒ Ⓓ	108. Ⓐ Ⓑ Ⓒ Ⓓ	138. Ⓐ Ⓑ Ⓒ Ⓓ	168. Ⓐ Ⓑ Ⓒ Ⓓ
19. Ⓐ Ⓑ Ⓒ Ⓓ	49. Ⓐ Ⓑ Ⓒ Ⓓ	79. Ⓐ Ⓑ Ⓒ Ⓓ	109. Ⓐ Ⓑ Ⓒ Ⓓ	139. Ⓐ Ⓑ Ⓒ Ⓓ	169. Ⓐ Ⓑ Ⓒ Ⓓ
20. Ⓐ Ⓑ Ⓒ Ⓓ	50. Ⓐ Ⓑ Ⓒ Ⓓ	80. Ⓐ Ⓑ Ⓒ Ⓓ	110. Ⓐ Ⓑ Ⓒ Ⓓ	140. Ⓐ Ⓑ Ⓒ Ⓓ	170. Ⓐ Ⓑ Ⓒ Ⓓ
21. Ⓐ Ⓑ Ⓒ Ⓓ	51. Ⓐ Ⓑ Ⓒ Ⓓ	81. Ⓐ Ⓑ Ⓒ Ⓓ	111. Ⓐ Ⓑ Ⓒ Ⓓ	141. Ⓐ Ⓑ Ⓒ Ⓓ	171. Ⓐ Ⓑ Ⓒ Ⓓ
22. Ⓐ Ⓑ Ⓒ Ⓓ	52. Ⓐ Ⓑ Ⓒ Ⓓ	82. Ⓐ Ⓑ Ⓒ Ⓓ	112. Ⓐ Ⓑ Ⓒ Ⓓ	142. Ⓐ Ⓑ Ⓒ Ⓓ	172. Ⓐ Ⓑ Ⓒ Ⓓ
23. Ⓐ Ⓑ Ⓒ Ⓓ	53. Ⓐ Ⓑ Ⓒ Ⓓ	83. Ⓐ Ⓑ Ⓒ Ⓓ	113. Ⓐ Ⓑ Ⓒ Ⓓ	143. Ⓐ Ⓑ Ⓒ Ⓓ	173. Ⓐ Ⓑ Ⓒ Ⓓ
24. Ⓐ Ⓑ Ⓒ Ⓓ	54. Ⓐ Ⓑ Ⓒ Ⓓ	84. Ⓐ Ⓑ Ⓒ Ⓓ	114. Ⓐ Ⓑ Ⓒ Ⓓ	144. Ⓐ Ⓑ Ⓒ Ⓓ	174. Ⓐ Ⓑ Ⓒ Ⓓ
25. Ⓐ Ⓑ Ⓒ Ⓓ	55. Ⓐ Ⓑ Ⓒ Ⓓ	85. Ⓐ Ⓑ Ⓒ Ⓓ	115. Ⓐ Ⓑ Ⓒ Ⓓ	145. Ⓐ Ⓑ Ⓒ Ⓓ	175. Ⓐ Ⓑ Ⓒ Ⓓ
26. Ⓐ Ⓑ Ⓒ Ⓓ	56. Ⓐ Ⓑ Ⓒ Ⓓ	86. Ⓐ Ⓑ Ⓒ Ⓓ	116. Ⓐ Ⓑ Ⓒ Ⓓ	146. Ⓐ Ⓑ Ⓒ Ⓓ	176. Ⓐ Ⓑ Ⓒ Ⓓ
27. Ⓐ Ⓑ Ⓒ Ⓓ	57. Ⓐ Ⓑ Ⓒ Ⓓ	87. Ⓐ Ⓑ Ⓒ Ⓓ	117. Ⓐ Ⓑ Ⓒ Ⓓ	147. Ⓐ Ⓑ Ⓒ Ⓓ	177. Ⓐ Ⓑ Ⓒ Ⓓ
28. Ⓐ Ⓑ Ⓒ Ⓓ	58. Ⓐ Ⓑ Ⓒ Ⓓ	88. Ⓐ Ⓑ Ⓒ Ⓓ	118. Ⓐ Ⓑ Ⓒ Ⓓ	148. Ⓐ Ⓑ Ⓒ Ⓓ	178. Ⓐ Ⓑ Ⓒ Ⓓ
29. Ⓐ Ⓑ Ⓒ Ⓓ	59. Ⓐ Ⓑ Ⓒ Ⓓ	89. Ⓐ Ⓑ Ⓒ Ⓓ	119. Ⓐ Ⓑ Ⓒ Ⓓ	149. Ⓐ Ⓑ Ⓒ Ⓓ	179. Ⓐ Ⓑ Ⓒ Ⓓ
30. Ⓐ Ⓑ Ⓒ Ⓓ	60. Ⓐ Ⓑ Ⓒ Ⓓ	90. Ⓐ Ⓑ Ⓒ Ⓓ	120. Ⓐ Ⓑ Ⓒ Ⓓ	150. Ⓐ Ⓑ Ⓒ Ⓓ	180. Ⓐ Ⓑ Ⓒ Ⓓ

PRACTICE TEST ANSWER SHEET

Test ____

1. Ⓐ Ⓑ Ⓒ Ⓓ	31. Ⓐ Ⓑ Ⓒ Ⓓ	61. Ⓐ Ⓑ Ⓒ Ⓓ	91. Ⓐ Ⓑ Ⓒ Ⓓ	121. Ⓐ Ⓑ Ⓒ Ⓓ	151. Ⓐ Ⓑ Ⓒ Ⓓ
2. Ⓐ Ⓑ Ⓒ Ⓓ	32. Ⓐ Ⓑ Ⓒ Ⓓ	62. Ⓐ Ⓑ Ⓒ Ⓓ	92. Ⓐ Ⓑ Ⓒ Ⓓ	122. Ⓐ Ⓑ Ⓒ Ⓓ	152. Ⓐ Ⓑ Ⓒ Ⓓ
3. Ⓐ Ⓑ Ⓒ Ⓓ	33. Ⓐ Ⓑ Ⓒ Ⓓ	63. Ⓐ Ⓑ Ⓒ Ⓓ	93. Ⓐ Ⓑ Ⓒ Ⓓ	123. Ⓐ Ⓑ Ⓒ Ⓓ	153. Ⓐ Ⓑ Ⓒ Ⓓ
4. Ⓐ Ⓑ Ⓒ Ⓓ	34. Ⓐ Ⓑ Ⓒ Ⓓ	64. Ⓐ Ⓑ Ⓒ Ⓓ	94. Ⓐ Ⓑ Ⓒ Ⓓ	124. Ⓐ Ⓑ Ⓒ Ⓓ	154. Ⓐ Ⓑ Ⓒ Ⓓ
5. Ⓐ Ⓑ Ⓒ Ⓓ	35. Ⓐ Ⓑ Ⓒ Ⓓ	65. Ⓐ Ⓑ Ⓒ Ⓓ	95. Ⓐ Ⓑ Ⓒ Ⓓ	125. Ⓐ Ⓑ Ⓒ Ⓓ	155. Ⓐ Ⓑ Ⓒ Ⓓ
6. Ⓐ Ⓑ Ⓒ Ⓓ	36. Ⓐ Ⓑ Ⓒ Ⓓ	66. Ⓐ Ⓑ Ⓒ Ⓓ	96. Ⓐ Ⓑ Ⓒ Ⓓ	126. Ⓐ Ⓑ Ⓒ Ⓓ	156. Ⓐ Ⓑ Ⓒ Ⓓ
7. Ⓐ Ⓑ Ⓒ Ⓓ	37. Ⓐ Ⓑ Ⓒ Ⓓ	67. Ⓐ Ⓑ Ⓒ Ⓓ	97. Ⓐ Ⓑ Ⓒ Ⓓ	127. Ⓐ Ⓑ Ⓒ Ⓓ	157. Ⓐ Ⓑ Ⓒ Ⓓ
8. Ⓐ Ⓑ Ⓒ Ⓓ	38. Ⓐ Ⓑ Ⓒ Ⓓ	68. Ⓐ Ⓑ Ⓒ Ⓓ	98. Ⓐ Ⓑ Ⓒ Ⓓ	128. Ⓐ Ⓑ Ⓒ Ⓓ	158. Ⓐ Ⓑ Ⓒ Ⓓ
9. Ⓐ Ⓑ Ⓒ Ⓓ	39. Ⓐ Ⓑ Ⓒ Ⓓ	69. Ⓐ Ⓑ Ⓒ Ⓓ	99. Ⓐ Ⓑ Ⓒ Ⓓ	129. Ⓐ Ⓑ Ⓒ Ⓓ	159. Ⓐ Ⓑ Ⓒ Ⓓ
10. Ⓐ Ⓑ Ⓒ Ⓓ	40. Ⓐ Ⓑ Ⓒ Ⓓ	70. Ⓐ Ⓑ Ⓒ Ⓓ	100. Ⓐ Ⓑ Ⓒ Ⓓ	130. Ⓐ Ⓑ Ⓒ Ⓓ	160. Ⓐ Ⓑ Ⓒ Ⓓ
11. Ⓐ Ⓑ Ⓒ Ⓓ	41. Ⓐ Ⓑ Ⓒ Ⓓ	71. Ⓐ Ⓑ Ⓒ Ⓓ	101. Ⓐ Ⓑ Ⓒ Ⓓ	131. Ⓐ Ⓑ Ⓒ Ⓓ	161. Ⓐ Ⓑ Ⓒ Ⓓ
12. Ⓐ Ⓑ Ⓒ Ⓓ	42. Ⓐ Ⓑ Ⓒ Ⓓ	72. Ⓐ Ⓑ Ⓒ Ⓓ	102. Ⓐ Ⓑ Ⓒ Ⓓ	132. Ⓐ Ⓑ Ⓒ Ⓓ	162. Ⓐ Ⓑ Ⓒ Ⓓ
13. Ⓐ Ⓑ Ⓒ Ⓓ	43. Ⓐ Ⓑ Ⓒ Ⓓ	73. Ⓐ Ⓑ Ⓒ Ⓓ	103. Ⓐ Ⓑ Ⓒ Ⓓ	133. Ⓐ Ⓑ Ⓒ Ⓓ	163. Ⓐ Ⓑ Ⓒ Ⓓ
14. Ⓐ Ⓑ Ⓒ Ⓓ	44. Ⓐ Ⓑ Ⓒ Ⓓ	74. Ⓐ Ⓑ Ⓒ Ⓓ	104. Ⓐ Ⓑ Ⓒ Ⓓ	134. Ⓐ Ⓑ Ⓒ Ⓓ	164. Ⓐ Ⓑ Ⓒ Ⓓ
15. Ⓐ Ⓑ Ⓒ Ⓓ	45. Ⓐ Ⓑ Ⓒ Ⓓ	75. Ⓐ Ⓑ Ⓒ Ⓓ	105. Ⓐ Ⓑ Ⓒ Ⓓ	135. Ⓐ Ⓑ Ⓒ Ⓓ	165. Ⓐ Ⓑ Ⓒ Ⓓ
16. Ⓐ Ⓑ Ⓒ Ⓓ	46. Ⓐ Ⓑ Ⓒ Ⓓ	76. Ⓐ Ⓑ Ⓒ Ⓓ	106. Ⓐ Ⓑ Ⓒ Ⓓ	136. Ⓐ Ⓑ Ⓒ Ⓓ	166. Ⓐ Ⓑ Ⓒ Ⓓ
17. Ⓐ Ⓑ Ⓒ Ⓓ	47. Ⓐ Ⓑ Ⓒ Ⓓ	77. Ⓐ Ⓑ Ⓒ Ⓓ	107. Ⓐ Ⓑ Ⓒ Ⓓ	137. Ⓐ Ⓑ Ⓒ Ⓓ	167. Ⓐ Ⓑ Ⓒ Ⓓ
18. Ⓐ Ⓑ Ⓒ Ⓓ	48. Ⓐ Ⓑ Ⓒ Ⓓ	78. Ⓐ Ⓑ Ⓒ Ⓓ	108. Ⓐ Ⓑ Ⓒ Ⓓ	138. Ⓐ Ⓑ Ⓒ Ⓓ	168. Ⓐ Ⓑ Ⓒ Ⓓ
19. Ⓐ Ⓑ Ⓒ Ⓓ	49. Ⓐ Ⓑ Ⓒ Ⓓ	79. Ⓐ Ⓑ Ⓒ Ⓓ	109. Ⓐ Ⓑ Ⓒ Ⓓ	139. Ⓐ Ⓑ Ⓒ Ⓓ	169. Ⓐ Ⓑ Ⓒ Ⓓ
20. Ⓐ Ⓑ Ⓒ Ⓓ	50. Ⓐ Ⓑ Ⓒ Ⓓ	80. Ⓐ Ⓑ Ⓒ Ⓓ	110. Ⓐ Ⓑ Ⓒ Ⓓ	140. Ⓐ Ⓑ Ⓒ Ⓓ	170. Ⓐ Ⓑ Ⓒ Ⓓ
21. Ⓐ Ⓑ Ⓒ Ⓓ	51. Ⓐ Ⓑ Ⓒ Ⓓ	81. Ⓐ Ⓑ Ⓒ Ⓓ	111. Ⓐ Ⓑ Ⓒ Ⓓ	141. Ⓐ Ⓑ Ⓒ Ⓓ	171. Ⓐ Ⓑ Ⓒ Ⓓ
22. Ⓐ Ⓑ Ⓒ Ⓓ	52. Ⓐ Ⓑ Ⓒ Ⓓ	82. Ⓐ Ⓑ Ⓒ Ⓓ	112. Ⓐ Ⓑ Ⓒ Ⓓ	142. Ⓐ Ⓑ Ⓒ Ⓓ	172. Ⓐ Ⓑ Ⓒ Ⓓ
23. Ⓐ Ⓑ Ⓒ Ⓓ	53. Ⓐ Ⓑ Ⓒ Ⓓ	83. Ⓐ Ⓑ Ⓒ Ⓓ	113. Ⓐ Ⓑ Ⓒ Ⓓ	143. Ⓐ Ⓑ Ⓒ Ⓓ	173. Ⓐ Ⓑ Ⓒ Ⓓ
24. Ⓐ Ⓑ Ⓒ Ⓓ	54. Ⓐ Ⓑ Ⓒ Ⓓ	84. Ⓐ Ⓑ Ⓒ Ⓓ	114. Ⓐ Ⓑ Ⓒ Ⓓ	144. Ⓐ Ⓑ Ⓒ Ⓓ	174. Ⓐ Ⓑ Ⓒ Ⓓ
25. Ⓐ Ⓑ Ⓒ Ⓓ	55. Ⓐ Ⓑ Ⓒ Ⓓ	85. Ⓐ Ⓑ Ⓒ Ⓓ	115. Ⓐ Ⓑ Ⓒ Ⓓ	145. Ⓐ Ⓑ Ⓒ Ⓓ	175. Ⓐ Ⓑ Ⓒ Ⓓ
26. Ⓐ Ⓑ Ⓒ Ⓓ	56. Ⓐ Ⓑ Ⓒ Ⓓ	86. Ⓐ Ⓑ Ⓒ Ⓓ	116. Ⓐ Ⓑ Ⓒ Ⓓ	146. Ⓐ Ⓑ Ⓒ Ⓓ	176. Ⓐ Ⓑ Ⓒ Ⓓ
27. Ⓐ Ⓑ Ⓒ Ⓓ	57. Ⓐ Ⓑ Ⓒ Ⓓ	87. Ⓐ Ⓑ Ⓒ Ⓓ	117. Ⓐ Ⓑ Ⓒ Ⓓ	147. Ⓐ Ⓑ Ⓒ Ⓓ	177. Ⓐ Ⓑ Ⓒ Ⓓ
28. Ⓐ Ⓑ Ⓒ Ⓓ	58. Ⓐ Ⓑ Ⓒ Ⓓ	88. Ⓐ Ⓑ Ⓒ Ⓓ	118. Ⓐ Ⓑ Ⓒ Ⓓ	148. Ⓐ Ⓑ Ⓒ Ⓓ	178. Ⓐ Ⓑ Ⓒ Ⓓ
29. Ⓐ Ⓑ Ⓒ Ⓓ	59. Ⓐ Ⓑ Ⓒ Ⓓ	89. Ⓐ Ⓑ Ⓒ Ⓓ	119. Ⓐ Ⓑ Ⓒ Ⓓ	149. Ⓐ Ⓑ Ⓒ Ⓓ	179. Ⓐ Ⓑ Ⓒ Ⓓ
30. Ⓐ Ⓑ Ⓒ Ⓓ	60. Ⓐ Ⓑ Ⓒ Ⓓ	90. Ⓐ Ⓑ Ⓒ Ⓓ	120. Ⓐ Ⓑ Ⓒ Ⓓ	150. Ⓐ Ⓑ Ⓒ Ⓓ	180. Ⓐ Ⓑ Ⓒ Ⓓ

PRACTICE TEST ANSWER SHEET

Test ____

1. Ⓐ Ⓑ Ⓒ Ⓓ	31. Ⓐ Ⓑ Ⓒ Ⓓ	61. Ⓐ Ⓑ Ⓒ Ⓓ	91. Ⓐ Ⓑ Ⓒ Ⓓ	121. Ⓐ Ⓑ Ⓒ Ⓓ	151. Ⓐ Ⓑ Ⓒ Ⓓ
2. Ⓐ Ⓑ Ⓒ Ⓓ	32. Ⓐ Ⓑ Ⓒ Ⓓ	62. Ⓐ Ⓑ Ⓒ Ⓓ	92. Ⓐ Ⓑ Ⓒ Ⓓ	122. Ⓐ Ⓑ Ⓒ Ⓓ	152. Ⓐ Ⓑ Ⓒ Ⓓ
3. Ⓐ Ⓑ Ⓒ Ⓓ	33. Ⓐ Ⓑ Ⓒ Ⓓ	63. Ⓐ Ⓑ Ⓒ Ⓓ	93. Ⓐ Ⓑ Ⓒ Ⓓ	123. Ⓐ Ⓑ Ⓒ Ⓓ	153. Ⓐ Ⓑ Ⓒ Ⓓ
4. Ⓐ Ⓑ Ⓒ Ⓓ	34. Ⓐ Ⓑ Ⓒ Ⓓ	64. Ⓐ Ⓑ Ⓒ Ⓓ	94. Ⓐ Ⓑ Ⓒ Ⓓ	124. Ⓐ Ⓑ Ⓒ Ⓓ	154. Ⓐ Ⓑ Ⓒ Ⓓ
5. Ⓐ Ⓑ Ⓒ Ⓓ	35. Ⓐ Ⓑ Ⓒ Ⓓ	65. Ⓐ Ⓑ Ⓒ Ⓓ	95. Ⓐ Ⓑ Ⓒ Ⓓ	125. Ⓐ Ⓑ Ⓒ Ⓓ	155. Ⓐ Ⓑ Ⓒ Ⓓ
6. Ⓐ Ⓑ Ⓒ Ⓓ	36. Ⓐ Ⓑ Ⓒ Ⓓ	66. Ⓐ Ⓑ Ⓒ Ⓓ	96. Ⓐ Ⓑ Ⓒ Ⓓ	126. Ⓐ Ⓑ Ⓒ Ⓓ	156. Ⓐ Ⓑ Ⓒ Ⓓ
7. Ⓐ Ⓑ Ⓒ Ⓓ	37. Ⓐ Ⓑ Ⓒ Ⓓ	67. Ⓐ Ⓑ Ⓒ Ⓓ	97. Ⓐ Ⓑ Ⓒ Ⓓ	127. Ⓐ Ⓑ Ⓒ Ⓓ	157. Ⓐ Ⓑ Ⓒ Ⓓ
8. Ⓐ Ⓑ Ⓒ Ⓓ	38. Ⓐ Ⓑ Ⓒ Ⓓ	68. Ⓐ Ⓑ Ⓒ Ⓓ	98. Ⓐ Ⓑ Ⓒ Ⓓ	128. Ⓐ Ⓑ Ⓒ Ⓓ	158. Ⓐ Ⓑ Ⓒ Ⓓ
9. Ⓐ Ⓑ Ⓒ Ⓓ	39. Ⓐ Ⓑ Ⓒ Ⓓ	69. Ⓐ Ⓑ Ⓒ Ⓓ	99. Ⓐ Ⓑ Ⓒ Ⓓ	129. Ⓐ Ⓑ Ⓒ Ⓓ	159. Ⓐ Ⓑ Ⓒ Ⓓ
10. Ⓐ Ⓑ Ⓒ Ⓓ	40. Ⓐ Ⓑ Ⓒ Ⓓ	70. Ⓐ Ⓑ Ⓒ Ⓓ	100. Ⓐ Ⓑ Ⓒ Ⓓ	130. Ⓐ Ⓑ Ⓒ Ⓓ	160. Ⓐ Ⓑ Ⓒ Ⓓ
11. Ⓐ Ⓑ Ⓒ Ⓓ	41. Ⓐ Ⓑ Ⓒ Ⓓ	71. Ⓐ Ⓑ Ⓒ Ⓓ	101. Ⓐ Ⓑ Ⓒ Ⓓ	131. Ⓐ Ⓑ Ⓒ Ⓓ	161. Ⓐ Ⓑ Ⓒ Ⓓ
12. Ⓐ Ⓑ Ⓒ Ⓓ	42. Ⓐ Ⓑ Ⓒ Ⓓ	72. Ⓐ Ⓑ Ⓒ Ⓓ	102. Ⓐ Ⓑ Ⓒ Ⓓ	132. Ⓐ Ⓑ Ⓒ Ⓓ	162. Ⓐ Ⓑ Ⓒ Ⓓ
13. Ⓐ Ⓑ Ⓒ Ⓓ	43. Ⓐ Ⓑ Ⓒ Ⓓ	73. Ⓐ Ⓑ Ⓒ Ⓓ	103. Ⓐ Ⓑ Ⓒ Ⓓ	133. Ⓐ Ⓑ Ⓒ Ⓓ	163. Ⓐ Ⓑ Ⓒ Ⓓ
14. Ⓐ Ⓑ Ⓒ Ⓓ	44. Ⓐ Ⓑ Ⓒ Ⓓ	74. Ⓐ Ⓑ Ⓒ Ⓓ	104. Ⓐ Ⓑ Ⓒ Ⓓ	134. Ⓐ Ⓑ Ⓒ Ⓓ	164. Ⓐ Ⓑ Ⓒ Ⓓ
15. Ⓐ Ⓑ Ⓒ Ⓓ	45. Ⓐ Ⓑ Ⓒ Ⓓ	75. Ⓐ Ⓑ Ⓒ Ⓓ	105. Ⓐ Ⓑ Ⓒ Ⓓ	135. Ⓐ Ⓑ Ⓒ Ⓓ	165. Ⓐ Ⓑ Ⓒ Ⓓ
16. Ⓐ Ⓑ Ⓒ Ⓓ	46. Ⓐ Ⓑ Ⓒ Ⓓ	76. Ⓐ Ⓑ Ⓒ Ⓓ	106. Ⓐ Ⓑ Ⓒ Ⓓ	136. Ⓐ Ⓑ Ⓒ Ⓓ	166. Ⓐ Ⓑ Ⓒ Ⓓ
17. Ⓐ Ⓑ Ⓒ Ⓓ	47. Ⓐ Ⓑ Ⓒ Ⓓ	77. Ⓐ Ⓑ Ⓒ Ⓓ	107. Ⓐ Ⓑ Ⓒ Ⓓ	137. Ⓐ Ⓑ Ⓒ Ⓓ	167. Ⓐ Ⓑ Ⓒ Ⓓ
18. Ⓐ Ⓑ Ⓒ Ⓓ	48. Ⓐ Ⓑ Ⓒ Ⓓ	78. Ⓐ Ⓑ Ⓒ Ⓓ	108. Ⓐ Ⓑ Ⓒ Ⓓ	138. Ⓐ Ⓑ Ⓒ Ⓓ	168. Ⓐ Ⓑ Ⓒ Ⓓ
19. Ⓐ Ⓑ Ⓒ Ⓓ	49. Ⓐ Ⓑ Ⓒ Ⓓ	79. Ⓐ Ⓑ Ⓒ Ⓓ	109. Ⓐ Ⓑ Ⓒ Ⓓ	139. Ⓐ Ⓑ Ⓒ Ⓓ	169. Ⓐ Ⓑ Ⓒ Ⓓ
20. Ⓐ Ⓑ Ⓒ Ⓓ	50. Ⓐ Ⓑ Ⓒ Ⓓ	80. Ⓐ Ⓑ Ⓒ Ⓓ	110. Ⓐ Ⓑ Ⓒ Ⓓ	140. Ⓐ Ⓑ Ⓒ Ⓓ	170. Ⓐ Ⓑ Ⓒ Ⓓ
21. Ⓐ Ⓑ Ⓒ Ⓓ	51. Ⓐ Ⓑ Ⓒ Ⓓ	81. Ⓐ Ⓑ Ⓒ Ⓓ	111. Ⓐ Ⓑ Ⓒ Ⓓ	141. Ⓐ Ⓑ Ⓒ Ⓓ	171. Ⓐ Ⓑ Ⓒ Ⓓ
22. Ⓐ Ⓑ Ⓒ Ⓓ	52. Ⓐ Ⓑ Ⓒ Ⓓ	82. Ⓐ Ⓑ Ⓒ Ⓓ	112. Ⓐ Ⓑ Ⓒ Ⓓ	142. Ⓐ Ⓑ Ⓒ Ⓓ	172. Ⓐ Ⓑ Ⓒ Ⓓ
23. Ⓐ Ⓑ Ⓒ Ⓓ	53. Ⓐ Ⓑ Ⓒ Ⓓ	83. Ⓐ Ⓑ Ⓒ Ⓓ	113. Ⓐ Ⓑ Ⓒ Ⓓ	143. Ⓐ Ⓑ Ⓒ Ⓓ	173. Ⓐ Ⓑ Ⓒ Ⓓ
24. Ⓐ Ⓑ Ⓒ Ⓓ	54. Ⓐ Ⓑ Ⓒ Ⓓ	84. Ⓐ Ⓑ Ⓒ Ⓓ	114. Ⓐ Ⓑ Ⓒ Ⓓ	144. Ⓐ Ⓑ Ⓒ Ⓓ	174. Ⓐ Ⓑ Ⓒ Ⓓ
25. Ⓐ Ⓑ Ⓒ Ⓓ	55. Ⓐ Ⓑ Ⓒ Ⓓ	85. Ⓐ Ⓑ Ⓒ Ⓓ	115. Ⓐ Ⓑ Ⓒ Ⓓ	145. Ⓐ Ⓑ Ⓒ Ⓓ	175. Ⓐ Ⓑ Ⓒ Ⓓ
26. Ⓐ Ⓑ Ⓒ Ⓓ	56. Ⓐ Ⓑ Ⓒ Ⓓ	86. Ⓐ Ⓑ Ⓒ Ⓓ	116. Ⓐ Ⓑ Ⓒ Ⓓ	146. Ⓐ Ⓑ Ⓒ Ⓓ	176. Ⓐ Ⓑ Ⓒ Ⓓ
27. Ⓐ Ⓑ Ⓒ Ⓓ	57. Ⓐ Ⓑ Ⓒ Ⓓ	87. Ⓐ Ⓑ Ⓒ Ⓓ	117. Ⓐ Ⓑ Ⓒ Ⓓ	147. Ⓐ Ⓑ Ⓒ Ⓓ	177. Ⓐ Ⓑ Ⓒ Ⓓ
28. Ⓐ Ⓑ Ⓒ Ⓓ	58. Ⓐ Ⓑ Ⓒ Ⓓ	88. Ⓐ Ⓑ Ⓒ Ⓓ	118. Ⓐ Ⓑ Ⓒ Ⓓ	148. Ⓐ Ⓑ Ⓒ Ⓓ	178. Ⓐ Ⓑ Ⓒ Ⓓ
29. Ⓐ Ⓑ Ⓒ Ⓓ	59. Ⓐ Ⓑ Ⓒ Ⓓ	89. Ⓐ Ⓑ Ⓒ Ⓓ	119. Ⓐ Ⓑ Ⓒ Ⓓ	149. Ⓐ Ⓑ Ⓒ Ⓓ	179. Ⓐ Ⓑ Ⓒ Ⓓ
30. Ⓐ Ⓑ Ⓒ Ⓓ	60. Ⓐ Ⓑ Ⓒ Ⓓ	90. Ⓐ Ⓑ Ⓒ Ⓓ	120. Ⓐ Ⓑ Ⓒ Ⓓ	150. Ⓐ Ⓑ Ⓒ Ⓓ	180. Ⓐ Ⓑ Ⓒ Ⓓ

PRACTICE TEST ANSWER SHEET

Test ____

1. Ⓐ Ⓑ Ⓒ Ⓓ	31. Ⓐ Ⓑ Ⓒ Ⓓ	61. Ⓐ Ⓑ Ⓒ Ⓓ	91. Ⓐ Ⓑ Ⓒ Ⓓ	121. Ⓐ Ⓑ Ⓒ Ⓓ	151. Ⓐ Ⓑ Ⓒ Ⓓ
2. Ⓐ Ⓑ Ⓒ Ⓓ	32. Ⓐ Ⓑ Ⓒ Ⓓ	62. Ⓐ Ⓑ Ⓒ Ⓓ	92. Ⓐ Ⓑ Ⓒ Ⓓ	122. Ⓐ Ⓑ Ⓒ Ⓓ	152. Ⓐ Ⓑ Ⓒ Ⓓ
3. Ⓐ Ⓑ Ⓒ Ⓓ	33. Ⓐ Ⓑ Ⓒ Ⓓ	63. Ⓐ Ⓑ Ⓒ Ⓓ	93. Ⓐ Ⓑ Ⓒ Ⓓ	123. Ⓐ Ⓑ Ⓒ Ⓓ	153. Ⓐ Ⓑ Ⓒ Ⓓ
4. Ⓐ Ⓑ Ⓒ Ⓓ	34. Ⓐ Ⓑ Ⓒ Ⓓ	64. Ⓐ Ⓑ Ⓒ Ⓓ	94. Ⓐ Ⓑ Ⓒ Ⓓ	124. Ⓐ Ⓑ Ⓒ Ⓓ	154. Ⓐ Ⓑ Ⓒ Ⓓ
5. Ⓐ Ⓑ Ⓒ Ⓓ	35. Ⓐ Ⓑ Ⓒ Ⓓ	65. Ⓐ Ⓑ Ⓒ Ⓓ	95. Ⓐ Ⓑ Ⓒ Ⓓ	125. Ⓐ Ⓑ Ⓒ Ⓓ	155. Ⓐ Ⓑ Ⓒ Ⓓ
6. Ⓐ Ⓑ Ⓒ Ⓓ	36. Ⓐ Ⓑ Ⓒ Ⓓ	66. Ⓐ Ⓑ Ⓒ Ⓓ	96. Ⓐ Ⓑ Ⓒ Ⓓ	126. Ⓐ Ⓑ Ⓒ Ⓓ	156. Ⓐ Ⓑ Ⓒ Ⓓ
7. Ⓐ Ⓑ Ⓒ Ⓓ	37. Ⓐ Ⓑ Ⓒ Ⓓ	67. Ⓐ Ⓑ Ⓒ Ⓓ	97. Ⓐ Ⓑ Ⓒ Ⓓ	127. Ⓐ Ⓑ Ⓒ Ⓓ	157. Ⓐ Ⓑ Ⓒ Ⓓ
8. Ⓐ Ⓑ Ⓒ Ⓓ	38. Ⓐ Ⓑ Ⓒ Ⓓ	68. Ⓐ Ⓑ Ⓒ Ⓓ	98. Ⓐ Ⓑ Ⓒ Ⓓ	128. Ⓐ Ⓑ Ⓒ Ⓓ	158. Ⓐ Ⓑ Ⓒ Ⓓ
9. Ⓐ Ⓑ Ⓒ Ⓓ	39. Ⓐ Ⓑ Ⓒ Ⓓ	69. Ⓐ Ⓑ Ⓒ Ⓓ	99. Ⓐ Ⓑ Ⓒ Ⓓ	129. Ⓐ Ⓑ Ⓒ Ⓓ	159. Ⓐ Ⓑ Ⓒ Ⓓ
10. Ⓐ Ⓑ Ⓒ Ⓓ	40. Ⓐ Ⓑ Ⓒ Ⓓ	70. Ⓐ Ⓑ Ⓒ Ⓓ	100. Ⓐ Ⓑ Ⓒ Ⓓ	130. Ⓐ Ⓑ Ⓒ Ⓓ	160. Ⓐ Ⓑ Ⓒ Ⓓ
11. Ⓐ Ⓑ Ⓒ Ⓓ	41. Ⓐ Ⓑ Ⓒ Ⓓ	71. Ⓐ Ⓑ Ⓒ Ⓓ	101. Ⓐ Ⓑ Ⓒ Ⓓ	131. Ⓐ Ⓑ Ⓒ Ⓓ	161. Ⓐ Ⓑ Ⓒ Ⓓ
12. Ⓐ Ⓑ Ⓒ Ⓓ	42. Ⓐ Ⓑ Ⓒ Ⓓ	72. Ⓐ Ⓑ Ⓒ Ⓓ	102. Ⓐ Ⓑ Ⓒ Ⓓ	132. Ⓐ Ⓑ Ⓒ Ⓓ	162. Ⓐ Ⓑ Ⓒ Ⓓ
13. Ⓐ Ⓑ Ⓒ Ⓓ	43. Ⓐ Ⓑ Ⓒ Ⓓ	73. Ⓐ Ⓑ Ⓒ Ⓓ	103. Ⓐ Ⓑ Ⓒ Ⓓ	133. Ⓐ Ⓑ Ⓒ Ⓓ	163. Ⓐ Ⓑ Ⓒ Ⓓ
14. Ⓐ Ⓑ Ⓒ Ⓓ	44. Ⓐ Ⓑ Ⓒ Ⓓ	74. Ⓐ Ⓑ Ⓒ Ⓓ	104. Ⓐ Ⓑ Ⓒ Ⓓ	134. Ⓐ Ⓑ Ⓒ Ⓓ	164. Ⓐ Ⓑ Ⓒ Ⓓ
15. Ⓐ Ⓑ Ⓒ Ⓓ	45. Ⓐ Ⓑ Ⓒ Ⓓ	75. Ⓐ Ⓑ Ⓒ Ⓓ	105. Ⓐ Ⓑ Ⓒ Ⓓ	135. Ⓐ Ⓑ Ⓒ Ⓓ	165. Ⓐ Ⓑ Ⓒ Ⓓ
16. Ⓐ Ⓑ Ⓒ Ⓓ	46. Ⓐ Ⓑ Ⓒ Ⓓ	76. Ⓐ Ⓑ Ⓒ Ⓓ	106. Ⓐ Ⓑ Ⓒ Ⓓ	136. Ⓐ Ⓑ Ⓒ Ⓓ	166. Ⓐ Ⓑ Ⓒ Ⓓ
17. Ⓐ Ⓑ Ⓒ Ⓓ	47. Ⓐ Ⓑ Ⓒ Ⓓ	77. Ⓐ Ⓑ Ⓒ Ⓓ	107. Ⓐ Ⓑ Ⓒ Ⓓ	137. Ⓐ Ⓑ Ⓒ Ⓓ	167. Ⓐ Ⓑ Ⓒ Ⓓ
18. Ⓐ Ⓑ Ⓒ Ⓓ	48. Ⓐ Ⓑ Ⓒ Ⓓ	78. Ⓐ Ⓑ Ⓒ Ⓓ	108. Ⓐ Ⓑ Ⓒ Ⓓ	138. Ⓐ Ⓑ Ⓒ Ⓓ	168. Ⓐ Ⓑ Ⓒ Ⓓ
19. Ⓐ Ⓑ Ⓒ Ⓓ	49. Ⓐ Ⓑ Ⓒ Ⓓ	79. Ⓐ Ⓑ Ⓒ Ⓓ	109. Ⓐ Ⓑ Ⓒ Ⓓ	139. Ⓐ Ⓑ Ⓒ Ⓓ	169. Ⓐ Ⓑ Ⓒ Ⓓ
20. Ⓐ Ⓑ Ⓒ Ⓓ	50. Ⓐ Ⓑ Ⓒ Ⓓ	80. Ⓐ Ⓑ Ⓒ Ⓓ	110. Ⓐ Ⓑ Ⓒ Ⓓ	140. Ⓐ Ⓑ Ⓒ Ⓓ	170. Ⓐ Ⓑ Ⓒ Ⓓ
21. Ⓐ Ⓑ Ⓒ Ⓓ	51. Ⓐ Ⓑ Ⓒ Ⓓ	81. Ⓐ Ⓑ Ⓒ Ⓓ	111. Ⓐ Ⓑ Ⓒ Ⓓ	141. Ⓐ Ⓑ Ⓒ Ⓓ	171. Ⓐ Ⓑ Ⓒ Ⓓ
22. Ⓐ Ⓑ Ⓒ Ⓓ	52. Ⓐ Ⓑ Ⓒ Ⓓ	82. Ⓐ Ⓑ Ⓒ Ⓓ	112. Ⓐ Ⓑ Ⓒ Ⓓ	142. Ⓐ Ⓑ Ⓒ Ⓓ	172. Ⓐ Ⓑ Ⓒ Ⓓ
23. Ⓐ Ⓑ Ⓒ Ⓓ	53. Ⓐ Ⓑ Ⓒ Ⓓ	83. Ⓐ Ⓑ Ⓒ Ⓓ	113. Ⓐ Ⓑ Ⓒ Ⓓ	143. Ⓐ Ⓑ Ⓒ Ⓓ	173. Ⓐ Ⓑ Ⓒ Ⓓ
24. Ⓐ Ⓑ Ⓒ Ⓓ	54. Ⓐ Ⓑ Ⓒ Ⓓ	84. Ⓐ Ⓑ Ⓒ Ⓓ	114. Ⓐ Ⓑ Ⓒ Ⓓ	144. Ⓐ Ⓑ Ⓒ Ⓓ	174. Ⓐ Ⓑ Ⓒ Ⓓ
25. Ⓐ Ⓑ Ⓒ Ⓓ	55. Ⓐ Ⓑ Ⓒ Ⓓ	85. Ⓐ Ⓑ Ⓒ Ⓓ	115. Ⓐ Ⓑ Ⓒ Ⓓ	145. Ⓐ Ⓑ Ⓒ Ⓓ	175. Ⓐ Ⓑ Ⓒ Ⓓ
26. Ⓐ Ⓑ Ⓒ Ⓓ	56. Ⓐ Ⓑ Ⓒ Ⓓ	86. Ⓐ Ⓑ Ⓒ Ⓓ	116. Ⓐ Ⓑ Ⓒ Ⓓ	146. Ⓐ Ⓑ Ⓒ Ⓓ	176. Ⓐ Ⓑ Ⓒ Ⓓ
27. Ⓐ Ⓑ Ⓒ Ⓓ	57. Ⓐ Ⓑ Ⓒ Ⓓ	87. Ⓐ Ⓑ Ⓒ Ⓓ	117. Ⓐ Ⓑ Ⓒ Ⓓ	147. Ⓐ Ⓑ Ⓒ Ⓓ	177. Ⓐ Ⓑ Ⓒ Ⓓ
28. Ⓐ Ⓑ Ⓒ Ⓓ	58. Ⓐ Ⓑ Ⓒ Ⓓ	88. Ⓐ Ⓑ Ⓒ Ⓓ	118. Ⓐ Ⓑ Ⓒ Ⓓ	148. Ⓐ Ⓑ Ⓒ Ⓓ	178. Ⓐ Ⓑ Ⓒ Ⓓ
29. Ⓐ Ⓑ Ⓒ Ⓓ	59. Ⓐ Ⓑ Ⓒ Ⓓ	89. Ⓐ Ⓑ Ⓒ Ⓓ	119. Ⓐ Ⓑ Ⓒ Ⓓ	149. Ⓐ Ⓑ Ⓒ Ⓓ	179. Ⓐ Ⓑ Ⓒ Ⓓ
30. Ⓐ Ⓑ Ⓒ Ⓓ	60. Ⓐ Ⓑ Ⓒ Ⓓ	90. Ⓐ Ⓑ Ⓒ Ⓓ	120. Ⓐ Ⓑ Ⓒ Ⓓ	150. Ⓐ Ⓑ Ⓒ Ⓓ	180. Ⓐ Ⓑ Ⓒ Ⓓ